READ ALL
ABOUT IT!

Published by First Stone Publishing,
a division of Corpus Publishing Ltd,
4-5 The Marina, Harbour Road,
Lydney, Gloucestershire, GL15 5ET.

First Published 2003

ISBN 1 904439 11X

Printed and bound by G. Canale, in Italy

10 9 8 7 6 5 4 3 2 1

READ ALL ABOUT IT!
100 Sensational Years of the Daily Mirror

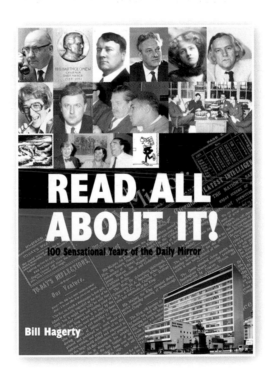

Bill Hagerty

CONTENTS

CONTRIBUTORS

DEDICATION

I am sorry more could not be mentioned by name, but this book is dedicated to all those men and women, from all departments, whose dedication and commitment contributed during its first century to the establishment of the *Daily Mirror* as one of the world's finest newspapers.

ACKNOWLEDGEMENTS

This book could not have been written without the assistance of a great many friends and colleagues, most of them past or present employees of the *Daily Mirror*. Thanks to them all and especially, for co-operation beyond the call of duty, to John Allard, Anton Antonowicz, Sly Bailey, David Banks, Revel Barker, Neil Bentley, Jessica Callan, Alastair Campbell, Charles Collier-Wright, Peter Cook, Lady Cudlipp, James Curran, Anthony Delano, Brian Downing, Eugene Duffy, John Edwards, Ian Gammidge, Christine Garbutt, Kent Gavin, Geoffrey Goodman, Philip Graf, Felicity Green, Dennis Hackett, Joe Haines, John Jackson, Derek Jameson, Sir Alex Jarratt, John Jenkinson, Gerald Kaufman, Ken Layson, Tony Miles, Tim Minogue, Mike Molloy, Jon Moorehead, Piers Morgan, Colin Myler, Brian Reade, Bernard Shrimsley, John Smith, Richard Stott, Bill Soutar, Ken Smiley, Keith Waterhouse, Ian Watson, Harry Weisbloom, Audrey Whiting, Peter (P.J.) Wilson, Jeff Wright, Sydney Young, Donald Zec and the late Sir Edward Pickering and Percy Roberts.

INTRODUCTION

It is a Monday in March 1995, and, towards the end of the morning in the faded but opulent surrounds of the National Liberal Club in London, an exceptional event is taking place. The men and women present are far from being in the first flush of youth, but are flushed nonetheless. Whether the collective rush of blood to many heads is due to the free-flowing wine or a general feeling of euphoria, it is impossible to say. Probably it is a combination of both, for those present are celebrating membership of one of the most elite groups in the history of national daily newspaper journalism.

Just over 30 years previously, they had been responsible for steering the popular tabloid *Daily Mirror* to a circulation in excess of five million copies. Five million copies *every day*. The then editorial director, Hugh Cudlipp, had been moved to change the front-page legend that, on occasion, had boasted BIGGEST DAILY SALE ON EARTH to BIGGEST DAILY SALE IN THE UNIVERSE. The chairman, Cecil Harmsworth King, had queried the change, asking, "But how do you know?" Hugh Cudlipp recalls amid laughter and the clinking of glasses in the Lloyd George Room.

A journalistic legend and, since his retirement, a peer of the realm, Cudlipp is, on this auspicious day, still a commanding presence among his own kind and a pugnacious critic of all things journalistic that he believes to be substandard. In his address, he castigates the current *Mirror* and its chief executive David Montgomery, the man he considers responsible for "the multi-coloured, kaleidoscopic upchuck" that appears on the paper's front page each morning. "We were all there, on St. Crispin's Eve, when the *Mirror* was about to thrust its way through the five million supersonic barrier," he tells his avid audience. "No newspaper in the world, popular or unpopular,

has lived on in the memories of its editorial creators at all levels more securely and nostalgically than the *Daily Mirror* in its proud, powerful and halcyon days. I say 'halcyon days' because it was a lot of bloody fun as well. Gathered in this room, I think it is fair to say, are the real, basic, Fleet Street whiz kids. There's never been a paper like it. But with all our flash and flamboyance and showing off, and gross immodesty, we were really trying to do something. I've forgotten what the bloody hell it was, but nobody's trying to do it now."

The room explodes. The old magician has done it again. The speech, scrawled on the aeroplane that had brought him back from his holiday home in Spain, will live on long after Cudlipp's departure for the journalists' Valhalla, where editions are never late and circulations never slip and there is always entertaining company with whom to share a bottle at the bar in The Angel.

* * *

Over at Canary Wharf, where the Mirror Group of newspapers had relocated long after almost everyone present at the National Liberal Club had moved on, retired or been ejected at the insistence of the management, the following morning's newspaper is coming together. The days when each issue sold more than five million copies, peaking in the second half of 1967 at an average daily 5,282,137, have vanished into the mists of time and the memories of those carousing across town at the Liberal Club. But even if the mid-1990s are not especially grand days for the paper – buffeted by the opposition, bled by staff cuts and the cost of ancillary media projects – most of those producing it are following the footprints of those dedicated men and women whose belief and talent shaped the modern *Mirror*.

In 1956, when it was little more than half-a-century old, the paper had stated its credo: "We believe in ordinary people… We rejoice in the good humour, the fine spirit and the success with which the British people are tackling the problems of modern life… We stand for equal opportunities for all children, good homes and robust health for everyone, a high standard of living for all. And we challenge every vested interest, whatever its political colour, that obstructs the realisation of that ideal… So we strive to smash every artificial barrier to full expression of the moral qualities of the British people… That is the faith that defines our daily purpose."

No matter how rocky the road has been since, some things don't change.

*   *   *

It is a Tuesday, a few days before Christmas 2002, and shortly past noon a steady stream of men and women, but mostly men, are clattering down a staircase into a basement club not far from the Tower of London. Most of them have hair as grey as the sky looks this day, although some of them have very little hair at all. The majority are smartly dressed and there are as many ties on parade as you would find at a regimental reunion. The analogy is apposite: this is the annual gathering of a rather special regiment of skilled craftspeople; officers and other ranks who have served – and, in a few cases, are still serving – in the formidable army that, for a century, has produced one of the world's great newspapers. To paraphrase the Duke of Wellington, I don't know what effect they have on the enemy, but by God they impress me.

I know most of them. They are of an age that determines they were working when I was in the now demolished red, white and blue giant matchbox of a building that dominated Holborn Circus, just inside the west edge of the City of London, for more than 30 years. There are not only journalists here, but circulation men, too, and promotions executives and secretaries, and others who contributed to success and fought against failure a little more than 100 yards from the celebrated newspaper thoroughfare of Fleet Street, christened the Street of Adventure by the eminent journalist and author Philip Gibbs. Today's event is colloquially known as the Old Mirror lunch, a gathering of almost 60 veterans of what, for much of its existence, was called Mirror Group Newspapers. Because of the number of staff necessary to produce a

publication with a propensity to appear on six mornings every week, rather than the requirement to muster on parade just once enjoyed by its leisured Sunday stable-companions, it is the *Daily Mirror* to which most of those present owe allegiance. Rose-tinted spectacles, although by no means mandatory, are very much in evidence.

This collective wandering down memory lane meanders all the way to this morning's issue for such as photographer Kent Gavin, television writer Tony Purnell and Terry Sanders, a media executive for the paper. But most have departed from the paper's employ, gathering together now only at this rekindling of old friendships.

The reunion is one of December's more pleasurable experiences, observes Murray Davies, formerly a reporter with the *Mirror* and a feature writer at its older but smallest sister, *The People*, and now a successful novelist. Everybody in the room believes they are still 35 years old, says George Thaw, one-time features sub-editor and then books editor. Brian McConnell agrees, although this veteran newsman was older than that when he stopped a bullet meant for Princess Anne after blundering into an attack on the Royal personage in The Mall.

These veterans drink to absent friends, those who died while still wearing the badge of office – crossed pens mounted on a bottle of champagne – or afterwards, plus ex-colleagues who have been otherwise sidetracked from attending, such as a former sub-editor currently incarcerated at Her Majesty's pleasure for having killed his wife's lover. As the afternoon grows long, there are toasts to present friends, too, and even to present enemies as old animosities are drowned in Chardonnay and Merlot.

Geoffrey Goodman, the venerable former industrial editor, rises to congratulate John Jenkinson, for many years the paper's publicity and promotions mastermind, who, along with a former member of his staff, Lesley Hutchins, organises this event every year. The gathering, says Goodman, represents a very special community. John Smith, a reporter in the paper's New York bureau before going on to even greater success as a *People* columnist, machine guns the assembly with jokes delivered with the expertise of a music hall comic, which indeed he once was. He proposes a toast to the spirit that has brought this diverse group together this day. To friendship, they chorus.

All three former editors present worked on the *Daily Mirror*. But whereas Eve Pollard went on to edit the Sunday title and I *The People*, Richard Stott claimed a special place in its history by becoming the only person to edit the daily paper twice. He gets to his feet to pay tribute to the *Mirror* as it enters its one-hundredth year and reminisces about his days in the newsroom, when reporters would compete for the Lunch of the Year title, a competition judged purely on length. John Jackson, now amiably looking on from a nearby table, was the most memorable winner, recalls Stott, having lunched with contacts from the Wimbledon All England Lawn Tennis Club until 3.45 the following morning. No other newspaper in the world could sustain an event of this kind, where the goodwill flows as copiously as the wine, says Stott. Happy days, says John Jenkinson. See you next year.

*   *   *

Over at Canary Wharf, a few miles to the east, the following morning's issue of the modern *Daily Mirror* is taking shape. Under the editorship of the mercurial, if controversial, Piers Morgan, old traditions are being followed and new traditions forged. This is not the *Mirror* of Cudlipp, or Stott, or any of those still re-bonding at the pertinently named English Martyrs Club. This is not the *Mirror* of its founder, Alfred Harmsworth, soon to be Lord Northcliffe, nor that of Harry Guy Bartholomew, the original architect of its greatness, nor of Cecil Harmsworth King, proprietor in all but the matter of ownership, nor Robert Maxwell, the owner who stole the eggs from his own golden goose after catapulting it back into serious Fleet Street contention with the introduction of colour. Nor is it the *Mirror* of David Montgomery, the driven chief executive who bridged the administrations of Maxwell and the present controlling company, Trinity Mirror.

Daily newspapers are ephemeral in that each new product is perishable within 24 hours, yet subsequently they are priceless as chroniclers of all aspects of civilisation's erratic progress. Newspapers, wrote Hugh Cudlipp, are not like any other business except in the sense that they must make a profit to survive. "Their death is the death of an idea, of an attitude to life, a service to the public," he commented about the closure of the once vibrant *News Chronicle*. The end of that paper, Cudlipp warned, was "the end of an instrument of political thought: when that doesn't matter, democracy doesn't matter."

Producing newspapers, as Piers Morgan and other editors have acknowledged, "is not rocket science", but to be properly practised it is a trade requiring integrity, crusading zeal, passion and the equilibrium of a tightrope walker, as well as stupendous energy. It is also a trade of romance: in 1923, just ten years after the birth of the *Mirror*, Philip Gibbs wrote of the "magnet" that drew him to Fleet Street: "The lure of adventure… The thrill of chasing the new story, the interest of getting into the middle of life, sometimes behind the scenes of history, the excitement of recording acts in the melodrama of reality, the meetings with heroes, rogues and oddities, the front seats at the peep-show of life, the comedy, the change, the comradeship, the rivalry, the test of one's own quality of character and vision."

A century of *Daily Mirrors* means more than 31,000 issues, each consisting of a cluster of editions to accommodate the special interests of the regions of Britain and news, no respecter of conventional hours, that breaks through the night. This is the story of what became and remains one of the world's great newspapers, the people who made it so and who accepted and passed on the baton through the 20th century and beyond. For those working in journalism, the unravelling of the past may confirm prejudices, destroy illusions, or bolster appreciation of the *Mirror*'s unparalleled record. For those looking in from the outside, it will reveal the truth about the paper that became part of the fabric of British life and introduce them to many of the memorable personalities – from vagabonds to knights (and damsels) in shining armour – behind it.

Welcome to the peep show of life.

1 THE DROWNING OF THE KITTENS

*I*t is a Monday in early November 1903 and the inaugural issue of the first ever daily newspaper for gentlewomen is launched on a public already bombarded by an unprecedented £100,000 promotional campaign.

The front page consists of picture-less advertisements for Victory's Furs, Tiffany's, Debenham and Freebody's sale of "mantles and jackets" and Peter Robinson's, of Oxford Street ("Ladies', gentlemen's and children's hosiery, gloves and underwear at one-half the usual prices"). On page 3, what passes for the paper's lead story is headed THE NATION'S SAFETY and begins portentously: "We are able to-day to

make an announcement of great national and imperial importance. The public will shortly be officially informed that a committee of three, with powers of the most liberal character, has been appointed for the reorganisation of national defences."

Beneath the Court Circular there is To-Day's News at a Glance: "M. Papazoglu, reputed the wealthiest man in Bulgaria, fatally shot himself in the presence of his parents." "Two men and a woman who are suspected of robbing and defrauding servants all over London, have been remanded at Southwark." "The entire Chilean cabinet has resigned." "The skating season at Prince's opened on Saturday." Also on a page totally free of illustration is the headline To-day's Reflections over a column signed by the proprietor, Alfred Harmsworth. He tells how the new paper has, in the months prior to publication, been ruthlessly studied and criticised by those who have created it. The soon-to-be Lord Northcliffe continues: "All that experience and preparation can do in shaping it has already been done, and the last feather of its wings adjusted; so that I now have only to open the door of the cage, and ask your good wishes for the flight."

He opens the cage. The fledgling newspaper flutters into the world just six weeks before Orville and Wilbur Wright achieve the first controlled flights in a heavier-than-air machine at Kitty Hawk, North Carolina. The Wright brothers' best effort carries them a distance of 852 feet in 59 seconds. The first issue of Harmsworth's ground-breaking 20-page paper sells out. But although on 2 November 265,217 gentlewomen of Edward VII's Britain buy the

No. 1 of

THE DAILY MIRROR

The First Daily Newspaper for Gentlewomen,

Will be issued on

MONDAY MORNING,
NOVEMBER 2.

Those who desire Copies should give immediate Orders to their Newsvendors.

ONE PENNY.

MONDAY, NOVEMBER 2nd.

Here she comes: A flyer heralds the new arrival.

Daily Mirror, *price one penny, the majority soon desert it. By 21 January, sales have dipped to just 25,563. The eagle has crash-landed...*

It had seemed a good idea at the time. Not that anyone was prepared to tell Alfred Harmsworth if they thought it was not: this was the publishing and journalistic genius who had bought and turned around the *Evening News* before creating the instantly successful *Daily Mail.* Born in Dublin of a barrister father and matriarchal mother who relocated to London, Alfred had six brothers and seven sisters. With so many mouths to feed, the family had little money, and, at 16, Alfred went straight from school into various publishing and journalistic jobs before, at the age of 22, launching *Answers to Correspondents,* the foundation stone of his success and wealth.

He was a genius. Why, hadn't Joseph Pulitzer been so impressed with the *Daily Mail* that, less than three years previously, he had invited Alfred to mastermind the relaunch of the *New York World* as "the newspaper of the future"?

Daily genius: Alfred Harmsworth, later to become Lord Northcliffe, had a magic touch.

Harmsworth had cut the broadsheet in half, slashed the length of the stories and written the front-page slogan "All the News in Sixty Seconds". He was also credited with hijacking from the firm of Burroughs, Wellcome & Co. the word "tabloid" to describe the compact size

Number one: The advert-filled front page of the new paper (left) and the first news page, page 3.

New look: But "Illustrated" would not last long in the title of the relauched Daily Mirror.

and shape of the new World. One of the founders of the pharmaceutical company had amalgamated the words "tablet" and "alkaloid" for the introduction of its Alka-Seltzer-ish fizzy reviver. But Alfred's audacity meant that "tabloid" instantly found a home in the newspaper publishing glossary, while the pharmaceutical industry was stuck with "tablet". Or "alkaloid". Alfred was a genius, all right. If he said a newspaper "written by gentlewomen for gentlewomen" – the French already had one, called *La Fronde* – would revolutionise the daily reading habits of the nation's females, then revolutionise them it would.

Only it didn't. The editor, Mary Howarth, who had previously been in charge of the women's pages at the *Daily Mail,* owes her place in history not to her achievements during a short-lived career at the *Mirror,* but for being the first female editor of a British national daily newspaper (there would not be another until Rosie Boycott was appointed at the *Daily Express* five years short of a century later). Despite the proprietor's dream of bringing daily news independence to emergent womanhood, Ms Howarth, officially "on loan" from the *Mail,* was paid just £50 a month, considerably less than her male counterparts elsewhere in Fleet Street (the paper's offices were at 2 Carmelite Street, just off the newspaper publishing artery). Her staff was described by Kennedy Jones, the

Spot the editor: One of the earliest photographs of Mirror staff playing the fool, taken within a couple of years of the paper's launch. In front in the wig is Harry Guy Bartholomew, destined one day to wear the Mirror crown, but then assisting Hannen Swaffer in the art department. Behind "Bart" (left to right) are a chap named Stewart – chief of the engraving department, Rich Richens of the art bench, Nixon from the art room and Bernard Wilson of the illustration bureau. Richens and Nixon were killed in the First World War.

Spin doctors: The Mirror staff of 1906 test their powers of invention with a primitive game of roulette, based on the office fan. Journalists usually make enthusiatic but unlucky gamblers, as those who joined a particular editor's poker school 70 years later would discover.

take-no-prisoners Glaswegian who had hitched his own talent-filled wagon to Alfred Harmsworth's star after persuading him to buy the ailing *Evening News,* as a "monstrous regiment of women".

Jones, known as "the most hated man in Fleet Street" (the title has been fiercely contested many times since), was one man who could stand up to Harmsworth, whom, to his great irritation, "K.J." addressed as "Alf". K.J., the man charged with managing the launch of the new venture, despaired of an office full of what he considered naivety and amateurishness. Every history of the popular press has recounted how he vetoed the story of the Drury Lane actor and actress who, married in the

afternoon, the *Mirror* reported, "before taking part in the usual performance in the evening". "You must have a horrid mind," whimpered the ladies when Jones killed it. Hamilton Fyfe, who was to supplant Howarth as editor, later wrote: "The *Daily Mirror* was not in the least like the women's sixpenny weeklies or *Home Chat...* It had an air of culture that those lacking in culture despised, and features designed to satisfy the latter, at which the women of taste and intellect shuddered." Concluded Fyfe: "In every department the wrong thing had been done."

One historian quoted an eyewitness as describing the atmosphere in the office as "a French farce, except all the ladies were plain".

Plain or pretty, they couldn't cut the mustard required by Jones and the man fast becoming known simply as the Chief. What's more, the *Mirror* was losing £3,000 a week. Something had to be done. Something had, in fact, already been done – Fyfe had been approached to replace Mary Howarth before the first issue had appeared, which

Star turn: The great opera singer Caruso (left) visited the Mirror's Manchester office in 1909, testing the Thorn-Baker telegraph by sending a caricature of himself over the wire to London.

suggests that Mary Howarth has been treated harshly by history. A flop though the paper most certainly was, it had always been intended that she would swiftly return to her job at the *Mail*. Harmsworth and his chain-smoking acolyte, Jones, saw Fyfe the day after launch and decided on him as the new skipper who would pilot the paper through the unanticipated choppy waters. Fyfe had made a name for himself as editor of the *Morning Advertiser* and Harmsworth had to settle the *Advertiser*'s claim for breach of contract with a £50 pay-off. Within a week, Fyfe was installed at Mary Howarth's desk.

Editorial changes were made immediately, with the paper being largely de-feminised. One of Kennedy Jones's early misogynistic observations about the *Mirror* was that women had no sense of humour and there were certainly no smiles evident as Fyfe set about decimating the staff – the slaughter of the guilty. He later famously wrote: "They begged me to be allowed to stay. They left little presents on my desk. They waylaid me tearfully in corridors. It was a horrid experience – like drowning kittens." The kittens, bedraggled rather than dead, received three months' pay in lieu of notice and departed in search of more comfortable catteries.

Meanwhile, as losses mounted, Harmsworth decided that another key figure in what had become a rescue operation would be the former editor of his magazine *Home Sweet Home,* an

Home base: The 1905 offices of the **Daily Mirror**, *in Whitefriars Street, just off Fleet Street.*

eccentric and frequently inebriated Hungarian named Arkas Sapt. A technical wizard, Sapt claimed he could publish photographs in a daily newspaper and print them perfectly on high-speed rotary presses. Until then, illustrative papers such as the *Daily Graphic* used mostly woodcuts and line drawings. However, newspaper historian Jeff Wright has correctly observed that the *Graphic* was already a proper illustrated newspaper when, in January 1904, the *Mirror* was diverted in that direction, replacing advertisements with illustrations on the front page. Other titles, including the *Daily Dispatch* in Manchester, also disputed the *Mirror*'s boast that it was the first paper to publish photographs on rotary presses.

But Sapt's development of half-tone printing certainly revolutionised the *Mirror* and its first published photographs – a studio portrait of Japanese Admiral Tora Ijuin and a picture of Japanese sailors at gun drill – appeared in the issue of 7 January 1904, a month before the Russo-Japanese war began. On 26 January the paper proclaimed "See the News Through the Camera" and "Yesterday's Events in Pictures" in two front-page boxes, but progress was slow and a technique popular at the time, where artists faithfully reproduced photographs in line drawing, continued.

On 8 February, as news of the war began to filter across the world, the *Daily Illustrated Mirror* – the masthead had been changed on 26 January and the price halved – dramatically harnessed this process. Alongside the headline WAR!, appeared a large and dramatic "drawn photograph" of Japanese sailors preparing to fire at a Russian ship. But, within two months, photographs had largely taken over and the first genuine front-page pictures appeared on 25 March, showing the funeral of the Duke of Cambridge at Kensal Green cemetery.

As the reproduction of photographs improved, the paper's circulation began to climb. Sapt was made a director of The Pictorial Newspaper Company, created as the holding company of the *Mirror* in March 1904. But, forever short of money and constantly fending off debt collectors, he commuted his commission on increased sales for, it is believed, a few hundred pounds, thereby turning his back on a fortune. By August 1909 his name had disappeared from the list of directors.

Of the appearance of the revamped title – the self-evident "Illustrated" addition to the title lasted only until the end of April – Jones proclaimed: "Fleet Street's most wonderful changeling uttered its first cry", proving he knew not only the rough and tumble of the newspaper business but also how to ensure a mention in the journalistic history books. Why someone with his experience and alleged flair had been unable to inspire the kittens to do a better job in the first place remains a mystery. Fyfe was later to suggest that Jones had little to do with the revamped paper and "in some moods would not have been sorry to see it killed". Unlike its treatment of Howarth, history, that old

misogynist, has been kind to Jones.

Thanks to Sapt's expertise and the presentational skills of one Hannen Swaffer, the paper's art editor, circulation very quickly jumped to 71,690 and reached 120,000 three weeks later. On 27 February, an elated Harmsworth felt able to confide the inadequacies of the original product to the paper's now burgeoning number of readers. Under the heading HOW I DROPPED £100,000 ON THE MIRROR, he wrote: "I had for many years a theory that a daily newspaper for women was in urgent request, and I started one. The belief cost me £100,000. I found out that I was beaten. Women don't want a daily paper of their own." The original *Mirror,* he asserted, was "up to the present, the only journalistic failure with which I have been associated. But the *Daily Illustrated Mirror* which has replaced it is certainly one of the simplest journalistic successes with which I have been associated." Finally, having acknowledged "flat, rank and unmitigated failure", the Chief trumpeted: "I then changed the price to a halfpenny, and filled it full of photographs and pictures to see how that would do. It did." The paper was still less than four months old.

In Carmelite Street, where the already muscular *Daily Mail* was also based, Fyfe continued to resuscitate the *Mirror*. His greatest strength was as a leader writer and his response

Pushing the boat out: Some notable* Mirror *faces (and hats) were on deck for this* Mirror *staff outing in 1912. Harold Harmsworth is smoking a pipe at the end of the front bench, with editor Alex Kenealy seated next to him. Harry Guy Bartholomew is perched on the lifeboat on the left, smoking a cigar. Hannen Swaffer, sporting an enormous flat cap and looking directly at camera, stands in the back row.

when a London coroner recorded "natural death" on a seven-year-old child who had died of starvation was to establish the paper's stance – by no means a constant, but a caring one that re-emerged to great effect many years hence – on social deprivation: "In the capital of the greatest empire in the world death from starvation is natural death. If this is natural, let us give up talking about the benefits of starvation… Is there no leading man in Britain who will come forward as the champion of the poor? Is there no one who can point a way and induce the nation to follow, no way of saving

the next generation from the same plight?" The socialist writer and editor Robert Blatchford seized upon Fyfe's radicalism, commenting: "It is so seldom one feels the warm pulse of human passion in a British newspaper."

Faster almost than the ink could dry, what had been a journalistic and commercial belly flop gained credibility and panache. As Robert Allen and John Frost recorded in their 1981 history, the paper reported on such disparate events as the return from a Government propaganda trip to Tibet by Colonel Younghusband; the "Queer Wee Man" – less than three feet tall, weighing nine kilogrammes, with a foot only four-and-a-half inches long – who had been discovered in Lower Burma and brought to London for the amusement of its citizens; the death of eight Britons in Aden when Captain Lloyd-Jones and 60 soldiers were surrounded by 1,000 tribesmen; highwaymen in Dagenham; a girl burglar in Birkenhead; and a workhouse in Clitheroe, Lancashire, that had become so popular that some 400 vagrants each week were seeking admission.

"Britain was a country of boisterous contrast in those days when the *Mirror* set out to record its affairs in photographs, pen-and-ink sketches and words," Hugh Cudlipp was to observe half-a-century later. This was a country with processions of unemployed men, children working long hours for a few pence a week, women working 17 hours a day for eight shillings a week as they made artificial flowers, and some men "labouring 12 hours on the railways for tenpence," he recalled. But "at the other end of the scale was a world of opulence, sables, orchids and folly" – the young Marquis of Anglesey spent £1million in three years and wore a £1,000 overcoat; a shoot in Hereford bagged 4,000 birds, including 1,324 pheasants; when Alfred Beit, the richest man in England

Start of the strips: W.K. Haselden *drew cartoons for the* **Mirror** *for almost 40 years.*

died, it was revealed that the businesses he controlled were worth a billion pounds.

So when Hamilton Fyfe wrote in a *Mirror* editorial: "How long can this butterfly-dance continue, this frivolity and pleasure-seeking of society?" he touched a nerve with thousands of ordinary men and women languishing on the wrong side of the tracks. A divided country was slithering through a deep trough of inequality towards a distant war that would decimate the population. Fyfe had already announced the paper's general support for the Labour Party, then the Labour Representation Committee – socialism was "the creed of the future", he wrote – and had campaigned for meals to be made available for schoolchildren. This concern for the less fortunate and a belief in social justice and human rights was to be the bedrock of the *Mirror*'s success during several incarnations.

A journalistic wunderkind, who years later would be largely responsible for the paper achieving true journalistic greatness, was already there as it struggled to its feet, if not yet to the skies. Harry Guy Bartholomew had come to work in the photo-engraving department just two months after the disastrous launch, producing line and, soon, half-tone blocks under the direction of Hannen Swaffer. Swaffer, who had been drafted in from the *Daily Mail,* was 24, "Bart" just 19. Together they formed a formidable double act that promised and delivered much.

Swaffer, who worked for ten years at the *Mirror*, would later become a pioneer gossip columnist ("I think I must have sunk to the

Edwardian pin-up: Beauty contests were regular Mirror *features. Here is 1908 winner Ivy Close.*

murky bottom of cheap yellow journalism," he was to observe of this role), editor of the *Weekly Dispatch* and then *The People*, drama critic of the *Daily Express*, a columnist on the *Daily Herald* and honorary president of the Spiritualists' National Union. Lord Northcliffe, previously Alfred Harmsworth, called him "The Poet" because "Swaff" always wore unkempt long hair upon which sat a wide-brimmed felt hat. A cigarette permanently smouldered between his lips. His trenchant columns in the *Herald* earned him another title, the Pope of Fleet Street, and the first proper awards for journalists, later to become the British Press Awards but created in the mid-1960s and originally administered by the Mirror Group, were named the Hannen Swaffer Awards in his memory.

Bart, about whom much more will be heard as the story of the *Daily Mirror* unfolds, was in his own way every bit as precocious a talent. Starting out at 14 as an office boy on the *Illustrated Mail*, he was to become editorial director and then chairman of the Mirror Group. That fate brought him and Swaffer together in 1904 was just one of the strokes of good fortune that enabled Alfred Harmsworth's shattered dream to be pieced together again. Sapt's intervention was another, as was the appearance one day of the Spanish-born cartoonist W.K. (William Kerridge) Haselden, who arrived with a portfolio of drawings and remained with the *Mirror* for the best part of the next 40 years. But then, even a genius, as many regarded Harmsworth, needs luck.

So successful had the paper become by the beginning of 1905 that larger premises were required. In January of that year, the *Daily Mirror* relocated to nearby 12 Whitefriars Street. The issue of 21 January was the last printed in Carmelite Street, and, in what the paper headlined "*Daily Mirror*'s Magic Move", 70,000lbs of equipment was transported by 300 men with carts in time for the following Monday's issue to be produced from the paper's new home.

Pictures continued to dominate the paper. The three Grant brothers, Bernard ("Bunny"), Horace and Tommy, were among the early star snappers and, as Hugh Cudlipp later recorded, another, David McLellan, created a "hullabaloo" when his faulty magnesium flash-powder exploded as he attempted to take the first ever night photograph of Piccadilly Circus from the balcony at the Swan and Edgar store. Fifty-two windows were blown out and a corner torn off the balcony in what other papers speculated was an anarchist bomb.

It was Tom Grant who managed to get appointed as assistant to the official court photographer for the funeral of Japanese Emperor Mutsuhito; dressed in top hat and formal dress, the man from the *Mirror* was in his place 12 hours before a ceremony where two men were killed and several others injured – experiments to boost the lighting had caused an explosion of vapour lamps. Grant got his pictures.

The stirrings of liberalism in the paper's views continued. In 1906, it broadly supported the suffragette movement; two years later, an article on the plight of the poor included the daily menu of a "dock worker", highlighting the enormous gulf between the haves and have-nots. And the paper's increasing superiority in the photographic field could not have been emphasised more dramatically than when King Edward VII died in 1910. The issue of Monday 10 May included, on the front page, a picture of the dead monarch at rest. Complaints that the *Mirror* had displayed atrocious taste by intruding on private grief were disproved when it

became known how Swaffer, overhearing in a public house that the picture had been taken, had reacted instantly by having the court photographer offered £100 to ask Queen Alexander if the paper could publish it. According to Swaffer's account, the Queen replied, "It can only go in one paper, the *Mirror*, because that is my favourite." The direct quotation today sounds as believable as the Queen having snapped her departed husband herself and given the image to Swaffer over a couple of gins-and-tonic in The Falstaff, but obtaining the picture was an outstanding coup. (The Queen may have been taken with the *Mirror*, but much of the aristocracy was unimpressed. Disdainful of both the *Mail* and its brazen, picture-powerful young cousin, Lord Salisbury was heard to remark that Mr Harmsworth had invented one paper for those who could read but not think and another for those who could see but not read.)

Another photographic scoop that same year was the discovery and publishing of the only known photograph of Ethel Le Neve, mistress of hunted wife-killer Dr Hawley Crippen. (In what became a notorious court case, the paper earned a dubious testimonial from Crippen, on trial after wireless telegraphy had been used for

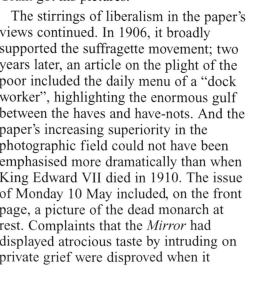

Danger man: Mirror *photographer* Horace Grant *being kitted out to dive on the wreck of the frigate Lutine.*

Steady as she goes: A woman learner driver reverses a 1914 runabout. This was part of a series of "men v. women" articles that sought to establish who was best adapted to learn the new skill of car driving.

the first time in crime detection to establish he and Ethel, who was disguised as a boy, were aboard an ocean liner. During a lull in proceedings, Crippen was seen reading a copy of the *Mirror*. He was hanged nonetheless.)

The paper was proud of its enterprise from the very beginning. In 1904, when the Holland-America shipping line announced it would carry emigrants from London to New York for an inclusive fare of £2, a *Mirror* reporter travelled steerage on the liner Potsdam from Rotterdam to write about the voyage. The following year the paper came up with an Unemployment Scheme, offering to pay out-of-work men 3s 6d (17½p) a day for sweeping the streets. With local councils rushing to become involved, £2,600 was raised and spent in wages and 15,000 unemployed men temporarily given brooms.

There were early forays into investigative journalism, too, including a report that tinned meat imported from the United States was so revolting it was inedible. The paper attacked the import of the canned health hazard and W.K. Haselden, normally not the most vicious of cartoonists, went for the American meat industry with pencil sharpened to lacerating effect. There were always off-beat tales to catch

the imagination, too: a clergyman attempted suicide by hiring a boat at Weymouth, rowing out to sea, taking poison and cutting his own throat before jumping into the water. He was rescued, whereupon a length of rope was found in his pocket – he had intended to throttle himself if his earlier attempts failed. They did and the story concluded: "The doctors state that there is hope of recovery." And the wacky, the frivolous, the audacious had their place. As Cudlipp later recalled: when an apiarist claimed that bees could live and thrive in a crowded city, two colonies of them – making 50,000 in all – were installed on the office roof. They were lightly powdered with flour so the public could spot them in gardens and squares within a two-mile radius.

The *Mirror*'s popularity was such that by now its name littered the conversation of the working class. Entertainer Gus Elen was quick to notice this and inserted into his act a song, *Wait Till the Work Comes Around*, that included the verse:

"If you ain't got a job, well you can't get the sack.
That's an argument that's always safe and sound.
Put your head upon the 'piller'
And read the Daily Mirror

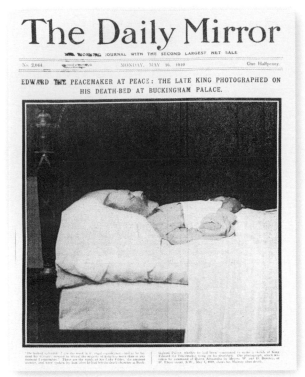

Scoop and scandal: The controversial picture of the dead King at rest in the issue of 16 May 1910.

Wrong place at the right time: A Mirror photographer was aboard the Sontay when she sank.

And wait till the work comes around."

Fyfe remained editor until 1907 – "Circulation raised from 40,000 to 400,000," his entry in *Who's Who* boasted – before departing to continue a distinguished career as a journalist and author that lasted throughout a long life. His replacement at the *Mirror* was Alexander Cockburn Kenealy. New York-trained but lured away from the news editorship of the *Daily Express* soon after Fyfe took control in 1904, the short, corpulent and ruddy-faced Kenealy had an aptitude for both news management and the extravagant editorial promotions for which the *Mirror* was fast becoming known.

Another *Mirror* historian, Maurice Edelman, told how, in June 1904, the *Mirror* celebrated the growing importance of the iron horse by organising a 26,000-mile non-stop motor car endurance test, with a Mr D.M. Weigal twice driving from the *Mirror* office to Perth and back and then making a round trip to Portsmouth. Other stunts included beauty contests (15,000 women who sent their photographs for entry in "the International Competition to find the Most Beautiful Woman in the World", won by Miss Ivy Lillian Close, were all awarded certificates of merit), baby contests, sandcastle competitions for readers' children, wireless tests from an aeroplane and the offer of a prize of 100 guineas for the first person to swim the

channel. Kenealy relished such profile-builders and under his editorship they continued to get the paper talked about. *Daily Mirror* Gala Days, jamborees to which readers were admitted on production of a coupon cut from the paper, had been introduced in September 1904, when the paper took over Crystal Palace and 100,000 people turned up. The following year's event was expanded to three days and then *Daily Mirror* Days were launched at seaside resorts, with special trains, with cheap fares, laid on to transport the readers. Then, in 1909, the paper proved that pigs could fly when, at the paper's instigation, aviator Moore-Brabazon took a porker for a short flip in his flying machine.

In 1911, the paper's Street Performers' Matinee competition at the Apollo Theatre was won by a boy violinist who received the immediate offer of an eight-week engagement on a major music hall circuit. And the paper began what was to become a long and sometimes chaotic association with live animals when, in 1909, "Roosevelt", a Syrian bear, was bought as a promotional pet for children. When he grew too large, the *Mirror* presented Roosevelt to a unit of the Army Service Corps as a regimental mascot and subsequently the animal was retired to the Zoological Gardens, where he died in 1913. So enthused was it by the bear that the paper next bought two Indian elephants, Jumbo and Jimbo, that toured the

THE DAILY MIRROR, Wednesday, May 21, 1913
CAPTAIN SCOTT'S TOMB NEAR THE SOUTH POLE.

The Daily Mirror 24 Pages

THE MORNING JOURNAL WITH THE SECOND LARGEST NET SALE.

No. 2,987.   WEDNESDAY, MAY 21, 1913.   One Halfpenny.

THE MOST WONDERFUL MONUMENT IN THE WORLD: CAPTAIN SCOTT'S SEPULCHRE ERECTED AMID ANTARCTIC WASTES.

Going places: The stunning front page of 21 May 1915, depicting the sepulchre of Captain Scott.

The Daily Mirror

THE MORNING JOURNAL WITH THE SECOND LARGEST NET SALE.

No. 2,648.   FRIDAY, APRIL 19, 1912.   One Halfpenny.

WHY WERE THERE ONLY TWENTY LIFEBOATS FOR 2,207 PEOPLE ON BOARD THE ILL-FATED TITANIC?

Horror story: The Mirror's *coverage of the sinking of the* Titanic *set a questioning tone.*

country, raising money for charity and visiting children's parties and hospitals. In 1912 the *Mirror* announced that "Baby Jumbo, the smallest elephant ever seen in England" would be collecting money for the paper's Christmas Pudding Fund for poor children. According to the paper, "Baby Jumbo is quite tame, of a very affectionate disposition, and especially fond of children", which must have come as something of a relief to parents. Jumbo and Jimbo also ended up in a zoo but, according to Hugh Cudlipp, another elephantine import, Babs, was one day let into the editor's office by "the high-spirited art staff" and promptly dropped dead. It is said that there are editors today who might have a similar affect on human beings.

On more serious issues, Lord Northcliffe's influence – Harmsworth had been created a baronet by Edward VII on the advice of Balfour in 1904 and became Lord Northcliffe in 1905 – was felt in the *Mirror*, but not frequently. It was the *Daily Mail* that the Chief used as a battering ram, although sometimes he would enlist the *Evening News* and his baby daily as reinforcements when pursuing one of the bees that buzzed not on the roof but constantly in his bonnet.

When Northcliffe decided the public was being asked to pay too much for a bar of household soap, Haselden was called up into the front line in the battle against William Lever MP, later Lord Leverhulme, the head of what was, to all intents and purposes, a soap trust that manufactured a variety of soaps, from Lux to Sunlight. The cartoonist's series of drawings introduced to readers "Mr Soap Trust", the pickpocket and cheat, and "Signor Soapo Trusti", the conjurer from "Port Moonshine" – Lever's main factory was at Port Sunlight – who, by sleight of hand, reduced a 16-ounce bar of soap by two ounces. With the big guns of the *Mail* and *Evening News* also firing venomously, the sales of Lever Brothers' products nose-dived and the 16-ounce bar of soap appeared once more on retailers' shelves. To celebrate victory, Haselden drew the British lion proudly standing over the defeated "Signor Soapo". (Lever Brothers subsequently sued for libel and won an action estimated to have cost Northcliffe around £200,000.)

An Overseas Edition was published from 1913, but two years before then the citizens – many of them English immigrants – of a new community in Canada, had been puzzling over what to call their town when one of them brandished a copy of the paper relatives and friends were still sending them from the old country. And so Mirror, Alberta, was born, and a cluster of streets were given names connected with the paper, although Whitefriars Boulevard and Northcliffe Boulevard have long since been

Death at the races: How a Suffragette Tried to Spoil the Derby was the Mirror's *headline in 1913.*

rechristened. Back in London, the paper's long-running leader page "This Morning's Gossip" feature, conducted by C.P. Little and crammed with society snippets, was ditched in November 1913 in favour of the jottings of "The Rambler", who concentrated on Parliament, gentlemen's clubs and the stage in serving up a scandal-free diet of harmless chitchat.

A picture exclusive when American journalist Harriet Quimby became the first woman to cross the English Channel by air was driven from the early news pages in April 1912 by coverage of the loss of the Titanic off Cape Race (WHY WERE THERE ONLY TWENTY LIFEBOATS FOR 2,207 PEOPLE? the paper wanted to know). A memorial pictorial issue after Scott and some of his party died on the way home from the Antarctic in February 1913 helped consolidate the *Mirror*'s position as a pugnacious new kid on the national newspaper block. A month later, in its 3000th issue, it published seven front-page pictures of the death of Emily Davidson, who had thrown herself under the King's Horse at Epsom (the headline, HOW A SUFFRAGETTE TRIED TO SPOIL THE DERBY, showed that the paper had yet to get fully into its compassionate stride). And in July 1914, editor Kenealy received a telegram from King George and Queen Mary congratulating the paper on achieving a daily circulation of 1,000,000 copies. The *Mirror* now

not only could claim to be the best, but the biggest, too.

But for Northcliffe the celebrations were muted. In January of 1914 he had sold his share of the *Mirror* to his commercially parsimonious younger brother, Harold, who was to become Baron Rothermere that same year. Northcliffe looked on the paper "as the bastard of his journalistic family", his official biographers later claimed, and certainly he was disappointed that the paper did not gain him the influence he craved in the corridors of power. He also appears to have been uncomfortable with the frequent light-heartedness of the paper – crucial to the popular morning journalism that media personality Francis Williams, himself a former newspaper editor, was years later to describe as "a three-ring circus, daily presenting to its patrons the greatest show on earth". The *Daily Mail* and now also *The Times* occupied most of Northcliffe's time and gave him more political muscle than the journalistic upstart he had founded. He received £100,000 from Harold for his *Mirror* shares – exactly the amount he claimed to have lost while the paper was suffering its birth pangs.

In his £3.5million will, Northcliffe was to reflect: "I invented the *Daily Mirror*. It was a failure at first, and Rothermere ran for his life. When it became a success, I sold it to him for nothing..." The will, written in pencil, began:

Drama afloat: A **Mirror** *photographer captures the scene after a Calais steamer runs aground in 1909.*

"I, Alfred Viscount Northcliffe, being in good mental state, though suffering from one dangerous disease, Indian jungle fever, and another unknown to any doctors in Great Britain, poisoning by ice-cream supplied on the Belgian frontier…" He died, of "infective or ulcerative endocarditis" rather than ice-cream poisoning and, some said, by now quite mad, on 14 August 1922 at the age of 57. Among those crowding the streets between Westminster Abbey, where the funeral service had been conducted, and St. Marylebone Cemetery were many of those gentlewomen for whom 19 years previously he had created a little bird of a newspaper they hadn't cared for enough to make it fly.

It must have seemed that the change of ownership would make little difference to the *Mirror*'s progress. The little bird had at last grown powerful wings and only the sky was the limit. None of those responsible were likely to miss the

Tube line: Lads man the early version of the tape room.

megalomania that had prompted Northcliffe to try on Napoleon's hat during a visit to Fontainebleau and, it is said, cry: "It fits!", or the ranting and the belittling of employees from whom he demanded total obedience (not the last time such behaviour was to rattle the windows at the *Mirror*) But there was to be a downside.

Unlike his brother, Harold was no journalist. Educated at the Philological School (later Marylebone Grammar) in Marylebone Road, London, where he shone at arithmetic, he had worked as a clerk at the Inland Revenue before joining Alfred in publishing. As a visionary, he was a first-class accountant.

War and carnage, obsession and arrogance, political miscalculation and editorial dissipation, and personal and professional tragedy were all just around the corner. Had seat belts been in vogue at the time, the exhilarated staff at the *Mirror* would have been wise to fasten them securely.

2 *THE WET BLANKET*

*It is a warm morning in July 1914 and the
Daily Mirror is loudly beating its own
drum. Such exercises in self-gratification
by papers of all complexions are to become as
familiar as the boasts of politicians over the
years to come, but today's claim establishes an
early benchmark in hyperbole: DAILY MIRROR
HAS WORLD'S LARGEST CIRCULATION.*

*Has the Mirror researched the sale of
newspapers in China, the Russias and the
Ottoman Empire? Well, no, and in the tub-
thumping text under the headline it is careful to
reduce its grand claim merely to having the
largest circulation of any paper in the English
language. There is no doubt that it has the
largest sale in Britain, and under Kenealy's
editorship it has maintained a heady
journalistic mix of eye-catching promotions,
awe-inspiring pictures from around the world –
from Italian atrocities in Tripoli in 1911 to a
balloon-crossing of the Alps – and cartoons,
often by W.K. Haselden, that have evolved into a
new enticing newspaper ingredient known as
"strips". The Mirror is no longer the youngest
pictorial paper, Edward Hulton having
launched the Daily Sketch against it in 1908,
but, this fine morning, Kenealy and the rest of
the Mirror team are at the peak of the Fleet
Street mountain.*

*If the new proprietor is elated by the paper's
record sales, he does not demonstrate his
pleasure with any celebratory extravagance.
Lord Rothermere is too busy applying himself to
reconstructing the company as an efficient
money machine (this, after all, is the man who,
when asked to look at the books of The Times
after his brother had acquired that famous title,
was so dismayed by the figures that he burst*

*into tears). But in the editorial offices and those
of the other departments that have achieved so
much inside a decade, there is a feeling of
festivity. A public holiday looms, and, on 28
July, the paper announces to its readers that on
the following Monday there will be a "Monster
Bank Holiday" issue. On 4 August, another
monster issue greets readers: Great Britain
declares war on Germany...*

The *Mirror* had a good World War,
dispatching to France and Belgium
correspondents and photographers, many of
them veterans of two conflicts in the Balkans
and the Italian-Turkish war, and keeping abreast
of the unfolding horror in words and pictures.
Soon the paper had become as important as
rations to the troops in the trenches. One *Mirror*
historian, Maurice Edelman, wrote that the
Mirror was distributed to the Army mainly by
children, who advanced as far as the reserve
lines, not much more than a mile from the
trenches, to sell the paper. Despite gradual
shrinkage, from 24 pages to eight, and the legal
suspension of sale or return by newsagents, the
Mirror surged ahead at home, too, by
graphically keeping wives and sweethearts
informed of what was happening to their loved
ones in the war to end them all. Cash prizes
were offered for readers' best war pictures and
the paper pulled off a major scoop by
publishing the first pictures of a new
revolutionary weapon, the tank. In July 1915, it
declared an average daily sale of 1,053,000 and
in 1917 was confident enough to double its
price, back to one penny. The *Mirror* looked
unassailable.

But commercial success was tarnished by the
illness and death of the editor and, for

Buy-up: *An early example of chequebook journalism secured the first pictures of tanks in action.*

Lord above: *Lord Rothermere's obsessions held the newspaper back in many different ways.*

Rothermere, by personal tragedy. Kenealy died at a nursing home in Haselmere, Surrey, on 26 June 1915, a Saturday – unusually bad timing for such a good daily newspaperman. So much was he revered that the *Mirror* published an eight-page "memorial number" to honour "The Man Who Made The *Mirror*". In a fulsome obituary the Monday following his death, the paper described the man known to friends and colleagues as "K" as "a born journalist" and observed: "He knew his work admirably, in all its detail, but never boasted of anything he had done".

The Kenealy that emerges from the *Mirror*'s reporting of his death was kind, gentle and a lover of children, of which he appears to have had none of his own (nor wife for that matter). Hugh Cudlipp later laid claim to information that suggested a rather different man, one with more recognisable journalistic traits: in his prime, "K" was apparently a saloon bruiser of some distinction, once having to pay $500 for broken glassware and furniture and his opponent's medical expenses after a bar-room disagreement with a cartoonist named Don McCarthy in the building that also housed the *New York World*. The gentleness mentioned after

his death may have embraced Kenealy following his return to England, for when, at the *Mirror*, Hamilton Fyfe once threatened to "knock his head off" in a verbal dispute over a story, "K" backed off, white-faced. "I would not have said it," the occasionally fanciful Fyfe later recalled, "if I had known the reason for his alarm – he was nervous of physical violence on account, I believe, of a weak heart."

Many years later, Fyfe wrote of Kenealy that he was "one of those men who get a great deal done without ever seeming to do anything in particular" (a skill shared by few editors, many of whom manage to do nothing at all while seeming always to be frenziedly busy) and recounted how he hated firing anybody. He did so with élan, however, on one occasion sending for a member of staff named Frank Rutter and asking: "You are an art critic, I believe, Mr Rutter?" Rutter did not deny it. "Then there is no need for me to point out to you the difference between painting pictures and house-painting," said Kenealy. "It is house-painting we want here, Mr Rutter. I am sure you understand what I mean." The unfortunate Rutter left at the end of the week.

Kenealy apparently possessed considerable

diplomatic skills, too. According to Maurice Edelman, in 1911 Northcliffe protested about the New York brashness – learned during the editor's early career in the United States – that had been introduced into the paper. In a duck and weave operation most editors would both recognise and admire, Kenealy replied: "I quite agree with your letter about the bad taste and ignorance of some of the things that appear in the *Daily Mirror*. I have been trying to stop them. Highly educated men, I find, as a rule have no sense of news. They always want to write about ancient Rome or what happened to Jupiter. They regard the death of King Edward as unimportant because it is recent. We have Oxford men here and Eton men. None of them can write gramatically [sic] or spell [look who's talking?], and they are woefully ignorant of anything that has happened since 42 BC."

Fyfe probably did better in evaluating Kenealy's undoubted qualities as an editor than all the posthumous praise poured on him by the *Mirror* when he wrote that when "K" worked on a Hearst paper in the United States, he saw a reader on the street pick up his morning *Examiner* and heard him exclaim "Gee whiz!" From then on, he strove for the "Gee whiz!" reaction every working day. He was only 51 when he died.

E.D. Flynn, an American and the most anonymous of all the *Daily Mirror* editors, succeeded his friend Kenealy. As the war progressed, the paper continued as it had previously, dramatically bringing home the

A talent to amaze: Alexander Kenealy edited the Daily Mirror **with a brashness bred in New York journalism.**

hostilities with powerful pictures and dispatches. The approach of Christmas in 1914 was marked by a front-page photograph of a soldier slumped in the snow, attempting to snatch some sleep, and a caption that reminded readers "There are no eiderdowns or hot-water bottles at the front". Graphic if ludicrously cheerful descriptions of the carnage in the mud at Flanders came from correspondent W. Beach Thomas, and a *Mirror* photographer travelling on the French liner Sontay when it was torpedoed in May 1917 was able to provide one of the most dramatic front pages of the war – lifeboats leaving the sinking ship and the headline: "VIVE LA FRANCE!" SHOUTS A CAPTAIN AS HIS SHIP SINKS.

The photographer, name unknown, had been smoking in his berth when the torpedo hit. He went on deck, returned for his camera, and in the four minutes that elapsed before the ship sank, took 14 striking pictures.

Rothermere, Director of the Army Clothing Department from 1916-17, was by 1917 correctly advocating the importance of controlling the skies. In November of that year he was appointed the first Minister for Air and began merging the Royal Flying Corps and Royal Naval Air Service into the Royal Air Force.

Rothermere had not been idle on the commercial front, either, having on 15 March 1915 reacted to a rumoured new Hulton paper, the *Illustrated Sunday Herald* (later the *Sunday Graphic*), by launching the *Sunday Pictorial*. Under the direction of editor F.R. Sanderson and his deputy, Alexander Campbell, the *Mirror*'s baby sister – it would adopt the family

Post-war line-up: Editor E.D. Flynn is the man in the front row wearing a bow tie in this 1919 staff photograph. Leigh D. Brownlee, then news editor, later editor, is on his left.

name and become the *Sunday Mirror* at the mature age of 48 – was hustled on to the streets at a clatter. Conception to publication took just eight weeks, but the *Pictorial* was an immediate success, reaching a circulation in excess of one million copies within six months.

One of Rothermere's first decisions as proprietor had been to close down the loss-making printing plant his brother had installed in Manchester – the paper may have had chutzpah, but it was shedding loose change at the rate of £600 a week in the north. With this saving, the continuing success of the *Mirror* and the rapid growth of the newborn *Pic*, Rothermere's financial stock rose. His personal life, however, was about to be devastated. The war arrived savagely in Whitefriars Street when two of his sons, Vyvyan and Vere, were killed in battle. Vere did not survive the Battle of the Ancre in November 1916, and, two years later, as the war ended, Vyvyan, the eldest, died of wounds sustained in the Battle of Cambrai. Earlier in the year, Rothermere had suffered a nervous collapse and resigned his ministerial post.

Shortly afterwards, back in the newspaper business full-time, he continued to look at plans for expansion, entrusting company chairman Bertram Lima with the development of an *Evening Mirror*. Sanderson and Campbell, the journalists who had made a success of the *Pictorial*, were selected to head up the new venture's editorial team, but Lima's death at the age of 35 in 1919 was another blow to the proprietor and effectively throttled the evening paper in the womb. The man chosen to replace Lima as chairman was John Cowley, who, following a disastrous publishing venture of his own, was as unadventurous as Rothermere was economically stringent (his Lordship could be

personally generous, however: Hugh Cudlipp recorded that Harold gave Rolls-Royces as presents to family members and thrust five-pound notes into the hands of beggars). Cowley considered the launch of the new evening title too hazardous for him to sanction.

Rothermere turned his attentions to the daily paper and, as Hugh Cudlipp later put it, "a wet blanket descended on the *Mirror*". Politically naïve and ultra-conservative on social issues, Rothermere disagreed in print with a proposed health scheme for every citizen and attacked

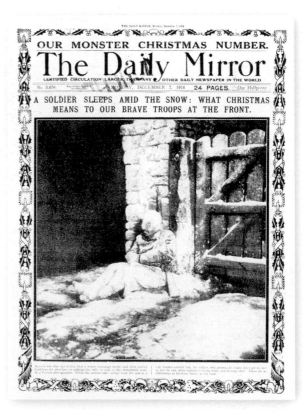

Heart of the matter: The Mirror *would always have a gift for bringing home the reality of war.*

labour exchanges as being clubs for pensioners. He alienated women readers with ponderous political and financial articles, and launched the *Mirror* down a cul-de-sac with a campaign against "squandermania", accusing Lloyd George's coalition Government of frittering away the nation's wealth. Richard Jennings, who was to become a key member of the *Mirror*'s radical editorial powerhouse in the years to come, wrote a polemic headlined Women Voters and Waste M.P.s: 'The Housewife's Protest Against Squandermania'. Rothermere formed the Anti-Waste League, with himself as president, and with some success sponsored parliamentary candidates. WASTE SPELLS MISERY, the *Mirror* told its readers, and continued to deliver the message with the subtlety of a battering ram. A special "Squandermania Number" on 9 December 1920, specifying how the nation's money was being wasted, infuriated the coalition Government. Unfazed, Rothermere

Alexander Campbell took over the editorship in 1920, but was unable to stop the paper's slide towards mediocrity.

personally practised what he preached, moving from the plush hotel suite where he lived to more modest accommodation and serving plain food in his dining room, with water to drink instead of wine. Fun, he wasn't, and although the *Mirror* was to make up for the deficiency in this area in later years, both the staff of the paper and the public soon began to grow tired of what had become an obsession.

It wasn't the only one of Rothermere's fixations with which readers were force-fed. His passion for, and belief in, the future of air travel, far-sighted though it may have been, spilled over page after page in the *Mirror* when Alcock and Brown made the first transatlantic

Hot wire: The Mirror of 6 July 1920 records the success of tests to send pictures by wireless.

Cover girl: The Daily Mirror of 7 March 1921 discovered Britain's most beautiful children.

Check mates: The readers in 1927 did not enjoy the best of accommodation.

flight in June 1919. (The paper, notably, had been the first to distribute an edition by air, Mr B.C. Hucks flying from Hendon to Bath with a cargo of *Mirrors* in May 1912.) Ponderous financial articles laced with dull gossip stories produced a daily cocktail with all the fizz of flat lemonade. In 1920, editor Flynn, having failed to follow Kenealy's example of stamping his personality on the paper, made way for Alexander Campbell, previously the *Evening Mirror*'s bridesmaid-in-waiting, but even the most alert newspaper junkie would have been forgiven for not noticing. The *Mirror*, no longer the only paper with picture power and in other areas having all the sparkle of syrup, continued its decline. It could now boast only "Certified Circulation Larger Than That Of Any Other Daily Picture Paper" – a far cry, or a sad whimper, from being a world-beater.

The death of Lord Northcliffe in 1922 prompted an issue packed almost front-to-back with eulogy. For two months the mental state of the founder of the *Daily Mirror* had been such that he was under constant surveillance in a rooftop hut above his Carlton Gardens London address. The last demand of the man later dubbed by Lord Beaverbrook (the Canadian mastermind responsible for the phenomenal success of the *Daily Express*) as "the greatest figure who ever strode down Fleet Street" was for a page reviewing his life and work in *The Times*. He did not mention the *Mirror*.

Upon his brother's death, Rothermere took charge of Associated Newspapers. The *Daily Mail, Evening News* and *Sunday Dispatch* jostled with the *Mirror* for his attention – *The Times* was sold, escaping into the welcoming arms of John J. Astor – and by 1928 there would be 14 daily and Sunday newspapers under Rothermere's control. Politically, the man now standing astride a newspaper empire of awesome power was a maverick, but he would have no truck with socialism – Fyfe's earlier liberalism and Rothermere's own support for the Liberal Party rapidly became dim memories. In the General Election of 1918, when Lloyd George's coalition romped home, the *Mirror* urged its readers to "Vote for the right man or woman (Coalition)". In November 1922, Ramsay MacDonald's Labour was conspicuous by its absence from a series of special *Mirror* issues spotlighting the various political factions. It was a time of political turbulence – the Conservatives, led by Bonar Law and Stanley Baldwin, brought down the Lloyd George coalition; Bonar Law became prime minister and upon his death only months later was succeeded by Baldwin. Rothermere was anti-socialist both in 1922 and in the election of December the following year, when the Tories were returned with a lead over Labour of 67 seats but no overall majority. When a combined Labour-Liberal vote torpedoed the Government a week later, Ramsay MacDonald formed the first Labour administration. Rothermere was mortified, but had not long to wait before the feared socialists were unseated. In the election of October 1924, in which the Liberal Party was destroyed as a major political force, the Tories routed Labour with 419 seats against the main opposition's 151. "The country's crushing verdict on socialism and red intrigues," crowed the *Daily Mirror*.

The General Strike of 1926 saw, on the night of Monday 3 May, the trade unions causing the *Mirror* to suspend publication for the first time in its history, although by no means the last. Two of the unions involved in production requested that the editor should amend a leading article hostile to the strike and remove a news paragraph they found offensive. The editor resisted. The paper failed to come out. By the following day the management had regrouped successfully enough to produce 80,000 copies of a single-sheet "News Bulletin", printed in a flat in Victoria by Gestetner machines on one side only and costing a penny. Dated 5 May, its "Point of View" was a rallying cry: "The *Daily Mirror* calls upon its readers to do all in their power to support the Government". Elsewhere on the page, the paper reported that Mr F. Saklatvala, the MP for North Battersea, had been arrested and charged with making a "dangerous and inflammatory speech".

Two days later, a strike issue containing pictures appeared and soon similar papers were being produced in addition to the Gestetner bulletins, with the print being spread around

Penny wise: John Cowley, Mirror chairman 1919-1944, as drawn by Ralph Sallon.

centres in Finchley, St. Albans, Croydon, Wimbledon, Soho and Holborn. The *Mirror* denounced the strikers, advised the Government STAND FAST! NO SURRENDER! and in a

The little presses roll: The issue of Tuesday, 4 May 1926 had been lost to strike action. Gestetner machines, set up in a flat in Victoria, were used to produce the first mini-Mirrors of the General Strike in May 1926. 80,000 copies of the first issue were successfully run off.

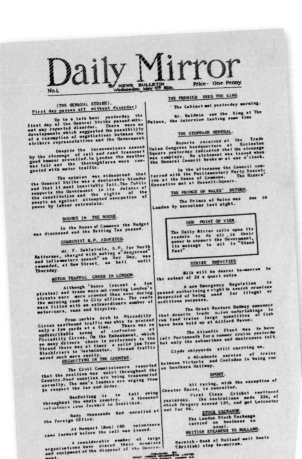

Taking on the workers: Samples of the General Strike miniature issues of the Mirror. Even though drastically reduced in size, room could still be found for Pip, Squeak and Wilfred.

Destined to rule: The first picture, published on 22 May 1926, of the Duchess of York with her first child, the future Queen Elizabeth II.

Tribute: Rothermere and the Hon. Mrs Esmond Harmsworth attend the unveiling of the memorial to Lord Northcliffe at St. Dunstan's, Fleet Street.

leading article railed: "The people expect the Government not to fail in its duty. If the Cabinet surrenders, democratic government will be forever impossible in this country." It greeted with undisguised glee news of those militants who decided the fight was futile and returned to work, and reported that "the public cheerfully and helpfully shouldered the inconveniences the strike brought in its train". The paper was later to boast that no member of the editorial staff went on strike, despite being "called upon to work most hours of the 24, in strange places, and often under stranger conditions". Its size may have been stunted, but the *Mirror*'s illiberal voice was undiminished.

Meanwhile, Rothermere's fortune continued to grow. He invested shrewdly, expanded his newspaper empire into the provinces, and poured money into the *Mirror*'s distribution structure so that its availability, if not its content, was superior to its rivals. He also could have become king of Hungary, but gracefully declined. Rothermere believed that the central European state had been badly treated in 1919 by the Treaty of Trianon, which basically redrew the borders of one of Germany's Great

War allies. The country had given up Croatia, which became part of Yugoslavia; Transylvania, which was added to Rumania; and Slovakia, which joined Bohemia-Moravia as the Czechoslovak Republic. After what Hugh Cudlipp described as "a chance social meeting" with the Princess Hohenlohe-Waldenburg, Rothermere embarked upon a course to right what he saw as the wrongs inflicted on a down-at-heel but noble country and many of its people.

A year after the General Strike, a fleet of Rolls-Royces carried Rothermere and a considerable entourage to Vienna, Budapest and Venice. Upon his return, he used the *Daily Mail* to instruct readers in the machinations of modern mid-Europe and urge that the frontiers established by the Trianon agreement must be revised. His campaign, which ran month after month in his newspapers, was greeted throughout Britain by the sound of quiet snoring. Only the Hungarians took notice, to the extent of naming much of Budapest after their English champion and showering him with gifts. The most extravagant of these was offered by Hungarian monarchists, who wanted

New home: On the left, Geraldine House, the new Mirror headquarters at Rolls Buildings in Fetter Lane. On the right, Rothermere with his sister, Geraldine (who shared the name of her mother, after whom the building was named). She was the mother of Cecil King, who inherited the looks of this fearsome female.

Rothermere to accept the crown of Saint Stephen. "I have never discovered how or when the proposal that this high honour should be offered to myself took place," he was to write, "…I was assured that, in the prevailing enthusiastic mood of the Hungarian people, a plebiscite in my favour would be practically unanimous." He said no, which may have been ultimately good for Hungary, although not necessarily so for the *Daily Mirror.*

At the paper, they were still required to count the paper clips, but at least had pleasant accommodation in which to do so: that same year, the daily and its Sunday sister were moved to a grand new printing plant and offices – named Geraldine House, after Rothermere's mother – at Rolls Buildings in Fetter Lane, a hundred yards or so north of Fleet Street. Alexander Campbell, destined to become the second longest-serving editor in the paper's first 100 years, had little opportunity to demonstrate what editorial flair he might possess, although he managed to retain a vestige of the paper's social conscience. He published a road safety campaign, attacks on the ways police obtained evidence and calls for an examination of the

powers of coroners' courts. But constantly suffering the vagaries of his capricious boss, Campbell was largely obliged to concentrate on the "soft" end of the operation, supervising giant giveaways and competitions to attract readers – those who spotted Captain Frass, the *Mirror* "Mystery Man" who wandered around the country, were rewarded with the sizeable sum of £50. Campbell was also the new and caring nurse of the toddler that was to continue to grow until it became both a mainstay of the *Mirror*'s later surge back to success and a permanent feature in popular papers everywhere: the strip cartoon.

W.K. Haselden, the former insurance clerk who had arrived at the *Daily Illustrated Mirror* with a portfolio of drawings under his arm, is credited by the marvellous archivist and social historian, the late Denis Gifford, as having by accident invented the strip (a story more comprehensively told elsewhere in this book). His pre-war linked-frame cartoons led to the debut of the hugely popular Big and Little Willie in 1914. But it was the introduction in 1919 of Bertram Lamb (alias Uncle Dick) and Austin Payne's The Adventures of Pip and

Squeak that saw the strip capture the imagination of the *Mirror*'s readership. Pip was a dog, Squeak a penguin, and this unlikely animal double act became a trio with the addition, the following year, of Wilfred the rabbit, whose vocabulary consisted of such exclamations as "Gug, gug" and "Nunc, Nunc". While this would have been highly articulate for a real rabbit, it made no sense, but this did not prevent the popularity of Pip, Squeak and Wilfred spreading like a brush fire. It was by no means only children who flocked to join the Wilfredian League of Gugnuncs (W.L.O.G.) and attend meetings, which began with members "chortling":

> *Gug, gug! Nunc, nunc!*
> *To friends of all degree.*

> *Give gugly hugs to nuncly gugs*
> *Of the W.L.O.G.*

It is not recorded whether or not Rothermere was a fan of P, S & W, but he had little time for jocularity and therefore probably even less for the chanting of a "Gug, gug! Nunc! Nunc!" refrain. His demeanour was becoming even more gloomy and his political judgement more suspect. Early in the ailing Bona Law's short premiership, Rothermere visited him in Downing Street to negotiate an earldom for himself and a cabinet post for his surviving son, Esmond, then MP for the Isle of Thanet, in exchange for Government support by Associated Newspapers. Bonar Law was not interested in the proposition, although he thought well of Esmond and considered him for

"Come back!" shrieked Squeak. "That isn't a hat, Auntie! You've taken my lamp-shade!"

MIRROR GRANGE, SHOWING THE FAMOUS TOWER IN WHICH, IT IS WHISPERED, "GHOSTS" OCCASIONALLY WALK.

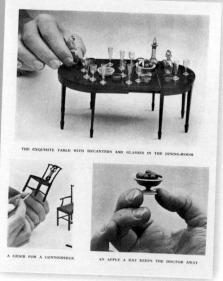

THE EXQUISITE TABLE WITH DECANTERS AND GLASSES IN THE DINING-ROOM

A CHAIR FOR A CONNOISSEUR   AN APPLE A DAY KEEPS THE DOCTOR AWAY

National treasures: The cartoon characters Pip, Squeak and Wilfred took Britain by storm. Left: Mirror Grange was a model "home" built for the famous trio. It was kitted out with exquisite miniature furniture.

a junior ministerial role. Rothermere would have none of this, dismissing Bonar Law as feeble and inadequate and lacking in leadership qualities. Later, when Baldwin, having succeeded Bonar Law, considered Esmond for a role in his Government, Rothermere wrote to his son that the prime minister had "neither the imagination, decision nor courage" to steer the country through turbulent times.

Rothermere had initially enthused about Baldwin, publishing a signed article in his newspapers that lauded the prime minister as "one of the greatest who ever held office". Within four years he was dismissing Baldwin as "a completely incompetent person who got into high office by an accident in post-war politics" and lashing out at the prime minister at every opportunity. As the 1929 General Election approached, Rothermere suggested to the Conservative Party that he was considering supporting Labour, even though his feelings for Baldwin bordered on the affectionate compared to his hatred of socialism. Then, even more foolishly, Rothermere demanded that he should be informed in advance of the composition of the next Tory cabinet. Baldwin rebuffed him, but saved his revenge for later.

Come the election – the first at which the voting age for women was lowered from 30 to 21, much to the disapproval of the paper founded for women – the *Mirror* urged: WOMEN'S DUTY TO VOTE TODAY AND TO KEEP SOCIALISTS OUT. But Labour was returned with 288 seats against the Tories' 260. Ramsay MacDonald formed his second Government and the *Mirror* commented: "Ought we to call this a plunge in the dark? Ought it not, after all, to be more accurately named a leap with eyes open – to suicide?" It was, in fact, a stumble in the half-light towards the precipice of the Wall Street Crash, lurking just six months ahead. The economic impact of America's economic collapse reverberated around the world. In Britain, unemployment was rising, the economy faltered and it became obvious that massive public spending cuts were required. At the *Mirror*, the proprietor maintained his rants against the Tories, while the pages of the paper were filled with reactionary social and political views and trivia: puzzles, competitions, free insurance offers and the nationwide tour of "The Guineas Man", a publicity drummer who dispensed fivers to train passengers in possession of that day's paper. The *Mirror* was now failing hopelessly to find the public pulse that it had so successfully monitored in the recent past.

Rothermere continued to huff and puff and flail. Having colluded with Beaverbrook in launching the United Empire Party to revive the rundown Tory Party, they claimed, he now decided to administer the coup de grace. He published in the *Sunday Pictorial* an article urging that Beaverbrook should replace Baldwin and, in January 1930, castigated the Tory leader for having added to "the country's burden of pensions and doles" and giving the vote to "millions of flappers who promptly helped to put the Socialists in office". At a public meeting of Tory faithful on 24 June, Baldwin retaliated, pulling from his pocket a document and telling a faithful audience: "Here is a letter from Lord Rothermere. 'I cannot make it too abundantly clear', he writes, 'that under no circumstances whatsoever will I support Mr Baldwin unless I know exactly what his policy is going to be, unless I have complete guarantees that such policy will be carried out if his Party achieves office, and unless I am acquainted with the names of at least eight or ten of his most prominent colleagues in the next ministry'." Baldwin paused for effect, then continued: "A more preposterous and insolent demand was never made on the leader of any political party. I repudiate it with contempt and I will fight that attempt at domination to the end."

Thunderous applause signalled Rothermere's humiliation, although he rallied briefly on 3 July with a *Daily Mirror* editorial headed WHO SHALL BE IN THE CABINET? which said of Baldwin's refusal to reveal the names of prospective ministers: "To appoint such men in privacy, and then to foist them upon the public after an election is grossly to abuse a power not conferred upon leaders by the law and custom of our constitution." Baldwin responded by going to the Commons that evening and asking for a vote of confidence from his Party, winning it handsomely.

In the spring of 1931, Baldwin used the power of Beaverbook and Rothermere as an issue in a by-election in the St. George's constituency in Westminster, dismissing them contemptuously as merchants of propaganda and famously declaring (with the help of his cousin, Rudyard Kipling): "What they aim at is power without responsibility, the prerogative of the harlot throughout the ages." Rothermere's last political throws of the dice where the *Mirror* was concerned had ended with the dice being thrown back in his face.

The following August the Government's attempts to balance its budget involved the possibility of severe cuts in unemployment benefit and split the Labour cabinet. MacDonald went to King George V with his Government's resignation and it was expected that Baldwin would be asked to form an administration. But with the support of the king, the Labour leader formed a national Government and the General Election of 27 October saw it secure 554 seats against Labour's 52. The following morning the *Mirror* observed that the Liberals were now in the "ludicrous position" of being able to ride to the Commons on a tandem: they had won just two seats. Doubtless to its delight, the *Mirror* was by now practically a Rothermere-free zone: disillusioned with his country and seeing a problematical future for a paper with a daily sale sliding alarmingly, he had in March started to sell off his interest in it and the *Pictorial* on the Stock Exchange. The eras of the first-generation Harmsworths was almost, but not quite, at an end.

The *Mirror* was fortunate in many ways to be out from under the Rothermere yoke. Harold's dejection and penny-pinching did nothing for morale; but his flirtation with Fascism, already demonstrated when the papers in his colossal stable were required to extol the virtues of Mussolini and Hitler, was becoming the fully fledged and hugely indiscreet love affair that was to sully his memory. But although he may have gone, he was certainly not forgotten, nor resisted by chairman John Cowley, the board representative of the man who still controlled a considerable holding in the company. "I wish you to understand most clearly," Rothermere wrote to Cowley upon his decision to distance himself from the papers, "that, in future, the *Mirror* and the *Sunday Pictorial* businesses are entirely under your and your colleagues' control." But almost three years later, in January of 1934, an article signed by Rothermere appeared in the *Mirror*. Headlined GIVE THE BLACKSHIRTS A HELPING HAND, it praised Oswald Mosley and concluded with addresses of Blackshirt

premises where readers could join. It wasn't quite Rothermere's swansong – a follow-up article proclaimed HURRAH FOR THE BLACKSHIRTS – but it was the *Mirror*'s political nadir.

It was also Rothermere's last hurrah. Believing that the *Mirror* – average sale now down to around 700,000 – might go out of business, he sold his remaining shares and those held by the Daily Mail Trust in 1935, totally severing his connection with the company. Later he was to visit Hitler and report that "There is no man living whose promise given in regard to something of real moment I would sooner take". He was, his nephew Cecil King was to write, "not a man of integrity and used his newspapers to boost the shares of the *Mirror* so that he could sell out." He was also a sad and unfulfilled man whose 17-year stewardship of the paper had seen it transformed from a groundbreaking, vital young buck of communication and entertainment to a prematurely middle-aged, middle-class dullard.

Rothermere's *Daily Mail* was propagating the Rothermere myth that Hitler was misunderstood rather than a megalomaniac right up until 1939. The proprietor himself was still sending flattering cables to the Nazi leader. Mercifully, perhaps, Rothermere did not live to see the German rape of much of Europe and the protracted battle to rid the world of the regime he had so misguidedly supported. His old political ally, Beaverbrook, now Minister of Aircraft Production, sent him on a war effort mission to Canada. Taken ill there, he repaired to Bermuda to recuperate but died on 26 November 1940. His last words were: "There is nothing more I can do to help my country now." He was 72.

At the *Daily Mirror*, his influence was by then no more than an uncomfortable memory. (When Rothermere took control, the *Mirror* was selling an average of 1,210,354 copies every day and by 1 March 1922 was able to record a sale of 3,005,430. In 1931, when he bowed out, the figure had tumbled to 987,080 – and the decline was accelerating.) There had been some changes made at Geraldine House since 1931, but through the early 1930s the paper continued to flounder like a whale struggling to stay away from the beach. The company, with interests in the Anglo-Canadian Pulp and Paper Mills in Quebec, which had taken a financial battering

Eyes down: Sub-editors at work in the new Geraldine House offices in 1927. This would be the Daily Mirror's *home until the move to Holborn Circus in 1961.*

in the Wall Street disaster, was still ticking over, but the tick was not very loud.

L.D. (Leigh) Brownlee, a former schoolmaster and an Oxford cricketing "blue", had succeeded Campbell as editor in 1931 – chairman John Cowley refused to accept the pugnacious Bartholomew in the role – but failed to reignite the *Mirror* flame during his three years in the chair. Cowley, a former cashier who had become general manager of the *Daily Mail* at its launch before branching out on his own and getting badly burned, remained chairman and was to do so until his death in 1944 at the age of 74. He was as unadventurous after Rothermere's departure as he had been before it and editorially made no contribution to the transformation that was to come. General Manager Wallace Broome was another executive with publishing experience but little drive.

Coming of age: **The Romance of the Daily Mirror** *was a book produced to celebrate 21 years of the newspaper.*

The circulation of the *Mirror* was now on what looked like an irreversible slide, possibly all the way to oblivion.

At a lower level on the board, however, were two men who would soon gallop to the rescue like a pair of avenging cowboys: Bartholomew and King, the *Mirror*'s answer to the Lone Ranger and Tonto. Bart may have lacked the charisma of the Masked Man, and the aloof King – Rothermere's nephew and the last conduit to the paper's founder – would have been horrified to be cast as the Native American sidekick. But this unlikely duo held the future of the company, and the *Daily Mirror*, in their hands and in terms of talent were both fast on the draw. Like many of those who live by the gun, they were both destined, in business terms, to die by it. In the meantime, however, there was a newspaper to be saved.

3 COME THE REVOLUTION

It is a Tuesday morning in November 1933 that ostensibly is like any other. But the paper that until now appeared to be dying of lethargy emerges on 29 November in a new suit of clothes: a striking whistle and flute that will catch the eye of the man and woman in the street while causing the diminishing number of middle-class, middle-aged, conservative readers who previously had considered the Daily Mirror *"their" paper to disapprove strongly and root through their own wardrobes searching for mourning attire.*

In heavy black type, the paper's front page proclaims: "TRIAL BY FURY – U.S. LYNCH LAW", with the subsidiary headline: "Frenzied mob storm another gaol. Soldiers' bombs defied". Illustrating the story are two photographs: one shows a lynch mob breaking down the doors of the county jail in San Jose, California; the other, the body of an alleged kidnapper hanging at the end of a rope. Apart from causing disquiet among many regular buyers of the Mirror *and apoplexy in the offices of advertisers peddling products of a genteel nature, the* Mirror's *new dynamism goes largely unnoticed. In Geraldine House, however, chairman Cowley looks as if he has lost a five-pound note and found fourpence, a catastrophic state of affairs for a man of such frugality. Could he have made a terrible mistake, he wonders? Should he have refused to sanction the appointment as editorial director of that vulgarian Harry Guy Bartholomew?...*

The revolution instigated and largely carried out by Bart was evident that morning, but the transformation of the *Mirror* took more than one eye-catching front page. The change of typeface, introducing the thumping, very black

New dawn: Harry Guy Bartholomew shows his hand with a new-look Daily Mirror.

sans serif that had come to Bart's attention in the *New York Daily News* and was subsequently to become a tabloid trademark worldwide, was only the first step. But the excitement generated by the permanent adoption the following year of exciting, undisciplined design and a sledgehammer style of headline writing – note the use of the word "frenzied" – brought about a rapid change in the paper's fortunes. A circulation that had taken to its bed with a headache suddenly decided it felt much better and clambered out again. No wonder, with the

New tech: Bartholomew developed the revolutionary Bartlane transmission device.

News by the bundle: The men of the Mirror publishing department in action at Geraldine House, March 1938.

toe of Bart's shoe making fierce contact with its behind.

The last time we spied Bart during the unfolding story of the *Daily Mirror* was when he was working with Hannen Swaffer, galvanising the picture department during the paper's early success. His unremitting enthusiasm and fierce competitiveness compensated for a lack of education bordering on illiteracy and a total absence of social graces. Of his ingenuity there can be no doubt. According to Maurice Edelman, at the Prince of Wales's investiture at Caernarvon Castle in 1911 Bart arranged for the plates from the cameras of the *Mirror* photographers to be thrown from the castle ramparts, caught in an outstretched blanket and sped to London by motorcycle, way ahead of the competitors. Chicanery, a permanent Fleet Street feature, came naturally to him. It is recorded that when, early in his *Mirror* career, a royal visit to Paris sparked a race between the British papers to get the pictures back first, Bart bribed a French train driver "to break the record for the run to Calais". Hugh Cudlipp wrote of a time when, to circumvent Northcliffe's instruction to hand over some prize pictures to the *Daily Mail*, the assistant art editor used greasepaint on his face to feign sickness and was promptly dispatched to hospital – taking the pictures with him. Harry Guy Bartholomew was a street fighter who didn't believe in coming second.

Sidelined in a reserve occupation during World War One – Northcliffe had made this rising star a director in 1913, when he was only 28 – he pulled strings to obtain a commission in the Canadian army and in 1917 was in France contributing to the photographic coverage of the British troops. Later, bored as a director with no particular portfolio at the *Mirror*, his resourcefulness and technical expertise saw him collaborate with a Captain Macfarlane, of the *New York Daily News*, on the development of a system of transmitting photographs by radio. The Bartlane process was superseded by more sophisticated equipment by the end of the 1920s – a reign short enough to decree that nothing about Macfarlane other than his name would survive – but it was used extensively, particularly in obtaining pictures from the United States. Cecil King was years later to declare that Bart, of whom he became an important partner in the resurrection of the *Mirror*, was a good photographer, a great picture editor, had a great understanding of strip cartoons and was full of ideas – most of them bad. Ungenerous to a fault, King sold very short indeed the human spark plug who, at the age of 51, took over editorial control that day in 1933.

From the moment he gained that control, but especially throughout 1934, Bart attacked with ferocity the stuffy image the *Mirror* had managed to construct for itself during Rothermere's reign. The prudish schoolmarm that the paper had become was summarily sacked and a jolly jack-the-lad, sensible but cheeky, supportive but a terrible tease, hired in her place. Had the word entered the lexicon by then, Bart's new *Mirror* could have been described as streetwise. It was also fun, with strip cartoons as a constant ingredient in the editorial mix. Bart loved them and recognised

BELINDA

GARTH

RUGGLES

Famous figures: Jane's Journal had brightened the life of the nation in 1932, and other cartoon characters would follow, including Belinda Blue Eyes, the Ruggles, Garth and Buck Ryan.

their appeal. An artist named Norman Pett had turned up in 1932 with "Jane's Journal, or the Diary of a Bright Young Thing" and now other characters began to be added to a cartoon cast that was to become as starry in their own way as the movie kings and queens at MGM. Buck Ryan, a clean-cut, chisel-jawed detective, Belinda Blue Eyes, Britain's answer to Little Orphan Annie, the first incredible hulk, Garth, and the Ruggles family would have had readers clamouring for autographs if only they could gain a third dimension and make personal appearances (as, indeed, Jane was to do).

Not that the new *Mirror* was all froth. After a period spent mostly locked away in the attic, the paper's campaigning spirit had both its pencil and its cutting edge sharpened, although its political stance would take years to discover itself. The paper fought for improvements in road safety, seeking the views of its readers – very much part of the editorial strategy – as it demanded tighter safety measures. Rothermere's promulgation of the Blackshirts in 1934 was a dark moment (and it was in January of that year that the *Mirror* hit the circulation nadir from

which it was to climb: 732,000). But the paper's editorials, so long dominated by the erstwhile proprietor's political inflexibility and remoteness from real life, began to rebuild their muscle under the discipline of Richard Jennings, the erudite son of a former *New York Times* journalist who subsequently had become a leader writer on *The Times* and an MP. Jennings had joined the *Daily Mirror* the year after its launch, but it was not until he was given his journalistic freedom by Bart that this bookish (he was an inveterate collector of fine volumes), left-leaning bachelor began to develop the spare, uncluttered style that became synonymous with the voice of the *Mirror*.

The revolution – conducted by Bart with advisers J. Walter Thompson, the American-owned advertising agency, at his elbow and the towering advertising director, Cecil Harmsworth King, emerging from his dynastic background to lend his not inconsiderable weight in support – continued apace. When two young men working for the Thompson advertising agency arrived to see him with some strip cartoons they had created, King was impressed enough – with the young men, rather than the cartoons – to recommend that they should be hired. One was an ideas factory named Basil D. Nicholson ("He was certainly among the half-dozen most brilliant men I ever met. He threw off ideas like a Catherine wheel," King was to recall), the other a copywriter named William Connor. Connor started at the paper on the same August Bank Holiday Monday in 1935 as sportswriter Peter Wilson from *The Times*. Already on board as part of the executive shake-up engineered by King was Nicholson, who, having reached the zenith of his advertising career by creating the Horlicks "night starvation" campaign had arrived at Geraldine House to take charge of features. He had, according to Hugh Cudlipp, little knowledge of newspapers but was brimming with populist ideas and a conviction that strip cartoons were an important weapon in the circulation war. Nicholson lost little time in recruiting a deputy features editor, placing an advertisement in the *Daily Telegraph* for a "bright assistant with ideas" who would be "able to take charge". Hugh Cudlipp, whose meteoric career had already taken him, at the age of 19, to the features editorship of the *Sunday Chronicle*, arrived to assist Nicholson on the same day as Connor and Wilson walked through the doors of Geraldine House – a coincidence that provided the compost to make the *Daily Mirror* grow as big and strong as Jack's beanstalk over the next 30 years.

Much later, Cudlipp wrote that when he arrived at the paper the *Mirror* was a "hotpotch of conflicting schools of thought, and schools of no thought at all". The editor, who had replaced the ineffectual Brownlee in 1934, was Cecil Thomas, a man whose greatest successs was to be survival – he remains the longest-serving editor in the paper's history – over 14 years of hectoring from Bart. But amid the turmoil Cudlipp noted a new, exciting paper was taking shape. The brilliant but hard-drinking Nicholson had uncompromising views about editorial content and the readership, believing a diet of strip cartoons and frivolity was all the masses needed (in August 1935 he introduced the remarkable Patience Strong, who wrote a daily poem, usually sentimental, that would have doubtless been sniffed at by poetry professors but which captivated readers for decades). Nicholson constantly questioned the validity of journalism itself – why had the profession

attracted such little talent and originality, he wondered to Cudlipp? Such thoughtful pondering, even if conducted over too many drinks in various London clubs, may have impressed King, but it cut no ice with Bart. Six months after hiring Cudlipp, Nicholson departed, leaving an intellectual legacy that formed an important part of the foundations of the revitalised *Mirror*. When he died of cancer in 1953, when only 45, Cassandra wrote of him: "Intelligent and daft… Brilliant and bemused. He has gone, but for those who appreciate mental explosions the dust will not settle for many years."

Cudlipp assumed the Nicholson mantle and began to make the features fizz even more. Features editor was the highest editorial executive position he ever held at the *Mirror* – later appointments embraced more than the daily title – and it was one in which he retained an intense interest throughout his long association with the group. While Cudlipp masterminded the features revival, night editor Roy Suffern, an Ulsterman who would become

Face of the future: The destiny of the Daily Mirror *would change with the arrival of* Hugh Cudlipp.

a director and editor of the group's fun and pin-up weekly, *Reveille*, set about overhauling the news operation. Also making their presence felt were such up-and-comers as Ted Castle, later to marry Barbara (Castle) Betts and become editor of *Picture Post* and an MP, Edward – later Sir Edward – Pickering, subsequently a distinguished editor of the *Daily Express* and Mirror Group editorial director and chairman, and Stuart "Sam" Campbell, who went on to edit *The People*.

One of Cudlipp's shrewdest signings, in the summer of 1936, was that of Godfrey Winn, a novelist and former actor who was engaged to perform daily in what Bill Connor dubbed "Cudlipp's Circus". Winn's simpering ramblings in his "Personality Parade" column, often concentrating on the personalities of his mother, dog or Surrey garden, do not today bear close scrutiny as examples of avant-garde journalism, but, at the time, Winn struck a unique chord with the readers he invited to share his indulgent lifestyle. He was constantly "dashing" hither and thither – to Grosvenor House to swim in the pool, to tea with Noel Coward, to Eton for a firework display. Compared to Winn, the not dissimilar provider of egocentric chitchat in the present-day *Mirror*, James Whitaker, is a model of restraint. Winn later reminded Cudlipp how he would make it a rule to go to tea with one of his readers every week, with, naturally, a photographer in tow. And when he opened his garden to the public to raise money for a charity – "It wasn't a big place, just a nice garden," he was to recall – 1,400 people flocked to meet him and his mother.

By 1937, the *Mirror* – for the time, a bulging tabloid, often of 32 pages – was boasting that Winn, still only 28, was "the most famous newspaper writer in the land". So famous was he that, after two years, his unique blend of homespun trivia, big name-dropping and occasional outrage (country gentlemen who supported cockfighting were "swine") was snaffled by, firstly, the *Sunday Express*, where he was required to write only once a week for much more money than the *Mirror* was paying, and then the *Sunday Dispatch*. Winn, a homosexual at a time when the closet doors remained firmly closed, became a war correspondent and then served in the Royal Navy as an ordinary seaman. He was to remain a highly-paid newspaper writer and author until

Simperingly super: Godfrey Winn managed to fit 1,400 readers into his "nice" garden.

his death on a tennis court in 1971.

With Winn, Cudlipp was appealing to a wide swathe of readers but especially targeting young women with aspiration as well as stars in their eyes: "Girls – working girls; hundreds of thousands of them, toiling over typewriters and ledgers and reading in many cases nothing more enlightening than *Peg's Paper*." The manoeuvre to snare a previously untapped section of society was strengthened with a plethora of women columnists: Emily Post, writing on etiquette; Eleanor Glyn on love and marriage; Dorothy Dix, an American syndicated precursor of Marje Proops in the advice business. Eileen Ascroft, who was to become the second Mrs Cudlipp, wrote a column headed "Sanctuary", with the claim "A message of peace and comfort", gossip by the bucketful and guidance on everything from boyfriends to the latest fashions.

The paper's attitude to sex was also enough to remind those new, young, female readers that they no longer had *Peg's Paper* in their hands. Despite chairman Cowley's misgivings and his constant imploring that the paper should not breach any taste barriers, the *Mirror* published

Leading light: The young William Connor joined the Daily Mirror August 1935. Soon his talent would begin to brighten a paper that was bubbling with exciting new ideas.

not only pictures of girls in bathing suits – not primarily aimed at the working girl, although it soon became apparent that women, too, were interested in the female form – but serious articles on birth control, dating and Can Marriage Be Happy Without Children?

Meanwhile, Bill Connor was applying his considerable talents to the *Mirror*'s Live Letters column, where, from 1938, the anonymous Old Codgers dispensed wisdom and offbeat philosophy to readers anxious to share their problems, seek guidance or simply vent their spleen. Created by Cudlipp as a rival to the paper's staid readers' letters column, the Codgers experienced a number of cast changes over the years in which they became something of a very British institution – their Saturday "Your prayers are asked…" panel attracted praise from an Archbishop of Canterbury – and the column remained in the paper until the old gents were shepherded off to retirement by then editor Roy Greenslade some 52 years later. The future of Bill Connor, however, was not to lie with Live Letters, no matter how lively he could make the Codgers' replies. Not long after he joined the paper, Bart had asked him if he thought he could write a column. The result was Cassandra, named after the mythological Greek prophetess, daughter of King Priam of Troy. It was to become the most famous and widely-quoted newspaper column in the world and to this day retains journalistic significance as a yardstick by which columnists are judged.

Much has been written about Connor, whose premature death from cancer at the age of 57 in 1967 preceded by only a few years the end of the *Mirror*'s golden age. For more than 30 years, with an enforced break for army service, he dominated opinion journalism, writing a column that ranged across every subject known to man and some that previously were not. His opening sentence when returning in 1946 to his beat after hostilities had ceased is one of the most quoted – and frequently misquoted – introductions in newspaper history: "As I was saying when I was interrupted, it is a powerful hard thing to please all the people all the time". His idiosyncratic prose, acerbic wit and pugnacious temperament in print combined to puncture the vanity, destroy the pomposity and invoke the ire of a legion of public figures, while at the same time informing and entertaining the readers who doted on his sometimes thrice-weekly appearances in the paper. Cassandra's column also landed him in the soup with government and, on one famous occasion – more of which later – resulted in an uncomfortable visit to the High Court.

In the office and the pub, so colleagues of the time testify, Connor aka Cass was hail-fellow-well-met unless he considered the fellow he was meeting to be an ignoramus. He was helpful to younger journalists and, certainly, kind to cats, which he adored. But sit him at a typewriter and he could unleash cold fury or withering scorn in sentences that machine-gunned those he believed to be enemies and left them for dead. Bill Connor came as close to genius as journalism can get, which usually is not especially close but in his case was a nuzzling intimacy. Rarely can writers be included as major players in a great newspaper success story. As a front-line general in the Bartholomew revolution, Cassandra could.

Towards the back of the paper, Peter Wilson was beginning to dominate sports journalism in the way that, further forward, Cassandra was overshadowing all other columnists. Soon a creative powerhouse in a different journalistic area came to join this elite group: Philip Zec, another recruit from the world of advertising. As a result of Bill Connor asking his former colleague's advice on who the *Mirror* should sign as a war artist, and then realising he was probably talking to the ideal candidate, the initially reluctant Zec was to become the country's foremost, and for a time most notorious, political cartoonist.

With Jennings' editorials rapidly developing the radicalism that was to be his strength until his retirement through ill health in 1942 and the *Mirror*'s signature for decades afterwards, there had now been gathered together a staff that could deliver the extrovert, reader-friendly, amiable elder brother of a paper Bart wanted. Not that the radicalism immediately stretched so far as to reflect the socialist beliefs of Jennings – his pseudonym, W.M., was assumed to be a tribute to William Morris – nor Bart's own political views. At the General Election of November 1935, the *Mirror* had supported Stanley Baldwin's predominately Conservative National Government, which cantered home with a 278-seat majority over Labour (although grass roots disenchantment was signalled in Seaham, Durham, where Labour's Emmanuel "Manny" Shinwell defeated former Party leader Ramsay MacDonald in a landslide). Unemployment stood at two million. The Government, which evolved into Conservative administrations under Chamberlain and Churchill, was to last for nine-and-a-half years. It was the last time the *Daily Mirror* would support any party other than Labour at a General Election.

If the paper's political line was still yet to be firmly established – its stance on the Spanish Civil War consisted of little more than hand wringing – from 1937 it began seriously to campaign on behalf of its readers against social injustice. Bart, Francis Williams was to write,

was a "daemoniac fury and a ball of fire." The journalists with whom he surrounded himself "invaded privacy shamelessly. They embraced every stunt however contemptible in terms of normal human dignity the public could be got to swallow and set practically no limits on what was permissible in print other than those imposed by the niggardliness of the law." But, Williams also noted, the *Mirror* "developed, whether by accident or design, a social conscience by no means inferior to that of many more respectable and high regarded journals."

It involved readers whenever and wherever it could – and not just by joining the free insurance reader incentive that many other papers also offered. Columnists were constantly inviting reader response and correspondence columns expanded to accommodate those anxious to obtain advice or proffer views on their daily lives. Cudlipp was later to claim that around 1,000 letters from readers arrived at Geraldine House every day. This was human interest journalism in its purest form, recording the interests of the increasing number of humans who were beginning to regard the *Mirror* as a friend and confidant with whom it could enjoy a cup of tea and a chinwag on six mornings every week. It could also, if it so wished, get in shape with the paper: a team of one-piece-swimsuited girls performing as the "*Daily Mirror* Eight" toured British seaside resorts during the 1930s, offering keep-fit lessons and organising team games. Each season's displays usually culminated in a spectacular event in London's Hyde Park.

Largely apolitical though it may have been, the paper had the assistance of royalty in displaying its beating heart. The formidable trio of Bart, Cassandra and W.M. spearheaded the *Mirror*'s forthright support of King Edward VIII during the abdication crisis of 1936. Cudlipp had kept the paper abreast of the King's dalliance with divorcee Mrs Wallis Warfield Simpson by monitoring the American newspapers that had no inhibition about publishing details of an affair about which the British public was so in the dark it might as well have been locked in a broom cupboard. Despite behind-gloved-hands gossip among the upper chattering classes, the then Prince of Wales's unwise dalliance was a closed book, or newspaper, to the majority of the British public. The *Mirror* didn't know much about what was

Crisis point: The Mirror, led by Bartholomew, waded into the abdication crisis of 1936 with considerable gusto. While other newspapers were whispering in the wings, the Mirror devoted powerful front-page coverage to get to the bottom of the issue that was to divide British opinion.

going on. The King was in constant communication with *Express* proprietor Lord Beaverbrook, who, ironically, had first learned from London *Evening Standard* editor Percy Cudlipp, Hugh's oldest brother, of Wallis Simpson's divorce action – her second – at Ipswich Assizes in October. Esmond, Lord Rothermere, successor to his father, the former *Mirror* chief, as chairman of Associated Newspapers, was also in the royal loop. As the King fought to minimise the influence Prime Minister Stanley Baldwin could exert on what was about to become a constitutional crisis, *The Times* began to receive daily briefings on the situation from Baldwin. What the King described as a "gentlemen's agreement" was reached with the press – it was to report the

divorce case without mentioning the connection between Mrs Simpson and the Monarch, which rendered the story about as exciting as yesterday's rice pudding and guaranteed Wallis would not suffer damaging publicity.

The *Mirror* was beholden to neither the King nor Baldwin. More importantly, steam began to emerge from Bartholomew's ears. When news of the King's relationship and the unseemly tussle between the monarchy and the state – the church had by now lined up alongside Baldwin in opposing the King's plans to marry his paramour – at last became public, the *Mirror* was noticeably out of step with the rest of the press. The others pussyfooted, disguising the seriousness of the situation with platitudes and innuendo. The *Mirror*, however, pulled on its hob-nailed boots, although not before chairman John Cowley, a carpet-slipper man in all matters, had departed from the office. The first two editions contained nothing at all about the King's predicament and the impending crisis.

Cudlipp later recorded how Bart telephoned him and outlined the scenario that would keep Cowley in the dark. This involved even making sure that Cowley's son, who worked for the paper at the time, would depart the premises early with a first edition tucked under his arm, just in case he was tempted to blow a whistle in the direction of dad. Night editor Roy Suffern was another trusted with the knowledge that Bart intended to explode a journalistic bomb before the night was out. The third edition alluded to a meeting between Baldwin and the King at which matters other than those governmental were discussed. Bart absented himself from the office for a while and, Cudlipp recalled, returned wearing a hat and a lounge suit pulled on over his pyjamas. The bomb went off with a loud bang in the last edition, printed too late for other papers to react to a big, black headline that read: THE KING WANTS TO MARRY MRS SIMPSON. CABINET ADVISES 'NO'.

The subsequent coverage of the story by the *Mirror* demanded that the King's "full demands and conditions" should be revealed by Baldwin and trumpeted: THE COUNTRY WILL GIVE YOU THE VERDICT. The paper was unequivocally on the side of the King, and when Cassandra joined the fracas, under the headline "I Accuse", he went straight for the jugular of the establishment: "I am writing about what I regard as the biggest put-up job of all time. I accuse leaders of the Church of England of putting our King in a position from which it was almost impossible to retreat. I accuse the Prime Minister and his Government of manoeuvring, with smooth and matchless guile, to a desperate situation where humiliation is the only answer." The issue of 3 December, when the *Mirror* alone named Wallis Simpson and published her photograph, splintered forever the cosy relationship that existed between the monarchy, government and the fourth estate. The subsequent campaign was historic in that it was the first time the paper gave over its front page to its opinion on an issue, forging a template for many more, including observations on the royals, in the future.

The Duke of Windsor was later to write of the *Mirror's* 3 December last edition that "the world can hold few worse shocks for a sensitive woman than to come without warning upon her own grossly magnified countenance upon the front page of a sensational newspaper". The *Mirror* was much criticised at the time for ignoring the "gentleman's agreement" to conceal the truth about a King who, as Maurice Edelman was to point out 30 years later, sympathised with the Nazis and disparaged the League of Nations. With hindsight, it is easy to see that the *Mirror* backed the wrong side in supporting an unworthy King as well as one who, despite the paper's vociferousness, was obliged to abdicate in order to marry Mrs Simpson. Its detachment from the opposing power bases – the Palace and Downing Street – led it into a blind alley where sentiment overcame constitutional authority. It wasn't the last time the *Mirror* would be wrong and at least on this occasion it was wrong with considerable panache.

The first real political test for the revolutionised *Daily Mirror* presented itself with the rise of Nazism in Germany and the threat of war. Here, there were mistakes, too. The paper's initial doubts rolled agonisingly slowly into a period of indignation and then on to raw fury (although it had been perceptive enough in 1933 to greet the appointment of the new German Chancellor with a headline prediction: HITLER MAY RULE AS DICTATOR). The paper had been warning against appeasement ever since 1932, when rumblings of German rearmament had prompted Winston Churchill to speak out. But "W.M." soft-pedalled the paper's way into the mid-1930s – following Hitler's 1935 speech at Nuremberg, the leading article stressed the Fuhrer's pledge "to injure none while tolerating injury from none" and ignored what was happening to German Jews. When, in October of that year, Mussolini invaded Abyssinia, a leading article questioned a Labour Party call for sanctions against Italy on the grounds that Labour had opposed rearmament and it was impossible for the country to impose sanctions if unarmed. This was no hangover from the Nazi sympathies of Lord Rothermere, who was now busy urging support of the regime in Germany and denying Nazi atrocities in the *Daily Mail*. Richard Jennings, the rare book collector and part-time literary editor who earlier in its life had published verse in the paper, was a cautious man who hoped, as Edelman later observed, "that reason would prevail even among the German and Italian leaders, and that they would draw back from the gulf of a general war".

But as the 1930s careered downhill, Jennings became more and more prepared to use an iron fist in an iron glove when he felt it necessary. When Hitler had Austrian Chancellor Dollfuss murdered by Austrian Nazis in 1934, "W.M." coined the phrase "international gangsterism" and commented: "Hitler's sympathies with the Austrian Nazis are known… We can only hope that behind each vapouring Dictator, whose own life is threatened by the hatreds his violence has inspired, are men who will at least attempt to understand the international complications that may follow from nationalist outrage. The hope is faint, like the last faint words of the dying Dollfuss, 'I only wanted peace'."

There were still major lapses. When, in February 1936, the *Mirror* obtained an interview with Hitler – a major scoop – it published it under the headline: HITLER'S 'LET'S BE FRIENDS' PLEA TO THE WORLD and behaved like a fan basking in reflected glory after obtaining the autograph of a star. It accepted without criticism the soft-soaping of a megalomaniac who was to order the invasion of the Rhineland just a week later. The paper's editorial twittered about "a glow of spring sunshine upon the wintry scene of European confusion". In March, the paper proclaimed: "It Must Not Be War. Hitler's Peace Plan Must Succeed" and laid down what Cudlipp was later to describe as "a pacifist's charter", beginning: "Who will be caught again by lying twaddle about war to end war, about our sacred honour and our solemn oath?"

Then, following a Saturday evening meeting early in 1938 with Cecil King at the Martinez restaurant in Swallow Street, just off Regent's Street, when, over a couple of bottles of claret, they forged a partnership that was to last for 30 years, Cudlipp defected. Still only 24, he was snaffled by King to edit the *Sunday Pictorial* and took sportswriter Peter Wilson and news executive Stuart "Sam" Campbell with him. Cudlipp's acceptance of the job infuriated Bartholomew, who had been rejected by Cowley for the position after Bart had been

Starstruck: The Mirror's *exclusive chat with the "man of destiny" saw judgement go out the window.*

unconsciously rude to him on two occasions when the editorship was discussed. Bart continued as editorial director of the daily title, with King filling the same role at the *Pic* while also supervising the political coverage of both papers. With Rothermere's departure, the *Mirror* and the *Pic* had been left bereft of political contacts. With Bart socially dangerous, it was left to King to repair the damage and it was he who contracted Winston Churchill to write a series of articles for the *Daily Mirror* in 1939.

With W.M. reaching the peak of his leader writing talents, the paper had, the previous year, at last discovered its true – and from then on – unwavering political soul. When, in February, Hitler made a public address lasting three hours, the *Mirror* dismissed it as "a rambling, interminable speech of Nazi self-glorification. Sneers at democracy, attacks on Jews and Christians with Bibles." And the following month, when Germany marched into Austria, the *Mirror* recalled Hitler's *Mein Kampf* and insisted: "He has never concealed his aims. They are all written in his book, the new Bible of Germany, written by Germany's new deity… To ignore them is as futile and foolish as it would be for a householder to open the door to

New boy on board: Cecil King was a towering figure – even behind a desk. His talents were vital to the Mirror's success, but initially he was so unpopular with other members of the board of directors that he had to use subterfuge to get his hands on the company's financial figures.

a burglar who had been obliging enough to announce his visit and the exact amount of property he intended to steal. Why, then, talk of talks with the burglar? Gangsters are not disarmed by talk." The *Mirror* celebrated "the one voice [that has] hammered home consistently, unswervingly the lesson must be strong" in October 1838 when it boasted: "Have you read what W.M. says about it in the *Mirror* this morning?' You've probably heard that remark made several times over the past few weeks of crisis. For that tribute to one man's far-sighted frankness has been paid by thousands of worried Britons during the fateful days that followed Hitler's speech at the Nuremburg National Congress."

The *Mirror* called for the introduction of a national government and national service, and for priority to be given to rearmament at home – "Arm, arm, arm", cried W.M. The paper demanded united military command with France. It lambasted *The Times*, which had emerged as the arch-appeaser of the national press. When Hitler threatened Czechoslovakia, the paper sent Bill Connor to Berlin and Prague and Cassandra's report from a country steeling itself for invasion appeared on September 14, the day before Prime Minister Chamberlain visited Hitler in Berchtesgaden and returned

with more false hopes of peace. "I was told that the authorities were fully aware that such an onslaught would probably mean anything from seventy-five thousand to one hundred thousand dead," wrote Cassandra. "'What do you do with the bodies?' 'Dig pits and fling them in.'…" Two days later, the paper was demanding: "Let us call Hitler's bluff."

News of Hitler's invitation to Chamberlain at the end of the month to visit him in Munich so cheered Ivor Lambe, the *Mirror*'s gossip columnist of the time, that he revealed how society dinner parties could now revert to their evening dress tradition, a habit given up by many because of the fraught international situation. This was a minor editorial hiccup. While expressing "immense relief" when Chamberlain returned waving a piece of paper as a written guarantee of peace, the newspaper was not totally convinced. It paid tribute to the abused Czechs – "We owe our brief respite to the humiliation and prospective ruin of a gallant people" – and praised First Lord of the Admiralty Duff Cooper, who had already resigned in protest at Chamberlain's trip. In an editorial, W.M. – soon to be described in the *Mirror* as "The Man Who Made All England Sit Up" – warned: "Do not relax your defence efforts. Redouble them… the world isn't a nice place ruled by kind men and old ladies who wouldn't hurt a fly. Large parts of it are ruled by men who have proved that they stop at nothing to gain their ends. At nothing but the certainty that if they strike, they will be struck." And the headline on a Cassandra column made the paper's position absolutely clear: SOME DAY SOMEONE WILL HAVE TO STOP HITLER: IT MAY BE US.

Throughout 1939, the *Mirror* continued to attack complacency and question every move made by Hitler and Mussolini. W.M. wrote of Hitler's "dark Satanic mind" and continued: "He stamps on the faces of his victims. We know his methods and we have studied his programme. Nothing that he does surprises us. What does surprise us is the surprise of our rulers here." Winston Churchill pronounced: "No further concessions can be made to threats of violence. We cannot pay Germany to leave off doing wrong." On Monday 4 September, war was declared and the following morning the *Mirror* got straight down to business: "For months, even years, past we have tried to warn the public concerning the aims, the threats, the secret intentions of Adolf Hitler," wrote Jennings in his editorial. "We have been accused of provoking those warlike thoughts that we have endeavoured to defeat by urging that readiness which alone can save us now. But we now forget these dissensions… to-day and henceforward and until the end, endure!" The front page proclaimed BRITAIN'S FIRST DAY OF WAR: CHURCHILL IS NEW NAVY CHIEF. Churchill, long admired by both Cudlipp and King ("He was an attractive personality with a good command of English, either written or spoken," King was to record with typical condescension), was a *Mirror* man, although the amiable relationship was not long to continue. Inside the paper, Cassandra's page proclaimed: WANTED! FOR MURDER… FOR KIDNAPPING… FOR THEFT AND ARSON. ADOLF HITLER. THIS RECKLESS CRIMINAL IS WANTED – DEAD OR ALIVE!

The *Mirror* rolled up its sleeves. So did its readers. Years later, A.C.H. Smith was to illustrate how the paper evolved from being a friend of its readers into a counsellor and moral guide by quoting an article written in late 1939 by Brian Murtough, a fine journalist later to grace the pages of the *Sunday Pictorial*, under

Evil identified: The Mirror **uses its punch to portray Hitler as an international criminal.**

the headline "I confess to my unborn son":

"…today, as I write, we are living on the edge of the world – never quite certain that there will be a tomorrow.

And I sometimes wonder if it is worthwhile fighting for a future that may never come. I grow afraid – for myself. Afraid at the thought of how everything I ever planned would be smashed if a certain German marches out of step.

Then I think of millions of other young men and women in the same position. Millions who would lose everything. And I am not afraid any longer.

I realise that only by carrying on with our plans and ambitions can we do our share in making the world a better place…

The moral of this is that you must cooperate. You must study other people and never forget that you are part of a nation, not a person on your own."

The *Mirror* had reached a point where it was doing more than its share to make the world a better place. It was on the threshold of the greatest period in its history. But first there was a war to be won.

4 WAR & PEACE

I *It is early in the morning of Friday 5 March 1942 and, unwittingly, the* Mirror *is sitting on another journalistic bomb that is about to explode. The incendiary in question is a cartoon by the brilliant Philip Zec, the latest in a short series in which he decries the thriving black market that continues to impede the war effort in this darkest of times for Britain. The drawing that appears in the paper this day is to become one of the most famous in the history of political cartooning: an exhausted sailor slumped upon a makeshift raft in the middle of an angry sea. But it is the caption to Zec's deft work that is the detonator responsible for the resultant blast: "The price of petrol has been increased by one penny." – Official.*

In Westminster this wartime morning, steam is rising not only from mugs of tea or overcooked toast. Winston Churchill, the Prime Minister, and his Home Secretary, the Labour politician Herbert Morrison, are convinced that the Mirror *is suggesting that seamen are risking their lives so that additional profits can be made from oil. "A wicked cartoon," observes Morrison. A puzzled Zec claims that he is only trying to show the importance of saving fuel because men are risking their lives every day to bring it across the seas. Beverley Baxter, MP for Wood Green and a former editor of the* Daily Express, *says in the Commons: "Is it not a little terrifying, both to the press and to this House, that appreciation of a cartoon by the Home Secretary, which has many variations of meaning, may result in at least a process of starting to ban that newspaper?" It is not the first time during this war that the* Mirror *has been in trouble with the Government. Nor is it to be the last...*

Chamberlain resigned and Churchill succeeded him as Prime Minister on May 11, 1940. The *Mirror* had been forthright since 1936 in promoting Churchill for Premier and attacking the "old men" whom it believed had failed adequately to prepare for war. Now it was to be generous in its praise of the new leader and former contributor – "We feel that our new Prime Minster has great gifts," the paper's editorial commented the day after Churchill took over – but such commendation was not to be slavish. The *Mirror* adopted the position of a friendly critic, a patriot but not a patsy, a supporter but not one who could be bamboozled or bullied. It gave Churchill no respite, continuing its criticism of the former appeasers who remained in the Government. On June 7, less than a month after he became P.M., Winston received Cecil King in the Cabinet room. King, as the political brain of the *Mirror*, was the company's representative in the corridors of power. Bart lacked the knowledge and the social skills to enjoy making house calls on the country's leaders and Cowley would rather be left at the office to fret. As it turned out, he had a lot of fretting to do.

On that day in Downing Street, Churchill defended the inclusion in the Government of many of those who had led the country astray in the 1930s and observed, for King to record in his diary, that "if one were dependent on the people who had been right in the last few years, what a tiny handful one would have to depend

Battle cry: The *Mirror*'s first issue of the Second World War delivered the news with telling force.

on". Two weeks later, the *Mirror* renewed its call for more drive and purpose from the Government. "Already here and there, fragments of the old complacency begin to peep out," wrote Jennings. Cassandra attacked "Army foolery", lampooning the senior officers' decrees that serving soldiers were not allowed to walk arm-in-arm with their girls. The Army – or, at least, the Army hierarchy – was livid.

No one could doubt the *Mirror*'s patriotic fervour. Dunkirk was recorded with the front-page headline BLOODY MARVELLOUS! and a Zec cartoon showing a wounded soldier being carried to safety by a sailor, with the caption, "This way, Chum!" Nor did it fail to give credit where it believed it was due. Churchill's "We shall never surrender" speech of June 4 was acknowledged by the paper as "the greatest speech ever made by a Prime Minister of Britain". But when the Cabinet was reshuffled in October, Jennings noted that "the sifting or shunting of mediocrities or reputed successes appears to have been directed by no principle plain to the outsider, unless it was the principle that new blood must rarely be transfused into an old body." Now the Government – or, at least, some members of the Government – were livid.

In October, Deputy Prime Minister Clement Atlee informed the Newspaper Proprietors Association that a Cabinet discussion on the press had deplored the *Mirror* and the *Sunday Pictorial* and that any further criticism of an "irresponsible kind" would result in legislation to introduce wartime censorship for all papers. The NPA had strongly resisted the proposition, but Atlee had described the *Mirror* and *Pictorial* as "subversive". Esmond Harmsworth, chairman of the Proprietors, lost no time in scurrying to Geraldine House to report the conversation to Cowley and Bartholomew.

As a result, the unholy alliance of the suspicious Bart and the aloof King visited Atlee in Whitehall. As German aircraft droned across the London skyline, the *Mirror* directors were shown to a basement air raid shelter, what King was to describe as "a gasproof room about nine feet square, where Atlee was sitting on a bed reading the *New Statesman*". The *Mirror* men spiritedly defended the position of its papers, stressing that the Group's policy was that Britain must win the war at all costs. Atlee's criticisms were so imprecise that the meeting broke up after only 25 minutes. Bart and King believed Atlee had been delivering Churchill's views rather than his own. Nonetheless, the incident contributed to the gathering storm over the *Mirror*'s view of the way the war was being conducted.

Early in 1941, there was another rumble of distant thunder. In a Commons debate following the Government's suppression of the *Daily Worker* and *The Week*, Aneurin Bevan let slip that only a few months previously the Government had warned two large circulation newspapers that they were considered subversive. He did not name the *Mirror* and *Pictorial*, but described the Government's tactics against the papers as "secret terror". An exchange of letters between King and Churchill in January enabled the Prime Minister to complain of "a spirit of hatred and malice against the Government… which spirit surpasses anything I have ever seen in English journalism". King saw Churchill in Downing Street again at the end of that month, when the Prime Minister accused the papers of "rocking the boat", which could be disastrous for the country. King later recalled: "Winston was very difficult to talk to… getting up and striding about, shooting remarks at me that often had

Penny dreadful: Zec's cartoon, helped by Cassandra's caption, was to cause a storm that threatened the very existence of the Daily Mirror.

"The price of petrol has been increased by one penny."—Official.

nothing whatever to do with his last remark or anything I was saying, sitting down again, leaning on the fire-guard or lighting his cigar."

Further letters bounced back and forth between the two men, ending in mid-February with pleasantries that established an uneasy truce. But with an ongoing feeling in Downing Street of mistrust in, and betrayal by, the *Mirror,* it is with hindsight not at all surprising that the events of 6 March 1942 dragged the conflict between Premier and paper into the public domain. Zec, having transported himself and his stricken sailor cartoon by bicycle from his Regent's Park home, showed it to his friend Cassandra. The caption read, "Petrol is Dearer Now". Cudlipp later recorded the dialogue between the two men, which, although probably fanciful, accurately credited the caption that appeared in the paper. "You're a genius," Cassandra is alleged to have told Zec, "but you want a stronger caption. You need to pinpoint and dramatise the

In the shadow of greatness: Cecil Thomas was editor – but with Bart and Cudlipp "upstairs".

extra penny charge." Cass promptly pinpointed and emphasised it and the cartoon went to press with sticks of dynamite strapped to its back.

The initial babble of inaccurate analysis and wounded complaint had died away before the editorial director, Bartholomew, and the editor, Cecil Thomas, received a summons to attend a meeting with Home Secretary Herbert Morrison – himself a recent *Mirror* contributor – at the Home Office. The meeting was documented in a letter Thomas wrote subsequently to a member of the paper's staff then serving in the RAF. Zec's cartoon was "worthy of Goebbels at his best", suggested Morrison, and was "plainly meant to tell seamen not to go to sea to put money in the pockets of petrol owners". He was unhappy about a Jennings leading article, too, although apparently objected only to one sentence in the editorial of 6 March, the same day Zec's offending cartoon had appeared. "He reminded us he had closed one paper, and said it would be a long time before it was opened," wrote Thomas. 'And that goes for you, too… If you are closed, it will be for a long time.' No further warning would be given. 'We shall act with a speed that will surprise you'." After they left Morrison, Bart and Thomas agreed that the Home Secretary had seemed to be relaying the threat of action against the paper, speaking, they felt, in his master's voice. "I spent the next few weeks in a kind of trance," Zec was to say. "It was hard to believe it was happening."

Most of the other national newspapers sided against the *Mirror* when Morrison made the rebuke public in the Commons later that day. Some of the *Mirror's* friends in the House called for a debate and on 26 March the serious, and, at the time, uphill business of winning a war was interrupted while the Commons discussed the Freedom of the Press. The debate is noteworthy mainly because of Aneurin Bevan's contribution. He roundly attacked Morrison and the restriction of press liberty, but commented: "I do not like the *Daily Mirror*, and I have never liked it… I do not like that form of journalism. I do not like the strip-tease artists [sic]… But the *Daily Mirror* has not been warned because people do not like that kind of journalism. It is not because the Home Secretary is aesthetically repelled by it that he wants it. I have heard a number of honourable Members say that it is a hateful paper, a tabloid paper, a hysterical paper, a sensational paper, and that they do not like it. I am sure the Home Secretary does not take that view. He likes the paper. He is taking its money." And Bevan waved a batch of Morrison's *Mirror* cuttings in the air. It was a cheap shot and a foolish one. Morrison immediately responded with: "If the honourable Gentleman wants to be personal, so is somebody closely connected with him." Perhaps it had momentarily slipped Bevan's mind that his wife, Jennie Lee, had the previous year become political correspondent of the *Mirror*.

George Orwell, a member of the Home Guard and at this time working for the BBC, recorded in his diary: "Terrific debate in the House over the 'affaire' *Daily Mirror*. A. Bevan reading numerous extracts from Morrison's own articles in the *D.M.*, written since war started, to the amusement of Conservatives who are anti-*D.M.*, but can never resist the spectacle of two Socialists slamming one another. Cassandra

announces he is resigning to join the army. Prophesy he will be back in journalism within three months."

That was, apart from the odd squawk as feathers were ruffled, the end of the 'affaire' *Daily Mirror*. The paper remained trenchant in its views, sometimes pointing out the follies of those directing the long-running battle against Fascism, but always urging the country forward, and supporting the brave men and women, of all ranks, who bore the main burden of doing the job. BRITISH GRIT IN A BRITISH SHIP BEAT THE LOT read its headline on the report of the attack by a German submarine on HMS Kelly and the refusal of Lord Louis Mountbatten – much later he was to figure, fleetingly but crucially, in the *Mirror's* history – to abandon ship. FARM BOY FOUGHT GERMANY WITH HIS PEN told of how a Yorkshire 12-year-old had won 4s 6d (22p) for a patriotic essay.

On 27 March 1942, Cassandra announced his departure from the paper in typical fashion:

"By 1938 I had graduated from pickle kings to Neville Chamberlain. I fought hard against him and I fought fiercely against Munich. I had been in Germany nearly every year from 1929 to 1938 and it seemed incredible to me then, as it does now, that anybody could possibly mistake Hitler's preparations as being designed for anything but gigantic war.

"I campaigned for Churchill, and my support was early and violent. But since he came to power, I have distrusted many of his lieutenants – and I have said so with scant respect either for their position or their feelings.

"Churchill told a former colleague of his that 'there are paths of service open in wartime which are not open in the days of peace, and some of these paths may be paths to honour.'

"I, who have not transgressed, am shortly following the Prime Minister's advice. I am still a comparatively young man and I propose to see whether the rifle is a better weapon than the printed word.

"Mr Morrison can have my pen – but not my conscience."

So with Captain W. Connor otherwise engaged on Army duty with the Royal Artillery and then the forces newspaper *Union Jack*, edited by Lieutenant-Colonel H. Cudlipp – Hugh had joined up in December 1940 – a new

Comrades in arms: serving soldiers Hugh Cudlipp (front row, second from right) flanked by Bill Connor (on his right) and Peter Wilson.

column by Garry Allingham appeared in the *Mirror* in 1942 and ran until 1945. Allingham was very much on the side of the serviceman, like a gruff but kindly sergeant-major, and did much in paving the way for the returning troops at the end of the war to continue taking the paper every day. Tom Wintringham, a political activist who had fought in Spain, and lobby correspondent Bill Greig, appointed by Bartholomew to provide a column about soldiers' grievances, were others writing for the forces from London. Greig's column was an instant success, attracting a deluge of correspondence from servicemen and, subsequently, their families. Soldiers complained about red tape and "bull". Their wives bemoaned the inadequacies of rationing. Greig was summoned to the War Office and told in no uncertain terms that such contentious material could demoralise the forces. Greig ignored the warning and so did Bart.

Bringing the news from the theatres of war was a team of correspondents who were, Cudlipp later recalled, always near the sharp end – "no shop stewards, no restrictionist practices and no days off". David Walker, whose adventures in Greece, Romania, Bulgaria and Italy were like something from *Boy's Own*, but deadly serious; George McCarthy, who was on a Normandy beach with British troops soon after D-Day; and correspondent Archer Brooks all

returned safely at the end of the war. Bernard Gray and Ian Fyfe didn't. Gray hitched a lift on a submarine to get back to Cairo from Malta, where he had gone to write about the fortitude of the Maltese during the Nazi onslaught on the island. The submarine didn't make it. Future *Mirror* star Fyfe, Donald Zec's companion during adventures in Manchester as young reporters before the war, volunteered for a ride on a different form of transport – one of the gliders braving heavy anti-aircraft fire over the coast of France on D-Day. Fyfe was never heard of again.

Meanwhile, the 56-year-old Bartholomew had joined the Auxiliary Fire Service and spent many evenings out on the streets with photographer George Greenwell, recording the devastation caused by enemy air raids. Having turned around the ailing *Daily Mirror,* Bart was, with the war, experiencing another finest hour of his own. With the backing of the Admiralty, he launched *Good Morning*, a daily newspaper for the submarine service of the Royal Navy. Between 1943 and 1945, 924 issues of the paper, numbered but undated and consisting of puzzles, pin-ups, cartoons and letters as well as articles, were printed in advance of the departure of subs for the war zones, dispatched to the Admiralty in batches of 28 and distributed while the vessels were at sea. *Good Morning* built up a remarkable relationship with

Man of vision: Philip Zec's explosive cartoons spoke directly to the people of wartime Britain.

News in depth: Good Morning brought a taste of home to the Navy's submarine crews.

its readers, interviewing the families of submariners and publishing the interviews, along with photographs, in issues that were handed out by the ships' coxswains on a strictly daily basis (although Cudlipp recorded that when one sub was depth-charged and sank, its engines out of action, the coxswain distributed the papers for "the tomorrows they did not hope to see". The engines were restarted and the sub

saved – but there were no more *Good Mornings* for the rest of the voyage).

As for Philip Zec, a socialist and a Jew, his cartoons continued to dominate the slim issues of a *Mirror* that had become the People's Paper and, most importantly, the paper of the serving soldier, sailor and airman (the historian A.J.P. Taylor was to write that the *Mirror* was the first ever daily paper to be read by "other ranks" in

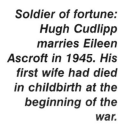

Soldier of fortune: Hugh Cudlipp marries Eileen Ascroft in 1945. His first wife had died in childbirth at the beginning of the war.

the Forces and at home). Zec had been one of those remarkable recruits who arrived on the *Mirror* when such talent appeared to be dropping from the skies. Having trained at St. Martin's School of Art, he had become a prominent commercial illustrator before being attracted to newspapers as a means of expressing his strong political and social beliefs. So wounding were his withering cartoon attacks on the Nazi hierarchy that, captured German documents later verified, he was to be arrested immediately Britain had fallen or capitulated. Fastidious of dress and a sparkling raconteur, he drew less frequently after the war – his brother, Donald, believes he became disenchanted with what he considered to be growing Left extremism in the Labour Party. But his often venomous wartime cartoons were as potent a weapon as could be employed on the home front.

If Cudlipp was right, it was not until after Jennings' retirement through ill health in 1942, when "The Man Who Made England Sit Up" was honourably discharged to spend more time with his books, that Bart's instincts, Zec's socialism, King's sympathies and the paper's rapport with the ordinary men and women struggling to survive in a world gone mad fused into an almost subliminal political commitment to the Labour Party. Jennings' replacement, the paper's former radio reviewer, Bernard Buckham – editorials now carried the initials BBB – carried on where his predecessor had left off in the pursuit of social justice for all, but for the first time the *Mirror* began to extol the virtues of Labour, describing the Party as "the nation's political hope" for "a fundamental change in the political scene".

George Orwell had noticed a shift in the paper's politics in April of 1941, when he had written in his London Letter to *Partisan Review*: "The tone of the popular press has improved out of all recognition during the last year. This is especially notable in the *Daily Mirror* and *Sunday Pictorial* ('tabloid' papers of vast circulation. Read largely by the army)… the *Mirror* and the [*Evening*] *Standard* are noticeably 'left'." But Cudlipp set 1943 as the year when it became clear that the then *Mirror* Group would throw its growing weight behind the Labour Party when the country emerged from the social as well as the literal debris of the war. Buckham wrote that "…the next

general election will record the verdict of a new Britain. This election, when it comes, may bring surprises." It certainly did, mainly for the Conservatives.

Although Cecil King still guided the *Mirror* politically, Bartholomew began to take a greater interest. Bill Greig introduced him to Labour politicians, including "Manny" Shinwell, whose no-nonsense approach to what needed to be done to ensure a rapid recovery after the war was couched in the sort of language the equally direct Bart understood. King had already decided that the Beveridge Report – the findings of the Commons-appointed committee chaired by Sir William Beveridge – was likely to be an important foundation stone for the welfare state in post-war Britain. Summoned towards the end of 1942 to the London flat of Lord Privy Seal and Leader of the House Sir Stafford Cripps, a fellow-Wykehamist (King professed to have hated almost every day of his time at Winchester and wrote "…there have been no great Wykehamists and a surprisingly small number of eminent ones"), King was given a broad outline of the Beveridge committee's plan to change the social face of the country. He thought it was a good thing and, fearful that there were those in the House attempting to block its progress, inspired a *Mirror* editorial calling for the report to be made public. A week later, the report, *Proposals to the Government*, was available in the Government Stationery Office and crowds flocked to buy it and learn its secrets.

But it was not until September 1944 that two White Papers on the social services, the offspring of the Beveridge Report, were published. The paper spread its arms to embrace their contents: "The *Daily Mirror* welcomes the Government's proposals for social security… We have at last arrived at a national scheme of insurance, and that in itself marks a big step forward in the social reconstruction of the country." But it went on cautiously to warn that "while the step is a big one, it is only the first one, and, in our view, represents not an end but a beginning" and emphasised that full employment, a rising birthrate and a state medical scheme were essential to success on the road to what would be a new world.

The mood at the *Mirror* grew more confident with each passing day, despite the mounting rubble in Fetter Lane. The area had suffered

Beginning of the end: Zec anticipates the fall of Hitler's "Fortress Europe" in this dramatic cartoon of June 1944. The caption reads: The Hour of Reckoning.

Then, in May 1941, an incendiary penetrated the roof of Geraldine House while fires raged on and around the building.

Cudlipp was later to leave it to an article written by Roy Lewis and published in *Persuasion* to encapsulate the paper's role in the war and it is worth recalling part of it:

"During the war," wrote Lewis, *"the* Mirror *went after, and told, the story of all wars, the story reflected in every individual experience, in the sense of loneliness, frustration and persecution that rises under tightened discipline and lack of channels for self-expression – the story of 'the man at the receiving end', the man whose job it is to do and die and not to reason why, although fifty years of elementary education and popular newspapers have made him into a reasoning animal... The* Mirror *settled down to fight his fight and air his grouse... As everyone now knows, the* Mirror *was in fact an integral part of Service morale. Its circulation showed it. Troops' welfare organisations swore by it. It was in touch with Service feeling as no other paper. It was the paper of armies without political commissars, of fighting men innocent of ideologies."*

heavy bombing and in September 1940 Birkbeck College, which adjoined Geraldine House, was set on fire and only the opening of a rarely used rear exit from the *Mirror* building enabled the paper to get out on time. That winter, what had become the *Mirror*'s favourite wartime pub, the Red Lion in Red Lion Court, was hit by incendiary bombs on a night when the body of the recently deceased fiancé of the landlord's daughter, Elsie, was in a coffin on the top floor, awaiting collection by the undertaker. "We can't leave Stan," wept Elsie as evacuation became necessary, so, at the height of the air raid, three *Mirror* journalists and two servicemen climbed the stairs to put out the fire and carry the coffin from the pub and through the streets to St. Dunstan's-in-the-West church.

Live Letters became another conduit for many servicemen to air their grievances – complaints were investigated and taken up with the ministries at the rate of 20 a week – but the column was also instrumental in helping servicemen in other ways. In four years, almost 70,000 games were sent to serving units. With tennis balls unobtainable, the Old Codgers cadged 2,000, had them refurbished and sent to units all over the world. During the last two years of the war, 570 small ships of the Royal Navy were "adopted" by readers and each Christmas hundreds of parcels containing gifts were dispatched to needy children of service personnel. Such munificence delivered a dividend for the *Mirror*: the hundreds of thousands of readers' letters that had poured into the paper – to the often pugnacious Codgers and elsewhere, including Questions in the Mess, now conducted by Barbara (Castle) Betts. The popular approach initiated by Bart in the mid-1930s enabled the paper to establish a touch so common to its readers that it was as if it was permanently shaking hands with them. Michael Christiansen, a future *Mirror* editor, was to disclose in a speech, when editing the paper's Sunday sister in the 1960s, that after Bartholomew became editorial director, the *Mirror* analysed the thousands of letters that arrived every week and adapted its editorial approach to what it learned from this invaluable running "survey". There could be no better way of formulating editorial policy.

As peace and the inevitable General Election approached, however, some of the allegations made in the paper's editorials were, in retrospect, outrageous – that Fascists in Britain were actively assisting the Conservative Party, and that "German big businessmen are praying for a Conservative victory". Robert Allen and John Frost observed years later that wars never bring out the best in newspapers – "they encourage deception, exaggerate hatred – and all from the very best of motives". There are those involved in the coverage of modern warfare who would argue against one or other of those counts, but there is no doubt that some of the language used by the *Mirror* in 1939-45 would today be considered intemperate. Come D-Day, however, – DESTINY'S HOUR, bellowed page one – however, the paper's clarion call was both understandable and appreciated by a weary and still apprehensive nation: "We can with reason select a sacred invocation for the battle-cry and say, with Montgomery: 'Let God arise, and let his enemies be scattered'."

John Cowley, having endeared himself to few at Geraldine House, died in 1944 and subsequently became no more than a dismissive note in histories of the paper. An obituary in the *Mirror*, written by former business partner Bernard Falk, described Cowley as "a rare genius – an all-round newspaper chief with the same competent understanding of the editorial side of a great Metropolitan 'daily' as of the commercial and mechanical." There were no recorded cries of "Hear, hear!" Falk also recalled how author Edgar Wallace and he had been Cowley's associates in an "ill-starred" weekly newspaper venture that evolved into a racing paper and "promised to yield us a fortune, but, mainly owing… to our inability to control Wallace, that promise proved illusory". Cecil King recorded that Cowley was so secretive that when he was dying and efforts were made to get in touch with his family, neither his long-time secretary nor his three sons could provide any information about his origins.

His timidity in the role of chairman was replaced by Bartholomew's aggression and impetuosity, undiminished at 61. Throughout that year, the *Mirror* was shepherding its readers towards the General Election that would swiftly follow the end of the war. A page headed "Readers' Parliament" opened up debates on matters of concern to the man and woman in the street. The paper began to educate its readers in politics, a subject that one may safely assume did not feature at the top of their lists of hobbies and pastimes. There could be no doubt which party the paper would back when it came time for votes to be cast. Labour had "ideas and flair", and despite failing one familiar *Mirror* test – the hierarchy was much too old – it was the party that would best deliver the by now familiar "new world". Labour's proposed post-war anti-profiteering, nationalisation programme, support for the United Nations and continued rationing would bring home the bacon, although shortages might determine there still might not be very much of that.

Then, the following May, as Cudlipp – busy in Rome ruffling political and senior military feathers with *Union Jack* – was memorably to observe, some "bloody fool declared peace. The roundabout suddenly stopped and all the lights went out in the fairground." Back home, the *Mirror* greeted news of Germany's surrender in Berlin with celebration and a warning – "Never must the slothful years return. Who shall say that there are not in the world other Hitlers waiting to rise up if the time comes ripe?" The following morning, Wednesday 9 May, a joyous front page proclaimed BRITAIN'S DAY OF REJOICING and pictured a jubilant Churchill in the centre of an estimated 50,000 crowd in Whitehall. It is not surprising that the Prime Minister felt a demonstrably grateful nation would entrust peacetime Britain to the care of the man with the nerve to outsmart and outlast Hitler.

Rejoicing with the nation: The Mirror celebrates Victory in Europe, as Londoners take to the streets.

The final act: Japan surrenders and the Mirror records the end of the Second World War.

Philip Zec's VE-Day cartoon of a bloodied and bandaged soldier thrusting a victory laurel wreath forward and exclaiming, "Here you are! Don't lose it again!" ranks among the greatest he ever drew and, for old soldiers and sentimentalists, can still bring a lump to the throat almost 60 years later. Two days after it appeared, the *Mirror* adopted a new slogan, which would appear under its masthead in every issue for the next 15 years and encapsulate the paper's relationship with its readers: FORWARD WITH THE PEOPLE. The war was not yet over – it would not be until Wednesday 15 August that the front page could announce PEACE over the subsidiary headline JAPAN SURRENDERS – ALLIES CEASE FIRE and one of the most welcome introductions in history: "Peace has once again come to the world". But from the moment of the German surrender, the *Mirror* was preoccupied with another battle – that for the custody of post-war Britain.

Churchill resigned as Prime Minister and requested the dissolution of Parliament on 23 May, just 22 days after the death of Hitler in his Berlin bunker. It was a decade since the last election, when the *Mirror* had been behind

Baldwin. Its stance was to be very different this time, in what was to become one of the most famous and influential newspaper election campaigns in history. The seed from which it grew had been sown by a Mrs C. Gardiner, of Ilford in Essex, whose reader's letter about the hopes she had when her soldier husband returned home was published on the front page of 25 June. It ended with the promise: "I shall vote for him". The *Mirror* seized upon the phrase and pondered: "How does a woman vote for a serving man who has no vote [the majority of the 2,867,836 "service voters" would still be overseas, of whom around two-thirds would have proxy votes; the remainder were disenfranchised]? How does she make sure that his fighting views get into the ballot box? The answer is easy. She puts them there herself using her own vote to do it." On 3 July, the paper returned to the theme: "To the electors we would say: You know what the fighting man wants. You know which party is likely to give him what he wants. You know the only way to make his future safe. Go then and do your duty. Vote for him."

Labour loved the slogan, even though the

Mirror at no time during a brilliantly orchestrated campaign – masterminded by left-wing journalist and editor Sydney Elliott, who was engaged as political advisor – directly urged its readers to vote Labour. Out of sight of the electorate, the party had the paper behind it in practical ways, too: members of staff such as Philip Zec and Ted Castle, the then picture editor, worked with campaign manager Herbert Morrison on the best way to harness the swell of public feeling for a new regime to guide the country in what was to be a brave new world. The readers had a major role to play in the paper's campaign: hundreds of letters were published, most of which indicated that the writers would not be voting Conservative. Gerry Allingham, who was to become a Labour Member of Parliament in the election, orchestrated the mail from those still in the services and told them in print: "Don't let the politicians get away with it this time. You fellows have the power. You have the power to fight – and you also have the power to vote." Not all of them did, but the unsubtle message continued to be unerringly delivered into the hearts and minds of a weary but hopeful nation.

In the last days of the campaign, Philip Zec drew a regular strip cartoon in which a soldier wrote home to his family, outlining his hopes and dreams for the future. It was simple but effective pro-Labour propaganda. And on 4 July, the day before the country went to the polls, the editor delivered the final front-page clarion call:

"Tomorrow the future of Britain and of yourselves is at stake, your hearths and homes, your families, your jobs, your dreams. Vote for them!

"For five long years the lusty youth of this great land has bled and died.

"Vote for Them!

"You women must think of your men. For five years you have depended on them. Tomorrow they depend on you. The choice is plain: to march forward to a better and happier Britain or turn back to the dangers that led to the brink of disaster.

"You know which way your men would march.

"Vote for Them!"

On election day itself the paper reprinted, "without apology", Zec's VE-Day cartoon: "Here you are – don't lose it again". Having

embraced peace with a fierce hug, what the public wasn't about to lose in those tentative early post-war days was its nerve. A turnout of 72.7 per cent elected Labour with a majority of 180 over the Tories and an overall majority of 146. To their amazement and horror, the Conservatives were swept away by a landslide and the *Mirror* reported, "the scenes at the Conservative Party H.Q. were reminiscent of the funeral of a millionaire at which all the mourners have just learned that they were left out of the will". How much had the *Mirror* contributed to Labour's victory? Almost certainly less than was imagined at the time: the wave of radicalism that had swamped the Tories had its own momentum. But after "the people's war" – Bartholomew's phrase – the women of Britain had indeed Voted for Them.

As chairman, Bart was now in total control of the company. Unsurprisingly, Cecil King had seen himself as the obvious successor to Cowley and later insisted that Bart had professed not to want the job before plotting with other board members to ensure he got it. King later recalled that "I told Bart he would make a very bad chairman," which must have done a great deal to improve his standing with the suspicious, scheming older man. Bart's unchallenged power meant that now his idiosyncrasies could go unchecked. The telephones of senior executives were tapped – more than 40 years would pass before another extraordinary character reintroduced the practice – and he enjoyed constantly manipulating and humiliating the staff.

At the end of the war, Bart had published, as did many companies, a celebratory in-house tribute to employees. Early in 1946, a copy of *The Call and the Answer* was presented to every member of staff, with their names printed on the front in gold lettering. In a fulsome tribute to "how *Daily Mirror* men [sic; once again the women were overlooked], wherever they were, in the office or out of it, did their bit". A roll of honour showed that 26 employees, from 11 different areas of the company, had been lost.

Cudlipp was still in Rome, as were Bill Connor, Peter Wilson, former news editor Mackenzie Porter, who won the Military Cross, and a second lieutenant named Clifford Davis, who was working with Army Broadcasting at its station in the suburbs of Monte Marino and would later claim his own place in *Mirror*

folklore. Back home, Bart, if not the *Daily Mirror*, was at his peak (as Robert Allen and John Frost were later to point out, the *Mirror* comprised eight pages and cost a penny when hostilities ended in 1945, exactly the same pagination and cost as at the end of World War One). The paper continued to surge forward and the *Pictorial*, as yet still under the wartime temporary stewardship of Stuart "Sam" Campbell, was also thriving. Bart bought *Reveille*, a struggling weekly, and installed the versatile Roy Suffern to transform it from a dull paper for dull servicemen into a cheeky, fun-filled rapid-read package that soon achieved a circulation soaring like an anti-aircraft tracer. This was probably the pinnacle of what Bart saw as his vocation, but he was incapable of enjoying it. The one-man ideas machine, driven by an inferiority complex and resentful of anyone and anything he thought might come between him and his personal mission to make

the *Mirror* the biggest newspaper in the land, had his eyes fixed firmly on the horizon, except when their beady gaze was turned in the direction of the latest unfortunate to attract his malevolence.

Untouched by post-war euphoria and true to his 'man of the people' image, Bart rejected a knighthood for his work when the Admiralty recommended that he should be honoured for his war effort with *Good Morning* (he also organised special laundry ships, so that submarine crews arriving in northern ports could get their clothes dried and ironed). The submariners' paper had been an important morale booster, especially through its pin-ups and the adventures of the skimpily dressed Jane, but it was also an educational instrument of sorts, dispensing information to be digested by ordinary seaman and officers too between wolf-whistles. Those who enjoyed *Good Morning* were potential *Mirror* readers and many gravitated to the paper when they came home. That was reward enough for Bart, although he did accept an OBE – having requested as lowly an award as it was possible to bestow – and then, so secretive was his nature, initially neglecting to mention the fact to his family.

When the *Mirror* had come under fire from the Government during the war, questions had been raised about its ownership. Suggestions that a controlling interest was held by the American press magnate William Randolph Hearst were refuted: "At no time in our history has this evil man Hearst had any financial or other interest in our newspaper." Claims were made also that Israel Sieff, of Marks and Spencer, and the reclusive multi-millionaire Sir John Ellerman, both Jewish, were pulling the *Mirror* strings. Ellerman did in fact own a little over 2.6 per cent of the company's shares in 1945, but not until the arrival of Robert Maxwell almost 40 years later did any one person or group hold enough equity to influence its policy, political or otherwise.

The revitalised *Daily Mirror* "had no proprietor", A.J.P. Taylor was to write. "It was created by the ordinary people on its staff, and especially by Harry Guy Bartholomew. The English people at last found their voice." So had Bart – and it was one to be heard very loudly over the next six years…

Destiny in their hands: The Mirror **urges its readers to vote for the soldiers – and social security.**

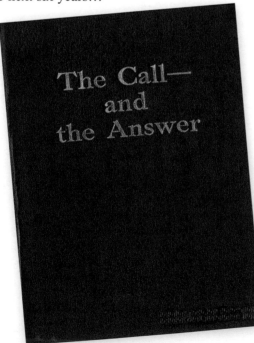

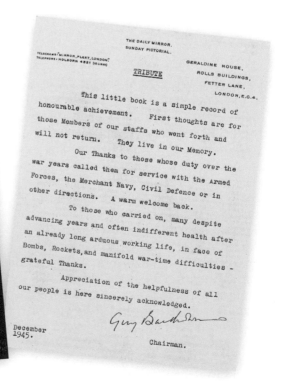

Lest we forget: Bart paid tribute to the Mirror *men and woman who battled through the war at home and overseas in the booklet* The Call – and the Answer, *which was distributed to staff at Christmas 1945.*

5 *THE GOLDEN AGE*

I *t is a March morning in Rome and*
Lieutenant-Colonel Hugh Cudlipp is
reading his mail. The war has been over
for more than seven months and Cudlipp is
fretting to get back to where he feels he truly
belongs – in a civilian editor's chair. He is not
unaware of what has been happening at the
Mirror *and* Pictorial *in his absence and smiles*
wryly when he opens an envelope containing a
guarded if ostensibly friendly letter from
Bartholomew. The postscript amuses him:
"When you reach England, see me before you
see anybody, even if you have to wait." Bart's
capacity for intrigue has not diminished in his
absence, reflects Cudlipp, who is certain that,
but for the Act of Parliament requiring
employers to reinstate employees returning from
the armed forces, Bart's welcome home would
be in the shape of a letter of dismissal.

He is tempted by prospects other than those at
Geraldine House. The second Lord Rothermere
has made it clear that he would welcome his
services, as has Arthur Christiansen, editor of
the mighty Daily Express. *But Cecil King has*
also written, warmly, and Cudlipp's inclination
is to pick up where he left off six years
previously, editing a Sunday Pictorial *that has*
been in the custody of Stuart "Sam" Campbell
– also no favourite of Bart, nor of King –
during most of the war. As he makes his
decision to return, Cudlipp contemplates his
future, concluding that Bart will never appoint
him editor of the Daily Mirror. *He is right, but*
for much of the golden age of the paper he will
be the main editorial driving force that enables
it to boast "The greatest daily sale in the
universe"…

The *Mirror*, concluded a research report, *The*
Popular Press and Social Change 1935-65
(1970), emerged from the war quite a different
newspaper from what it had been in 1940 – "It
had learned to handle the news in terms of
demotic radicalism… The *Mirror* did not
'decide' to support Labour, whatever happened,
once the war ended: it learned to speak to its
readers a certain way, and in doing so placed
itself in a position to hear, and then to articulate
(in what must be counted as one of the most
sustained instances of journalistic ventriloquism
ever practised), what its readers were feeling
and thinking."

During the war, the paper had reflected the
thoughts of the majority of those serving
overseas and the women left to fend for their
families on the home front. When peace broke
out, the paper was able to address itself to a
different kind of war: the one between the
privileged few and the rest – those who quickly
discovered that, despite victory over the Axis
powers, the battle for social equality at home
was far from over. But there was much to
lighten the post-war austerity caused by
continued rationing and the painful rebuilding
of a country that had been driven almost, but
not quite, to its knees. GLAMOUR IS BACK
FOR WOMEN AT LAST, the *Mirror*
announced in May 1946 above a story reporting
on "reappearance of famous brands, more
corsets, and nicer clothes with all the pleats,
tucks, embroideries and other gay fripperies of
pre-war days". The following year in Paris, Dior
introduced the New Look, with long skirts, and
in 1948 the American tennis star "Gorgeous"
Gussie Moran caused a sensation by arriving at
the Wimbledon championships wearing lace-
trimmed knickers – GAME, SET AND

Rising star: Hugh Cudlipp was said to look on Cecil King as the father he never had. Mirror director Ellis Birk said King sent Cudlipp "lots of books. Hugh pretended to read them, but never actually read a single one."

UNDIES! chortled Joanna Davey's story. (The *Mirror* had adopted a new look of its own in September 1947, introducing the seven-column page format. It had been fixed at five columns per page in January 1940 and redesigned to accommodate six the following April.)

Levity was the order of every day in the paper, but not necessarily in the office: Bart was as driven as ever. Cudlipp, who never did reveal whether or not he went to see the chairman "before talking to anyone else" upon arriving in England from Italy, resumed his helmsmanship of the *Sunday Pictorial*, his partnership with King and his uneasy stand-off with the firebrand who had been elevated to chairman during Cudlipp's required absence. Sam Campbell left for the rival *People*, where later he would become one of its most distinguished editors. And in 1948 the mild-mannered Cecil Thomas departed as inconspicuously as he had arrived after almost 15 years of responding to his master's voice from behind the editor's desk at the *Mirror*. Bart replaced Thomas with Sylvester Bolam, a Durham University graduate who had taken the sub-editorial route to success and had risen to night editor and then deputy to Thomas. When Bolam took over, he published a

front-page statement of intent: "The *Mirror* is a sensational newspaper. We make no apology for that. We believe in the sensational presentation of news and views, especially important news and views, as a necessary and valuable public service in these days of mass readership and democratic responsibility. We shall go on being sensational to the best of our ability…" He was, according to Cudlipp, "a friendly, wiry bird". He was to be the editor when the *Mirror* steamed past the ostensibly omnipotent *Daily Express* to become the country's biggest-selling newspaper – and also, in fittingly sensational fashion, the first and only national newspaper editor to serve a jail term while in office.

In March 1949, what became known as the "acid bath murders" was a story that gripped all but the ultra squeamish among the population. An investigation into the disappearance of 69-year-old Mrs Olive Durand-Deacon became a murder inquiry that led to the discovery of a series of horrific killings. The murderer had tried to dispose of Mrs Durand-Deacon's body in a bath of acid and had, *Mirror* Scotland Yard reporter "Jeep" Whittal was told by a police contact, drunk the blood of his victims through a straw. Following the arrest of John George

Tough guy: Harry Guy "Bart" Bartholomew enjoyed putting the fear of God into reporters.

Inside story: Editor Sylvester Bolam spent three months in jail after the Haigh contempt trial.

Haigh, Scotland Yard issued a warning to the press that comment on the case could prejudice the trial. The *Mirror* had been running the story with macabre relish: VAMPIRE HORROR IN NOTTING HILL was the headline over a report Clifford Davis had knitted together from information obtained by Whittal and other staff reporters, including Howard Johnson, later chief reporter, and Donald Zec. "Play up the human vampire stuff," managing editor Cyril Morton told Davis. And even after the police cautionary notice had been received on 3 March, several editions of the following morning's paper were produced with a front page proclaiming THE VAMPIRE CONFESSES which, although not mentioning Haigh by name, contained quotes from the "monster" and the names of five other people he claimed to have killed.

The story was changed during the night to remove the offending material, but the *Mirror* was clearly in contempt of court – "It is difficult to think of a matter more calculated to prejudice a fair trial," said Haigh's counsel, Sir Walter Monckton KC, when proceedings were brought against the paper and its editor in a court presided over by the Lord Chief Justice, Lord Goddard. The *Mirror* admitted an error of

judgement and was fined £10,000 plus costs. The slight figure of Bolam was dispatched from the courtroom to Brixton for three months, a period during which Bartholomew, Philip Zec and Cudlipp visited in a Rolls-Royce to confer with Bolam on an editorial matter – "I bet that's the first and last meeting of newspaper directors held in jail," said Bart, without apparent sympathy. As for John George Haigh, he failed to impress in the courtroom, too, and went to the gallows.

The circulations of the *Mirror* and *Pictorial* continued to flourish, but the company was becoming more and more vulnerable to Bart's caprices. In 1937, when Cudlipp had moved to the *Pictorial*, Bart had said, "I'll tell you this, you'll not get any help from me – no help at all", and he was patently a believer in the maxim that revenge is a dish best served cold. Towards the end of 1949, when the *Pictorial* was making considerable inroads on the circulation of the *People* – the *News of the World* was, as it remains, comfortably the market leader – Cecil King inadvertently provided the chairman with the opportunity to repay what he still considered gross disloyalty by Cudlipp. King travelled to Lagos to see how sales of the group-owned *Daily Times* could be expanded in Eastern Nigeria. He flew on to Enugu, where he stumbled upon a story – a dozen black miners had been killed in a riot. Although journalistic skills were not at the forefront of King's undoubted abilities – he was so shy with people he would have great difficulty ever putting a question to them, Cudlipp later told author Ruth Dudley Edwards – he pieced together the story and cabled it to the *Pictorial*, where it arrived at 10pm on a Saturday evening – "…[Cudlipp] was not one in the ordinary way to miss a world scoop, but for reasons never explained spiked the story," a pained King wrote. "I lost my one bid for a world scoop and Cudlipp was fired."

Bearing in mind how close the two men were, and were to be again – "Cecil was Hugh's father substitute," Mirror Group director Ellis Birk was to observe – the phrase "for reasons never explained" is extraordinary. Presumably King never asked Cudlipp why he did not consider the story worthy of inclusion (the paper was running late that night, he later revealed, and "Nigeria… was a country far away and Enugu was not close to our readers' hearts or to mine"). Whether or not King protested to Bart about his main lieutenant's dismissal, which took place only after the *Pictorial*'s editorial director had returned from Africa, is another mystery – "What sort of fight, if any, Cecil put up for his editor is unknown," Cudlipp was to write. The picture painted by the whole unsavoury episode is of a cowed King and a defeated Cudlipp who accepted without question Bart's vindictiveness.

This scenario is substantiated by Cudlipp's observation, in a reply to King's "pleasant letter" regretting the end of their association, that "now there is only one cockerel in the barnyard I suppose Bart's hens on the *Mirror* will all know even more clearly when, and how often, to lift up their skirts." Cecil Thomas wrote to Cudlipp, too, showing more gumption in retirement than he ever had as Bart's factotum: "One thing I am certain of is that Bart has done himself no good at all."

Philip Zec, he of the 1942 Price of Petrol fracas, took over at the *Pic*. Cudlipp picked up a telephone and within two hours of his dismissal had, metaphorically and almost literally, crossed the Street – the black palace where Lord Beaverbook's newspapers were headquartered

was all of 200 yards away. As assistant to the editor, John Gordon, and subsequently managing editor of the title, Cudlipp was to spend a little over two years at the *Sunday Express*. Back at Geraldine House, there was some cause for jubilation despite the exit of the journalistic crown prince. In 1949, the 12-page *Mirror* – newsprint rationing was still not entirely relaxed – achieved an average circulation of four million copies and surged past the *Daily Express*, which was never to regain its position as Britain's biggest-selling daily paper.

What were to be Bart's last great journalistic flings came with the General Elections of 1950 and 1951. Since 1945, the *Mirror* had broadly supported the Labour Government, although by no means blindly – industrial correspondent Harold Hutchinson was unequivocal in his belief that the 1949 industrial dispute in London docks could have been averted had the Government stepped in early to deal with long-festering dockland grievances and was attacked in the Commons for daring to say so. But the *Mirror* was "of the Left and so is the vast majority of the nation".

When Prime Minister Clement Atlee called an election for 23 February 1950, the paper positioned itself directly behind Labour and ran a campaign that left no doubt as to its allegiance. It dismissed Churchill's pledge that the Conservatives would abolish petrol rationing as "a stunt" and on its centre pages ran pictures and text contrasting the pre-war dole queues with the full employment the country was enjoying under Labour. Even the popular strip cartoon the Ruggles was roped in to aid the paper's campaign (years later it was suggested that Andy Capp should urge readers to "Vote Labour", but his creator, Reg Smythe, refused and the idea was abandoned).

Two days before the country was to go to the polls, the *Mirror* published an editorial headlined "Where We Stand". Whereas in 1945 it had not endorsed Labour by name, this time the message was unambiguous: "The *Daily Mirror* supports the Labour Party at the General Election… This is a critical moment in our history and the world's. It is not a time for starting to dither and go backwards; we must go forward determined to make secure the future of our great nation. Economic difficulties are bound to be ahead. We believe that the Labour

First person IAN WATSON

Good sports: Ian Watson (far left) raises a glass to Peter Wilson at his book launch in 1977.

Ian Watson was born in 1928 in Streatham, London. He joined the Daily Mirror *from the* Portsmouth Evening News *as a sports sub-editor in March 1952, aged 24, at a salary of 14 guineas (£14.70) a week. Later, he became chief sub, deputy sports editor and sports editor (1978-1985). After helping to set up the dummy issue of a "secret" proposed cheap colour newspaper* Good Day – *an aborted project – in the last few months of 1985, he accepted redundancy terms from Robert Maxwell and left in January 1986.*

After World War Two, it took some time for paper rationing, which determined pegged circulations, to be ended. But in the early 1950s, Fleet Street returned to the days of free for all. All circulation departments regarded the sports pages as vital in putting on sales, and the *Daily Mirror* started its sports build-up when Tom Phillips was moved from the news night desk to take charge of the sports department. Jack Hutchinson, an amateur boxer of some distinction, came to London from the *Mirror* in Manchester, and worked his way up to sports editor, where he remained until his retirement in 1973. With Jack manning the office, Tom Phillips was free to enjoy the sporting life as an executive at large, covering major events all over the country. He achieved some fame as a racing tipster – thousands of readers followed his advice to back the Aha Khan's Tulyar to win the 1952 Derby. Next morning, Tom's photograph appeared on Page 1 alongside the headline: WHAT DID I TULYAR! But Philiips developed a penchant for writing fictional stories about a hard-drinking character, "Harry Hollowlegs", which meant real sporting stories had to be minimised or left out altogether. Increasingly, Tom gave the impression of modelling the role of Harry Hollowlegs too closely on himself.

When Hugh Cudlipp returned to the Mirror Group from the *Sunday Express* in 1952, his old friend and wartime colleague, sports writer Peter Wilson, came with him. There was obviously no room for two big names on *Mirror* Sport – Tom Phillips had to go. When he moved to write for the rival *Daily Herald,* his new role was generously (and uniquely) announced on the *Mirror*'s front page. Cudlipp, who had dubbed Peter "The Man They Can't Gag", decreed that he could fill two columns only on the sports pages – not exactly a gag, but a sensible limit to any excess. Old Harrovian Wilson, following in his father's footsteps in writing

Continued on page 68

Party is the only one that can deal with them. We support the Labour Party because it has kept its promises and earned our trust."

A centre spread urging readers to cast their votes for Labour appeared the next day, but although the *Mirror* supported and trusted Labour, the country wasn't quite so sure. The highest turnout in 40 years saw Labour edge home with a majority over the Tories of 17 and an overall majority of just five. "The mood of the country has never been more thoughtful," commented the *Mirror* with a less than memorable summing-up of a major political upheaval. It is probable that its role had been as crucial as a newspaper's was ever to be in an election – the paper's strident voice during the days immediately before polling might just have tipped the balance. But despite Labour's efforts about sport – Freddy Wilson was cricket and rackets correspondent on *The Times*, where Peter's own journalistic career started – was to prove an invaluable asset to the *Mirror* for years to come.

The *Portsmouth Evening News* proved a fertile nursery for the *Mirror* in the late 40s and early 50s. Those arriving in the sports department from there included Don Canadine-Bate, as a rugby writer and chief sports sub-editor in the late 40s. He took over as sports editor when Jack Hutchinson retired. Other Portmuthians who moved to Fetter Lane were James Stagg, football writer Derek Wallis, sub-editor Frank Eyles, and me, a young sub only a month past his National Union of Journalists' junior status. New writers who strengthened the team of football reporters in London at this time included a youthful, ambitious Frank McGhee, later to become the *Daily Mirror*'s Voice of Sport when Peter Wilson retired.

The other outstanding recruit was ex-professional footballer Ken Jones, whose playing career ended with an injury while with Hereford. He came to the Mirror via Dixon's, a Fleet Street sports agency, in September 1958 and moved into the top football writing job reluctantly when his friend and colleague Bill Holden succumbed to a severe chest illness. Later, Ken was to move to the *Sunday Mirror* as its sports columnist and then to *The Independent*, whose pages he still graces.

Peter Laker, a young cricketer who had once turned out for Sussex, mixed reporting rugby with sub-editing before succeeding Brian Chapman as the paper's cricket writer. Laker was still playing and coaching in the West Country in 2002 when in his mid-seventies! Bob Rodney arrived from the Sheffield Telegraph as a sub and cycling reporter, and was later to help Noel Whitcomb manage the highly successful Punters' Club, which provided bargain racing trips at home and abroad for *Mirror* readers.

Deputy sports editor George Harley, a former Press Association reporter with an encyclopaedic sporting knowledge, was the *Mirror*'s man at athletics, football, golf, show jumping and gymnastics. He was also the football pools expert. In those pre-Lottery days, all the

papers devoted considerable space every Wednesday to publishing advice, perms and exclusive plans, hoping to forecast a line of eight draws among the following Saturday's matches. George compiled the pools page under the byline "Longsight", but, on 6 May 1954, appeared woefully shortsighted when sports history was made without the Man from the *Mirror* in attendance.

For years, athletes had dreamed of running a mile in under four minutes, and, on that day, word got around that an attempt was to be made by a select group of middle-distance athletes at the Ifley Road track at Oxford. When the early staff came on duty on the *Mirror* sports desk at 11am that Thursday, George arrived to announce that he would not be going to Oxford as the weather and track "were all wrong" (there was a cold wind that day), that "no historic mile record will be achieved today" and that "I've got other things to do". He removed his jacket and lit the first of a chain of Craven A cigarettes.

In the early afternoon, the teleprinter machines alongside the sports desk began stuttering their FLASH messages and the telephone rang. It was Fenton of Oxford, the local freelance, asking if we would like him to file to the *Mirror* the story of how 25-year-old medical student Roger Bannister, supported by fellow graduates Chris Chataway and Chris Brasher, had set a new world mile record of 3 minutes 59.4 seconds. It was a rare lapse by George, whose chain-smoking claimed him some years later as a cancer victim.

Circulation climbed steadily throughout the 1950s – television sport was still in its infancy – as the *Mirror* brought the big sports stories vividly into people's homes: American Maureen ("Little Mo") Connelly winning her first Wimbledon women's singles title at the age of 17 in 1952; the Czech Emil Zatopek collecting three Olympic golds in Helsinki; the most famous of all FA Cup Finals, when 38-year-old Stanley Matthews turned Blackpool's 3-1 deficit into a 4-3 victory over Bolton Wanderers in 1953; another veteran, newly knighted Gordon Richards, claiming his first Derby win on Pinza just a month later.

Circulation received a further boost with the decision to print the *Mirror* at Withy Grove Manchester as well as

to lift the country out of a post-war gloom brought about by restrictions and controls, a swelling body of opinion within the electorate wanted more and wanted it now.

Within 18 months – during which time the price of the *Mirror* leapt from one penny to a penny-halfpenny (less than 1p) – an administration buffeted at every turn by its tiny advantage in the House was falling apart in mind and body. The *Mirror* warned Atlee that his ageing cabinet should be transfused with new blood from the backbenches. But when a

General Election was called for 25 October 1951, the paper once again rode to the rescue, this time at a canter that produced one of the most famous front pages in the history of political journalism and culminated in a libel writ from Winston Churchill.

With the Korean War into its second year – it was not to end until July 1953 – and the Russians beginning to catch up with the Americans in nuclear weapon development, Prime Minister Atlee's December 1950 visit to the United States for discussions with President

Making the Grade: The teenage Michael Grade in the Mirror's sports department. "His father is Leslie, his uncle is Lew. Look after him," said Cudlipp.

London, enabling the paper to compete on equal terms with its rivals in Scotland, Ireland and the north. In February 1956, it also saved Frank McGhee's life, but at the expense of that of football writer Archie Ledbroke. Ledbroke was one of the journalists inherited by the *Mirror* from Kemsley's closed down *Daily Dispatch* in the Withy Grove deal, and he claimed that his contract entitled him to follow Manchester United to Belgrade to report their European Cup semi-final. Young McGhee wanted to go, but Ledbroke was adamant. It was several hours after the Munich disaster that we learned that he was among those who died, along with seven other journalists and ten of the United party, including seven "Busby Babes".

One of those seriously injured in the crash was *News Chronicle* sports reporter Frank Taylor. After a long and painful recovery, Frank suffered the additional trauma of the abrupt closure of the *News Chronicle* by the Cadbury family. He eventually came to the *Mirror* via the IPC *Sun,* and much later it was Frank who would be at the forefront of the paper's adoption of back page sport, something

the paper's rivals had enjoyed for years, but had been resisted in Holborn Circus.

With the arrival of the 1960s, *Mirror* Sport for the first time enjoyed having a dedicated photographer, at first Charlie Ley and then Monte Fresco. Monte revolutionised sports photography with his keen eye, inventive brain, technical talent and an ability to jolly the office-bound darkroom staff into adding that little extra magic to his prints. Another newcomer to the staff was less well received – at least for his first few weeks on the *Mirror*. Jack Hutchinson was called up to Cudlipp's office one morning to be told he was getting a new member of staff, a 16-year-old with no journalistic experience.

"Who *is* this boy?" asked a miffed Jack – Fleet Street was not considered to be a training ground by those who had served their apprenticeships in the provinces. "Michael Grade," said Cudlipp. "His father is Leslie, his uncle is Lew. Look after him!" The future television magnate was greeted with suspicion. He had never hung around in draughty stadiums on Saturday afternoons, waiting to get a quote from a manager or player – he had a seat in the directors' box at Leyton Orient. On his first day, Michael arrived in style – in a Rolls-Royce! But if he had the ear of Cudlipp, as far as we knew he never once tried to whisper into it. He was young, bright, enthusiastic, unaffected and keen to learn.

Michael Grade's appearance on the sports desk was one of the few instances of senior *Mirror* executives interfering in the department's affairs. Almost all the editors of this period, from Sylvester Bolam to Richard Stott, were content to let *Mirror* Sport look after itself – just as long as the editions were produced on time and the pages did not give rise to writs. Only Mike Christiansen, during his brief editorship, took a serious journalistic interest in what was going on in the world of sport. Otherwise, sport was a paper within the paper, with Jack Hutchinson looking after the administration by day and Don Canadine-Bate supervising the content and design of the pages each night.

Within the "paper inside a paper" was another

Continued on page 70

Truman on the atom bomb had prompted the *Mirror* to ask: WHOSE FINGER DO YOU WANT ON THE TRIGGER WHEN THE WORLD SITUATION IS SO DELICATE? Obviously the paper recognised that the sentence had a resonant ring, for as the election campaign gained speed it published an editorial under the headline WHOSE FINGER? with the comment that "…in spite of our esteem for Mr Churchill we must point out that there are forces at work in the world which he dangerously misunderstands… Mr Churchill

suggested that we need not worry – because only Russia or America was in a position to pull the trigger. But we do worry, precisely because he can make such statements. They make our hair stand on end." This and a succession of further "Whose Finger" features, all of which suggested that Labour would be safer custodians of the atomic bomb option than the Conservatives, angered Churchill and he finally erupted, pulling the legal trigger, when, on polling day, the *Mirror*'s front page featured a Jack Dunkley drawing of a revolver and the

First person   IAN WATSON

autonomous, esoteric section – Racing *Mirror.* "Newsboy", the byline under which Bob Butchers wrote and topped tipster charts for many years, still survives, as does "Bouverie", the byline then disguising the identity of tipster Pat Murphy. Racing editor David Phillips and his staff squeezed into the pages a fund of information about the prospects facing racehorses and Greyhounds, and prepared four-page pullouts for big race days. One famous Grand National tip did not appear in the racing pages but in the "Sportlight" column, written by golf and boxing reporter Ron Wills after the late John Bromley's departure. Wills, to everyone's amazement, advised a flutter in the 1967 Grand National on no-hoper Foinavon. After the field was decimated by falls at the early fences, the Irish horse stayed upright to win at 100-1. At this time, the *Mirror*'s back page was still devoted to news. Sport took over by degrees, first occupying the two columns under the *Daily Mirror* red seal. Don made an inspired choice in choosing Frank Taylor as writer of a column that was to reflect what the average man in the pub was talking about. This was meat and drink to Taylor, although his meat and drink was usually a sandwich and a half of bitter. Thus fortified, he would happily sound off on any topic.

With increasing competition from the Rupert Murdoch *Sun* and with late-night football under floodlights becoming commonplace instead of exceptional, the two columns of sport were soon extended to the whole back page. At last, the *Mirror* was on equal terms with the rest of the Fleet Street popular papers and the circulation continued to rise, helped by British sporting triumphs such as the three gold medals, won by Ken Matthews, Lynn Davies and Ann Packer, at the 1964 Tokyo Olympics, and England's World Cup victory in 1966. Big stories – big sales.

In 1972, Jack Hutchinson took early retirement, and Don Canadine-Bate became sports editor, with me as his deputy. Then in October of the same year, the *Mirror* was deprived of the full-time services of the writer who had outshone all others in Fleet Street for so many years – Peter Wilson. He stoically accepted his doctor's revelation that he had contracted lung cancer, stopping smoking

immediately, and from then on restricted his alcoholic intake to wine. But there was nothing he could do about the English weather. The doctors told him he must live abroad in a fresher, warmer climate and he and his wife, Sally, went off to Majorca, where his life was extended by almost a further ten years.

In those distant pre-television days, Fleet Street's sportswriters were the eyes of their readers: Desmond Hackett on the *Daily Express,* Jim Manning on the *Daily Mail*, Clifford Webb on the *Daily Herald*, the monocled Gerard Walter (later to join *Mirror* Sport) on the *News Chronicle*, Scottie Hall on the *Daily Sketch.* But Wilson in the *Mirror* had the biggest audience of all. Peter Dimmock, BBC-TV's former *Grandstand* presenter turned television executive, once described Peter as "The man who bestrides Fleet Street like a colossus".

In his time, Wilson reported from five continents, touch-typing his copy at ringside, trackside, courtside, snow slope, soccer or rugby press box – never taking his eyes off the action. Some of his datelines were more exotic than others. Once, back in the days when "rude" words were not printed in family newspapers, Wilson – never over-sure of himself – was concerned that one particular dateline should not give offence to readers. Reporting one day from a dreary, drizzling town in Sweden, he sought my approval for his opening sentence under the dateline:

BASTAAD, Wednesday.

"This place," wrote Wilson, "was not idly named..." I reassured him that the readers would be chuckling too much to take umbrage.

It was the readers that Wilson cared about. He had no time for slippery politicians, bumptious sports officials, greedy promoters and dishonesty of any kind in sport. He had plenty of targets to aim at – often on the *Mirror*'s front page. Peter enjoyed a lifetime's front seat at all the major sporting events around the globe. He covered all the summer and winter Olympics, big fights at home and abroad, rugby and soccer's biggest games and, each summer, the Wimbledon fortnight, where he was rewarded with membership of the All-England Club. He also received an OBE for his services to sport.

headlines: "WHOSE FINGER? Today YOUR finger is on the trigger. VOTE FOR THE PARTY YOU CAN REALLY TRUST. The '*Daily Mirror*' believes that party is Labour."

As an example of newspaper political propaganda, the page was a masterpiece that, because of his deserved reputation for such flamboyant presentation, is even today credited as the work of Hugh Cudlipp. But Cudlipp had not yet returned from the relative anonymity of his role at the *Sunday Express* and his only, slender connection with the "Whose Finger" brouhaha was that he happened to be in Lord

Beaverbook's office when Churchill called for advice on whether or not to sue (Beaverbook said yes). The *Mirror*'s campaign was Bart's, a display of journalistic panache that was to be his swansong and a failure at that – the Tories were victorious with 26 more seats than Labour and an overall majority of 17.

Churchill's libel writ raised the possibility of him having to appear in the witness box and be subjected to cross-examination when the *Mirror* went into court to defend its headlines. But the matter was settled after the action was diverted to embrace an earlier story about Churchill's

The great and the greatest: Peter Wilson with Muhammad Ali.

Don Canadine-Bate arranged for Peter to come to London for Wimbledon each year and to be at the ringside for the occasional big fight. Wilson also contributed several sporting series, particularly on boxing, that kept his name in front of the public for almost another decade. Don sat with him in the back of the car that took him to hospital in Majorca when time finally ran out for Peter in October 1981.

When Peter left *Mirror* Sport in 1972, television was vigorously challenging the old order. No longer did readers have to rely on the ability of newspaper writers to capture the scene – they could watch it happening in their living rooms. It was time to switch to a different tack. Deputy editor Geoff Pinnington walked into Don's office one morning and told him, "Start spending." "When do I stop?" asked the new assistant editor (sport). "When I tell you to," said Pinnington.

Don set about signing sports "names" in the news: stars such as George Best (for £100 per column), new Manchester United manager Frank O'Farrell, extrovert soccer star Malcolm MacDonald, Champion National Hunt jockey Jonjo O'Neill, rugby's Bill Beaumont, cricket legend Ian Botham and many more.

In the 80s, after more than 30 years of being responsible for producing the *Mirror*'s sports pages, Don and I were joined by night desk executive and keen sports fan Ted Graham, switched to sport to bring in fresh ideas. And then came Maxwell. "Mad Max", who regarded himself as a sporting guru, demanded excessive space for Oxford United – which he happened to own – and anything else that took his personal, momentary fancy. The new publisher might have understood printing, but he knew nothing of newspaper deadlines and urgency. Foreign trips had to be approved by him personally and on one occasion he refused to let me send football writer Harry Miller to a European match in Brussels because of the cost, even though it would have been cheaper than going from London to Manchester. Then, through Harry Harris, who had joined the football staff from the *Daily Mail* and appeared to have his ear, Maxwell launched a savage front-page attack on then England manager Bobby Robson.

With a large staff clear-out threatened, anyone aged over 55 knew their days were numbered. Don was called to Maxwell's office to discuss his impending departure and the end of a sporting chapter in the *Mirror* story. "You know, Don," boomed Maxwell, "I can't find one person in the whole of this office who has a bad word to say about you." For once, Maxwell wasn't lying.

assertion, at a private dinner party in Paris, that, under certain circumstances, a preventative war against Russia might be necessary. The *Mirror* had, according to Cecil King, been given the story by the French Foreign Minister on the understanding that the paper would not reveal its source. The *Mirror* paid up: £1,500 plus costs.

Despite his occasional bursts of editorial flair, Bart's powers were waning and his day-to-day control of the papers was further hindered by what had become a serious drink problem. Philip Zec tried without success to persuade the chairman to resign before the election. Soon after Churchill became an elected Prime Minister for the first time, Bart departed for Australia to try to solve a business problem of his own making with the under-performing *Melbourne Argus*, into which he had bought. King, whose grasp of inter-office warfare tactics had been honed by observing Bart, was not about to let such an opportunity pass by ("Cecil set about his task with his usual patience and ruthlessness," Cudlipp was to recall, even though he wasn't there at the time). King later wrote that "towards the end of his

Making the point: the Mirror's "Whose Finger" **campaign reaches its climax in the 1951 election.**

reign I got more involved in our West African papers and Bart's spirit and influence became more and more perceptible in the paper [the *Daily Mirror*]. Eventually his drunkenness reached such proportions that something had to be done."

King approached each member of a board that totalled only seven as Bart undertook the long haul back from Australia. King obtained enough support, including that of disillusioned editor Bolam, to warrant mounting a putsch, but the key to its success would be Philip Zec, the only remaining figure of consequence who needed to be convinced. King called Zec and told him that he and three other directors believed that Bart, now 67 years old, should be unseated. Then, according to King, "early one morning (he was usually incoherent by 9.30am) I told him [Bart] he had lost the confidence of the board and must vacate the chair… He lingered on… weeping maudlin tears into his whisky in the company of the hall porter."

Zec's story, recounted to Labour politician and future minister Richard Crossman, was different. He said that, over lunch, King convinced him that Bart's departure was inevitable and the same afternoon Zec told the

chairman he had no alternative but to leave. Bart broke down in tears and the two men shared a bottle of commiserative whisky. "How could Bolam do this to me?" cried Bart of the editor he created and believed would remain loyal. *World's Press News*, the trade paper of the time, recorded that an official statement recorded Bart's resignation – "accepted with regret" – was motivated by "an earnest desire to promote the advancement of younger men". In reality, Bart bitterly resented having to depart and a lump sum pay-off of £20,000 and £6,000 annual pension organised by Zec did nothing to mollify him.

There was an irony pleasing to many who had fallen foul of him that Bart was put to the sword shortly before Christmas. Francis Williams was later to write that "He was altogether lost without the *Mirror*. And indeed he was its true creator." As is the way with those who succeed great men – no matter how much they may achieve themselves – King was slow to give Bart full credit for turning an ugly duckling of a *Mirror* into a swan. It was not until after he, too, had been ousted that King acknowledged: "It was really the triumvirate of Bartholomew, Nicholson and Cudlipp who created the new *Mirror*, while I supplied the ballast, the sense of direction and continuity that were very necessary."

King had barely settled his large frame behind the desk in the chairman's office before he wrote to Cudlipp: "Let's get together and make a dent in the history of our times." They did too.

Hugh, now 37, returned at the beginning of the new year to relieve Philip Zec of the *Sunday Pictorial* editorship, taking charge at the paper for the third time (Zec, sidelined by Cecil King, was to leave for the *Daily Herald* in 1958 and, as a passionate supporter of the Common Market, later became editor of *New Europe*. Blind during the last three years of his life, he died in London in 1983 at the age of 73). The following year, Cudlipp became editor-in-chief of the *Pic* and the *Mirror,* and King began to consider appointing a new editor of the Sunday title, in order to release Cudlipp for a wider role, and also, at Cudlipp's instigation, for the *Mirror* – Bolam's reward for backing the coup that removed Bart was to be found only in heaven, to which he was to depart shortly after leaving.

One of King's early important decisions was

First person **BERNARD SHRIMSLEY**

Bernard Shrimsley was born in 1931 and educated at Kilburn Grammar School, Northampton. He joined the Press Association as a messenger in 1947 and moved to the Southport Guardian *as a reporter the following year. He joined the* Daily Mirror *in Manchester as a reporter in 1953, moving to the* Sunday Express *in 1958 as news editor, later becoming deputy editor. From 1961 he was again with the* Daily Mirror, *as assistant editor, associate (night) editor and northern editor. He was transferred to London as assistant editor features and was for a short time publicity director before leaving to edit the* Liverpool Daily Post. *He was subsequently deputy editor of* The Sun, *associate editor of the* News of the World *and editor of* The Sun, News of the World *and the* Mail on Sunday.

Call me lucky: Bernard Shrimsley started in the northern newsroom.

'I joined the *Mirror* in 1952 after writing to Kenneth Hord, the news editor. Like me, he had begun as a human carrier pigeon (aka "reporter's telephonist") at the Press Association. Unlike me, he was the son of an editor. And unlike me, he had risen high in the RAF, demobbed as a Wing Commander.

"Tell me all about yourself, chum."

"Well, I joined the PA in 19…"

"Start at the beginning."

"I was educated mostly at Kilburn Gra…"

"I said the beginning."

"I was conceived in Belgium, where my parents were on holiday."

"Whereabouts in Belgium?"

While I talked, Hord was shuffling through my cuttings: "Not as impressive as I had hoped." I translated that as 'thank you and goodbye'.

"What do you expect in the Southport Guardian – Dostoyevsky?"

"Okay, chum. Take a week of your holidays and come and see if you like working with us. We'll pay you 15 guineas. And if we don't suit you, there's no harm done."

I got the job and joined a fine reporting team in the northern newsroom that included Desmond Wilcox, Derek Lambert, Jack Stoneley, William Marshall, Angus Hall, Ian Skidmore and Margaret Clayton. I got a reputation for being a lucky reporter. In a train, I would find myself sitting next to the witness the murder squad was looking for. A fugitive couple would choose my hotel. An alleged singing dog that had stayed dumb for earlier rivals would sing for me. And when I was sent to Dublin to find the tycoon at the centre of a City scandal, a stranger came up to me in a bar.

"You're looking for the Big Fella, right?"

"Right."

"I'll take you to him."

"Thanks. You're on a nice little earner."

"Keep your money. Just make sure it gets a big splash in the *Mirror*. All I want is to double-cross the *Daily Mail*."

Continued on page 74

to take the printing of the northern editions of the company's newspapers back to Manchester, from where, to save money, Rothermere had withdrawn almost 20 years previously. After a complex deal with the Kemsley organisation, printing started at Withy Grove in November 1955 and that same month, after long negotiations, the new chairman bought the *Daily Record* and *Sunday Mail* in Scotland, slightly denting the circulation of *Mirror* and *Pic* but rapidly establishing a thriving business in Glasgow. Later, at the very end of 1958, he

would move into magazines with the acquisition of Amalgamated Press, which became Fleetway, and three years later take over Odhams to establish the biggest publishing house of its kind in the world. The acquisition of West of England Newspapers, soon to be home to the Mirror Group journalists' training scheme, followed in the summer of 1965. King also had the foresight to make an early and highly lucrative investment in Associated Television at a time when newspapers were still suspicious of TV and had yet to harness the medium's content as the boost

First person BERNARD SHRIMSLEY

In 1955, Cecil Harmsworth King did the deal that gave the *Mirror* a Manchester print base so that it could at last compete in the north of England on even terms with the long-established *Express, Mail, News Chronicle* and *Herald*. Kemsley Newspapers would close down its *Daily Dispatch* to free its huge Withy Grove plant for the *Mirror* to rent. A hundred Dispatch journalists were given jobs on the *Mirror's* expanded northern team, which had until then consisted of a news editor and a dozen reporters and photographers. Hugh Cudlipp remarked wryly on the flexibility of journalists: one day producing a Tory broadsheet, the very next day bringing out a Labour tabloid.

Progress in the north was sluggish for five years, until King appointed the ambitious Percy Roberts as northern manager. Roberts introduced me to King over dinner, and within days I was promoted from night editor to northern editor. The appointment was made without Cecil consulting his editorial supremo, a Borgia practice which runs in the Harmsworth dynasty, whose Vere Rothermere twenty years later appointed me editor of *The Mail* on Sunday without consulting editor-in-chief David English.

The northern editorship was my big break. I was 31. I worked like mad, fuelled by the immediate surge of the paper's northern sales, which Roberts put his massive shoulder behind, with circulation managers Jim Wallace and Desmond Bracken and publicity manager Ron Clarke. I was in the office by 9am, before the news editor, and left around 2am when there were no more editions to edit. I slept in the railway station hotel across the road, getting home to Southport only for short weekends.

Night after night, I put out opportunistic district editions to excite local interest: special pullouts for the Isle of Man TT races, Eisteddfod spreads for north Wales, front-page cross-references to flag up local titbits. My biggest stroke of luck was that my arrival in the chair coincided with the Beatles phenomenon taking off. Our souvenir editions were snapped up by local fans and the army of Beatlemaniacs touring the north with John, Paul, George and Ringo. Cudlipp was no fan of the Fab Four and it was heresy to suggest to him that hitting five million was

principally the triumph of the *Mirror's* northern set-up.

When the editorship of the *Sunday Mirror* became vacant, King wanted me but Cudlipp wanted Mike Christiansen. Mike got the job and I got Mike's assistant editor in charge of features, though Cudlipp reduced it in the executive pecking order while I was on the train down to London to take the job. Noel Whitcomb said to me: "Hugh's only happy with people who need his patronage. You don't seem to fear for your mortgage and all that." I said I was a helluva sight more working class than Hugh had ever been. He'd never sat on an outside toilet.

Cudlipp always regarded me as a King's man. Eventually, after declining his offers to go into internal exile as editor of the Glasgow *Daily Record* ("You'll be chairman there within five years"); or to become a director of the magazine division; or to take over from the group publicity director, I jumped at the chance of editing the *Liverpool Daily Post*.

"Can't understand you," said Hugh. "Why leave us for Liverpool?"

"To re-enter journalism," I said.

King was a throwback to a bygone age. Dinner chez Cecil was like taking part in a Galsworthy period piece. Dame Ruth actually took the wives off while the gentlemen smoked a cigar. Later, Cecil actually said: "Shall we join the ladies?"

When I mentioned that I was off to Nigeria, accompanying Cecil King on his annual progress check, Noel Whitcomb recalled his trip there with the chairman, and this exchange on the journey:

"Noel, what are you reading?"

"*Old Goriot,* Mr King."

"In English, I suppose."

"Not at all, sir. I've always thought Balzac ill-served by his translators."

Percy Roberts told me of a bizarre trip with King around the company's Caribbean papers. They had been sweating an hour on the runway in an island-hopping plane. The pilot came on to explain that there was one

to sales it can be today (although TV listings had been introduced into the *Mirror* in 1937).

Even radio had been relatively ignored by the press as a source of news and it was not until the late 1940s, when Bartholomew heard an item on Woman's Hour and rebuked the news desk for not covering it as a news story, that Robert Cannell was appointed the *Mirror's* radio and television correspondent. When, towards the end of 1950, Cannell departed for the *Daily Express*, writer Eric Wainwright replaced him. Canadian Wainwright, who would

become legendary as the *Mirror* features writer who, towards the end of his career, visited the office only to draw advances against his expenses, was unsuited to the role. His forte, as he was to prove, was writing features where he was part of the story – if a *Mirror* journalist was required to jump from an airplane or take the place of a circus lion tamer, they sent for Wainwright. Radio and TV needed someone with a more finely tuned nose for news, so when Wainwright floundered, they sent for Clifford Davis.

Money for nothing: Cecil King towers over George Brown, the industrial advisor who never offered advice.

more passenger aboard than on the manifest. He couldn't get clearance to take off until the check-in clerk had finished his lunch. King mopped his boiling head. "Roberts," he said. "Get off the plane."

King was guest of honour as the Emir of Ilorin laid on a welcome befitting the proprietor of Nigeria's most influential daily. We were given yellow, claret and black tribal robes to wear over our European suits. Aladdin lamps lighted the town square in front of the Emir's palace as his troupe of sword dancers did its perilous stuff. The leader performed a series of fantastic leaps, flips, and forward and backward somersaults and came to rest on his knees before us, eyes popping, sweat running down his face to glisten on the blade between his teeth.

Magical... until Cecil turned to me and said: "Give him a quid."

We sometimes stayed at Government rest houses. As we signed a register, I said to King, "Pity you didn't take a peerage."

"Why is it a pity?"

"You could have signed yourself King – and not even the Queen can do that."

He was supposed to laugh, but he just shook his head at my peasant ignorance. "There is a Lord King."

Cecil had arranged for Labour's unseated deputy leader, George Brown, to join the *Mirror* payroll as an "industrial adviser." The *Mirror*, like all Fleet Street groups, was in constant battle with the print unions. I wondered out loud how much help Brown had been to the *Mirror*. Cecil sighed: "During the period Mr Brown was industrial adviser to the *Daily Mirror,* he neither gave any industrial advice nor was any sought."

When Beaverbrook's death was announced, King rubbed his hands as he walked the length of the newsroom: "It's not every day Lord Beaverbrook dies," he said.

Back from a stint in the Paris office, Davis let it be known that he had worked with Army Broadcasting during the war, an experience that news editor Ken Hord and editor Bolam saw as an obvious qualification for the job. Davis was also a part-time magician and harboured a yearning to be a television performer, an ambition realised years later when he became the prototype "Mr Nasty" panel member on the search-for-talent show *New Faces*. In tandem with writing about television and building up a department that grew to house half-a-dozen

journalists – and along the way coining the phrase "chat show" for television multi-guest interview programmes – Davis performed as a magician on cruise liners and in cabaret. His was a full and eclectic career that was watched with amused indifference by Eric Wainwright from the Italian waiters' Soho drinking club to which, for many years, he repaired most afternoons.

The renewed partnership of King and Cudlipp may not have been a marriage made in heaven, but it appeared to be one made especially for

Fleet Street. Charles Wintour, himself a distinguished editor of the *Evening Standard*, was to write: "King gave Cudlipp every encouragement... He now delegated to him, subject only to King's litmus test of *Mirror* journalism – whether or not a story was intelligible to a bus driver's wife in Sheffield." That Cecil King could even accurately identify a Sheffield bus, let alone the wife of the driver, is arguable, but he knew that Cudlipp could. Not that the editor-in-chief's role was restricted to the London-based newspapers. King's delegation included sending Cudlipp and his wife, Eileen, to Australia for several months with the brief to solve the ongoing problem of the loss-making *Melbourne Argus* – the paper ultimately went to the wall – and involve himself with a chain of radio stations that Bartholomew had also speculatively acquired.

It was while Cudlipp was away in Australia, and while negotiations to buy the Kemsley Scottish titles proceeded, that a flurry of cables between the two men resulted in King restructuring his editorial hierarchy. "As I see it your role must be to give the papers direction and drive without becoming encumbered with day-to-day routine," he told Cudlipp, who replied with the recommendation that Jimmy Eilbeck, a precocious but particularly undisciplined talent, should be appointed to run the paper's features – "Too immature for *Pictorial* editorship" was the view from Melbourne – while Colin Valdar, a former *Pic* man who had moved to the *Daily Express*, should be brought back to edit his old paper. Cudlipp also advocated that Bolam should be replaced as editor by his deputy, Jack Nener, and that either Bolam or Roy Suffern should be put in charge in Glasgow when the deal was done. As it was, the company severed its connection with Bolam, Suffern went to Scotland, where eventually he became

chairman, and the verbally volcanic Nener became Cudlipp's conduit to what he loved most – the *Daily Mirror* editorial floor.

Of all *Mirror* editors, Nener is probably the one who came closest to matching the tabloid stereotype of the demanding, unsophisticated, hard-bitten, foul-mouthed tyrant with a heart of gold, probably because he was all these things other, Audrey Whiting, the *Mirror* reporter who married him, would argue, than unsophisticated. But even she acknowledges that he was "an absolutely awful man to work for" and others who spent time around him would claim that any sophistication in Nener's character was buried so deep it would have taken dynamite to uncover it.

The story that best epitomises the bow-tied terror of Geraldine House has been recounted many times in books and bar-rooms but demands retelling here. Gathered with senior members of his staff sitting and drinking around a table in an elegant lounge, Nener's language became so colourful that a respectable fellow customer sitting quietly with his wife was moved to approach the newspapermen and complain: "Excuse me, sir, would you please curb your language – there are ladies present?" Nener, momentarily unaware that the world was occupied by any species other than journalists, stared with contempt at the upstart and bellowed: "Do you know who I am? I'm the fucking editor of the fucking *Daily Mirror*." "Yes," said the man quietly, "I rather thought you might be."

Similar anecdotes about Nener, a rough diamond but more rough than diamond, abounded at the *Mirror* until long after the editor's departure. Crashing through the doors on to the editorial floor at Geraldine House one day, he spied sub-editor George Laing wearing a neckerchief rather than a tie. "Who's the fuckin' Tarzan?" he bellowed, and Laing was sent home

First person AUDREY WHITING

Audrey Whiting was born in 1927 in Hull, Yorkshire, and educated at local schools before joining the Hull Daily Mail *and then the* Yorkshire Evening Post. *She arrived at the* Daily Mirror *as a junior reporter in 1948, was appointed Paris correspondent in 1950, New York correspondent in 1952 and chief European correspondent, based in Paris, in 1953. She subsequently married* Mirror *editor Jack Nener and transferred to the* Sunday Pictorial, *as, at that time, husbands and wives were not encouraged to work on the same title. She rejoined the staff of the daily paper in 1970, eventually leaving in 1985. She now lives in retirement in London.*

'When the news editor, Ken Hord, and managing editor, Cyril Morton, wanted me to go to Paris for the paper, they asked what my French was like. I said, "Not bad", but they sent me to language school for a week, and when I was tested there, I realised I couldn't really speak French at all.

Then, in 1952, Cecil King sent me to the United States to "educate yourself", but the trip was cut short when I was made New York correspondent. I was back in Paris in 1953 when I was told that the new editor was coming on a European trip; I was to collect him from the airport and arrange whatever meetings he wanted. Jack Nener had been in Paris only a short while when I received a tip-off that there was to be a strike that would paralyse the city. I said he had better go back, but he refused – he wanted to see some of France.

When eventually he decided to return to London, I took him to the airport. You could get right alongside the planes in those days, and as he went up the steps, he turned round and said: "Will you marry me?" He had been divorced from his first wife for seven years by then. I said no, and after three months of pressure from London, I still said no. But in the December, I was in London and he took me to a drinks party at the Cudlipps'. When I went into this room, full of VIPs, Hugh said: "Congratulations!" Jack had told him we were going to marry. I didn't know what to do, but then I decided that I quite liked him really. Sure, he effed and blinded a lot in the office, but he was a highly intelligent and serious man. He could tear the arse off you, he could make you feel an inch high, but he also had that old journalistic ability to get on with anybody. We married in February 1954.

He was also intensely loyal. He had been with Cecil King on a trip around America, and Cecil asked him if he would become editor. Jack said no, because he felt a loyalty to Sylvester Bolam, who had been in jail following the Haigh murders story. He did become editor when Bolam left, not long after Cudlipp returned from his stint at the *Sunday Express*. Jack was very much against the paper's stance over Suez, and he and Hugh had a stand-up row over it. Jack knew it would lose sales. They were two fiery Welshman but a good combination – Jack was the brake that Hugh

On form: Audrey and Jack enjoy a day at the races.

needed put on his enthusiasms every now and again.

By 1961, Jack had developed corns on his feet and walked rather badly. King said he didn't look well and they retired him on the grounds of ill health. He went without a fight and with a terrible pension. He was a man with no sense whatsoever of money – he never saved a penny. When he left, I did his final expenses – for about £80 – and he tore them up.

We went to live in Cannes, from where I wrote features and series for the *Sunday Mirror*, until 1970, when he did become ill and we had to return to England. The paper didn't have a proper royal correspondent then, but I had been writing royal stories for both the *Sunday* and *Daily Mirror* during the 1960s and had a lot of royal connections. It was very different then – the stories you sat on were more memorable than those that were published. I covered the royals for quite a long period, but I never did a royal tour because I didn't want to leave Jack at home alone. He died in 1982.

In 1985, not long after Maxwell had taken over the company, I met him in the lift. He said to me: "You'd better watch it or you'll be out on your neck!" So I walked out after almost 40 years with Mirror Group.

When the *Mirror* moved from Geraldine House to Holborn in 1961, Jack and I heard that the editor's desk was to be thrown into the junkyard. It had been the editor's desk for years and Jack was horrified. So, after a lot of negotiation, we bought it – and I still have it here at my home.'

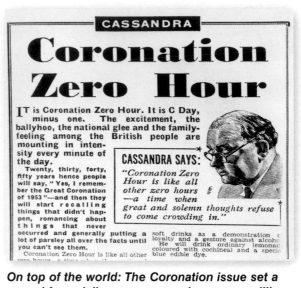

On top of the world: The Coronation issue set a record for a daily newspaper sale – seven million copies.

to fetch the required neckwear. Nener, a divorcee, was tamed slightly, but only slightly, when he married Audrey Whiting, an extremely tall *Mirror* writer – "The night of the long wives," Cudlipp is supposed to have wryly observed of the nuptial evening and a competition among executives to come up with a phrase to describe the liaison was won by "Jack and the beanstalk".

As the 1950s had begun to gather momentum, the Festival of Britain came and went, the Conservative Government increased the meat ration to 1s 7d (about 7p) a week, and the King – the real one – died. Cudlipp was back in Britain in January 1953, in good time to prepare the papers for Queen Elizabeth II's historic 2 June appointment at Westminster Abbey. It was a day of rejoicing that delighted the nation and, especially, the *Mirror*, whose Coronation issue set a world record for a daily newspaper when it sold more than seven million copies ("Twenty, thirty, forty, fifty years hence people will say, 'Yes, I remember the Great Coronation of 1953' – and then they will start recalling things that didn't happen, romancing about things that never occurred and generally putting a lot of parsley all over the facts until you can't see them," wrote Cassandra).

Also in 1953, the Prime Minister's doctors ordered him, at the age of 78, to rest. It is unlikely that a primary cause of Churchill's

health problems was his continuing irritability with the *Daily Mirror*, but: "The *Mirror* is suggesting I am past it and that I ought to resign," he told his doctor, Charles Moran. "…Why do I waste my time over this rag?" The "rag" was in fact riding high and on 2 November, 50 years to the day since it had tottered into public view, a grand jubilee ball was held at the Grosvenor House Hotel in London. As 500 guests ate filet de sole bonne femme and suprême de volaille Maryland, they listened to speeches constructed as if Dickens' *A Christmas Carol* had been used as a guide: Hannen Swaffer spoke about *Mirror* past, Cecil King about *Mirror* present and Hugh Cudlipp gave his vision of *Mirror* yet to come. Then there was cabaret featuring a "ballet" from the Folies Bergere, "forces sweetheart" Vera Lynn and gap-toothed comic Terry-Thomas. The orchestras of Geraldo and Edmundo Ros provided music for dancing, and television personality McDonald Hobley compered. In terms of lavishness, the evening set the standard for *Mirror* events that would be maintained for decades.

In 1976, Cudlipp wrote that the greatest decade in the history of the paper could accurately be charted: beginning in 1954, it was a period when the paper "enjoyed the maximum of approbation and obloquy, a healthy state of affairs… and a sale of five million copies a day

The Jubilee Ball

Showstopper: The boat was pushed out so far to celebrate the Daily Mirror's 50th birthday that it's surprising it ever got back to shore.
Top row: Donald Zec and his wife, Frances; Ken Hord; Cecil King and his wife cut the extraordinary Festival-of-Britain inspired birthday cake.
Middle row: Mr & Mrs John Monk; the stylish menu.
Bottom row: Michael King; Ailsa Garland.

Donald Zec was born in 1919 in London and was educated at Upton House School in north-east London. He says he forsook higher education in the hope of becoming a concert violinist, but turned to journalism, and, in 1938, followed his elder brother, the cartoonist and editor Philip, to the Daily Mirror. *He returned to reporting with the paper after war service, then became a feature and entertainment writer, specialising in interviewing major stars around the world but especially in Hollywood. He won a British Press Award and was awarded the OBE for his services to journalism. He has written ten books since leaving the* Mirror *in 1972.*

'I joined the paper on a three-day try-out in 1938. It was close to a disaster, actually, but quite funny. I had been introduced to the paper by Bill Connor – my brother knew Bill. Up till then I had been selling space in a magazine called *Floor Covering Review* and before then I had worked at the *Evening Standard* as a clerk. Then I walked into Geraldine House on this trial, and, after three days, I knew I had been so embarrassingly bad that I wasn't sure whether to come in again or not – and I think they were too embarrassed to tell me not to!

I had to go and report on a fire in Soho. It's a fair indication of the way the *Mirror* operated then. The news editor was a Scottish-Canadian named Douglas Mackenzie, who was straight out of Hecht and Macarthur's *The Front Page*. A wonderful character. I was sent out on this fire and actually came back and wrote, to my shame, something like: "Firemen were called to a blaze…" Mackenzie started reading it and said, "This is shit. Have a word with Dudley Hawkins." Hawkins was a reporter and I showed it to him. When the story appeared, it read something like: "So-and-so, an 18-year-old hostess, climbed along a 30ft parapet in her scanties to rescue her pet cat in a fire at a Soho nightclub last night." In that short introduction you had drama, sex, courage – and pets. The whole caboodle.

Anyway, I did come in after my trial and I stayed 35 years. I was sent up to Manchester until 1939. I went with a Scots reporter named Ian Fyfe, who became a war correspondent and went over with the gliders on D-Day and was killed. The editor in the north was a man named Chapman. Manchester was something like the *Daily Mirror's* Siberia then – if you were on probation, or if you got drunk or transgressed in some other way, you would be banished to the north for a few months.

Ian Fyfe and I were given £25 advance expenses and sent to Manchester to make names for ourselves. The night we arrived we both spent our entire £25 in a place called the Carlton Bar, opposite the Post Office. There was a small orchestra playing and as I used to play the fiddle, I went up – I was mildly drunk – and said I would like to play. The leader was moonlighting from the Halle Orchestra and he wasn't too sure, but people in the bar were shouting out, "Let the fooker have it", meaning the fiddle, so he did. Then Fyfe dragged me off to a telephone booth in the bar and got through to Chapman at the office. Fyfe said, "You've got to hear this fucking music – it's fucking brilliant." And I started to play *Vienna City of My Dreams* to the northern editor of the *Daily Mirror* over the telephone. The following morning, Chapman called us in and he said to me: "If your ambitions lie in music, I suggest you try for an audition with the Halle. On the other hand, I think you were sent up here to raise the circulation of the *Daily Mirror* and judging by your performance on the fiddle last night…"

I joined the Territorial Army in 1939, as did a lot of journalists, and when I went into F Company of the London Irish Rifles there was Mackenzie Porter, a tall, thin, red-haired journalist of enormous talent who was by then news editor of the *Mirror*, a Welsh reporter named Cyril Jones and an Irish reporter named Brian Murtough.

The editor before the war was C.E. Thomas, a very cultivated, quiet Welshman, and the leader writer was Richard Jennings, one of the real driving forces behind the paper. Soon after I came out of the Army, I worked as a reporter and sometimes royal reporter. Sylvester Bolam was editor. I had a phone call one day from a man who gave me his name and started to talk about Buckingham Palace. I asked how he knew anything about the Palace and he said, "I'm a boilerman there." He gave me two major scoops during his not unlucrative reign as my informant at the Palace: one on the Queen's Coronation, when he told me he had had to put 12 hot-water bottles in

at the end of it, a suitable reward. Tabloid journalism stretched its wings and they were not singed." Later, he observed that: "During its vintage decades the *Daily Mirror* was a campaigning newspaper with a social conscience, but the causes of its phenomenal success at that time… were its ebullience, its insolence, its irreverence, in brief, its sense of contemporaneous humour. It was the jester at Court, the mocking clown at the tail end of the Emperor's procession."

All true, but he neglected to point out that the *Mirror* also began on occasion to stray towards the respectable and earned plaudits from those very members of the establishment who criticised much of the populist menu the paper supplied to supplement its readers' daily bread. A series of learned pamphlets entitled "Spotlight", dealing with such subjects as The Common Market, Defence, Education and Britain's Voice Abroad, were especially well received. Even Lord Goddard, the Lord Chief Justice who only five years before had sent the editor to the slammer, was impressed enough to write with his mainly favourable views on this *Mirror* initiative.

Glam rock: Donald Zec in 1957, admiring the ring given to Liz Taylor by husband Mike Todd.

the Queen's coach, and then on the morning Prince Charles was born, when we got details of the birth, including the weight of the baby, 25 minutes before PA. I remember he said, "The waters burst at ten past seven." I thought the boiler had gone up!

Eventually the Palace launched an investigation. They wanted to know how, on his salary of four pounds nine shillings and threepence a week, or whatever, the boilerman could call for taxis outside the side entrance of Buckingham Palace. That's how it ended.

Howard Johnson was there, a very good journalist who became chief reporter. And Jack Greenslade was a top-class reporter and there was a man called Whittall, who was the crime man and really highly respected. They were very hard-working men in those days.

After I did the royal thing, I was a crime reporter for a very short period when I became involved in the John George Haigh – the so-called acid bath murderer – case, which sent Sylvester Bolam to jail. I was the last person from the *Mirror* to interview Haigh and the picture that appeared at the time was one he gave me the night he was arrested. That night I had gone to the Onslow Court Hotel, where Haigh lived. The whole of Onslow Square was crowded with police cars. I was in his hotel room and he was still, as he had all the time, protesting his innocence. I walked him over to the window, pointed to the cars and said, "Look, you've convinced me, but your problem is convincing all these police." He didn't say anything but went to a drawer and opened it very slowly – I knew at this time that he not only murdered his victims but also drank a glass of their blood as part of the ritual, so I was a bit apprehensive – and took out this picture. He gave it to me and said, "I think this might be very useful to you in the next 24 hours." He pleaded guilty to five murders, I think. He was probably guilty of about nine, but I think he should never have been hanged – he was as mad as they come.

The *Mirror* then published the story that got Bolam sent down for contempt of court. We ran the story about vampire killings and on the same front page something like " John George Haigh was yesterday arrested in connection with…" The juxtaposition of the two stories was sufficient for the Lord Chief Justice, Lord Goddard, to declare it was contempt of court. When Bolam was in Brixton, I seem to remember Bartholomew going with Cudlipp and my brother, Philip, to see him about some company business and saying, "Don't worry, you're going to be the only editor who's ever edited the *Daily Mirror* from prison."

Bolam was a man with an enormous range of interests. The *Mirror* kept an apartment in Clifford's Inn, at the bottom of Fetter Lane, where Bolam had a piano – he played quite well. I used to go down to the apartment occasionally and we would play some Corelli sonatas, with Bish on the piano and me on the fiddle. Whatever people's view of the *Mirror* at that time, it didn't include

Continued on page 82

A key figure in the production of these pamphlets and in the paper's growing political astuteness was Sydney Jacobson, another major figure in the *Mirror* story. Educated at King's College in London, Jacobson had worked on the *Statesman* in India before the war and won the Military Cross during his Army service. He was a special correspondent on *Picture Post* and then edited *Leader* magazine before meeting Cudlipp early in 1952. As soon as he was appointed editorial director, Cudlipp brought Jacobson to the *Mirror* as its political editor and began a journalistic association that was to last

more than 20 years – "We called it the collaboration of the minorities, the Welsh and the Jews," Hugh was to write. Jacobson was the motivator of many of the paper's campaigns and it was his and Bill Connor's conviction that determined the *Mirror*'s strong anti-capital punishment line – Cassandra's front-page condemnation of the hanging of Ruth Ellis in July 1955 remains a tour de force of emotive rhetoric – and swung public opinion enough for hanging to be suspended in Britain in November 1965. Sydney, the urbane antidote to Cudlipp's abrasiveness, would go on to edit the *Daily* the editor playing Corelli in Clifford's Inn with the paper's crime reporter. It really made me sad when he went to jail – he was a sensitive character.

Back then the paper had a film critic named Reg Whitley, but his sole interest was reviewing films and we were missing a great many stories about films and film stars. I was asked if I would do something about that, so I did. As a musician and coming from an artistic family, I'd always liked entertainment, so I just did it. It was a hugely untapped source of material for the *Mirror*, because at that point the stuff appearing in the paper was very bland, almost like publicity handouts. The *Mirror* was becoming a paper of some importance. It was becoming more realistic and less escapist, and it was essential that that should be reflected in our attitude to showbusiness.

So I took a fairly sardonic view without being malicious and it seemed to strike a chord. And it fitted with Cudlipp's attitude to showbusiness, which was that if people had great talent, let's say so, but those who didn't, let's not be taken in by them. We'd make the distinction between the real McCoy and the phoney-baloney. It was a wonderful time – I used to fly to New York and back just to review films, so that our reviews appeared before anybody else's. And you could say whatever you wanted to say without being afraid, unlike some other papers where if a famous entertainer was offended he or she would phone the proprietor and complain. If that happened on the *Mirror*, they got short shrift. I wrote a review of Carl Foreman's *The Victors,* which I disliked and also wrote the headline, All Trite on the Western Front. Foreman complained to Cudlipp and Hugh said, "I know – I'm having such trouble with my writers!" Everybody on the paper felt with Cudlipp that they could flex their muscles. There were just two provisos: it had to be written in an entertaining style and it had to be right, it had to be accurate. Then Cudlipp would back you all the way, right or wrong.

I don't think Piers Morgan should try to recreate the old *Daily Mirror*, but where I think he is right is in trying to recreate the ethos of the paper then – to coin a phrase, without fear or favour. As someone whose entire

professional life was spent on the paper, I believe that ethos is an infinite thing and must remain. We used to pay our own way everywhere, too. If the story was worth publishing, we'd fund it ourselves – money was no object if the project was worthwhile. The company was awash with money then.

A great example of Cudlipp's creative impertinence, where he would take one bizarre comment and turn it into page one and a spread in the paper, was when, in 1955, R.A. Butler, then Chancellor of the Exchequer, was trying to tell the British people that they could no longer live the extravagant existence they'd become accustomed to. And he actually said, "We must not drop back to easy evenings of port wine and over-ripe pheasant." The notion was too much for Hugh, who called me and told me to take out a dozen people and give them a meal of over-ripe pheasant and vintage port. One would have thought it would be reasonably simple to find twelve people and take them to the Savoy Hotel, where I had booked a private room. In fact, I had great difficulty. I remember ending up in the Finchley Road in the pissing rain, leaning over a parapet where four navvies were digging a gas or water main. They were shovelling all this shit over my shoes and I heard myself say, "I wonder if you would all care to come and have dinner with me at the Savoy Hotel tonight?" Cudlipp absolutely fell about when he heard about it. But this was the sort of nonsense that made the paper absolutely unique.

I went a lot to Hollywood. When I arrived at the Beverly Hills Hotel on my first visit, the paper was the largest selling daily paper in the world and the Americans always respected numbers. Within 20 minutes of my arriving, Humphrey Bogart, with whom I'd had lunch in London, came on the phone and said, "I thought I told you to call me when you got here." I said, "I've only been here 15 minutes." He said, "Twenty minutes by my count." I was in this room with stacks of liquor, sent with welcome messages by just about every press agent in Hollywood. Bogart came over and looked at all this and said: "I see those assholes have got to you already!" He invited me on to his boat, the Santana, so I asked if there was anything I could bring. He looked at the liquor and said,

Herald and its successor, the IPC *Sun*, and fill senior directorial roles at Mirror Group before being ennobled as Lord Jacobson of St. Albans in 1975 after his retirement.

In 1954, Cudlipp switched Labour politician and intellectual Richard Crossman, who had been writing a column for the *Pictorial*, to the daily paper and there were other recruits to the ranks of the *Mirror*'s political team. Soon to become the third journalist member of the paper's policy think tanks – editor Nener was seldom involved in heavyweight discussion –

was Alan Fairclough, a brilliant scholar and the man who was to pick up and run with the leader-writing baton passed on by Jennings and Buckham. And the genial Michael King, son of the chairman – but "His character is his own," wrote Cudlipp – was appointed foreign editor, a role he filled conscientiously even though his wife's family recoiled at the thought of him working for what they saw as a scandal sheet (Malcolm Muggeridge, then editor of *Punch*, recorded in his diary that, in January 1954, he visited "Conradine Hobhouse, and her daughter

"Let's bring all this."

We were halfway down the freeway to Catalina when he suddenly said, "We've forgotten the liquor" and did a u-turn, almost, and went back. As we were coming back out of the Beverly Hills Hotel, our arms full of all this liquor, the doorman looked at us and said: "Have a nice weekend, Mr Bogart." He was great fun and a wonderful host. When we came back, not having shaved for two days and pretty hungover, we went to his house on Mapleton Drive where his wife, Betty [Lauren] Bacall, was having a meeting with some very upper class, WASP-type charity committee. So we crawled in on our hands and knees so as not to disturb them. Betty saw us and said, "Hi Bogey – had a nice weekend?" "Yes, darling," he said as we crawled to go upstairs and shave.

The power of the paper – rather than my personality – was such that I had John Wayne come and pick me up and take me to some ranch he had, and met Clark Gable, Cary Grant, Spencer Tracy, Marilyn Monroe, Greer Garson, Alfred Hitchcock... I went to America almost every year, for at least six weeks each time. Those were the great days of Hollywood and of the *Mirror*, I think. The paper's success when I was there, and especially when it was selling five-and-a-quarter million copies a day, was partly because celebrities were actually impressed by the paper's own celebrity.

I decided to leave when I began to find it physically hard travelling to and from Hollywood, and the people I had written about were beginning to die off. The strain of writing under pressure got to me after a while and I suffered some heart trouble. Also, I was beginning to run out of people to interview and I was recycling. If I saw Cary Grant coming towards me, I'd disappear down a manhole because I didn't know what to say to him any more. So I decided it was time to call it a day.

Star gazer: Zec shares a joke with Marilyn Monroe in 1960.

Libby and son-in-law Michael King. Speaking of Michael being on the *Daily Mirror*, which his father Cecil controls, Conradine said she wouldn't allow it in the house, but had felt bound to get it for the servants, though, she added, she feared it was read above, before going below, stairs.)"

Despite its burgeoning sense of responsibility, the *Mirror* and controversy still walked hand-in-hand. In 1955, with the Queen's younger sister faced with the dichotomy of whether to marry the divorced Group Captain Peter Townsend or follow the Church's urging and put duty before love, Cudlipp produced a striking and sensational front page. COME ON MARGARET! Please make up your mind! the *Mirror* audaciously demanded. He had, Cudlipp admitted to television interviewer Desmond Wilcox years later, gone too far: "It was really meant to be a friendly shout from the crowd, but I was torn to shreds. On the whole, and on second thoughts, that was justified. It was a mistake."

The paper's stance over the Suez crisis the

Cheek: The "make up your mind" front page was supposed to sound friendly, not hectoring.

Chilling: A stark and simple layout framed Cassandra's view on the death penalty.

following year was considered by many to be even more notorious and cost the paper 70,000 copies in (temporarily) lost circulation. But retrospectively it was politically and morally sound. When, on 26 July 1956, President Nasser of Egypt nationalised the Suez Canal and collusion between the British and French made armed retaliation likely, Cudlipp and Jacobson together visited Paris to meet with senior French journalists and politicians. Back in London, there followed a *Mirror* "policy conference", which, according to Cudlipp, was minuted by Jacobson "for the archives". King believed Nasser was a threat to world peace and that the paper should support Prime Minister Anthony Eden (Churchill's departure from office in April 1955 was during a 25-day union stoppage in Fleet Street and therefore went unrecorded in the press) if he decided that force was the only option. Cudlipp and Jacobson argued that the *Mirror* should condone the use of force only if it was sanctioned by the United Nations and supported by the Commonwealth and the United States. They pointed out that "the *Mirror* had for many years spoken out against gunboat diplomacy," Jacobson recorded. "…We have

spoken out against colonial wars and in support of independence movements in Asia and Africa. Were we now to crash into reverse?" And Jacobson reminded those present that "the *Mirror* was a Left-wing paper," and "the whole of the Left in Britain – Labour, Liberal, progressive Toryism – would be against force."

King agreed that the paper should back international action to keep the Canal open to shipping, but not support aggression by Britain (editor Nener warned Cudlipp that an anti-retaliation line might harm circulation, but was ignored). On 10 August, the paper's editorial advised: "If Nasser blocks the Suez Canal or endangers British lives in Egypt, then Britain must use force against him. Short of such an emergency, it is folly for Britain to think of 'going it alone' in the face of world opinion." The unrelenting determination with which the *Mirror* criticised Eden's policy during the crisis was to be repeated almost half-a-century later when the paper refused to support the American and British invasion of Iraq. The results of both *Mirror* campaigns were the same: a significant number of readers deserted the paper because they disagreed with its stance. Journalistically, the Suez anti-war crusade delivered a front page that even the paper's strenuous denial of the need for the 2003 Iraq conflict could not match. It proclaimed: "SI SIT PRUDENTIA. This is the first headline ever to appear in the *Mirror* in LATIN (and we hope the last!). What do these three Latin words mean? We'll tell you. They mean: 'If there be but prudence'." (the phrase was the motto on Eden's family crest).

By early November, the British, French and Israelis had invaded Egypt. In the House of Commons, an increasingly exhausted Eden was being battered by the Labour opposition, with leader Hugh Gaitskell condemning "Eden's war" as an act of "suicidal folly, whose consequences we shall regret for years" (when King wrote to congratulate him, Gaitskell replied with praise for the "wonderful job the *Daily Mirror* has done in rousing public opinion on this issue"). Among the British press, *The Times*, the *Daily Mail* and the *Daily Express* backed the Prime Minister. The *Mirror*, *The Guardian*, the *News Chronicle* and, with as much conviction as that mustered by the *Mirror*, *The Observer* did not and, later, Harry Evans, then editor of *The Sunday Times*, was to remark: "The *Mirror* was as brave as *The Observer*, as right as *The Observer* and, I think, somewhat more readable than *The Observer*. It was Cudlipp at his best."

International pressure brought about a ceasefire and Britain withdrew with a bloody nose. Anthony Eden, his health failing, resigned in January 1957, and, the following April, the Suez Canal was reopened to shipping. It had been an inglorious episode in the nation's history, but not in that of the *Mirror*'s.

Notoriety continued to stalk the paper, although its next costly visit was occasioned when Cassandra opened the door and gestured for it to enter. The American entertainer Liberace incurred the columnist's wrath in 1956 simply for being what he was – "a deadly, winking, sniggering, chromium-plated, scent-impregnated, luminous, quivering, giggling, fruit-flavoured, mincing, ice-covered, heap of mother love", although there were those, Liberace included, who would challenge "deadly" and wonder exactly what "ice-covered" was meant to imply. It was, however, another Cassandra sentence that drove Liberace to seek redress in court: "He is the summit of sex – the pinnacle of masculine, feminine, and

neuter. Everything that he, she and it can ever want." Twenty-two words, as Cudlipp was to point out, "that proved to be the most expensive William Connor ever penned".

Three years after the offending column appeared, the libel case was heard at the Royal Courts of Justice in The Strand before Mr Justice Salmon, with Gerald Gardiner QC, a future Lord Chancellor, appearing for the *Mirror* and Gilbert Beyfus QC for Liberace. The star, shorn of glamour and glitz for his day in court, lied under oath in protesting his heterosexuality "on my word of God, on my mother's health". Connor, his confidence rattled, was an unconvincing witness – "Cassandra did not have the voice for public appearances, in court or on TV," reflected Cudlipp. And despite the occasional bon mot, Cudlipp – volunteering to represent the editor during Nener's absence abroad – was thoroughly drubbed by the wily Beyfus, who used selective extracts from *Publish and Be Damned!*, the book the editorial director had written to celebrate the *Mirror*'s half-century, to paint the *Mirror*, in the Cassandra-speak Beyfus used in his closing remarks, as "vicious and violent, venomous and vindictive, salacious and sensational and ruthless and remorseless." Cassandra could probably have written the speech with more flair, but didn't have the opportunity. The case cost the paper £8,000 in damages, plus £27,000 in legal costs. Liberace, honour satisfied and sense of humour intact – "I just love the *Mirror*," he told this author some 20 years later – quivered and minced his way back to the United States, where he was to die of Aids in 1987.

If the *Mirror* was bruised by the Liberace experience, it didn't show. As the Faltering Fifties turned into the Swinging Sixties, the passing carnival of society, from rock and roll to international affairs, was recorded with the blackest of headlines, short and sometimes shocking sentences and pictures with juggernaut impact. Stunts organised with aplomb and extravagance by Tommy Atkins – a Charladies' Ball at the Savoy, two *Mirror*-sponsored National Pets' Club lunches, at one of which Cudlipp made a speech with a parrot perched on his head – tickled the public's fancy. (The Pets' Club, for years run by chain-smoking former reporter Betty Tay, was to scamper on until 1981.) Writers such as chatty columnist

Facing the music: Bill Connor and his wife attend the Liberace trial at the High Court.

Noel Whitcomb and Marjorie Proops – lured back from the *Daily Herald* in 1954 to the paper on which she had started out as a fashion artist – had become household names.

So had Peter Wilson, often cutting a dash with his silver-topped swordstick. Donald Zec recalls: "I was in Rome when Randolph Turpin was boxing there and I met Peter Wilson outside the Excelsior Hotel and he asked if I would like to go to the fight. I went to the arena and the boxers had just entered the ring and I was looking down to see where Peter Wilson was and I couldn't see him. As they came out of their corners I saw that famous camel-haired coat and homburg hat settling at ringside. I saw the homburg hat come off, I saw a telephone lifted up and put to one ear, I saw his left finger going into the other ear – and then the fight was over. I then watched Peter Wilson talking into the phone for the next ten or 15 minutes. It was the lead on page one, going over to the back page. He had managed somehow to take it all in on his way to the ringside, managed somehow to get through to London and managed somehow to dictate what must have been 1,500 words, a totally off-the-cuff account of a sensational fight that had lasted one minute and 57 seconds. It was one of the greatest examples

of newspaper journalism I ever saw."

Zec's own showbusiness interviews, acerbic and often gloriously funny, had made his another famous *Mirror* by-line; Keith Waterhouse was writing features from 1949, and Donald Wise came from the *Daily Express* to develop into a great foreign correspondent.

Berlin-born Victor Weisz, who, as Vicky, was the greatest political cartoonist of his generation, began a four-and-a-half-year residency at the *Mirror* early in 1954 (the man his friend Michael Foot described as "a Twentieth Century Don Quixote", and who left the *Mirror* for the *Evening Standard*, died tragically by his own hand in 1966). Responding to a demand from Cudlipp for a new cartoon character that would appeal to northern readers, Reg Smythe's Andy Capp made his debut in the north in August 1957, being promoted to all editions 18 months later. But Andy's flat cap and four-ale bar culture wasn't indicative of the direction the paper was taking. Proudly producing its first 32-page issue since the war in September 1959, the *Mirror* kept ahead of the field with the introduction of new features that reflected the changing tastes and requirements of its readership. On 8 March 1960, Derek Dale introduced a new column devoted to "the world of money". Dale's most un-*Mirror*-title: City Editor.

Even the news' subs table of the late 50s and early 60s became legendary to succeeding generations: when others talked about a sub trying to finish his book, ran the fable, it more often than not meant he was writing rather than reading one. Certainly the likes of the veteran Bill Leonard and young pretenders Larry Lamb, Bob Coole, Ken Eastaugh and Harry Weisbloom were superior members of a branch of the trade that backbench executives Dick Dinsdale, Bryan Parker and Joe Grizzard were used to bawling out for the slightest misdemeanour. "What cunt subbed this?" Dinsdale yelled towards this elite crew one busy evening. "What cunt wants to know?" answered Coole.

Having a trial on the 50s subs' desk was the most terrifying experience, remembers Ken Smiley, whose career on the *Mirror* took him from subbing to the New York bureau and then on to West Africa as Cecil King expanded his empire there. Nobody spoke much around the table. Smiley sat next to a sub who never spoke

First person JOHN SMITH

Fairytale of New York: John Smith, the reporter who started out as a music-hall stand-up comedian.

John Smith was born in 1936 in London and educated at Stationers' Company's School, a grammar, in Hornsey, North London. He was a Fleet Street messenger with the Westminster Press Group at 16, then a reporter with the Muswell Hill Record. *National Service in the RAF began a dalliance with show business in a comic double act and he worked in music halls around Britain after demobilisation. He returned to journalism with the* Paddington Mercury *and worked for the* Evening Argus, *Brighton, and the* Evening World, *Bristol, before joining the* Daily Mirror *in 1962. He was in the* Mirror's *New York bureau 1965-73 and with* The People, *as a roving correspondent and then columnist 1973-96.*

'In the 1950s and 60s, the *Daily Mirror* was hungry for news from America. Fads and fashions born in Hollywood or New York were quick to make an impression in Britain, especially among young people, and it was important to keep up with these transatlantic trends. Rock 'n' roll, The Twist, hoola hoops, crew cuts, blue jeans, bobby-soxers, heavyweight boxers, glamorous film stars, flash motor cars, electrical gadgets – almost anything stamped "Made in the USA" was welcome in a United Kingdom looking for a little excitement in the aftermath of World War Two.

This was reflected in the growth of the *Mirror*'s New York bureau. By the early 60s, the paper had five correspondents working in New York, based in the skyscraper offices of the New York *Daily News* building on East 42nd Street in Manhattan. However, the time difference meant London lost interest about 3pm Eastern Seaboard time, so 'work' was carried out from Costellos', a newspaper bar frequented by British correspondents and *Daily News* staff and adorned with genuine James Thurber murals. A full-time contracted freelance, Donald Ludlow worked out of Washington DC.

In the 50s and throughout much of the 60s, television had still not taken over as the main news medium. The immediacy of satellite links and other forms of instant global communication were not available to the TV networks, and film of major events in the USA had to be air freighted to the BBC in London from its American correspondents. Often film aired on the evening news was a day old. With wired photographs and on-the-spot accounts, newspapers could very often beat them to the punch, and dispatches under a Dallas or Denver dateline still bore the whiff of front-line reporting that could match anything TV then had to offer.

As a result, the reporters in the *Mirror*'s New York bureau were constantly on the road. In my time there, I provided on-the-spot accounts of race riots in Los Angeles, Detroit and Washington, followed the train taking Bobby Kennedy's body from Los Angeles to Washington after his assassination, watched astronauts blast off from Cape Kennedy in the

continuing race to put a man on the moon, spoke to terrorists who had kidnapped British diplomat James Cross in Montreal, saw former London Black Power activist Michael X sentenced to death for murder in Trinidad, interviewed Muhammad Ali in his Chicago home after he was stripped of his heavyweight title for refusing to fight with the U.S. Army in Vietnam, trudged behind the mule-drawn funeral cart carrying the assassinated civil rights leader Dr. Martin Luther King through the streets of Atlanta, Georgia, and shadowed golfer Tony Jacklin every stroke of the way as he won the U.S. Open championship in Minnesota.

The veteran bureau chief was Ralph Champion, appointed to the New York job in the early 1950s by his mentor, Hugh Cudlipp – as teenagers they had worked on rival papers in Penarth, south Wales. With his distinguished, swept-back grey hair and immaculately tailored Brooks Brothers suits, Ralph looked more like a diplomat than a newspaperman. He maintained the image by living in ambassadorial style. His home was a huge, luxurious apartment opposite Gracie Mansion, official residence of the mayors of New York, on Manhattan's upper East Side. The *Mirror* provided him with an equally impressive Lincoln limousine, and his expense account enabled him to dine in New York's finest restaurants. Ralph was a man who enjoyed a drink or nine and the main daily task for his four-man team was to ensure that at least one of them was free at 1pm to accompany Ralph to Renato's Italian bar, just off Second Avenue and just a few minutes' stroll from the office.

There Ralph would consume copious amounts of Scotch and soda, fielding phone calls from London at the telephone on the bar. Untouchable because of the Cudlipp connection, Ralph was a law unto himself. He hated sport and could see no reason why his New York staff should be involved in its coverage. He considered this the province of visiting firemen like the great Peter Wilson, who made regular trips to New York to cover boxing and tennis. When Tony Jacklin swept into a commanding lead in the U.S. Open golf championship in Chaska, Minnesota, in June 1970, there were urgent calls from the sports desk in London to provide as much detail as possible – no one from

Continued on page 88

London was there. I managed to scramble something together, but it was obvious that if we were to provide the close coverage that London was demanding, we would have to send someone to Chaska. Ralph would have none of it. "Those buggers should have sent someone from the sports department in the first place," he observed.

In secret, I phoned Jack Hutchinson, the sports editor in London, explained the situation and advised him that only a direct order from London would ensure that someone was sent. A few minutes later, the Telex in the office chattered into life with a message for Ralph: "Editor orders that we send staff man to Minnesota soonest." A furious Ralph ordered me on to the next plane, convinced that my trip was a total waste of time. When, three days later, Jacklin won the tournament by seven strokes, the first Briton to win the U.S. Open for 50 years, my story of his triumph took up most of the front and back pages, plus the centre spread. "Hmm," said Ralph, browsing through this coverage. "Good job I decided to send you."

New York was a plum posting for any aspiring *Mirror* journalist. Among those to win this journalistic jackpot were Desmond Wilcox, later to become a TV executive and famous interviewer, *Daily Mail* columnist John Edwards, political columnist Chris Buckland – currently with the *News of the World* – Sydney Young, subsequently a long-time *Daily Mirror* correspondent based in Bristol, the Australian Tony Delano, later a professor of journalism at the London College of Printing, and David Wright, who liked America so much he came home only briefly and returned to work for the *National Enquirer* in Florida.

Although there was great competition among the correspondents, there was also a great sense of camaraderie. Malcolm Keogh, a very talented young writer from St. Helens in Lancashire, was struck down with a mysterious illness. While he was undergoing tests in Columbia Presbyterian Hospital, Brian Hitchen and I decided to cheer him up with an unusual visit. The two of us hired clergy outfits from a fancy dress costume store. Complete with dog collar, purple vest and a huge, high-crowned Native American-style hat, I was the "Bishop of

Fine diner: The young Ralph Champion.

Arizona". Brian, all in black with a dog collar, a pipe and a bible tucked under one arm, looked like an avuncular Catholic priest out of *Going My Way*.

Our arrival at the hospital caused quite a stir, and we were ushered into Malcolm's room, where his wife, Jennie, was at his bedside. She sprang respectfully to her feet and was spluttering a confused welcome when suddenly she recognised us and addressed us in a torrent of somewhat un-holy language before collapsing with laughter. Sadly, Malcolm was diagnosed with a rare and incurable blood disease and died a few weeks later.

If they wished, *Mirror* men posted to the American bureau sailed to New York, with their families, as first-class passengers on the old Queen Elizabeth. Ralph Champion's perks included paid-for membership of a swish country club on Long Island and the seal of approval for newly arrived correspondents was to be invited there for Saturday lunch.

While he was content to leave the day-by-day coverage to his four-man staff, Ralph was assigned to the White House Press Corps and travelled on almost every major trip abroad made by successive American presidents. As befitted his ambassadorial style, Ralph considered his most important role in New York was as meeter and greeter for the *Daily Mirror*'s most prominent VIPs, chairman Cecil King and editorial director Hugh Cudlipp, who regularly came to the city. Preparations for either of these dignitaries resembled those for a royal visit. Hours were spent anguishing over which restaurant to take them to, which venue to book for a "meet the troops" staff

at all, but who one night slipped him a piece of paper on which was written "I can get you a trial at *The Express*". He didn't last.

If there was even just one typographical error in the paper, let alone an error of fact or some unsupported surmise, a head would roll.

The hierarchy had the usual titles but their jobs tended to be more free-ranging. Joe Grizzard was the chief sub who was inclined to give Smiley stories of which Dick Dinsdale, the night editor, was unaware. Dinsdale's standards

were terrifyingly high, and he, like Jack Nener (and future editor Tony Miles), called everyone Cock, particularly when decimating their stories.

One day, when Smiley was still on trial, Dinsdale gave him a new splash. He subbed it, went off on his break, came back and found someone else working on it. Trouble. The corridor from the back bench to the executive offices was known as the golden mile, a route taken by anyone about to be fired. Dinsdale called Smiley, said it was the first big story he'd

Riding high: The New York bureau's favourite "staff car" was shipped to the Holborn office in the Seventies. The beast is flanked here by Bill Hagerty, Tony Miles, Kent Gavin, Tony Delano, Mike Molloy and Keith Waterhouse.

cocktail party, arranging limousines, theatre tickets etc. Cecil King would arrive with a personal assistant at the Waldorf Astoria Hotel like some visiting potentate. On one occasion in the 1950s, he was driving to the airport to catch his flight home when he spotted a large shop as the car travelled through an especially rundown section of Brooklyn. "Champion, what is that shop?" inquired King. "That, sir, is called a supermarket," said Ralph. "I don't believe you have them in Britain yet." "I would like to see this 'supermarket'," said King. "Stop the car."

The gleaming limousine slid to a halt, causing a great deal of interest on the shabby high street. King swept imperiously into the shop, trailed by his PA and Ralph. The supermarket owner, sensing some kind of high-powered takeover bid for his modest establishment, eagerly escorted them around as King poked at packets of butter, smelled the cheese, squeezed the vegetables and sniffily examined the shelves. Unimpressed, he headed for the door, to the bewilderment of the attentive owner. "Er, don't you think we ought to buy something?" inquired Ralph. "I don't think so," snapped King, marching for the exit. Ralph mollified the owner with a five-dollar bill.

Ralph retired in 1975 and returned to live in England until his death. He'd seen the best of the United States operation: although later the Mirror was for a while to maintain a correspondent in Los Angeles – Jill Evans, Paul Connew and Barry Wigmore occupied that enviable berth at different times – economies and the revolution in communications made the idea of such a large-scale U.S. presence redundant.

Like most British papers, the *Daily Mirror* now has just one America correspondent, working out of his apartment. And even Costellos' isn't there anymore.

given him and that he'd made a cat's arse of it. Smiley said "What do you mean, the first big story. I've done the front, spread and back today." And, since he reckoned he was going to be fired anyway, added the word 'cock'. They went back through the files, Smiley had made his point and was taken on the payroll with the customary lack of grace – no welcome to the *Mirror* staff. The only comment from Dinsdale was "Well, sorry I spoke, cock."

Those running the features operation as the paper gathered momentum in its charge towards the magic five million daily circulation barrier included Mike Randall, later to edit a *Daily Mail* admired by journalists but not, alas, by the public (Randall later recalled how, in 1954, he couldn't fill the Christmas Eve issue. Keith Waterhouse wandered away and returned with a 1,200-word short story that later became the basis for his autobiographical novel of childhood, *There Is a Happy Land*). Later, after the group's papers had moved into new state-of-the-art offices in Holborn, one of the least successful features executives ensured he

A reader writes: Keith Waterhouse, then a feature writer, in 1957.

became one of the most memorable by, after his professional demise, writing a novel about his experiences. On a trip to Ireland, Cudlipp met the genial Tony Gray and invited him to London, hiring him as features editor, it was claimed, during a congenial breakfast at which the two men shared a bottle of Irish whiskey. When it became apparent that Gray was out of his depth, he was taken to the pub across the road and fired. By the time he returned, his office – constructed of easily manipulated metal panels – had been dismantled. Personalities and places were only thinly disguised in his hilarious fictionalised version of his time on the paper, *The Real Professionals*.

With George Brown, a future deputy leader of the Labour Party and cabinet minister, on board as a political adviser – rarely used, King recalled – and Crossman's columns ruffling as many feathers within his own party as he did

Troubled lines: Vicky (Victor Weisz) spent the second half of the 1950s at the Mirror, drawing matchless political cartoons. Michael Foot was to speak of him as a Twentieth Century Don Quixote. He committed suicide in 1966. Right: Vicky's self-portrait alongside his cartoon of Cassandra.

CASSANDRA AND VICKY

First person

KEN LAYSON

Drawing the crowds: In March 1975 an exhibition of the work of **Daily Mirror cartoonists opened at a gallery in Piccadilly. Here David Langdon kicks off proceedings with a lightning sketch. Also featured are Reg Smythe (Andy Capp), Dennis Collins (The Perishers), Bill Tidy (The Fosdyke Saga), Jack Dunkley (The Larks), Frank Bellamy (Garth), Mike Molloy (Virginia), David Rowe (Playboy), and political cartoonist Keith Waite.**

Ken Layson was born in 1946 and educated in Bromley, Kent, at Downham Secondary Boys' School and at the Camberwell College of Art and the London School of Printing. He joined the IPC Sun in 1964 and moved to the Mirror strips department when Rupert Murdoch acquired The Sun. Originally a lettering and strips background artist, he was appointed cartoon and crossword editor in 1993.

‘When I joined the department there were between 15 and 18 people working in it. I was given the job when John Allard, who stayed on an extra three months to complete 50 years with the company, retired and now where a strips and puzzles department is concerned, I'm it! I'm responsible for putting together two pages a day, six days a week, and I didn't even get a salary increase.

When new technology took over, all I got was three days' training on a computer and that was that. And when the company moved from Holborn to Canary Wharf, everybody forgot about me. I got a phone call asking me where I was! There was a move to end the daily strips page and place the strips throughout the paper, but I fought against that because I knew it would mean the strips eventually being dropped. There's still enormous interest in the strips and the puzzles – it's still true that even the smallest error in the crossword makes the phones go mad.

Forever Andy: As well as his traditional headgear, Andy Capp wears the crown as the Mirror's most successful cartoon character.

Continued on page 92

There have been lots of changes over the years, with many of the old favourites being dropped and new strips introduced. Mandy, which is now at the top of the strips page, came about when Brendon Parsons, the then deputy editor, wanted Reg Smythe to create Mandy Capp, daughter of Andy. Reg had a fit. Well, it just didn't go with Andy's image and everybody knows that he and Florrie had no children. But Parsons insisted, so I got Roger Mahoney to draw it and Carla Ostrer to write the stories and dialogue. Soon it replaced Andy as the strip at the top of the page, which really upset Reg. But the word Capp didn't last long on the new strip and she became simply Mandy.

Reg Smythe was quite remarkable and an absolute professional. When he died, in June 1998, he left over two years' worth of original Andys. After living in London for a while he had gone back to his home town, Hartlepool, several years before and hardly ever ventured south again. On the rare occasions he visited he wouldn't come to the Canary Wharf office. We'd meet and he'd have a few gin and tonics and a roast lunch.

I went to see him in Hartlepool a few times. He's supposed to have based Andy and Florrie on his parents, but Reg and his wife, Vera, were just like the strip characters. They had no children either. On one trip we were sitting in his kitchen while she bustled around and Reg said, 'There's something wrong, pet.' 'What's that,

pet?' Vera asked and Reg nodded at his coffee cup. The handle was facing the wrong way, so he couldn't pick it up without turning the cup. Without a word, she turned it round for him.

Reg and I went to a working men's club in Hartlepool at about five o'clock and it was practically empty. I went to sit on a stool in the corner and Reg said, 'Don't sit there.' I pointed out that there was hardly anyone in the place and sat down. Five minutes later a huge shadow fell over me and a very large ex-miner said, 'That's my seat – I've been sitting there for fifty years.' So I moved!

Reg and Vera lived in a very nice bungalow, quite lavish but still very Andy – there was a snooker table in the hall. He was very rich of course through syndication fees, which were always paid a year in advance. Vera died and Reg's long-time girlfriend, Jean, whom Vera had known about, moved in with him. Then, although he'd stopped smoking in 1983 – so did Andy and he hasn't smoked since, although people still think he's always with a cigarette – Reg got lung cancer and died. Jean telephoned me on a Saturday morning to tell me he had passed away – and that they had been married three days previously.

Now the *Mirror* and Hartlepool Council are co-funding a bronze statue of Andy Capp, life-size and characteristically leaning on a bar, which the town hopes will attract tourists, particularly Americans because the

Terrific tripe: Bill Tidy's The Fosdyke Saga developed a cult following.

elsewhere, the paper maintained its position as a critical friend to Labour. It was a good and generous friend – Cudlipp, Jacobson and Crossman produced the party's policy pamphlet in the run-up to the 1959 General Election – but backing losers was not its style; at least, not Cudlipp's or King's. Labour had lost 18 seats in the 1955 election, increasing the Tory majority to 38. Now, while King dickered with ditching Labour for a neutral political stance, Cudlipp warned Hugh Gaitskell that he could not expect unwavering support if the party was badly

beaten again. On 8 October the Tories romped home, winning a further 21 seats, 19 from Labour, and increasing their overall majority to 100.

Cudlipp had masterminded a lively and totally committed pro-Labour campaign in the paper, during which the *Mirror* advocated lowering the voting age to 18, but come defeat he was as good as his word. The slogan FORWARD WITH THE PEOPLE disappeared from under the *Mirror*'s masthead on 12 October, Crossman's column was ditched – his strip still syndicates all over the United States. Initially the statue was going to be of Reg, but he hated the idea – he was a very shy and modest man.

Long before we used up the strips Reg left, I commissioned new ones from Roger Mahoney, with Roger Kettle providing the words, and feathered them in so that the changeover wasn't really noticeable. Andy has been modernised a bit – we've had him talking on a mobile phone and soon he'll be taking a trip to the United States – but he's still that chauvinistic, northern layabout that Reg created.

Of the other strips, Scorer is very popular. It was introduced 11 years ago as a foil to Striker in *The Sun* – the only time the *Mirror* has followed *The Sun*'s lead on a strip, whereas they stole from us such concepts as Garth – theirs was a girl named Scarth – and Andy Capp, under the name of The Waggs, when Murdoch launched the paper. Barry Tomlinson, who also does Roy of the Rovers, writes Striker and the computerised art work is done by John Gillatt, with David Pugh handling the backgrounds. Scorer's hero plays for England and we do contemporary story lines featuring real people. The strip has been greatly enlarged in size and now dominates the page.

The most recently introduced strip is Real Life, which is done by Tom Johnson. Piers Morgan brought Johnson

and now the *Daily Mirror* doesn't have a regular political cartoon or cartoonist, a great shame when you remember the paper's great history in that area – Philip Zec, Vicky, Stanley Franklin, Keith Waite and Charles Griffin. We don't produce books the way we used to, either. There hasn't been an Andy Capp book for about ten years and the puzzle books, once very successful, have stopped. And spot jokes – individual cartoons to liven up a page – disappeared about six years ago for budgetary reasons.

Pip, Squeak and Wilfred, a famous *Mirror* strip in its day, made a reappearance for about six months not many years ago. Piers Morgan had met the Queen Mother, who said that the strip had been Prince Charles's favourite cartoon when he was very small and used to look at Children's *Mirror*. Wilfred, the rabbit who didn't speak but went "nunc nunc", was an inspiration for Spike Milligan when he was creating what would become *The Goon Show*. And the central figure of Captain Reilly-Ffoull in Just Jake, another early *Mirror* strip, was a model for John Cleese's Basil Fawlty – Reilly Ffloull even had a butler he used to whack, just as Fawlty ill-treated Manuel.

The department may have changed beyond recognition, with some of the strips being done on screen from pencil outline original artwork, but the cartoons appear to be as well read as ever. They help cement readers to the title, I think. Not long ago our Mandy strip featured a wedding and someone called to say that coincidentally he and his girlfriend had married on the day the strip appeared and that they even had the same names – Roger and Donna – as the characters in the drawing. "How much for the original, mate?" Roger said. Fortunately we do have originals of Mandy, so I had it signed by the artist and writer and sent to them, without charge of course. I try to keep as many originals as possible. They're an important part of the paper's history. **"**

Top kids: The Perishers was an inspired take on the Peanuts strip.

researcher, a young Gerald Kaufman, stayed on as a political writer until leaving to pursue his own political career – and domestic party politics were replaced by a drive to attract younger readers (a weekly "Teen Page" was subtitled "For the young of all ages"). Subsequently, Cudlipp argued that the decision to drop the front-page slogan and dispense with Crossman – Jane, once the world's most talked-about strip, exited at the same time – had been made prior to the election. But he was piqued by Labour's ineffectuality and King told *The*

Observer: "Women readers particularly have had a bellyful of politics."

Cudlipp's inspiration was undiminished, however, as he continued to use the front page as a canvas for some of the greatest creative popular journalism of all time. The most famous page one contained no text and no picture: MR. K! (If you will pardon an olde English phrase) DON'T BE SO BLOODY RUDE! PS Who do you think you are? STALIN?

It is not known whether the Soviet leader,

Union gap: After a national newspaper strike involving the Amalgamated Engineering Union and the Electrical Trades Union, which lasted nearly four weeks, publication of the Mirror *was resumed on 21 April 1955. Left: Returning to work at Geraldine House.*

whose anti-American outburst in Paris had seen the May 1960 Summit collapse, was impressed, but the public was and so was the rest of Fleet Street.

Shock Issues, long to be a part of the *Mirror's* editorial armoury, were launched with devastating exposés of child neglect, ecological rape and the slaughter of endangered species, death on the road and, just before the 1964 General Election, poverty. And the paper's campaign in favour of the Common Market, of which both King and Cudlipp were dedicated supporters, began June 1961, a year during which much else was happening to divert the attentions of both chairman and editorial director.

King moved in on the struggling Odhams Press and, after a running battle with Roy Thomson, proprietor of *The Sunday Times,* acquired the *Daily Herald,* which was part owned by the TUC, plus *The People* and a cluster of magazines ranging from women's weeklies to *Farmers' Weekly* and a host of trade and technical titles. Parliamentary objections to

the deal and the concerns of Labour leader Gaitskell that the struggling Labour-committed *Herald* was under threat were solved by the International Publishing Corporation, as the group would now become, guaranteeing the paper's survival for seven years and two pledges written by Cudlipp: the future of the *Herald* as a separate entity would be fought for with the utmost energy; and, no amalgamation of the *Daily Herald* and *Daily Mirror* would ever take place during the Mirror Group's control of Odhams. King might as well have been signing a blank cheque and Cudlipp, named as chairman of the *Herald,* was stepping on to a whirligig that, before the end of the decade, would pitch him flat on his face.

Also in 1961, Nener made way for 47-year-old L.A. Lee Howard, the paper's tenth editor. Nener occupied the editor's office only briefly when, in February of that year, the company relocated to its new custom-built headquarters, designed by Wembley Stadium architect Sir Owen Williams and built at a cost of £11million at the apex where Fetter Lane and New Fetter

First person GERALD KAUFMAN

Gerald Kaufman was born in 1931 and educated at Leeds Grammar School and Queen's College, Oxford. He was assistant general secretary of the Fabian Society and became a research assistant to Richard Crossman when Crossman began writing a twice-weekly column for the Daily Mirror *in 1955. Kaufman joined the political staff of the paper and remained there until 1964. He subsequently wrote for the* New Statesman *before becoming Labour MP for Manchester Ardwick in 1970 (Manchester Gorton from 1983). He was a government minister and later shadow Home and Foreign Secretary. He chaired the House of Commons 2003 Culture, Media and Sport select committee inquiry into privacy and intrusion.*

Take me to your leader: Gerald Kaufman learned the value of disciplined writing.

' I did a lot of factual stuff for Richard Crossman. He saw his job as teaching people about what was going on in the world in a highly readable way. I can't imagine people being taught anything by what's in the papers of today. The Crossman column went soon after the 1959 General Election, when Hugh Cudlipp got fed up with it. I stayed, writing leaders of about 240 words that had to be comprehensible to people who had left school at 15 – writing a Mirror leader was as stylised as writing a sonnet, in terms of discipline. The *Mirror* really respected its readers, which I think few papers do today.

I shared an office with Alan Fairclough and Keith Waterhouse. Fairclough was brilliant, a miner's son with a double first from Balliol and an absolute master at writing *Mirror* leaders – the voice of the most important popular newspaper in the country. Keith was a star feature writer then, a genius with a wonderful gift for memorable phrases. When I think of him and Donald Zec and Peter Wilson, well, I don't think it is simply nostalgia when I say that there is no one around to touch them today. And Vicky, of course, the best political cartoonist in the world. I used to see him every day. It was a wonderful office. When I fought Gillingham in the 1959 Election, Keith helped me write my election address and Bill Connor – Cassandra – actually came to speak for me, even though he hated public speaking. And later, after I had left and was standing for the first time in the Manchester constituency where I was elected, Marje Proops came to speak at my eve-of-poll meeting.

After the *Mirror* moved to Holborn Circus, I used to drink with Alan Fairclough and Bill Connor at the Stab [the White Hart] across the street. They were remarkable people to learn from – working for the paper was the best school I ever attended. My job was never really defined. I worked mostly to Sydney Jacobson and later to [political adviser] John Beavan and also to Cudlipp.

Hugh Cudlipp was the greatest single journalist I have ever had anything to do with. He was a man of principle and very courageous, especially over Suez in 1956. But one of the reasons I was happy to leave the

Mirror when the time came was that when I wrote a leader and Cudlipp took an interest, I could be there until two in the morning. He would go home to Strand-on-the-Green in Chiswick, where he was living at the time, and the leader would have to be biked out to him. Hugh found it very unattractive that the Labour Party kept losing elections. He hated it. After the Orpington by-election of 1962, when Eric Lubbock won for the Liberals while Sydney Jacobson was on holiday, Hugh decided to switch the paper's allegiance to the Liberal Party. Sydney soon put a stop to that when he returned, but whenever Labour lost, Hugh would always go very cool and put very little politics in the paper for a while.

When I resigned to go to the *New Statesman* as political correspondent, Cudlipp said he was about to make me chief leader writer. He also said, "Now you're leaving, I suppose you will be criticising the *Mirror*." I said, "No, I won't – I am a great admirer of the paper." And I never have. '

Up front: No pictures, just hard-hitting words and dynamite typography give Kruschev the message.

Fighting cock: R.L. "Dick" Dinsdale would tear stories and staff to pieces.

Powerhouse: Picture desk, art desk and night desk at Geraldine House, 1960. Picture editor Simon Clyne talks into one of his many phones. Art editor Bill Soutar is in shirtsleeves on the left. Night editor Bryan Parker is in the middle ground, back to camera.

Lane joined Holborn. This new paper palace, where the *Mirror* was to remain for more than 30 years, rose from the rubble of a derelict bombsite where had stood the Thomas Wallis department store until it was destroyed by fire during the Blitz. The company bought the one-acre site in 1946 but it was not until April 1956 that Cecil King had turned the first spade of earth and construction began of a building with the most highly mechanised publishing room – it and the press room were deep underground – and, among floors of offices and the requisite support services, a library containing four-and-a-half million cuttings, a million photographs, half-a-million negatives and 15,000 books, pamphlets and reports. Cudlipp prowled the editorial floor, fitted with sound-deadening ceiling panels. "Bloody quiet, innit?" he observed to the news subs.

Although only a hundred yards or so from Rolls Buildings, the move radically changed the staff's social habits. Number 10, or Winnie's, where features journalists had often lingered over drinks into the afternoon, was replaced as the department's out-of-office base by the White Hart, which quickly became known as "the Stab-in-the-Back" because of the firings, hirings and inter-office intrigue that went on

Empire building: The new base of the Daily Mirror and Sunday Pictorial at Holborn Circus was opened in 1961. Although few found the building beautiful, it was designed to produce and print a modern newspaper in a way that would be the envy of its rivals. The building was demolished at the start of the 21st century, the site becoming the head office of the Sainsbury's supermarket chain.

Best seller: Stet, the company's house newspaper, celebrates the Mirror breaking through five million.

Uncovered: Britain may have never had it so good, but the Mirror's Shock Issues told a different story.

John Jenkinson was born in 1928 and educated at the Bec Grammar School, Wandsworth, south London, and Westminster Technical College. He joined the Mirror Group in Manchester as an assistant in the publicity department in 1957 and was transferred to London to promote the Sunday Mirror's National Exhibition of Children's Art. He became manager and then director of publicity and promotions before being fired on several occasions by Robert Maxwell – the last time, in 1991, permanently. He subsequently acted as a consultant to the company.

'The legendary Tommy Atkins was the head of promotions when I came to London and until he retired towards the end of the 1960s he was responsible for organising most of the wonderful stunts dreamed up for the *Daily Mirror*, usually by Hugh Cudlipp. We worked for all titles and there was always some grand promotion going on – it was like a fun factory.

We were very big on boats. There was an American sailor named Robert Manrey crossing the Atlantic in a 30ft boat and I called him by radio telephone and arranged to display his boat, Tinkerbell, in the big window of Orbit House, the building we owned across the street from the main Holborn building. He arrived on Friday, the boat was in the window by Sunday morning and by 9am people were queuing to get in. After that, we did the same thing with Francis Chichester's *Gypsy Moth* and the boats of Robin Knox-Johnson and Alec Rose. We even put Sheila Scott's aeroplane in the window after she completed a newsworthy flight. And we would do things like rent trains and fill them with readers – we took the Andy Capp Special from Manchester to Blackpool one bank holiday and it was a huge success.

Great promotions – Boom Cities, the search for Mrs Britain, themed tribute dinners to various industries and the rest – were seen as the way ahead for the *Mirror*. They produced no revenue whatsoever and they were incredibly expensive, but the paper was seen to be involved in all aspects of modern life. The Boom Cities dinners at the end of the 1960s were amazing. They all had themes – passenger liners in Southampton, Concorde in Bristol, commerce in Manchester, steel in Sheffield, shipbuilding in Newcastle – and the one in Liverpool has become the most famous of them all because that is when Hugh Cudlipp had the ship the dinner was being held on turned round at enormous expense.

Many of the promotions we did were tied to features in the paper. The *Mirror* Pets' Club, run by Betty Tay, was very popular and on two occasions we had Cudlipp-inspired Pets' Club lunches in the Napoleon Room at the Café Royal. It was a madhouse – there were dogs and goats and bears and a chimpanzee and, at one of them, old man Steptoe's horse from the *Steptoe and Son* TV series. We put a tranquilliser of some sort down on the floor to keep them quiet. The tables had aquariums as centrepieces and Freddie Reed, a great *Mirror* photographer who usually specialised in royals, wanted to photograph a Pekingese belonging to Xenia Field, the gardening columnist, on top of one of them. The dog fell in. After the lunch, an elephant we had brought along wouldn't get into its trailer and started to run off down the street. We made the later editions of the *Evening Standard: Elephant runs amok in Piccadilly.*

The *Mirror* also organised the first and only supersonic awayday. We chartered a Concorde for a day as part of our celebration of the Queen's silver jubilee in 1977. Some 80 readers and a group of staff went to New York and were back the same day. Except for some of the staff, that is – Mike Molloy, editor at the time, Marje Proops, Felicity Green and the photographer, Kent Gavin, stayed on in New York for a few days!

When Felicity Green left to work for Vidal Sassoon in 1978, I became director of the department. We were locked in a circulation battle with *The Sun* and still doing a lot of big stunts – *The Sun* didn't compete in that area, all its money went on TV advertising.

We used the late Tommy Cooper on one promotion and he came into my office and asked for coffee – said he wasn't drinking. Then a drinks trolley was brought to my Orbit House office from the hospitality area in Holborn, but Cooper said he would like a pint of beer, so we sent down to the pub, the Stab, for one. Then he was hungry –

there. The almost equally close proximity of the three public houses on the other side of the building meant that there was no shortage of watering holes for the growing company's work force and a rush of extra prosperity came to the White Swan, Printer's Devil and White Horse (the latter colloquially known as "Barney's" after the publican whose attachment to the premises was such that, when eventually called upon to retire, died in the taxi carrying him to the railway station).

The reason given for the end of Nener's reign as editor, during which, apart from minor blips, the circulation had continued to climb, was that his health was considered suspect, although his wife, Audrey Whiting, denies to this day that he was no longer fit to continue. Lee Howard – Lee to those senior enough to have progressed beyond calling him Mr Howard – moved from the *Sunday Pictorial* to begin a decade as editor, during which time he would witness the *Mirror* reach the peak of its success and then begin the gradual descent from the lofty heights of "the greatest sale in the universe". The philosophical Howard, winner of a DFC as a wartime flyer and the author of several successful novels, was to be a remote figure to many of his staff, rarely leaving his office during working days that

Let the good times roll: John Jenkinson promoted the good name of the Daily Mirror across the land in the far-off days of fun and largesse. Here (centre) he presides over a beautiful barmaid contest.

Continued on page 100

often lasted 16 hours. He took few holidays and, although towards the end of his term was drinking far more than was good for even his hefty build, never appeared to be drunk. Like his predecessor, he was minimally interested in politics, which was just as well. Cudlipp, now approaching 50 and, despite the personal turmoil that came with the deaths of his wife, Eileen, and eldest brother, Percy, in 1962, was still firing on all cylinders. With the assistance and counsel of Sydney Jacobson and, from 1964 when he relinquished the role of editor of the *Daily Herald*, political adviser John Beavan, Cudlipp ran the political show and would do so

until he took his top hat and whip and bowed out of the circus.

King, now 60, showed little sign of slowing down, either. From his spacious ninth-floor office in Holborn – not as big as a tennis court, but only just – he could survey a publishing empire consisting of 12 British newspapers, including two national daily and two national Sunday titles, 11 overseas papers, 75 consumer magazines, 132 trade and technical journals, and several book publishing imprints. It had interests in a score of print sites, TV and radio companies and other diversifications, and employed some 30,000 people in home and

JOHN JENKINSON

so we got him a plate of sandwiches. Then he attacked the trolley – he must have drunk an entire bottle of brandy. Later on, Tommy said he would like to meet the editor. We'd been drinking all day. I telephoned Mike Molloy, who invited us to his office. I said I didn't think that would be a very good idea and suggested we met in the Stab. Cooper ordered a pint of Guinness. The pub was packed with printers but they didn't acknowledge him. He'd refused to do a magic trick all day, but suddenly went into his act. After a few more drinks with Mike, he opened an attaché case of props he was carrying and did about 20 minutes in the bar. It was hilarious.

The bingo craze was the beginning of the end for major promotions. Bingo started well, but became repetitive – like Kentucky Fried Chicken, it was always the same. The first print run of *Mirror* bingo cards cost £65,000 and then there was the cost of distribution and the prize money – which had to match that being offered by the opposition – on top. The odds against winning were ridiculous, but for a while it seized the imagination of the readership throughout the country.

But it was when Maxwell took over the company that the most unproductive time for promotions during my years there began. Soon after he arrived, he said to me: "I must get out and meet my public". I said: "Why don't you get a train and tour Britain?" I didn't mean then – it was January – but he said, "Get it now!" The first carriage had to be refitted with first-class sleeping quarters and a lounge for RM. And we put in a conference area, staff quarters and eating areas – it cost around £55,000. The entire editorial team was against the idea, but they had to go.

First stop was Plymouth, where it was raining after there had been snow and ice. Not surprisingly, very few readers turned up. RM travelled with his own entourage, including a butler, plus fax machines and telephones that had to be taken and set up in a hotel where he might stay for only an hour. In Bristol, I introduced the *Mirror* team on the platform – RM, Mike Molloy, Marje Proops and other senior people – and invited questions from the audience. Maxwell answered them all, so there was nothing for the others to do. A member of the audience with a grievance

over something that had happened in a local magistrate's court asked why the *Mirror* hadn't had a reporter there. Maxwell glowered at Syd Young, the district man who was at the meeting, and said: "You there! In future you will cover all magistrate's courts and report back directly to me."

In Coventry we arrived late and the staff wanted to go out and get something to eat. Nonsense, said Maxwell, we would all eat in the hotel restaurant, which I pointed out was closed. "I don't think so," said Maxwell, and he had the kitchen opened to prepare a meal of smoked salmon and sirloin steaks, together with wines and brandy. He insisted Marje sat alongside him, and Anne Robinson, who was then a *Mirror* columnist, opposite. Anne went to light a cigarette and RM said: "No one smokes cigarettes at my table – what you will have is a proper cigar after the meal." She agreed and when the coffee and brandy came up, Maxwell gave her a torpedo of a cigar, worth about £40. Moisten the end with brandy, he told her – "Stick it in Jenks's glass, he won't mind." She managed about four puffs.

Maxwell could be a nightmare. When we ran a promotion to win £50,000, there were 50 boxes, one of which was supposed to have a cheque for £50,000 in it. The contestant had a 49-1 shot at picking the right box, but when it was time for the cheque to be placed in one of the boxes, Maxwell used to tell me to go away – he did it alone. So we never knew if the cheque was actually in a box at all.

He was extraordinary. Once he met a competition contestant who had a growth on his face. "Why don't you get it removed?" said Maxwell and he paid £5,000 for the operation. He wasn't beyond generosity like that, although he did make sure the story was given to the local papers in the area where the man lived. But he could be a monster, too. He publicly bollocked his daughter, Ghislaine, when she was 15 minutes late turning up to draw the winning entry in a competition. She was in tears. When eventually she pulled out a winner, Maxwell looked at it and said: "He's from the north-west – do we want someone from the north-west, is it a good circulation area?" He rejected about ten entries that were

---

international businesses stretching from West Africa to the Caribbean. At the first annual general meeting of IPC, shareholders were cheered by the announcement of profits of £6.5million.

As for the group's flagship, it looked unstoppable. On Tuesday 9 June 1964, the *Mirror* was able to announce a world record average daily sale of five million copies – a readership, it claimed, of 14 million, which meant that one in three of every adult in the

country was now seeing the paper.

It was necessary for only one more milestone to be reached for the *Mirror*'s Golden Age to be gift-wrapped and the champagne corks to pop with even more than the usual frequency in Holborn Circus. Cudlipp and King's disenchantment with party politics had softened since 1959 and when Sir Alec Douglas-Home – the 71-year-old former 14th Earl of Home, who, the previous year, had renounced his peerage to succeed Harold Macmillan as Prime Minister –

The eyes had it: Chalkey White toured the seaside towns and Britain's leisure attractions, ready to dispense a fiver to the Mirror reader who saw through his disguise.

drawn before he found one he thought was right to win £100,000.

The winner lived in Manchester and reporter Ron Ricketts and photographer Andy Hoosier were dispatched north with instructions to be at the lady's house at 9.30am, by which time Maxwell would have called her to deliver the good news. He didn't, of course – when they got there, she knew nothing about it. Ten minutes later, Maxwell came on the phone to tell her she'd won and that a reporter and photographer would soon be there, and she said, "They're here now." They got a severe bollocking on the woman's phone for not allowing him to break the news.

Maxwell loved going on TV. On one occasion when we were due at Thames Television, I was in his flat at the top of the building while he was getting changed – he was running around in just a white shirt, revealing his huge, flabby legs. When we arrived at Thames, the commissionaire asked for RM's pass, and of course he

didn't have it. So he was told he couldn't go in, but he looked at the decorations on the man's uniform and said: "The India Star, eh. Marvellous! What would the world do without men like me and you?" Next thing, the other commissionaire came over and said, "I've got the Africa Star, sir." And there was Maxwell, his arms around both their shoulders, pointing at people in the street and saying, "If it wasn't for men like us, these people wouldn't be living in freedom." And in he went, without a pass. But they wouldn't let me go in until I'd found mine.

He fired me many times, but then I would get a call asking me to go into the office. "Never mind about that," he would say when I pointed out that he had fired me. Eventually he accused me of not having done something and said, "You and I had better part company" – that was his ultimate firing phrase. Everything had changed by then. But it was mostly enormous fun while it lasted.

,

called a General Election for 15 October 1964, the paper swung behind Labour with renewed vigour. By now, the Tories had been in office for a debilitating 14 years. Labour had a relatively young front bench team led by Harold Wilson – "a brilliant Leader of the Opposition and, at that stage, readier to listen," King was to write of the man who would be instrumental in his own downfall. "I was not particularly impressed by the promise of a Labour Government, but quite convinced that it was

time for a change." Whatever his reservations, they did not prevent King displaying a red pennant with the message "Vote Labour" on the bonnet of his Rolls-Royce in the run-up to polling day. (Cudlipp's support was more practical, providing Wilson with the phrase "the white heat of the technological revolution" for the leader's masterly 1963 Labour Conference speech.)

The *Mirror* did not begin its own campaign until 28 September – "Who's finger on the

Big feature: Reg Payne, assistant editor (right), Tony Gray, features editor (left) and Freddie Wills, deputy features editor (sitting) in July 1960.

Music man: Ken Smiley, a sub who could make stories sing, playing with the Fleet Street jazz band.

tranquillizer?" it cheekily inquired in reporting a Tory plan to downplay the election – but, from then on, it reminded readers almost every day of governmental failure and incompetence during the previous 13 years. It also, as A.C.H. Smith observed in *The Popular Press* and *Social Change*, continually used the class card in its arguments, with the powerful voice of Majorie Proops telling readers: "…when I contemplate the three or four million who still, in 1964, have to trudge down backyards, or share squalid outside lavatories with countless other citizens, I am overwhelmed with scorn for you [Douglas-Home] and the rest of the never-had-it-so-good brigade. Has your lady, Sir Alec, ever had to lug hot water to a tub in the kitchen to bath her young? Or herself? Or you, come to that?"

Labour edged home in a nail-biting finish, with 317 seats to the Tories' 303, with the Liberals and others winning seven: an overall majority of four. Home, pronounced Hume, went home, pronounced home, and Wilson, at 48 the youngest Prime Minister of the century so far, moved into Downing Street – "Nice place we've got here," he said. "Brothers, we are on our way," said his deputy and former *Mirror* consultant George Brown. Had it been

the people's paper that had tipped the balance in favour of the people's party? Many prominent Labour figures certainly believed so.

Just 17 months later, during which time Labour's majority had fluctuated between five and just one, Wilson decided to seek the support of the country. In the election of 31 March 1966, Labour gained 47.9 per cent of the vote and an overall majority. The people's party was, for the time being, secure in Government. The *Mirror*'s cup runneth over.

But soon the cascading champagne would be replaced by a non-sparkling red substance, and it wasn't claret. As Cudlipp was to recall: "Wilson barely had time to hang up his Gannex in Downing Street, say good morning to Marcia [personal and political secretary Marcia Williams] and light his briar before Cecil King began to monitor his shortcomings as Prime Minister." The *Mirror* was about to enter a period of turmoil that would see it lose control of its own destiny and ultimately be thrown carelessly into the arms of one of the most colourful, and disreputable, figures in a history already littered with characters splashed with every shade and hue. Imperceptibly, the Golden Age was about to slip through the fingers of time.

6
THE SUN ALSO RISES

It is the morning of 7 April 1967 and there is a sombre air in the Mirror *offices. Bill Connor, now Sir William and author of the best-known newspaper column in the land, is dead, having succumbed to cancer in St. Bart's Hospital, London, the previous day. The shock felt by colleagues and Cass's millions of readers is not caused by the suddenness of his departure: Connor had been ill for some time and on 6 February movingly concluded a series of thoughts on the subject of insomnia in what was to be his final piece for the paper. Under the headline Plenty of Time, Cassandra had written: "Normal service in this column is temporarily interrupted while I learn what any babe can do with ease and what comes naturally to most men of good conscience – sleep easily o'nights…" Unlike the interruption he suffered during World War Two, this one turned out not to be temporary.*

Cass's departure, 20 days short of his fifty-eighth birthday, is, for many, hard to accept. This, after all, was the man who neither the British Government nor the Nazis could shut up; the man who interviewed presidents and movie kings and queens and Senator Joseph McCarthy while a dentist drilled the Senator's teeth ("I told the dentist that I dearly hoped he would hurt the Senator"); the man who was on HMS Alert, near Christmas Island, when the British A-bomb was tested there; the man who watched Eichmann brought to justice in a glass dock in Israel; the man who covered the funeral of Churchill and bade farewell with very different, but just as memorable, sentiments to Bernard Shaw and Josef Stalin; the man who found a bar inside St. Peter's Basilica in Vatican City; the man who claimed to have shunted tons of rail freight all over London when his telephone number was so similar to that of Camden Town Goods Station that he was continually rung up at night to be asked "most peculiar questions, such as what I proposed to do with forty-seven sheets of corrugated asbestos in Siding Seventeen".

Hugh Cudlipp's observation that "He'll be flaming angry now that he won't be able to write a column about Judgement Day" is the perfect epitaph. Yes, it is a sad day today. But tomorrow is another newspaper…

As the most socially defining decade of the second half of the 20th century found its feet – what is popularly referred to as "the sixties" did not really begin until 1963 – the *Mirror* worked hard to keep up with it. Sometimes the paper's capability to understand and adapt to social change had all the appearance of competitors in a three-legged race struggling not to be left behind by a champion sprinter, but efforts were made to embrace the new youth culture with pages devoted to rock and roll, mod fashion and teenage angst. Despite some antipathy towards the icons of the age – Cudlipp had snubbed The Beatles at the Albert Hall ball with which the *Mirror* celebrated its five million triumph and Cassandra abhorred the "furry twanging" of a group he considered "as unskilled as a quartet of chimps tarring a back fence" – the paper tried to keep its finger on the pulse of the nation, even if, at times, it had difficulty in locating it.

The location was certainly awry, it was to transpire, when Cudlipp became convinced that a population benefiting from a vastly improved schools system and the widespread opportunity for further education required the *Mirror* to move up a gear in its coverage of more serious issues. Editor Howard was not so sure. The mood in the country was upbeat and optimistic, feelings heightened by England's World Cup victory in 1966 – by now the paper more or less left Scotland to the *Daily Record* – but Howard could detect no sign that this constituted a desire by readers for the *Mirror* to springboard upwards from the editorial mix that had served them so well in the past. As happened with many editors during the reigns of Bart and Cudlipp and others who were to run the newspapers in the years ahead, Howard's opinion metaphorically went straight on to the spike. What could possibly go wrong at a paper that, in the second half of 1967, returned a record circulation figure of 5,282,137?

Cudlipp instigated World Spotlight, an admirable attempt to interest readers in foreign news. The old-fashioned Rex North gossip column was transferred to the *Pictorial* and the relatively sophisticated Inside Page launched in its place under the editorship of Tony Miles, a bright young features writer whose potential Cudlipp had spotted soon after Miles arrived from the *Brighton Argus*. And the introduction of Mirrorscope, initially a once-a-week four-page section containing news analysis and interviews of great length by *Mirror* standards, saw Miles shifted to edit it and the appointment of Mike Molloy, the former *Sunday Pictorial* office boy who had swiftly risen to become features art editor, to oversee its design and projection. Cudlipp,

Under the influence: Lee Howard found his views overruled by Cudlipp and King.

Fame abroad: The young John Pilger reported from Rhodesia and Jerusalem.

explaining the philosophy of these up-market elements to Molloy, said that as the *Daily Sketch* offered no real competition to the *Mirror*, the paper must attack the *Daily Express* to win more readers. Even examined from a distance of 35 years, Mirrorscope is a substantial piece of work. Ellis Plaice reporting from South Korea, John Pilger from Rhodesia and Jerusalem, Peter Stephens from Paris on the delayed Concorde project, John Checkley from Rome on the Catholic church and the birth control pill, a James Cameron profile of Ho Chi Minh, another, of Indira Gandhi, by Dom Moraes, and detailed but easy-to-comprehend financial analysis by city editor Robert Head.

The paper by now also had a new globetrotting writing star whose name was fast becoming as revered, and sometimes reviled, as any in *Mirror* history. Hired as a sub-editor by then assistant editor Michael Christiansen on the erroneous assumption that any male Australian must be a useful cricketer – Christiansen's passion for the game rivalled his enthusiasm for newspapers – John Pilger had willingly transferred to Manchester to pursue his ambition to write. Cudlipp shipped him back fast after a series on British youth had heralded a major new talent, and for his outstanding reporting of conflict around the world, the paper and Pilger were rewarded with National Press Awards as descriptive writer of the year in 1966 and, in 1967, journalist of the year as well as *What the Papers Say* reporter of the year.

First person FELICITY GREEN

Fields of Green: Felicity came to the Mirror as women's editor and associate editor.

Felicity Green was born in Dagenham, Essex. After an inadequate local education, she became a shorthand typist. She then wrote to the editor of Woman & Beauty magazine and was given a job as a gofer, walking the dog and making tea. In two years she became fashion editor, then left to set up a PR department for Crawfords advertising agency. Two years later, she joined the Mirror Group as associate editor, first of the Woman's Sunday Mirror, *then the* Sunday Pictorial *and then the* Daily Mirror. *Hugh Cudlipp appointed her director of publicity – the first woman to sit on the main board of a national newspaper. After a brief respite from journalism as managing director of Vidal Sassoon's European hairdressing business, she returned as editorial consultant at the* Daily Express *and then* The Daily Telegraph. *For many years she has been editorial and creative consultant to contract publishers Redwood.*

Woman's Sunday Mirror was up and running when I got a call from Hugh Cudlipp. Phyllis Digby Morton, my boss at *Woman & Beauty,* knew him well and was a guest at his wedding to Eileen Ascroft. I remember his being fairly off-hand the first time we met. I had the impression that as he had started a newspaper for women staffed almost entirely by senior men, he thought he had better have a senior woman on board – and I don't think he cared which particular woman it was. After an extremely brief interview he said okay, I could start any time I liked as women's editor. I said it seemed a bit odd being called women's editor of a paper aimed wholly at women. This was the first time I irritated him. What did I want to be called? I suggested associate editor and he speedily agreed since it obviously wasn't a matter of great import to him.

Thus began a tour round the Mirror Group that lasted 21 years. My first editor was Jimmy Eilbeck, a wunderkind from the north with the cleanest nails and hands I had ever seen. He took me to lunch at a nearby Italian trat on my first day. He was replaced by Lee Howard, whom, as associate editor, I followed first to the *Sunday Pictorial* and then the *Daily Mirror*. Lee was my mentor and his first piece of advice was to "learn to write in a fucking straight line". I have been trying to do so ever since.

When I arrived on the *Daily Mirror* I became both women's editor and associate editor and a very green field awaited me. I set up a fashion department with a talented team that included Jean Dobson, Penny Vincenzi, Penny Portrait in Paris and Terry Keane in Dublin – only much later did I discover her red-hot and long-term affair with Charles Haughey. My best-loved best colleague and best friend was, of course, Marje Proops. When she arrived, my most cynical male colleagues stood back and waited for the sparks to fly between us. None flew and Marje and I became, and remained, the best of friends all our working lives.

Maybe it was a bit dumb of me, but I expected a warm welcome when I first arrived at the Daily Mirror. But misogyny was more alive and well than I knew. After I had been there about six months, the very friendly deputy features editor, Freddie Wills, who initially had unwisely provided me with a range of bow-trimmed borders for the women's pages, asked if I was pleased that "all that hatred had disappeared?" What hatred? "You mean you didn't feel it? Just about everyone was ready to loathe you." I thought that was a bit premature... they might at least have waited till they knew me.

Continued on page 106

Frippery and fun were not discontinued. Veteran music writer Pat Doncaster – a fine piano player who was proud to count Errol Garner among his friends – and bluff reporter Don Short covered the pop and rock beat, and associate editor Felicity Green – a Lee Howard import from the *Sunday Pictorial* – masterminded the fashion coverage. Marjorie Proops, although writing a light-hearted advice column for Jodi Hyland – she had become Mrs Hugh Cudlipp in 1963 – at Woman's *Mirror* and, after its closure, *Woman* magazine, had established herself, complete with equally famous spectacles and cigarette holder, as one of the country's biggest journalistic stars with celebrity interviews and off-beat reports from around the world. Describing her travels, she wrote: "I have eaten man-sized steaks with man-sized men in the log forests of Canada, had cinnamon toast for tea at Rumpelmayer's in New York, fallen over Groucho Marx in Hollywood, watched nude ladies and gentlemen sunbathing in Stockholm..." Marje was on her way to becoming a national treasure.

First person　　　FELICITY GREEN

There were of course still some nasty moments and the macho male was in evidence everywhere, flexing his professional muscles inside nylon shirts in those pre-deodorant days. I don't think I will ever quite get over the moment when a very senior male colleague came into the features room during my first week, sniffed and said, "Great smell of cunt in here". To be fair, I wasn't the only one moderately horrified, and, in fact, much later on I grew to like him a lot!

In those days, the *Mirror* was full of hard drinkers and it was difficult to find anyone stone cold sober after lunch. If you needed a decision, it was best to get it before lunch, before the ubiquitous fridges opened and white wine flowed like whisky in every senior executive office (and some not so senior). Then came the edict from on high – chairman Cecil King, the reformed heavy drinker, decreed that, as of now, the building would be dry. Grief and disbelief abounded. Hugh, enjoying a last white wine, and as always banging the glass against his bottom front teeth, was despondent: "There'll be no one in the office next week except Cecil and Felicity Green."

Among Hugh's more quixotic tendencies was the fact that he hated both cripples and anyone with a beard, and behaved so badly in their presence that anyone with limited mobility or a hairy face was advised to give him a wide berth. He also didn't like people being ill. Arriving back at the office after a nasty encounter with a blood clot, I must have looked less than my best. "What the fuck's the matter with you?" he demanded. I made the details very brief. "Right," he said. "I'm sending you off to Barbados for a couple of weeks." And he did just that. Ah, the delights of those budget-free days.

When Hugh was around, there was always excitement and never more so than when a boardroom coup removed Cecil King from the chairman's chair. None of us on the shop floor knew anything about all this behind-the-scenes drama until we heard it on the lunchtime television news. I don't know if the word gobsmacked existed then, but gobsmacked we certainly were. The silence was broken by one backbench journalist, Fergus Linane, who had recently been verbally assaulted by the

condescending Cecil on one of his rare appearances in the newsroom. "That'll teach him to tangle with me," murmured Fergus.

One colourful bird of passage who arrived at the *Mirror* from the more sophisticated world of the *Express* was Harold Keeble. Already past his brilliant journalistic prime, Harold, a design and projection genius, had become an alcoholic. "Sad, really," he admitted, "because I was always at my best after at least one bottle of champagne." There were, however, some marvellous *Mirror* moments when Harold returned to his unsurpassed best, like when the Queen opened Buckingham Palace to the public for the first time and Harold wrote the headline CLICKETY CLICK GO THE TURNSTILES AT BRITAIN'S STATELIEST HOME. Harold was also the one responsible for bringing brilliant black-and-white fashion photography to the sludge-coloured newspaper pages of the time.

Harold was also a swine. He loved women and he loved to cause trouble, so I was on the lookout for those telltale signs, which were not long in coming. He came into my office one morning, cuddling his upper arms and rocking, a sure sign he was up to no good. "I've just had this great idea," he explained, "and you're the only one round here who could possibly bring it off. I want to do a spread on the fact that all women are either owls or larks – morning or night-time birds. Just think about it." So I did – and then I asked myself why he hadn't asked Marje, who frankly would do a much better feature on this than I ever could. So I went to see Marje and guess what? He had spun her the same line – and was now standing back to see us kill each other. We went for the kill all right, but it was his not ours. We marched into his office, hand in hand, and told him that if he ever tried such a mischievously dirty trick like that, we'd have his guts for garters. Or words to that effect!

So there I was, still learning the trade and having a wonderful time, when my life underwent a sea change. On a Friday afternoon, I was arguing with a photographer about whether or not a picture was worth the £75 he was asking when I got a call from Hugh. Would I come and see him as early as possible on Monday morning as he

---

The highly visible spending of company money also continued unabated. If he had not been a newspaperman, Cudlipp would have been a marvellous promoter of a real circus – he understood showmanship and the techniques necessary to attract customers. To this end, and to support Labour's transition from no-hopers to a party of government that, the *Mirror* predicted, would make Britain great again, he dug deep into the dressing-up box and the paper became a journalistic John Bull, talking up the country's strengths. In 1967, a series of a dozen

lavish Boom City dinners, saluting the endeavours and successes in various provincial locations, were organised by the publicity and promotions staff and given full editorial support. They were spectacular events even by *Mirror* standards and were backed up editorially by squads of writers and photographers descending on the cities to file countless positive stories and features. "The one in Leeds was especially notable because of the great words and pictures it produced," recalls Neil Bentley, a reporter in Manchester who was

Bare essentials: Felicity made her mark on the Mirror with features that captured the fun and freedom of the times.

WHICH TWIN WOR[E] THE BIKINI THAT LETS THE SUN SHINE THROUGH?

STORY: **FELICITY GREEN**
PICTURES:

had some very important news for me? A natural pessimist, I spent an uncomfortable weekend preparing for the worst. I entered his office at 9.30 precisely. "Right," he said with his usual dramatic lack of preliminaries. "From now on, you're on the main board as Director of Promotions and Publicity. What do you think of that?" To be truthful, I don't even remember what I thought – it's another moment to rely on "gobsmacked". I don't know what my fellow directors thought, either, but the finance director came down to my office immediately to tell me that my annual departmental budget was £3,500,000 and to enquire whether I knew what it meant when a figure was in brackets. I did. Just.

I really enjoyed running the publicity department. In those heady, much-moneyed days, I was allowed to design and furnish my own office. So avoiding all those ocean-going desks and clubby armchairs, I bought myself a bright red desk, lined the walls in mirror glass, and filled the room with rubber plants. Smirks and condescending smiles all round until I got a call to advise me that the boss of one of the biggest, bossiest print unions had seen my office and wanted one just like it. So for a moment back there I became an interior decorator with no budgetary restrictions. What a different world it all was!

Fast-forward five highly enjoyable years to the moment when I discovered that I was earning precisely half what the newest male appointment to the board was getting. I was cross. And so I left to join Vidal Sassoon, who I had known since our sizzling 1960s days in Swinging London; me a fashion editor and Vidal the cutter to the stars. Did I miss journalism? You bet and I couldn't wait to get back. But the wonder days of the *Mirror* – the worldwide respect the paper enjoyed, the campaigns to be espoused, the Shock Issues designed both to shock and achieve results and the daily sale of five million copies – are all long gone.

,

seconded to the Boom Cities roadshow when northern editor Bernard Shrimsley was transferred to London as an assistant editor. Bentley, who himself was soon to be sent for by Lee Howard to become an editorial fixer working from London on these kind of projects, seized upon the Leeds story of a Romanian surgeon who was using pigs' heart valves in his work and taking them home for his wife to modify with needle and thread before they were used in operations. No such journalistic gems came from a further series of dinners Cudlipp

presided over at the end of the decade, when tributes were paid to such thriving areas of British culture as the fashion and horse racing industries, but they were every bit as extravagantly staged.

With Cudlipp now chairman of Odhams as well as deputy chairman and editorial director of IPC, Edward Pickering, a former editor of the *Daily Express*, was appointed editorial director of the national newspapers in 1964, strengthening a senior executive team that had been weakened by Sydney Jacobson's

National treasure: Marje Proops quickly established herself as an indispensable asset.

appointment as editor of the *Daily Herald* two years previously. The paper marched on, launching a Northern Ireland edition in April 1966. But Michael King, no admirer of Lee Howard's isolationist style of running the paper, departed in 1967, having earlier speculatively written to his father to suggest four replacements for the editor: himself, Jacobson, city editor Derek Dale or Charles Wintour, editor of the *Standard*. Gordon Jeffrey, tough as they come but minus one leg due to a road accident, became foreign editor and remained so until, several years later, he was killed when attempting to hobble across a multi-lane highway in Los Angeles.

In other areas, the paper recruited, mostly with success, although Cudlipp's choice as successor to Cassandra of George Gale, a Cambridge double-first history graduate who had distinguished himself as a foreign correspondent and pundit during 12 years with the *Daily Express*, was not wholly so – his column "did not fit the paper as we envisaged it," Lee Howard was to say with gentlemanly understatement when Gale departed after three years. (Gale had, however, demonstrated his superlative writing skills when filing a report of the shooting of Bobby Kennedy at the

Ambassador's Hotel in Los Angeles in June 1998. So brilliant was his copy that this author, then a sub-editor, kept the original dispatch.)

With the backlash that would come from the editorial move up-market still beyond the horizon, the *Mirror* carried on in its own profligate and cavalier but successful fashion. Soon it became clear, however, that there was a major problem brewing in the paper palace: the chairman. It was not King's decision to give up alcohol on medical advice that was irking those ensconced in the directors' enclave on the ninth floor, although Cudlipp did not celebrate the conversion, or take kindly to being advised by his boss to stop drinking. Nor was it the magisterial behaviour of King's second wife, the founder of the National Youth Orchestra, Ruth Railton, who, apart from engineering substantial *Mirror* sponsorship for the orchestra, had ordered other directors' wives around at the 1964 election night party as if she were queen of King's kingdom.

The chairman's flaw was that he had developed delusions of grandeur. Grand he most certainly was, but he was not the proprietor of the *Mirror,* and when he became increasingly disillusioned with Harold Wilson's performance as Prime Minister, discovered to his great cost that he should not try to behave as though he was. In gratitude for the *Mirror*'s unwavering support during the 1964 election, the new Prime Minister had offered King a life peerage. It was refused, as was the offer of a second-string government job of Minister of State in charge of exports at the Board of Trade. But King became

Gale warning: In the opinion of Lee Howard, George Gale, formerly of the Express and a gifted writer, did not make a perfect fit with the Mirror.

Before the storm: Cecil King with Harold Wilson at the launch of Maurice Edelman's book, The Mirror – A Political History *in 1966.*

a director of the Bank of England in 1965 and it was not long before he began to lose interest in the running of the company and devoting much time to examining the ills of a country he felt was on the skids and fully expected to seize up amid social disintegration and violence.

He began to advocate to Cudlipp that the *Mirror* should urge the removal of Wilson and the installation of an "Emergency" Government of industrialists and businessmen, himself included, led by Lord Mountbatten of Burma, the former First Sea Lord and Chief of the UK Defence Staff. At this time, Cudlipp recorded, a number of fellow directors approached him with the suggestion that it was time for Cecil to go. Early in 1968, King told Frank Rogers, then managing director of IPC, that he expected to be playing some part in the running of the country, and other newspapers began to speculate that King was the driving force behind shadowy plans to replace the Government. It was that February, according to Cudlipp, that it became "acknowledged within the Corporation that the close of King's reign might have to be timed by a reluctant palace revolt against his will rather than by a gracious abdication".

Mountbatten was of the Something Must be Done school of thought and told Cudlipp, with whom he was friendly, that he believed Barbara Castle, then Secretary of State for Employment, was the person to rescue the country. Cudlipp pointed out that any approach to Castle would result in her immediately telling the Prime Minister. But he relayed Mountbatten's views to

King and the bizarre conspiracy-that-never-was came to a head when, at King's behest, Cudlipp arranged a meeting between the chairman and Mountbatten at Mountbatten's London home on Wednesday 8 May. Mountbatten, a cousin of the Queen and already determined not to become directly involved in any alternative government, invited Sir Solly, later Lord, Zuckerman, the Government's chief scientific adviser, to attend the meeting in Kinnerton Street, S.W.1. King and Cudlipp subsequently had very different recollections of what happened that afternoon.

King observed that Zuckerman left early and that "Dickie does not really have his ear to the ground or understand politics" but had revealed that the Queen was "desperately worried about the whole situation". Mountbatten asked him if there was anything he should do and King advised that there might be occasion for the Crown to intervene or for the armed forces to have an important role. "Dickie should keep himself out of public view so as to have clean hands if either emergency should arise in the future," wrote King.

Cudlipp, however, recalled Cecil waiting for Zuckerman to arrive before giving his views on the parlous state of the nation and the need for urgent action. He envisaged "bloodshed in the streets" and the involvement of the armed forces. In such circumstances, would Mountbatten agree to be the titular head of an emergency administration, King inquired? Mountbatten then asked Zuckerman what he thought and Sir Solly, heading for the door (presumably in an effort to put as much distance as possible between himself and the mad plan), paused long enough to say: "This is rank treachery. All this talk of machine guns at street corners is appalling. I am a public servant and will have nothing to do with it. Nor should you, Dickie." After Zuckerman had left, Mountbatten told King that his participation was "simply not on".

Zuckerman would later say that perhaps he should not have used the word "treachery". Cudlipp charitably expressed the opinion that King might not have heard Zuckerman's condemnation of the plan. Whatever the truth, what should have stopped King's obsessive mission dead in its tracks did nothing of the sort.

Two days later, the morning following Labour's battering in local elections around the country, the chairman commandeered the front page of the *Daily Mirror* (and those of the *Daily Herald* and *Daily Record* in Scotland) to publish his personal and soon to be infamous message alongside the election results: "ENOUGH IS ENOUGH By Cecil H. King".

The Prime Minister and his Government had lost all credibility, wrote King – "The Government which was voted into office with so much goodwill only three-and-a-half years ago has revealed itself as lacking in foresight, in administrative ability, in political sensitivity, and in integrity." A new leader was necessary, King thundered, and concluded: "It is up to the Parliamentary Labour Party to give us that leader – and soon."

The culmination of an obsession that had been occupying King's thinking for more than a year, the article was a gross act of folly. Politically, it was a hand grenade that the Government could have done without, but inflicted a wound so minor it could be treated with a small strip of verbal Elastoplast. Financially, it was far more damaging, for it included a paragraph in which a director of the Bank of England claimed the country faced "the greatest financial crisis in our history" that could not be removed "by lies about our reserves". Sterling and the equity market took a tumble. King had in fact resigned his bank directorship by letter the evening before Enough Is Enough appeared, but a weary Chancellor of the Exchequer, Roy Jenkins, did not realise fully its significance until he saw the morning newspapers the following day.

Enough is too much: The front page that was to bring about the end of Cecil King's reign.

King was done for. On Friday 10 May, the day of the *Mirror* issue that was effectively a professional suicide note, he invited to dinner some of the Group's newspaper editors and political specialists, and recorded in his diary that the editors present all approved of "the line taken" in his front-page piece. Once again, King's version of events differed to those of others present – Sydney Jacobson recollected telling the chairman that the effect of his broadside would be to rally Wilson's cabinet around him, at least for the time being.

The following Monday, Cudlipp instigated and the *Mirror* published a page-one piece headlined NO VENDETTAS. This stated that King would not retract what he said in the Enough Is Enough article and a follow-up article in similar vein in the previous day's *Sunday Mirror* (the paper had ceased to be the *Pictorial* in 1964). But it pointed out that the same issue of the Sunday paper had also carried critical replies to King from Government ministers and "Mr Wilson's boldness, whenever it is exercised, will continue to be fairly reported – and encouraged and applauded".

Meanwhile, in a scenario not dissimilar to that when Bartholomew had bitten the dust little more than 15 years previously, the IPC directors were individually and then collectively coming to the conclusion that it was King, not Wilson, that must go. The ripples caused when King had thrown his stone into the political pond continued to lap at the *Mirror*'s front door. The paper had been made to look foolish.

Legally the directors could remove the chairman by a majority vote, but from the board only unanimously. Cudlipp set about rounding up the full set for a meeting on 29 May, to be held at Orbit House, the company's satellite building on the other side of New Fetter Lane (shortly a three-storey bridge would link the two). While Cecil and Ruth dined in his office suite before going to a concert, "every director was invited to say his piece in front of every other director and did so," Cudlipp recorded. Paul Hamlyn, who had headed IPC's book division since the company had bought his publishing company in 1964 and who greatly admired King, was a lone voice in supporting the retention of the chairman. Eventually he bowed to peer pressure.

The resignation request was signed by them all and delivered to King's Hampton Court home by the company secretary, John Chandler, the following morning. The chairman was shaving when it arrived. Later that morning, Cudlipp, Frank Rogers and Don Ryder, chairman of the IPC-controlled Reed Paper Group, were summoned to King's opulent office, with its Adam fireplace over a coal fire grate, antique writing tables and Chippendale armchairs. The chairman, sitting behind his enormous octagonal desk, refused to resign. The directors retreated, regrouped – and sacked him.

King's removal was a big story. ITV interrupted its racing coverage to transmit a newsflash, which is how those *Mirror* members of staff in the building – including the editor and his executives – learned what had happened. National Union of Journalists members were at a chapel meeting a short distance away and heard the news only when I wandered in to deliver it, having passed through the office on my way there. Father (chairman) Ron Ricketts abandoned the meeting and the journalists headed at a trot for the office or the Stab, which for once had not been a hotbed of rumour concerning the impending regicide on the ninth floor.

King made the most of his last flurry of fame, appearing on television and giving press interviews – "I was stabbed in the back for my views," he told the *Sunday Express* – and succeeded in eliciting some sympathy for what he presented as the savage way in which he had been treated. At the IPC annual meeting in early June he shook hands cheerfully with shareholders, many of whom had been disappointed with their dividends in recent years but were not about to mention it to him, and listened to a speech by Cudlipp in which the new chairman claimed that King had not been fired over the Enough is Enough episode. The decision had been taken, said Cudlipp, because of "the quantity, the preoccupation, the personal intervention in national affairs" that were detrimental to the company. King responded by describing the board's action as "a conspiracy of a particularly squalid kind". But there was no overt rancour and the famous profile photograph of King and Cudlipp, grim face to grim face and apparently a study in belligerence, proved only that the camera can sometimes lie.

As the turmoil subsided, Cudlipp delegated all his editorial responsibilities to Ted Pickering and entered what was to be the least successful period of his career. Initially he appeared to be a highly capable chairman and, according to Pickering, established a genial relationship with the City. But by the end of the year it became obvious that *The Sun*, "The Paper Born of the Age We Live In" with which IPC had replaced the ailing *Herald* in September 1964, was not shining the way Cudlipp and Jacobson, its creators, had anticipated. In fact, it was almost obscured by dark clouds of debt and was threatening the future of the company. Drastic action was required.

Initially created in response to market research that suggested the public wanted more mature and intelligent newspapers, *The Sun* was now edited by former *Mirror* backbench firebrand and deputy editor Dick Dinsdale, an executive of the Jack Nener school of vocabulary, who had succeeded Jacobson when he moved up to become Odhams' editorial director. But the paper continued to wither – "We couldn't play a new tune on the old *Herald* fiddle," Cudlipp was to recall. And the term of IPC's guarantee of survival for the *Herald/Sun* had expired.

Head to head: it may look like a scene of confrontation and defiance, but in reality relations between Cudlipp and King at the IPC AGM in 1968 were not as hostile as this photograph suggests.

The fledgling chairman had choices: he could relaunch the paper as a popular tabloid and let it compete head-to-head with the *Daily Mirror;* he could shut it down, at the cost of 2,000 jobs and political and trade union wrath; he could merge it with the *Mirror,* which IPC had promised not to do when it took over Odhams; or he could sell it. In retrospect, the most sensible solution was probably that previously advocated by Cecil King, who thought the IPC *Sun* should be taken downmarket while the *Mirror* continued subtly to move towards less titillation and more edification. But this would mean replanting to change the text-size paper into a tabloid and Cudlipp did not fancy either the capital outlay that would be required or the prospect of eroding the sales of his beloved *Mirror.*

Hovering in the wings were a disparate pair of suitors for *The Sun*: Robert Maxwell, the eastern European, self-made, technical publishing millionaire, and Rupert Murdoch, the journalistically-trained Australian who had already purloined the *News of the World* from under Maxwell's nose. Maxwell wanted to turn *The Sun* into a Labour-supporting paper published only in London. He would demand staff cuts and promised to put the supervision of the title in the hands of a trust. With the presumption that was his trademark, Maxwell even canvassed for an editor, offering the job to, among others who dickered or promptly made themselves scarce, *The People*'s Bob Edwards

and Mike Randall, then of *The Sunday Times*. But the trade unions turned down flat the Maxwell plan and ran into the arms of Murdoch, a journey that retrospectively can be likened to a turkey flinging itself in the direction of Bernard Matthews.

Maxwell retired to fight – and win – another day. IPC picked up the footling sums of £50,000 plus weekly payments that took the total price to around £800,000. Murdoch walked away with a title that was still selling not far short of 900,000 copies a day and relaunched it over a weekend under the editorship of ex-*Mirror* night editor Larry Lamb, with former *Mirror* northern editor and London features executive Bernard Shrimsley as deputy. The new tabloid *Sun* shamelessly aped the old *Mirror,* even resurrecting the FORWARD WITH THE PEOPLE slogan that Cudlipp had jettisoned in 1959. There was a Livelier Letters column to compete with the *Mirror*'s Live Letters, strip cartoons that ripped off Garth and Andy Capp and even a Son of Cassandra column written by Bill's offspring, Bob Connor. And there was sex – lots and lots of sex.

Here, romping out of its cage, was a feisty puppy that would snap at the heels of its older pedigree rival until supplanting it as top dog. Yet it is difficult to see how Cudlipp could have prevented Murdoch's invasion of the popular daily market: had he not sold him *The Sun,* the Australian would have launched a downmarket

Biding his time: in January 1969 News of the World shareholders met to decide between rival bids from Rupert Murdoch and Robert Maxwell. In this telling study by Mirror *photographer Tom King, a quietly confident Murdoch listens as Maxwell puts his case. The shareholders rejected the £34 million offer from the man who would one day own the* Mirror.

tabloid from scratch and its editorial mix would still have copied that of the earlier, less grown-up *Mirror*. Former *Guardian* political editor Ian Aitken recalls asking Hugh why he "handed Murdoch the loaded blunderbuss with which he would blow away the Cudlipp *Mirror*". Cudlipp said that the print unions had advised him that if he failed to accept Murdoch's offer and attempted to close down *The Sun*, they would stop all IPC publications. "In other words, the print unions created the conditions which led to their own destruction at the hands of Rupert Murdoch. I feel there is a satisfying touch of poetic justice in that," wrote Aitken.

All this was far from Cudlipp's mind in 1969. He was, wrongly, unperturbed when, late in the evening of Sunday 17 November, the first issue of Murdoch's *Sun* arrived on the editorial floor in Holborn. He invited comments from the *Mirror*'s senior staff, but only the editor had the foresight and courage to dispute Cudlipp's mocking dismissal of this brash upstart. In his Bouverie Street building, Murdoch was telling Lamb that *The Sun* would pass the *Mirror* within five years. Lamb reckoned it would be more like ten. It took eight-and-a-half. (A poignant note was struck in 1975 when, in its written submission to that year's Royal Commission on the Press, the *Mirror* observed: "The advent of Mr Murdoch's *Sun* should dispel romantic illusions about the willingness of masses of people to respond to a higher

journalism if only the popular newspapers would raise their sights.")

If the early months of his chairmanship had been uncomfortable for Cudlipp, the pressure was not about to be relaxed. The weekly *Daily Mirror* Magazine, the first full-colour supplement to accompany a national daily paper, had set high editorial standards since its first issue on Wednesday 4 October but was failing to attract enough advertising to make it viable. Inspired by the successful *Sunday Times* Magazine, the *Mirror*'s had been launched to the advertising industry on 18 June with the paper's traditional razzmatazz – a champagne breakfast at the Royal Festival Hall and then two more lavish presentations, in Birmingham and Manchester, on the same day. The advertising agency then retained by the paper, Hobson Bates, had predicted that ad revenue for the project would be £13.5million a year – a stunning figure for the time. Even had the forecast been correct, the magazine would have struggled – the customary inflated trade union demands in most areas meant guaranteeing a weekly loss from the start.

Dennis Hackett, a highly successful former editor of Nova and by then editorial director at Newnes, part of the IPC empire, had been shipped on to the Newspaper Division board as head of publicity and promotions and director in charge of the project. Hackett, an aggressive Yorkshire Catholic, who, in temperament, was too much like Cudlipp for his own good, had previously volunteered to edit the IPC *Sun* when a replacement for John Beavan was first mooted. Paul Hamlyn took him to the Savoy Hotel and said that Cudlipp had rejected him, saying, "I'm not going to hang an albatross round that talented young man's neck." Later, when an irritable Cudlipp was complaining that "You young men don't know what you want to do", Hackett responded by saying that he knew – he wanted to edit a national newspaper. Cudlipp was not impressed. "How can I give a national newspaper to someone who is likely to turn round and tell me to fuck off," he said.

"Then, when he told me to do a dummy for the Magazine, I said to Cudlipp that I didn't think it would work," Hackett recalls. "I knew they would be pitching the ad rate too high and I didn't think the plant at Watford, where it was to be printed, had the capacity to handle a run that would be more than five million. Cudlipp looked at me and said, "Just do the fucking thing." IPC were attracted to the venture because it would be an enormous fillip for the Watford plant and a boost for Don Ryder's Reed Paper, which would supply all the newsprint. But the projected profits were wildly optimistic.

Mike Molloy, aged 28, was appointed editor, and a handful of *Mirror* journalists, including me, were merged with designers and production staff from Newnes. Searching for a bright young fashion editor, Hackett and Molloy hired Eve Pollard (who much later would edit the *Sunday Mirror*) through a misunderstanding – each nodding at the other during the interview and Hackett taking what was an expression of interest by Molloy as a commitment. Fortunately the confusion paid off: Pollard's fashion pages were an outstanding feature of a magazine that was deliberately pitched up-market of the *Mirror,* and in concept, content and look was ahead of its time.

Brian Downing, a go-ahead advertising executive, came from Newnes to head up the department that hoped to convince agencies to pay the highest page rate in British newspaper periodical publishing. Text and pictures were mostly commissioned from freelancers, although writer Russell Miller was contracted and Delia Smith, who had been working as an assistant to early celebrity chef Clement Freud, arrived to contribute a food column and subsequently marry deputy editor Michael Wynn Jones.

Former Transport Minister Ernest Marples wrote a column on "Money and how to make it", and when I, as the executive responsible for his copy, visited his Ebury Street home, would invariably open a bottle of wine for us to share while we talked over ideas. When his contract ended, he submitted a hefty expenses claim for having entertained me – Marples knew how to make money all right. Dixon Scott, a former top *Daily Mirror* features writer who had made the mistake of leaving for an assistant editorship at the *Daily Sketch,* where he had failed to settle, wrote for the Magazine as a freelance. (It was said that when Dixie informed Lee Howard that he had been offered a substantial increase in salary to go to the *Sketch* and asked Lee how

Sex sells: The advertising for Mirror *Magazine was designed to shock – but in a sophisticated way.*

Mag mania: Mike Molloy flanked by Mirror Magazine staff in September 1969. Left to right: Michael Mayhew (art assistant), John Salt (managing editor, production), Bill Fallover (art assistant), Eve Pollard (fashion editor), Herbert Pearson (copy chief), Carol Bennett (assistant art editor), David Johnson (sub-editor), and Lynn White (sub-editor). Lynn is still on the editorial staff of the Mirror.

much the *Mirror* would offer to retain his services, Lee replied, to Scott's dismay, "I wish you well at the *Sketch*, darlinck".)

Jeffrey Bernard, Soho drifter and a great but totally undisciplined writing talent, arrived to contribute features erratically and, briefly, a sports column – but only after vanishing to Spain, where I tracked him down and talked him into returning. Most mornings, Bernard's jacket was on the back of his chair when the rest of us arrived. In the carriage of his typewriter was a sheet of paper blank but for a few words of total bluff: "Bernard 3. And furthermore…" Bernard would be in the pub downstairs, having probably already enjoyed a liquid breakfast in a Smithfield Market hostelry. He continued to exert great charm, borrow money from the largely female design team, accompany the senior Magazine staff on lunchtime forays to The French House and Wheeler's restaurant in Soho – Bernard rarely had the cash to pay his way – and, in years to come, waste his gifts until the drink eventually did for him.

Patric Walker, who, like Bernard, had worked for Hackett at *Nova*, contributed an astrology column, and the gay and giggly John Crueseman, a Dunkirk veteran and former prisoner of war, who, at 50, was easily the

Out to launch: Dennis Hackett and Mike Molloy celebrate the arrival of the new baby, Mirror Magazine, at the Savoy.

oldest on a staff with an average age considerably lower than my 29, arrived from the *Daily Express*, where he had worked on the William Hickey column and as a celebrity interviewer.

The most important signing for the Magazine, at Cudlipp's prompting, was Keith Waterhouse,

First person KEITH WATERHOUSE

Keith Waterhouse was born in 1929 in Leeds and educated at Osmondthorpe Council School and Leeds College of Commerce. He joined the Yorkshire Evening Post *in 1949 and moved to London and the* Daily Mirror *just after his 23rd birthday – he was later to write that the* Mirror, *with its raffish reputation, "was regarded in some journalistic quarters… as just about as low as it was possible to sink professionally, short of working for the house magazine of a brothel". In 1958, he left to concentrate on novels, film scripts and stage plays, returning to write an award-winning column briefly for* Mirror Magazine *and then the newspaper, 1970-86. That year, he moved to the* Daily Mail *where his column still appears.*

Hands off: Keith Waterhouse.

‘There was a motley crew in the features room at Geraldine House when I arrived from Leeds. Giles Romilly, a nephew of Winston Churchill, was there – he was the one who famously was ashamed to work for a tabloid and used to introduce himself as being from "the newspaper of the times", so that whoever he was speaking to might think he said *The Times*. James Cameron was there for a while, but he didn't do much. He was on the wrong newspaper, but he could have been the *Mirror*'s John Pilger of his day if he had played his cards right.

And then there was Peter Baker, later a TV producer for David Frost, Mary Brown, a former cleaning lady who had become the paper's agony aunt, and Eric Wainwright, who in his spare time – and there was lots of that for everybody – was secretary of a drinking club for Soho waiters. Later on, there was a day when Eric stormed out of the office after an argument with the features editor and I was sent to find him. I knew he would be at the waiters' club and when I got there he was seated at a table with a drink. I sat down and opened my mouth to deliver a message instructing him to return to the office, but he straight away took a swing at me and knocked me out of my chair. He was a strong man, Eric.

The pub used by the features staff then was No. 10 Fetter Lane, or Winnie's, as it was known. It was a great bar billiards centre and the hang-out for most of the writers. There used to be these academic, almost donnish

discussions in the pub – like, What is the average time? The tradition was that everyone would come back sozzled soon after three o'clock, before which nothing much was ever done. Those days remind me of Wilde's remark to Bosey: "After I met you, I was never entirely drunk, but never entirely sober." That was the *Mirror* – I even wrote leaders occasionally when pissed and the paper was edited in a sort of semi-pissed state. But somehow it worked.

Features were mostly done on the day, with the features editor, Jimmy Eilbeck, writing headlines like "The town that died of shame" and then someone writing a piece to justify it. Jack Nener, who became editor in 1953, was like a Mississippi gambler impersonator without the accent.

Hugh Cudlipp had turned up the previous year, back from the *Sunday Express* where he had turned me down for a job. I still have the letter. He took a shine to me when I went to cover the murder of a little girl in Brighton. I went to this dreadful housing estate, high in the town overlooking the beach, and wondered to myself if a child of her height could have seen the sea from there. I crouched to make myself her height and realised she just about could have done if she had stood on tiptoes. I put all this in the piece and Cudlipp was very taken with it – he kept quoting bits of it for years.

Cudlipp's idea of popular journalism was bread and circuses, and I was fortunate to be able to do both. I remember that when Nener gave a lunch for Hugh, Marshall Pugh, who was chief features writer but really loved writing about country matters, thought that as Hugh

back in the fold he had left to become a freelance in 1958. He was now 40 and had developed into a one-man words factory – the phrase he uses still to describe his workroom at home – that turned out high-quality novels and, often in collaboration with Willis Hall, equally classy plays and television scripts. His *Mirror* Magazine column, published inside the back cover every week, was a joy, but Waterhouse also became an integral part of the office culture, turning up for lunches and parties,

competing in the Great Hopping Race from the Wig and Pen Club in Fleet Street back to the office at Christmas 1969 and, with such successes as *Billy Liar,* the hit comedy *Say Who You Are* and sketches for *That Was The Week That Was* already under his belt, was never hesitant to pitch ideas and offer advice to whoever would listen, which was everybody. It was the renewal of an association with the *Mirror* that would last another 16 years and the beginning of a Waterhouse column that

Donkey work: It's 1958, and Waterhouse works as a luggage porter (and reporter) on the Costa Brava, researching a piece on British holidaymakers.

had a reputation of liking boats, he might give him a countryside column. He pitched it over lunch and Cudlipp said: "Gentlemen, there are too many fucking tent pegs on this paper." Pugh left shortly afterwards and I became, willy-nilly, chief features writer. Nobody knew except me, I think, but I had the title and became a sort of travelling foreign correspondent, mainly filing to news but always expected to bring back a couple of features, too.

More people were fired in those days. Michael Parkin, later of *The Guardian,* was fired for filing a story in verse. I'm not bloody surprised, come to think of it. And Cudlipp could be difficult, especially at the political party conferences. He used to pick on people – it was one of his less admirable traits. Lon Jackson, the industrial corer, and Alan Fairclough, a brilliant leader writer, were his favourite targets.

When I decided to leave after writing *There Is a Happy Land,* Cudlipp came up with this brilliant idea of paying me £1,000 a year not to write for any other paper. I wanted Cassandra's job, but it appeared he wanted it, too, so I decided to go off and do other things. I wrote the occasional features series, but it wasn't until the launch of the weekly colour magazine in 1969 that I really returned to the *Mirror.* My original arrangement was to write six – many columns start that way – and six became 12 and then, just before the magazine was closed, Cudlipp called me in and said, "What if *Mirror* Magazine was to appear twice a week on newsprint – would you write a twice-weekly column?" I took the hint. George Gale had just been fired and my column replaced his and stayed there for 16 years.

Bob Maxwell was the reason I left. I knew he would interfere with my column, so I accepted the offer from the *Mail.* Maxwell – I invented the Cap'n Bob nickname after Roy Hattersley recalled that when he was an MP the old charlatan always liked using his army rank – was always trying to bribe me or cajole me to return. "What's your pension like?" he would ask me, "I could enhance it for you." And whenever I saw him he would say, "Time to come home, Keith."

But it wasn't home anymore, not with him there. And I think the great *Mirror* period had gone. It was a class thing – what used to be the working class that was the bedrock of the *Mirror*'s readership lost its base. In the *Mirror*'s heyday the readers had jobs to go to. They were craftsmen. *The Sun* attracted a different kind of people – white van man rather than the old labouring class.

As for the charmed lives we lived when I first joined the paper, I think they are gone forever.

continues – sadly in the *Daily Mail* rather than the *Mirror* – today.

There were detractors from the moment the Magazine was announced. Members of the *Mirror* editorial staff resented what looked like the pampered young crowd located on the sixth floor of Orbit House, where Sue Wade's art staff would hold al fresco lunches on the balcony and the whiff of smoke drifting down the corridors sometimes smelt strangely different to that produced by Benson and Hedges or Senior

Service. Neither Lee Howard nor Tony Miles, earmarked by Cudlipp to be Lee's successor, lent their combined considerable weight to the project. Lee, especially, was uncooperative in supporting the Magazine in the newspaper. He thought the gap between the Beatle-mopped Magazine and a newspaper more compatible with short-back-and-sides was too great. He was probably right, but had the good grace some years later, when retired to Rome, to apologise to Hackett for his attitude at the time.

First person   BRIAN DOWNING

Brian Downing was born in 1933 and educated at Sutton County Grammar School, Surrey. He joined Kemsley Newspapers as a mail order advertisement salesman in 1954 and worked at the Manchester Daily Dispatch *and the* Sheffield Telegraph *before joining* House Beautiful *and then* Woman's Own – *soon to become part of IPC – where be became advertising manager. After moving to the newspaper division as advertisement sales director of* Mirror Magazine, *he subsequently became advertisement sales director of the* Daily Mirror, *group advertisement director and group marketing director. Later, he worked at IPC, Extel, Benn Brothers and United Newspapers.*

'In 1969, there was an IPC Magazine Division launch at the Talk of the Town nightclub in London. Arnold Quick, chairman of the division and on the main board, was one of the presenters and I was another. It was all very theatrical – I was walking about with a microphone in my hand. Unbeknown to me, sitting at the back of the audience were Hugh Cudlipp and Hugh Holker, the newspaper division's ad director. I'd never met Cudlipp, who had just taken over from Cecil King as chairman of the company. After the presentation I was told that Cudlipp wanted to meet me and the first words he spoke to me were something like: "You don't want to bugger about with these magazines, Brian, you want to come and work in newspapers. You must come and join us."

I'd just finished eulogising about the virtues of magazines. The last thing on my mind was going to the *Daily Mirror*. But a few months later, I was called into Arnold Quick's office and he said: "Right, you've got to work the whole weekend. We are going to do a colour magazine for the *Daily Mirror* – I want a complete plan on Monday morning. It's the biggest thing we've ever done and you are going to head it up on the advertising side. And you will report directly to me."

So I worked all over the weekend and on the Monday morning I got a phone call from Edward Pickering, chairman of IPC Newspapers, who asked me to go to see him at the *Mirror*. When I got there, 'Pick' said, "Hugh Cudlipp is very keen on you. We want you on board with this project – and you will report directly to me." I said,

"Hold on, one minute I'm being told I'm reporting to Arnold Quick, the next to you." Pick explained that Dennis Hackett would be director in charge but said again: "Brian, you report directly to me." So, on the spot, I said that I wouldn't take the job. He said, "I promise you, we want you to do it and you will be working here in Holborn." I said, "Fine, you had better tell Mr Quick."

As a result, there was the most enormous row between the magazine and newspaper divisions, which Cudlipp won, of course. So, on Monday, I found myself in Holborn, and from that moment, Arnold Quick virtually withdrew his support. He'd told me, "You name it, you can have it." The situation culminated in quite an ugly scene when there was a meeting of Percy Roberts, Pick and Quick, and other senior directors, and Quick accused me of pinching staff. Of course, I was. Quick was very aggressive to me and he walked out of the meeting. I think it would be fair to say that the magazine division worked against *Mirror* Magazine from then on.

I used to have to go and see Lee Howard, the paper's editor, and he would mutter to me, "This magazine is out of sync with the newspaper, it's different" and he refused to signal on the front page of the paper that we had a magazine. *The Sunday Times*, with a lagging circulation, had been the first to do it – the *Mirror* was the second. You could see the logic behind it – why don't we put a magazine in the *Mirror* and we'll have a mass newspaper market answer to television? They said, "We've got this fellow, Hackett, he was originally with *Nova*, he's dynamic – it should work." Even to this day, it makes sense; it was just way ahead of its time.

Some of the traditional *Mirror* people didn't take kindly to me arriving with all these bright young blokes I had handpicked. We introduced much more creative selling, taking on television advertising, but the ad rate was the highest in the industry. The target for the first year was colossal at 1969 prices – £7million. We were unlucky in that a recession was coming, which meant a reduced spend on advertising everywhere, and, anyway, agencies were not used to paying £7,500 a page. Yet we took out of this receding market £4.5million, which was huge. But still the overall loss in the first year was £3million.

If the Magazine was also seen as an added-value attraction that would keep the new *Sun* at bay, it didn't work – those *Mirror* readers defecting to the new paper were not the kind who wanted to read Donald Zec conducting an imaginary interview with Sigmund Freud, or Nancy Banks Smith and Sheila Duncan, a former *Mirror* education correspondent, examining mixed marriages between those of different race and religion. Nor were the deserters interested in the sociological study introduced on one of the most memorable

covers – a grimy hand with a cigarette held between finger and thumb and cupped in the palm, with the cover line: Are Your Manners Working Class? They were working class. The Magazine wasn't.

After the staff had been together for a year and publication of the Magazine was in its ninth month, an issue devoted to a Guide To Sexual Knowledge was put together for 18 July, complete with a parental warning on the cover and, for the time, explicit sexual information

So, in July 1970, the magazine was folded. We had worked on it for a year. The closure was exacerbated by board disapproval of an issue which was all about sexual problems, which turned out to be the last issue and was never distributed. But it was more to do with the losses. Cudlipp was under pressure from some directors, including Don Ryder, the chairman of Reed, and when they saw a quite explicit poster for the sex issue they pulled the plug. I had no warning of it. The general feeling

Getting the message across: Brian Downing makes one of many presentations on the Mirror.

in the trade was one of sympathy and there were those who believed that if the company had stuck with the project, it would have worked. Ryder said he had no criticism of the editorial and taking £4.5million for advertising was described in the trade press as an astonishing performance.

The casualty of the closure was Dennis Hackett, whose demise was a blow. The winners were Mike Molloy and Brian Downing and others who remained with the company. Mike became an assistant editor on the paper and I was made advertising sales director of the *Daily Mirror*.

During my time, we broke every record there was going. Cudlipp wrote to me in October 1973 congratulating me on achieving a record revenue figure of £336,816 for a week in September – at that time the highest weekly figure ever for the *Daily Mirror*. Actually, Cudlipp didn't like ad people. He rather looked down on them and saw advertising as something of a necessary evil. For some reason, he took a fancy to me, but my own experience working for him was that he found it extremely difficult to say thank you, or well done.

One day, I went to Tony Miles, who was editor, and I had ten requests – ad sites, different ad shapes, my usual sort of rubbish. He was distinctly unhappy about these and said, "I'm sorry, I'm opposed to all this, the chairman will have to decide." Next thing, I get a call to go and see Cudlipp, who had Tony with him. He said, what's all this? So I went through every one with him and he gave me the biggest bollocking of my life. He was shouting at me and he turned down every request – "I'm not having advertising fuck up this paper," he said. As I was leaving, he followed me to the door and he was still shouting at me as I went down the corridor.

Continued on page 120

and illustration inside. Mildly contentious in that it was a daring excursion for popular journalism, the issue provided the chairman with an excuse to close down what had become a serious loss-maker. Hugh Cudlipp, however, was no longer the chairman.

The previous January, an increasingly disaffected Cudlipp had accepted a suggestion from Frank Rogers that an internal reverse takeover should be manipulated with the IPC-partly-owned Reed. Reed became the

controlling company of IPC in what was a radical, if demeaning, solution to Hugh's reluctant and ineffectual chairmanship. Cudlipp could stand the heat of humiliation if it let him out of the managerial kitchen and back into journalism. Sydney Thomas Franklin Ryder, the Reed boss known by his childhood nickname of Don, was appointed chairman of the new company, Reed International, and it was he who decided the Guide To Sexual Knowledge, and, more crucially, the losses of £1,945,000 the Magazine had suffered so far, were

First person **BRIAN DOWNING**

The next day, twelve o'clock, the phone rings: "Brian? Hugh Cudlipp. Come up and see me." Tony was there again. Cudlipp said, "These bloody ideas you were putting to me – we can't have that." And then he started going through them again, saying things like, "That point there... well, yes, I think you can have that", and "I think I can agree to that..." Out of the ten, he agreed four of the points, and then he said, "We'd better have a glass of wine." Later, I walked out of the office with Tony and he said, "You realise you've won, don't you?" I developed enormous affection for Cudlipp.

In March 1978, I became the first marketing director of Mirror Group Newspapers and only the second in Fleet Street. I ran not only advertising, but circulation, research, promotion, the lot, with an enormous budget. Percy Roberts, the chairman, said, "Brian, you owe me 170 million quid – this is the biggest appointment I have ever made." I told him that I wouldn't take the job until the editors of all the Group's titles, and the editorial director, came to his room and, in front of him, told me that they wanted me to do it. With the exception of the editor of *The Sporting Life,* they all turned up in Percy's office and I said that if I was going to do the job, I wanted to go to editorial conferences, I wanted to be a lot more involved, and would have a lot of opinions about editorial. And unanimously they said they wanted me.

In editorial, there was a lack of understanding of advertising's role and, in some ways, a lack of respect. My philosophy from the moment I got the job was that editorial must come first and I said all over the place that if the editorial was right, we could sell copies and we could sell ads. I developed friendly relationships with the editors and got to know the department heads and the writers. Mike Molloy said I was in Bomber Command: "What the bloody hell are you up to – who are you bombing now?"

It wasn't all easy. Roger Bowes, who had taken over as ad director, came to see me one day and said he had been to see Richard Stott, a *Mirror* features executive then, and Richard had told him to fuck off. Roger felt insulted and offended and wanted me to take up the

matter with Mike Molloy. I said, "Roger, I'll tell you what I would have done – I would have told him to fuck off back. And a couple of hours later, I would have called him and said, 'How about a glass of wine?'"

I reduced the ad ratio from 50 to 30 per cent advertising against editorial and in return the ad rate was hardened. We started to do 40-page papers and Young and Rubican did two marvellous television campaigns for us. Then I persuaded Mike Molloy and the board to increase the price of the paper so that we were 2p more expensive than *The Sun.* I went to the retailers and talked about profit – I said, "Look here, the *Mirror*'s worth a bomb to you." Soon we were no longer production led – we became a marketing and editorial-led company.

In December 1980, I was transferred to IPC. Out of the blue, Doug Long, the chief executive and deputy chairman, said to me, "There is a big job at IPC – they need a managing director of the magazines and you're up for it." I said I didn't want to go, but I was asked to go and speak with the chief executive. I told him I loved being marketing director of the *Mirror* and that I was being foisted on him. Then I came back and kept my head down, but, after a couple of weeks, Long said, "Come on, what about this job? We're all waiting on you." I said, "Doug, I really am not keen. I have been at the *Mirror* 14 years and I really love it." I think it might have been that, among some people, I was seen as a potential chief executive. I think it might have been convenient for Doug Long to see me go. Anyway, I was summoned by Les Carpenter, the chief executive of Reed, and he pulled no punches. He told me that he wanted my agreement to become managing director of the women's magazines and indicated that if I didn't take the job, I was out.

So, very reluctantly, I left. The day I walked out of the *Mirror* building the gap between the *Mirror* and *The Sun* was 12,000 copies. Sadly, my first job as marketing director two-and-a-half years earlier had been to remove "Britain's largest daily sale" from under the masthead.

It wasn't my last contact with the *Mirror.* Three or four days after Maxwell got it, he went to The Oval as a guest to a lunch that I was at. I knew him a bit because IPC was

unacceptable. The issue was pulped and surviving copies are now collectors' items. The staff was properly paid off, except for those offered jobs with the *Daily Mirror,* a saddened but grateful group that included Molloy, me, Eve Pollard – seconded to Felicity Green's women's department – and Brian Downing, who became the paper's advertising sales director. And Waterhouse's column smoothly crossed New Fetter Lane to appear twice a week in the space previously occupied by the axed George Gale.

Campaign, the advertising industry trade magazine, quoted an advertising executive on the Magazine's closure: "If Ryder had publicly guaranteed publication for a period of something like two years, it could have succeeded – the fact that it achieved £4million of a £7million target in the first year is a strong indication that it would have succeeded given time." The advertising revenue demanded was, in the circumstances, ridiculous: the average cost of reaching 1,000 housewives through women's magazines was then 12s 9d (about

A pitch in time: Advent *was a slick promotional tool for* Mirror *advertising. This "magazine" aimed at ad industry insiders featured a guest editor who singled out his favourite advertisements appearing in* Mirror Group *papers.*

his biggest client. During the lunch he banged on a glass and announced that he was thrilled to own a national newspaper group and that on this very day he was making his first senior appointment. He said, "I am really delighted to announce that Brian Downing is to become deputy chairman of Mirror Group Newspapers." Of course, he hadn't asked me. I called out, "You're joking, Bob." For an hour after lunch, I drove around with him in the back of his Rolls-Royce. I can feel his big hand on my knee even now. He was saying, "Come on, Brian, we'll do this together", and I was saying, "Bob, it won't work, because I am an opinionated chap and at the first board meeting the relationship will blow up." But he persuaded me to sit down and overnight lay out a complete sales, marketing and promotional plan and to go and see him the following day at three o'clock.

The next day, I was ushered into his ante-office, where there were about 30 people either sitting or standing, waiting to see him. A secretary rang through and I went straight into Maxwell's office. He said, "Right, are you coming?" I said no, as I had given my word to join the board of Extel. "I'm sure you'll understand that," I said. He said, "Well, have you done my document?" I sat down and went right through it very carefully with him and he didn't interrupt once. When I'd finished he said, "Very, very good" and went to his desk and got out a chequebook. He said, "What do you want for it?" I looked at him and said, "You insult me, Bob." He said I had done him a big favour and offered me money in Luxembourg, money in Switzerland… I said, "Bob, I wouldn't take a penny." And he said, "Well, everybody else does."

63p); the cost of reaching 1,000 readers through the *Daily Mirror* Magazine more than double, at 27s 6d (£1.38p).

Heavy losses in Paul Hamlyn's books division probably contributed to forcing Ryder into the premature abandonment of what could have become a powerful weapon in the circulation battles of the future. Mike Molloy recalls that the circulation of the paper fell by around 40,000 copies a day when the Magazine was withdrawn, suggesting that it was adding some 200,000 to sales every Wednesday. Not

surprisingly, the name of whoever came up with the idea in the first place was never revealed. Cudlipp went so far as to deny in print that it was his project. Hackett quotes the warning to all entrepreneurs: "Success has a million fathers, but failure is an orphan."

Hackett became the fall guy for the Magazine's losses and the horrendous expense of the *Daily Mirror* World Cup Rally, a massive promotional and editorial venture even for the *Mirror* that saw motorcars, competitors and dozens of staff hit the road from London to

First person   PJ WILSON

Peter Wilson, known when he worked at the Daily Mirror *by his initials, P.J., in order to avoid confusion with the paper's star sportswriter, was born in 1938 and educated at West Norwood County Secondary School, South London. He joined the* Norwood News *as a trainee reporter, then ventured into Fleet Street as a sub-editor on the* Daily Sketch. *He became a* Daily Mirror *reporter in 1965, followed by spells as a* Sunday People *reporter and* Daily Express *news desk assistant. He was* Sunday Mirror *news editor 1978-84 and subsequently news editor of the* Daily Mirror *and then the* Sunday People. *He left the company in 1987 following a stormy relationship with Robert Maxwell and moved to the Scottish Highlands to run a holiday business. He continued his journalistic career at long range as an editor with Globe Communications in the USA, 1993-95, and then as assistant news editor/foreign editor of the* Sunday Express, *1995-96.*

Rallying call: Peter (P.J.) Wilson.

In retrospect, The Great World Cup Rally had all the elements of a Scoop of the auto age. But at the time it was a newspaper stunt that surpassed even the legendary *Daily Mail* air races of an earlier era. As a rally, it certainly was great – great enough to fascinate a huge section of the British public and go down in history as one of the longest, toughest and richest car rallies ever to hit the road. It also cost an absolute fortune.

Officially billed as the *Daily Mirror* World Cup Rally 1970, the project – hugely ambitious and imaginative – attracted top drivers from all over the world. The route would not only cross Europe and take in some Eastern bloc countries, it would continue on to South America to tackle some of the highest and most dangerous roads possible to imagine. The route through Europe would total 4,500 miles to cover the countries competing in the World Cup. These would include Germany, Austria, Hungary, Yugoslavia, Bulgaria, and Italy and then Portugal, where the cars would be ferried from Lisbon to Brazil for the most dramatic part of the rally – an 11,500-mile drive through South America to Mexico City.

The cars would begin their arduous journey from Rio de Janeiro and then race through Uruguay and then

Argentina, where they would speed over the flat terrain of the Pampas on to what was known as the Inca Trail. This would take them over the Andes, where in Peru the competitors would tackle the highest point on the rally – a 15,870-ft-high pass. They would battle on to Ecuador and Colombia and then take a steamer through the Panama Canal, to continue through Costa Rica, Honduras, El Salvador and Guatemala before a triumphant finish in Mexico City.

It had all started in 1969, when World Cup fever – England would be the defending champions – gripped the UK. Wylton Dickson, a London promoter connected with the English Football Supporters' Association, came up with the idea of a "rally to carry the World Cup from Wembley to Mexico". The hierarchy at the paper enthusiastically supported the idea. But there were doubts that the difficult and dangerous crossing of the Andes from south to north could actually be done.

An urgent call was made to *Mirror* news editor Roly Watkins and it was agreed that the way to find out would be to send experienced rally drivers John Sprinzel and John Brown to navigate the route in the same weather conditions as the rally cars would encounter. Then, another snag. This was South and Central America – what about communications? It would be disastrous in those pre-satellite phone days if news of the events could not speedily be got back to the *Mirror*. It was decided that a reporter should go with them and it was then that fate smiled on me.

Mexico in the summer of 1970. Hackett says there was also "a difference of opinion" over the promotional response to *The Sun*, where Murdoch was spending £3.50 for every £1 the *Mirror* was prepared to allocate. "But I always thought the last straw for Hugh was my remark to him that he couldn't have his 'Hot Pants Ball' at the Dorchester or Savoy because of shortage of money, and that if he insisted on holding it, he would have to make do with the Lyceum," says Hackett. In its eternal quest for younger readers, the paper was ready to celebrate hot

pants, the fashion rage of the time. But dancehalls, which is what the Lyceum then was, were not Hugh's style. Hackett was sacked by letter on the day following Easter Monday 1971. "Couldn't you have made it Good Friday?" he said when eventually getting to see Cudlipp.

With the staff dispersed and the Orbit House offices soon occupied by other departments, all that remained of the Magazine was the regular Thursday night Stab-in-the-Back revelries that had slowly attracted many of the *Mirror* staff –

These were the days when long lunches were the norm, but as a relative newcomer to the staff I was always on the lookout for the big story and wouldn't stay out too long. I was the only journalist in the third-floor newsroom when Roly got the call that a reporter was needed to go to South America. The mission, in effect, was to time how long it took to get phone calls back to London from the various countries the rally would pass through. I rushed off to the BOAC offices in Victoria for a whole batch of vaccinations, and hasty arrangements were made to get visas from all the countries concerned. And I was given cash – dollars, hundreds of them.

Within two days, I was on my way in a British United VC10 to Argentina with a concertina of air tickets a yard long and instructions to get the second part of my yellow fever jab in Buenos Aires. Unfortunately, the doctor misunderstood my request, with the result that I was given a second smallpox jab. I retired to my hotel room feeling distinctly unwell and spent the next few days in a coma-like state with a high temperature. Fortunately, Sprinzel and Brown were delayed and by the time they arrived I had recovered enough to start on the big drive.

Sprinzel and Brown picked up a massive Ford Falcon from a local Ford dealer and we set off at full speed over some of the worst and most dangerous roads possible. First, the straight roads of the Pampas, where several times the local horse riding gauchos had to help tow us out of mud. Then followed the horrifyingly tortuous roads over the Andes where we were hit by the debilitating effects of altitude sickness and constant repairs to the car were required – including fixing a leaking fuel tank with Wright's Coal Tar Soap.

We stayed at remote inns, some where the loo consisted of a cardboard box out in the yard and others with electricity that was switched off at 9pm. One night, a rat sitting at the end of my damp bed awakened me. I was terrified – there were no lights and all I could see was a shape in the gloom. I had a

Out of this world: The sheer scale of the Daily Mirror *World Cup Rally 1970 would drive a present-day newspaper financial director right round the bend. Here lavish promotional material shows the South American leg.*

Continued on page 124

especially those from the features department – despite the general dislike of the project. Nicknamed Nights of Magic, they involved the bonding of Magazine staff and, thereafter, those from other areas. Heads became sore and marriages and other apparently permanent relationships frayed as strong liquor and the heady tonic of youth were swigged to excess in the less than salubrious surrounds of the long, narrow bar. Pat Doncaster played cool jazz piano, and features chief sub-editor Desmond Lyons, a Rabelaisian character in a blazer liberally sprinkled with dandruff, would pound out more singalong material. These were magical nights, too, for manager Bill Pierce, for whom the ringing of the cash register was even grander music to his ears. (It was Pierce's wife, Lesley, who owned the particularly irritating Chihuahua that, one evening when she paraded it through the bar, Keith Waterhouse snatched from the floor and, calling for two slices of bread, threatened to turn into a dog sandwich.)

Once the fall-out from the collapse of the

rubber torch with me, which, quite stupidly, I threw at the creature. The torch went out and I was left to sit up in my bed wide awake for the rest of the night, convinced that this huge rat would go for my throat.

At one part of the route, in Colombia, we were advised to take a gun with us. I asked a policeman why. "Well, senor, there are many banditos out there. They may pick-a your pockets and steal your money." "If that happens, my office will send me more dinero," I feebly told him. "No, senor, you not understand. They go bang bang and shoot you first – and then they pick-a your pockets."

Our car, battered and bruised, eventually gave out with a shattered wheel and terminally damaged fuel tank in some remote village. We parked it outside a seedy looking police station and told an incredulous cop: "You can keep it, senor."

Despite all this, it was decided the rally would go ahead. It started on 19 April from Wembley Stadium with a great media fanfare and 96 cars setting off for a ferry from Dover in what would be a 25-country, 24-day spectacular. The competitors were not only famed rally drivers like the "Flying Finn", Hannu Mikkola, and Paddy Hopkirk – it caught the imagination of all sections of society. Two brothers set off in their Rolls-Royce Silver Cloud and Prince Michael of Kent was among several teams of Army competitors. Star footballer Jimmy Greaves took his seat as navigator in the Ford team.

For the *Mirror*'s London-based team of reporters, it was an unforgettable time. The office was denuded as we were dispatched to various stopping points of the rally to file stories about its progress. We could have covered a war with the manpower involved. A rally desk was set up in the office, headed by editorial co-coordinator Neil Bentley. The entire event was incident-packed: it had to be hastily re-routed when snow blocked the Peruvian mountain pass and then a French driver died in Panama after a head-on crash.

My first rally assignment was in Italy, where I sat with an official in an autostrada toll booth. I was supposed to interview the drivers as they stopped, but they were in such a hurry they barely said a word. So I went on to South America, where, with *Mirror* photographers Eric

Piper and Kent Gavin, I took an airliner to the interior of Argentina. The plane was hit by a tremendous storm and the air stewardess began to cry and crossed herself as it was thrown around the sky. Then she walked along the aisle giving us not glasses – but bottles – of whisky! Eventually, we were diverted to an airport far from our destination. Elsewhere I had to act as translator to arrange nursing for an injured Australian competitor in a tiny village hospital and was then invited by the friendly English-speaking surgeon to watch them remove the appendix from a local patient.

For the *Mirror* team the assignment was wonderful fun, but keeping up with the fast-moving drivers was a nightmare, and when it was over we were all pretty shattered. We celebrated in a big way in Mexico City and then, to our horror, we had a call from the Rally Desk in London – it seemed no one had been assigned to write the story of the finish. There was a frantic rush to the phones. Of the 96 cars that left Wembley, 23 made it to Mexico City. The main prize, £10,000 and the *Daily Mirror* Trophy, went to Hannu Mikkola and Gunnar Palm, who drove a Ford Escort entered by *The Daily Telegraph* magazine.

Despite the astronomical cost of the operation, the management decided to treat its rally staff generously. I had covered the last stages with ex-Paris staffer Kenelm Jenour, and when we made our final check call, Roly Watkins told us: "Come back to the UK via anywhere you like, as long as it's more or less on the way home." Kenelm and I chose Acapulco, where we stayed at the best hotel, chatted up the local lovelies and impressed them with our big spending ways. There was one especially wonderful moment, when we were both dining with some girls in a splendid open-air restaurant beneath a moonlit sky and some exotic looking trees. Kenelm, who thought of himself as a ladies' man, switched to his best chat-up mode. He dressed like an over-the-top James Bond – including a white silk shirt with a frilly, ruffled front. Suddenly, a large fruit fell from the tree above us into his soup, splattering the shirt with red mush. It remains one of my most vivid memories of the World Cup Rally.

Magazine and the resultant upheaval in the features department subsided – Molloy became assistant editor and I replaced Doncaster as features editor – the *Mirror* continued with the serious business of fending off the growing threat of *The Sun*. Waterhouse's column, and his continued involvement in planning and ideas, bolstered a features operation that already boasted the estimable Proops, Donald Zec and Pilger. Christopher Ward – later to edit the

Daily Express – wrote a column and other youth-oriented features, and there was a squad of talented writers too numerous to ensure that any of them appeared in the paper very often. Mike Ewing and then John Knight and Tony Delano, back from the New York bureau via a stint as an executive at the *Sunday Mirror*, ran The Inside Page, which under Miles' direction had won television's *What the Papers Say* award as column of the year in 1966.

First person   JOHN JACKSON

John Jackson was born in Wood Green, North London in 1935 and educated, as a World War Two evacuee, at the village school in Spaxton, Somerset, and then Tollington Secondary Grammar School for Boys, Muswell Hill, London. He started out in journalism with The Scout *magazine and worked on the* Birkenhead Advertiser; Orillia Daily Packet and Times, *Ontario, Canada;* Auckland Star, *New Zealand (twice);* Manchester Evening News; Hamilton Spectator, *Canada; Rand* Daily Mail, *South Africa;* Daily Herald *and the IPC* Sun *before the* Daily Mirror, *1969 to 1993, and then* Today.

One to one: John Jackson chats to the Princess Royal.

6 When it comes to world impact, the two biggest stories I covered were the 1972 Munich Olympics massacre and the release of Nelson Mandela in 1990. At Munich the *Daily Mirror*'s experienced team sprang into action once the early morning news of the killing of Israeli athletes in the Olympic Village reached the nearby press centre. Well, most of them sprang, but Frank Taylor went for a long lunch and Ron Wills went off to play golf – "This is down to you, Jacko, nothing to do with sport."

Peter Wilson, our legendary sports columnist, immediately volunteered to act as a runner, even abandoning his place in the laundry queue because of the enormity of the tragedy. Two newsmen took control. Bonn correspondent Dennis Martin, with his obvious command of German, stayed at the main press centre to monitor the wires, local TV and hurriedly called press conferences. I sped to the sealed-off Village and managed to gain entrance with the connivance of Britain's former Olympic long-jump champion Lynn Davies (he repeatedly pulled his jockstrap and dirty clothes from his bag each time the baffled guards asked for his identity pass, so allowing others to slip past unquestioned).

Later, I followed by road, in a hastily summoned taxi, the helicopter carrying the Arab terrorists and their hostages to Fürstenfeldbruck airport. I was there when the shooting started, the helicopters were blown up and the death toll rose to 16. Then it was back to the press centre for the 3am final press conference.

Back in London, Hugh Cudlipp had decided that the main spread should be written by Peter Wilson. After all, The Man They Couldn't Gag had seen it all. His first Games had been in Berlin in 1936, with Adolf Hitler taking centre stage, and here he was at the age of 60, ending his Olympic career in the same country, with this horrendous terrorist attack. So, in Munich, Wilson sat down at his typewriter (which at one point had made the Guinness Book of Records as the most travelled typewriter, and was double its weight because of the wodge of airline labels still attached to the case), stressing to colleagues that he had no intention of making out he arrived to cover sport and finished up reporting a war. "None of that, old boy," he said.

Cudlipp had different ideas. The copy was sent straight to him on arrival in London and he made the odd change (not the sort of subbing Peter Wilson would normally entertain). And on Wednesday 6 September 1972 Wilson's first-person account of the Munich Massacre appeared with the intro: "I came to Munich as a sportswriter. Today, I'm a war correspondent." Wilson simply shrugged and ordered some more whisky.

Cudlipp had also been keeping an impressed eye on the amount of copy from Dennis Martin. In fact, *Daily Mirror* readers on that Wednesday would have thought Martin and Wilson were the only *Mirror* men in Munich. Unknown to everyone, especially me as I filed

Continued on page 126

Nights of Magic continued to fill the Stab every Thursday for months. They probably lasted longer than the career of the Greyhound of that name, bought as a puppy by art editor Paddy O'Gara and me on behalf of a features consortium during an executive visit to the *Mirror*'s Belfast office. The dog, trained at the White City, won once and then dead-heated for first place in a race where it was just unable to

forge ahead of its nearest challenger. It was a situation the *Mirror* itself was soon to experience.

With Ryder's elevation, Cudlipp's editorial powers had been totally reclaimed. The *Mirror* had fought its customary vigorous campaign in the June 1970 General Election, but a late swing had seen the Conservatives returned to Government with a slender overall majority reams of copy from all the action spots, Martin had instructed the copytakers that every piece of phoned copy from Germany had to have his name on it.

The only by-line I received was on a few paragraphs of interview with Mark Spitz, the American swimmer who won seven gold medals but was removed from the Olympic Village urgently as he was Jewish. And that copy was actually filed from Heathrow Airport by reporter Tom Merrin! Martin's "great work" was rewarded by Hugh Cudlipp, who invited him and his wife to enjoy an all-expenses-paid holiday anywhere in the world. They chose Israel.

On to 1990, when to stand at the gates of Victor Verster Prison, 40 miles outside Cape Town on February 11, a ferociously hot Sunday, and witness Nelson Mandela walking to freedom, hand in hand with then wife Winnie, was the fulfillment of a dream. I could paraphrase the famous report from the BBC's Brian Hanrahan during the Falklands War: "I counted them out, I counted them in". I am sure I was the only one standing on the road, surrounded by deliriously happy Africans singing and dancing, who could boast: "I saw him in, now I've seen him out". And if I ever get a chance to meet the great man, I will inform him that the first move he made as a free man was to step into a chauffeur-driven limousine – and drive over my foot.

Twenty-seven years earlier, I had been a staff reporter on the *Rand Daily Mail* in Johannesburg. My wife, Barbara, and I lived near to Rivonia where Mandela was standing trial. Apartheid ruled, and life was nasty. My next visit to South Africa did not come until the start of 1990, when I flew out with Mike Gatting and his team of cricket rebels for a disastrous tour of a country still banned from international sport. I must have been the only reporter with a travelling international cricket team who was under instructions to write not one word about the on-field play. Mind you, I need not have worried about a possible dearth of news stories, as Gatting was to manage far more faux pas than centuries.

It was Gatting who was on my mind when the amazing news that Nelson Mandela was about to be released was flashed around the world. I was sitting in the press box at

the splendid Wanderers ground in Johannesburg on a hot Saturday afternoon with South Africa and England locked in yet another unofficial Test Match battle. England lost two early wickets and once again we had skipper Gatting heading for the crease.

Cricket followers will know that the walk from the dressing rooms at the Wanderers is especially long. As Gatting stepped from the dressing room, the Reuters man in the Press Box yelled: "Mandela will be freed at 3pm tomorrow". I lunged for the telephone and dialled the *Mirror* office in London. As it was a Saturday, I went through to foreign editor Nick Davies, who was assisting the *Sunday Mirror*. He suggested I phone the editor, Roy Greenslade, at his home in Brighton.

Gatting had reached the boundary and was striding toward the middle. By the time I had got through, Gatting had taken guard and was facing his first ball. The phone was answered by Roy's wife, *Daily Mirror* feature writer Noreen Taylor, and my immediate desk-mate in the editorial office. I watched what was happening at the wicket with horror as she exclaimed excitedly: "Isn't it wonderful!" Instinctively, I replied: "No it's not. Gatt's just been bowled first ball".

So it was an evening flight to Cape Town, a rush drive to the prison, another back to Cape Town for the amazing celebrations, followed by a Monday return to ensure a place in the main stadium for Nelson Mandela's triumphant return to Soweto. Who cared about cricket after that? Even the rebel cricketers packed up and went home.

I was lucky enough to work on many great stories. After John Stonehouse's disappearance and re-emergence, the first indication that the Postmaster General and his secretary, Sheila Buckley, were an item came after some brilliant ferreting around hotels in Hawaii by Syd Young, then in the *Mirror*'s New York bureau. He discovered phone calls had been made by Stonehouse to a small hotel in Hampstead. On receiving this news, night news editor Dan Ferrari said he would send "a small team who will quietly go through the place".

And that's how Ed Vale (at 17 stones), Terry O'Hanlon

of 30. This time, Cudlipp did not petulantly turn his back on politics, although, as it transpired, it would be the last General Election in which he would guide the *Mirror*'s coverage.

Internally, he still dominated the papers. With his approval, I was appointed features editor by Tony Miles and taken only later to meet the editor for the first time. Lee Howard was magnanimous and encouraging – the days of "What cunt subbed this?" and the bullying of staff had all but been eradicated under his editorship. Except, that is, for the occasions

when Cudlipp, normally with too much drink inside him, used the erudite Alan Fairclough as a ventriloquist's doll, humiliatingly perching him upon his knee, or berated others whose efforts or behaviour he felt unworthy of the greatest popular newspaper in the history of journalism. (At the 1972 Labour Party conference at Blackpool, I had the temerity, or stupidity, to attend wearing a beard. Hugh loathed beards, and at a dinner table crowded with other executives rasped, "Who does he think he is – Jesus Christ?" and then started

Tartan army: Jacko prepares for the Wembley walk that thousands of Scots would undertake on Saturday 24 May 1975, heading for the England v Scotland International.

(another heavyweight), Revel Barker (hugely tall), John Jackson (then a slim 13 stones), John Penrose (a lightweight), Ronnie Maxwell and Nick Davies (both smaller than the rest of us), went through the front door like a whirlwind. The smallest of all, photographer Harry Prosser, probably the most accident-prone man ever to hit Fleet Street, walked straight into the glass interior door, was temporarily knocked out and alerted everyone in the place.

A few days later, I was the first reporter to knock on Sheila Buckley's door. She appeared impressed. Although saying nothing at first, constantly denying she had been anything other than Stonehouse's secretary, she asked me to return later, dismissing notes offering huge sums of money being pushed through her letterbox by such heavies as Peter Earle, of the *News of the World*. I

returned at the same time as colleague Nick Davies, who was also allowed entry as he was from the *Daily Mirror*. After a few moments, Sheila Buckley asked me: "How can one paper have such opposites – a Mr Nice and a Mr Nasty?"

By this time, two other reporters had gained access along with Buckley's parents: Keith Deves, from our great rival, *The Sun*, and a certain Anne Robinson from *The Sunday Times*. Robinson was no threat as she would not be writing for several days, but Deves had to be removed. I knew he would follow me wherever I went, so Mr Nice left the house, leaving Mr Nasty with Buckley. Deves chased after me and the Nice-Nasty combination worked perfectly – the next day, the *Mirror* had the exclusive splash confession: "My Love for John Stonehouse".

When news came through of the Pan American 747 explosion over Lockerbie, the *Daily Mirror* editorial department was enjoying its Christmas party in the first-floor Rotunda restaurant in Holborn. Editor Richard Stott was summoned to the phone, then turned to all his reporters and without saying a word, thrust both thumbs in the air to signal everyone to return to the third-floor newsroom. Glasses were promptly downed. It was obvious this was serious.

At the very time as the reporters were heading upwards, publisher Robert Maxwell was on his way down to join the fun. He arrived to find an all-female party made up of secretaries and the odd wife and girlfriend. But having a flamboyant proprietor was a plus that day for everyone except Stott's driver, John Brockington, who was stopped for speeding in the Hyde Park under-pass as he ferried reporters and photographers to Maxwell's appropriated private jet at Heathrow.

verbally to crucify me. With the honourable exception of Felicity Green, who chided him for his bad temper, the rest of those present understandably attempted to make themselves invisible.)

The news operation, under long-time servant Roly Watkins, and production area, from which veteran Geoff Pinnington had been plucked to become Lee's deputy after Bryan Parker had departed, still functioned like athletes that had no doubt they were world class. But Lee, overweight, over-tired and far from

overwhelmed at the prospect of a drawn-out battle with *The Sun*, was ready to bow out once he had completed ten years in office. Cudlipp had already promoted Miles to associate editor so that he could leapfrog Pinnington into the editor's chair. Lee's dubious health determined that he didn't quite complete his decade, and, on 29 January 1971, he was applauded the length of the editorial floor when he walked to the backbench for a farewell presentation. The reception was generated by genuine affection, but also through the deference of some

On your marks: Lee Howard in the editor's chair for morning conference in his Holborn office.

members of staff who were seeing the editor in the considerable flesh for the first time. Lee's appearances in the newsroom were rare indeed.

Photographs of each department had been mounted in a handsome presentation album (when the features personnel had gathered in the office studio, Molloy and I met, for the first and only time, Sidney Tremaine, whose job was answering the editor's letters and of whose existence, let alone his inclusion on the features payroll, we were unaware). Lee accepted his gifts graciously, stayed only briefly at his farewell party upstairs in the Printer's Devil, then went home and shortly afterwards left his wife, easing his bulk into a Mini and departing for Rome to marry and spend happy years with *Mirror* correspondent Madalon Dimont.

With Miles settling uncertainly into the editor's chair, the staff acknowledged the end of a *Mirror* era that had seen the paper achieve apparent omnipotence. Then it rolled up its collective sleeves to deal with the threat that

had come whistling from further than out of left field – all the way from Australia. But if *The Sun* had a dynamic proprietor in Murdoch, the *Mirror* was comforted by the continuing presence of the man long acknowledged as the finest popular journalist of all time.

Unfortunately – or not, depending on one's regard for him – the finest popular journalist of all time had other ideas. In October 1972, Cudlipp announced that he would retire at the end of the following year, by which time he would have turned 60. He thought it right to make way for younger men, he said, and later was to observe that one of his editor brothers, Percy Cudlipp, Herbert Gunn (editor of the *Evening Standard, Daily Sketch* and *Sunday Dispatch*), Percy Elland (*Evening Standard*) and Arthur Christiansen (*Daily Express*) all died years before they were 60 – "I was the one who got away". But where was the *Mirror* to go without him?

7
THE MINK-LINED COFFIN

*I*t is a festive Saturday evening in 1973 and the Daily Mirror *is preparing to bid farewell to Hugh Cudlipp. There have already been several parties to pay tribute to the enormous contribution he has made to the Group's newspapers over the years, and there will be several more. But tonight's affair is the grandest of them all: a dinner in the Painted Hall at Greenwich, to which the guests – practically the entire editorial staff of the daily paper – are ferried from Charing Cross Pier by Thames riverboats. Once on board, the already boisterous hacks are handed glasses of champagne, which continues to flow as the boats proceed downriver. By the time they nose towards the landing stage at Greenwich, it is obvious that the unlimited hospitality may mean the event does not go exactly according to plan.*

Some of the journalists do not even reach the Royal Naval College. Teddy Prendergast, who works in editorial liaison between London and Manchester offices, is lost for several days, reappearing to sing the praises of a number of Greenwich public houses. At dinner itself, bread rolls are thrown, glasses are smashed and the odd drunken skirmish breaks out. Venerable gardening columnist Xenia Field is hit in the eye by an airborne Brussel sprout. When science correspondent Arthur Smith, whose nose is always of a slightly more crimson hue than the rest of his face, is struck by a flying radish, Richard Stott, the reporter who within a little more than 12 years will be editor, picks it up and cries, "Hey, Arthur, you've dropped your nose." The speeches are barely audible, partly because of constant interruption but also because the speech of many of those getting to their feet is hopelessly slurred.

The return boat journey, which managing director Percy Roberts, in fear of his life, refuses to undertake, brings the evening to a chaotic conclusion. Features writer Eric Wainwright falls asleep in a flowerbed before he reaches the Savoy Hotel room he has booked for the night. This shindig and other events held up and down the country are later estimated by Sunday Mirror *editor Bob Edwards to have cost around £50,000 – upwards of £350,000 at today's values. The following Monday, those who can remember being at the great Greenwich debacle agree that it was money well spent...*

Cudlipp's decision to retire had not been opposed by Reed. Alex Jarratt, the number two civil servant at the Department of Employment who had been the Government representative during the reverse merger with Reed, had been drafted in as IPC managing director in 1970. Jarratt was waiting in the wings to assume the chairmanship, but Cudlipp wanted a journalist to succeed him and told a number of senior *Mirror* executives that he had the very man, "Mr X", in mind. This was Harold Evans, celebrated editor of *The Sunday Times*, who met with Cudlipp, Ryder and Jarratt at Reed's Piccadilly headquarters and was offered the job of editor-in-chief. Evans went away to ponder the proposition, and several days later met Jarratt and Ryder at the Holborn building and lunched with Cudlipp. Evans, still heavily involved in his paper's now historic thalidomide exposé, decided not to accept the offer, but did not leave empty handed, Cudlipp having suggested over lunch that Evans should put the protracted court proceedings over the thalidomide series into a book. He duly did so,

Mr X: Harold Evans of **The Sunday Times** *was targeted by Cudlipp for the* **Mirror** *chairmanship.*

but not before being approached for a second time at the end of 1974, shortly before Ryder had left Reed for the National Enterprise Board and Jarratt had replaced him as chairman, when the title of chief executive was discussed. Again Evans declined, feeling he could not sever his ties with *The Sunday Times*. Cudlipp was deeply disappointed that his grand plan had not worked out.

Hugh may have gone, but his *modus operandi* was not forgotten. The *Mirror* was used to spending money like there was no tomorrow and the fact that tomorrow was obviously going to be a lot less rosy than yesterday initially made little difference. As features editor, I do not recall ever being presented with a contributions budget. Salaries were not over-generous, but personal expenses were colossal. When I had been drafted temporarily into the features writing team before the launch of *Mirror* Magazine, I was told to ask features editor Pat Doncaster about "exes". "Thirty pounds a week," Doncaster told me – this was 1968, the year after I had joined the paper as a sub-editor on £47 per week. After a tantalising pause, Doncaster added: "…unless you have to

spend anything", and then wisely counselled that what was the equivalent of a massive salary increase should not be used to pay the mortgage. "It's fun money," he said, correctly recognising the damage that could be caused to the financially foolhardy when the gravy train was eventually derailed. When columnist George Gale was about to depart several years later, it was discovered that he owed thousands of pounds in advances against expenses that he had never justified. Gale sighed, took the proffered claims sheet and wrote: "To expenses from…" followed by the starting and finishing date of his *Mirror* employment. There was nothing the management could do but accept it.

The system of drawing advances against expenses from the hatch in the wall of the tenth floor "bank in the sky" was extraordinary. On Friday evenings, a queue of editorial staff members and the secretaries of executives would form outside the hatch as sums ranging from ten to several hundred pounds were collected to see the recipients through the weekend. Those who fell behind in submitting detailed expenses claims were denied such advantages unless an executive of at least assistant editor rank – possessing the "golden arm" – signed their advance "chits". Assistant editors tended to vanish on Fridays as marauding "out-of-date" reporters, writers and senior sub-editors – for a period even some desk-bound subs were allowed expenses – searched for the signature that would provide weekend beer and, perhaps, groceries money.

If expenses were spinning almost out of control, the availability of taxis to take home those on late shifts was also in need of radical surgery. For a while, a telephone call from almost anyone on the editorial staff was all that was needed for a cab to be ordered. When it was realised that taxis were not only taking subs and writers to their homes, but sometimes also to someone else's home where the cab would be kept waiting outside for as long as whatever was going on inside took, executive authorisation was introduced. At around pub closing time – not necessarily the licensing law hour, but whenever a pub decided to stop serving – senior executives were once again required to take to the hills.

Des Lyons, the enormously talented but wayward chief features sub-editor, helped necessitate even stricter control of the late car system by frequently diverting drivers to the Press Club, where Des would remain for several hours as the meter ticked away out in the street. He was rarely required to work especially late but often would not make it home to Kent at all. After one office Christmas party, he returned to the features room with a set of identical young female twins, both of whom lisped. They danced for Des on the subs' table before whisking him off into the night, doubtless providing him with an unforgettable experience while at the same time saving the company the price of a cab.

Just as it was careful with salaries, the *Mirror* policy regarding company cars was initially stringent, with only the editor and his deputy being provided with vehicles as part of their salary packages. As the 1970s progressed, this was, through various in-house arrangements, relaxed to the point where, it seemed, few were junior enough *not* to qualify for a company car. Later, one director was rumoured to have two. Whether or not this new strategy cut down on taxi bills was never revealed.

But despite sneers of those working on rival newspapers that the *Mirror* had become "a mink-lined coffin", the paper was still producing good journalism and, for much of the 1970s, refused to acknowledge that *The Sun*'s formula for success could permanently dent a popular journalism culture that had been developed by some of the greatest talents in the business over six decades. Mink-lined it may have been, but the *Mirror* was not ready to be buried.

Tony Miles, brusque, uneasy around women journalists and – the last to follow what had been an executive tradition – prone to address all male colleagues as "cock", had early in his tenure manipulated the removal of his deputy and former rival for the top job, Geoff Pinnington, who went to edit *The People*. Michael Christiansen, the often journalistically inspired but also wildly erratic editor of the *Sunday Mirror,* had blundered once too often and Cudlipp fired him, replacing him with *The People*'s Bob Edwards and offering Christiansen the choice of a generous pay-off or the deputy editorship of the daily paper. To the surprise of everyone and the horror of some, Christiansen accepted the latter and transferred his skills and quirky personality from the fifth floor to the third.

Miles wore the editor's crown almost apprehensively, and with some reason. Morale among his journalists may have remained buoyant, but the decade had begun turbulently for the *Mirror* – in 1971, the IRA had blown up the company's £2,000,000 printing plant at Dunmurray, just outside Belfast, which, although covered by insurance, put paid to a bold initiative – and for Fleet Street itself, where a series of industrial disputes had seen millions of copies of several titles lost. Some of these at the *Mirror* involved the editorial staff, which in the late 1960s had become the first national newspaper chapel (in-house branch) to win the right to negotiate "house agreements", rather than accept the blanket deals made by the National Union of Journalists.

In 1971, a NUJ house strike over salaries and conditions collapsed when senior executives managed to bring out a 16-page paper. That September, a National Graphical Association Fleet Street dispute, during which chapel meetings were constantly held in production time at the *Mirror,* lasted for more than a week and resulted in the loss of millions of copies and millions of pounds of lost revenue. *The Sun* was hit only slightly. Engineers then halted the *Mirror* for a day in November. But these were minor skirmishes compared to the industrial unrest of 1973-77, which included another journalists' strike, in Manchester and Glasgow in February 1974, that saw IPC withdraw temporarily from the Newspaper Publishers Association as a precautionary measure against losing the paper during the forthcoming General Election.

Dozens of editions were lost in London or Manchester, and often at both printing centres, as the print unions responded to what the *Mirror* described to the 1975 Royal Commission on the Press as management seeking "to eradicate the traditional proprietorial paternalism expected by employees where all decisions are made at the highest level". Union reaction was to demand that many decisions were made at union level. Overmanning in production areas alone was costing the company £5.3million in 1975.

Then, in November 1977, the print unions agreed to allow what was the speculative installation of computer typesetting only after negotiating an increase of £3,000 per man. The journalists were ignored. Steve Turner, who had succeeded the shrewd but less militant Bryn

Tony Miles was born in 1930 and educated at High Wycombe Royal Grammar School. He joined the Daily Mirror *as a feature writer in 1954 and ran The Inside Page column and Mirrorscope before becoming assistant editor (features) in 1967. He was associate editor, 1968-71, editor 1971-74, editorial director 1975-84, deputy chairman 1977-79 and, briefly, also in 1984; and chairman 1980-83. After leaving the group, he became executive publisher of Globe Communications in Florida, USA. He now lives in London and Somerset.*

'Features was a good department when I joined in 1954. Keith Waterhouse was there, and Douglas Howell and Fergus Cashin, who went to the *Daily Sketch* – it was a really strong team and the papers were quite small. I was an ordinary feature writer, but I did some series and then a few things for Cudlipp. Then he gave me The Inside Page, which I started. I stuck out for the name, which Cudlipp wasn't too keen on. But the morning it started, Cudlipp was going up in the lift with Cecil King, and King said: "Any fool can kill a column, but it takes skill to produce a much better one." That was the accolade and Hugh loved it. The Inside Page went on in its first year to win the *What The Papers Say* column of the year award.

Next, I went on a trip to Africa with Cudlipp. I was taken aside before we left by Roly Hurman, the industrial editor, and Michael King, the foreign editor and Cecil's son, who said, "He'll be tricky – if there is any trouble, phone us immediately." Cecil King's brief to Cudlipp had apparently been, "Investigate the Chinese influence in Dar-es-Salaam". That was his mission! I had my typewriter with me and Hugh would send messages back to Cecil, who was acting like a potentate. We met all the African leaders except in South Africa, where nobody from the government would meet us. Hugh had a natural curiosity, although he was never a news man – he wasn't interested in news as such. At the paper, when there was a big news story, I never once saw him come down from his office and say, "Right, we'll do this and that". Never. The only major stories I remember him masterminding were royal weddings. He was a brilliant tabloid journalist but he'd have nothing to do with news.

I didn't see much of Cecil. No one saw much of Cecil.

He gave Hugh a bit of a rough ride – Hugh really did stand to attention when Cecil came on the phone to him. Nobody really saw King's demise coming. On the day it happened, I was in Lee's [Lee Howard's] office watching the racing on television and suddenly there was a newsflash – Cecil King was leaving. So the first thing the editor knew about it was when it interrupted him watching the racing on TV. No one on the paper had an inkling of it.

People say that Hugh went in the wrong direction when he introduced Mirroscope, but he thought the public was becoming more educated and also he wanted the paper to move away from *The Sun* – the same policy Piers Morgan adopted, really. Hugh was very proud of Mirroscope, which was his idea. I edited it and Mike Molloy was very much involved.

There has been a lot said and written about Lee Howard being fired, but he wasn't. It wasn't a firing – he felt he'd done ten years and had enough, and Cudlipp thought he'd had enough, so there was an agreement that they would call it a day and the paper would look after him. I think if Lee had said he didn't want to go it might have been a problem, but he was quite happy about it. I was then told, about three months before he left, that I would be taking over.

From the start, Geoff Pinnington resented me – it was the old news versus features battle – and I wasn't getting on with him as my deputy, so I moved him out. Suddenly there was a vacancy for an editor at The People – Bob Edwards was going to the *Sunday Mirror*. Hugh said, "God, what are we going to do about *The People*?" and I said, "I know just the man to edit it – Geoff Pinnington." "Brilliant," Hugh said, not knowing that it was the best thing I could possible have wangled for myself. In fact, it wasn't a good idea – I think *The People* was softened under Geoff. He didn't keep its campaigning heart.

The vacancy at *The People* had arisen because Mike Christiansen had gone slightly bonkers at the *Sunday Mirror*, running a series on magic mushrooms, and Hugh said, "We've got to do something about this". Mike was offered the choice of leaving and getting a pay-off or becoming my deputy. Many years before, I'd been a young boy working for him, but when it was put to him he said, "I'll work for Tony".

Jones as Father of the NUJ Chapel, demanded parity, but chief executive and newly installed chairman Percy Roberts argued that the company could not afford such a demand. Badges demanding "Three Grand In My Hand" were worn throughout a series of disruptive meetings that stopped the paper. Roberts responded by suspending publication and issuing dismissal notices. Editor Mike Molloy, although broadly sympathetic with the journalists' claim, remains bitter that circulation gains on the back of three powerful series – Joe

Haines on Harold Wilson, publicist Chris Hutchins on Tom Jones and Engelbert Humperdinck, and Richard Stott's damning exposure of match fixing by soccer boss Don Revie – were destroyed by giving *The Sun* a free run for 11 days.

Media commentator Roy Greenslade, himself briefly a *Mirror* editor at the beginning of the 1990s, has disputed the claim, pointing out that the drop was not significant, and soon reversed, and that the following summer *The Sun* was not

Here's to us, none like us: Tony Miles (right) raises a glass with Bob Edwards (centre) and Percy Roberts.

I was editor for about three-and-a-half years, which wasn't long enough really, but Cudlipp went early in 1974 and Sydney Jacobson was going to leave and I succeeded Sydney as editorial director. We had to decide who was going to be editor, and Christiansen had been a good deputy and had overcome his magic mushrooms phase. I said I thought he could be a very good editor. He was full of enthusiasm and he encouraged the troops, so, once again to everyone's surprise, he was made editor and Mike Molloy became his deputy. But after only a few months, Mike Christiansen was taken ill, on my wedding day actually, 1st May 1975. Because of our entry into the Common Market, he was editing the paper from Paris. He was invited to the wedding, and he and Mike Taylor were to drive back. Christiansen had a heart attack in France and they got him back to Folkestone and into hospital. Ted Pickering, who had come in as chairman, had to tell him that he wasn't fit enough to come back to the editorship, which was exactly what he had had to tell Mike's father, Arthur Christiansen, when Pick was his deputy at the *Daily Express*.

The reason I became chairman was that I chucked my hat in the ring when it looked as if Douglas Long [another senior director] might get it. I was very lucky – I was in the right place at the right time. I moved up so quickly I didn't

Continued on page 134

published, also for 11 days, when its journalists were in dispute over pay. But Molloy is adamant: "The *Mirror* lied about its circulation figures at the time because they did not want the trade to know just how badly we had been damaged. Tony Griffin, then in charge of circulation, had told me the paper would soon be back over 4 million, but the journalists' dispute left us with a sale of 3.1 million. I was a director of the company, and know full well that in those days circulation figures were often faked. They were padded by printing enormous amounts of copies and then, when a genuine rise in sales occurred, losing previous 'waste' in the returns. It was bloody difficult to discover the true figures." Whatever the culpability of the NUJ chapel, by the end of November 1977 *The Sun*'s circulation glided past that of the *Mirror* and from then on only rarely had to look over it shoulder.

Back in 1972, Tony Miles had experienced his own trades unions nightmares. The introduction of the Industrial Relations Act had provoked the really get my feet under the table where I really wanted to. I had a fair amount of time as editor of the Mirror, but things were tough in those days with both the unions and the lack of proper investment in promotions. Being chairman was all right – I got £60,000 a year – but I hankered to have a hand in the paper and you can't really do that as chairman. I was sort of chairman and editorial director really, concentrating on the editorial side. Hugh had hated being chairman of IPC because that wasn't his thing. He only did it because there was no one else around and he didn't like it. When he left, Reed were quite glad in a way because he was in charge of the whole shooting match and he wasn't really a businessman. He felt a bit frustrated. I'm sure if he had not been chairman of IPC he would have stayed on, as editorial director, after he turned 60.

When we realised Reed wanted to unload Mirror Group we got in Clive Thornton. That was, in fact, a mistake. He wasn't the right man for it. There were other people hovering around, such as Tiny Rowland, looking to buy the group. We asked Bob Head, the *Mirror*'s city editor, and he came up with this name. Thornton was the boss of the Abbey National and all our readers knew of him – many of them bought their houses through him. He was sort of flavour of the month and was a popular choice with readers and in the City, but he wasn't right for the *Mirror*. He suddenly decided he wanted to do things that Reed didn't want him to do. He came up with this idea of the golden share, which could be used to vote against anyone getting sole control of the company. It would have acted like a veto and would have made it impossible for it to be sold to any one person. He wanted it owned by the workers, by everybody. But Maxwell got to hear of it and realised he had to strike then.

I stood down as chairman and Thornton came in on 1 January. I got on all right with him but he wasn't a man who fitted into tabloid newspapers. He didn't drink and he had no idea how newspapers worked. He was supposed to take over the job Percy Roberts had done, running the place. He was a nice man and he meant well, but he thought he could talk to the unions –

"We're all in this together, boys, and you'll all have a share…" Good stuff, but in the reality of life the print unions didn't give twopence about the paper, they only cared about their money.

I learned about the Maxwell deal only on the morning of the day it happened, when he moved into a suite at the Ritz Hotel opposite the Reed building. We basically knew only what we read in the papers – Reed wouldn't tell us anything. We had been assured by Reed that they would not sell to any individual. Jarratt phoned me at midnight in the office. We had been having dinner with the people who had been put forward as non-executive directors of the new Mirror Group when we floated it. Suddenly, at midnight, the telephone rang and it was Jarratt. He said, "Well, we've sold to Maxwell, sorry about it. But he has promised he will not come to the building tonight." I wasn't angry – there was no point. But I think it probably was a massive betrayal on their part and also very bad business – they gave it away. Whether there were that many people queuing up to buy it is another matter, but Maxwell basically got the company for the price of the building.

Then there was a phone call saying that Maxwell was coming in through the front door. So I went home, but, when I got there, my wife said Douglas Long had been on the phone and that he thought I should go back. I did go back, by which time Maxwell had been wandering around the editorial floor. Days later, he said he wanted me to be his deputy chairman but that I couldn't be editorial director because he wanted direct access to the editors. But I knew that when Reed had sold to him, one of the deals he'd had to sign was that if he offered me or Douglas Long any job different to the ones we were already doing – if our job descriptions were changed – he'd have to pay us off. It was a contract he'd already signed. Whether he knew it, whether he'd read the small print or not, I don't know. Nor whether he gave a damn. So I asked him to put his offer in writing and he called in a secretary and dictated it in front of me. She typed it up and he gave it to me, and I said, "Okay, you've broken my contract – I'm going and you've got to pay me." **9**

unions to what was sometimes violent action, and in July of that year five dock workers were jailed within the terms of the Act. This resulted in the IPC Newspapers SOGAT chapels deciding that they would not work until the dockers were released from Pentonville. Other unions then withdrew their labour. The total loss of copies of the company's titles was 24 million, and, when the men returned to work, there were demands for payment for some of the lost time, on the grounds that this had been a "strike of conscience". SOGAT even demanded extra

payment for doing the work they should have done during the stoppage.

The litany of what were ultimately suicidal demands by the print unions makes depressing and, today, barely credible reading. At the *Mirror*, the combination of traditional extravagance, the fierce competition of *The Sun* and what was becoming a union stranglehold saw the company's profits nosedive. In January 1975, the management called all FoCs to a meeting where it intended to report on the serious financial state of the company and

First person PERCY ROBERTS

In a place of strife: Percy Roberts surveys a demonstration in Holborn.

Percy Roberts was born in 1920 and educated at Brighton and Hove Grammar School. He joined the Sussex Daily News *as a reporter in 1936, spent 1939-45 as an army officer in France and the Middle East, and worked as a journalist on the* Egyptian Daily Mail, *Cairo, and the* Mid-East Mail, *Palestine, before returning to Sussex in 1948. Following a short spell with the* Liverpool Daily Post, *he went to Nigeria as editor of the* Nigerian Citizen *and joined Mirror Group in 1952 when it took over the* Nigerian Daily Times, *where he became managing director. He was managing director of Mirror Group in the Caribbean and general manager in Manchester and London before becoming managing director and, ultimately, chief executive and chairman from 1977 until his retirement in 1980. He died while on holiday in Kenya in February 2003.*

❛ During my time in Manchester, we increased the circulation by about 25 per cent. We also started printing in Belfast. We built a web-offset plant there and became the first paper in Britain to use facsimile transmission – the whole of the *Daily Mirror*

could be transmitted in under an hour. Circulation in Ireland rocketed and then the IRA blew up the plant. Actually, I don't think they meant to destroy it, only to put it out of action for a few weeks. But the force of the explosion in a confined space blew the walls apart and the walls fell in on top of the presses.

We never would have been able to get insurance a second time, so we decided to close the plant down. Subsequently we found out that one of the telephone operators, a girl, and her sister were members of the IRA. The IRA had been armed with machine guns and had ordered the staff out of the building. Later there was a warning from the IRA that they were going to get me – I've never got to an airport so fast in my life!

I was regarded as Cecil King's bright boy, although that didn't do me any good, really. Cecil had a great affection for Nigeria and all the European ex-pats working for the group there, as long as they lasted the pace, which was quite considerable. We were resented

Continued on page 136

outline the principles on which it hoped to formulate a revised industrial policy. The NATSOPA chapel officers refused to attend and the meeting was cancelled. Instead, a management statement was issued pointing out that IPC Newspapers had lost £894,000 in the year ended 31 March 1974 and that losses for the first nine months of the current financial year were £558,000. A total of 31,657,025 copies of all group titles had been lost between 1 April and 31 December 1974, and with newsprint prices having increased by 11 per

cent, the company was facing a loss for the third consecutive year. And this on an annual turnover of around £100million.

Yet if the ship was holed, the *Mirror*'s editorial crew could not feel the water lapping around its ankles. House agreements saw the four-week holiday allocation become five, and later six; sabbaticals and maternity leave were introduced; most senior executives had refrigerators and small bars in their offices; and the paper's expansive style was still very much in evidence. Promotions, such as the search for

First person   **PERCY ROBERTS**

in the *Mirror* organisation at one time, when we were known as the Black Mafia. We didn't bring any of the Nigerians to Britain to train because we didn't want them contaminated by the British trades unions. Eventually the operation was handed over to the Nigerians. Then I was sent by King to buy up every paper in the Caribbean – well, one paper on every island. We set up a plant in Trinidad, but political trouble eventually forced us to sell out to Roy Thomson and he eventually lost them all.

In Manchester we used a lot of London-produced stuff, of course, including the leading article. I was nearly fired over the leader. Cudlipp used to take all day to write an editorial and one particular day it was so late the paper would have missed a lot of trains, so I published without it. I think he forgave me in the end but it was traumatic at the time.

Hugh and I had a love-hate relationship. I was devoted to him in a lot of ways – he was a genius at producing a tabloid newspaper – but he made some horrible mistakes, particularly over *The Sun*. When he launched the Odhams *Sun* he made it clear from the very outset that he was not going to let it compete with the *Mirror*, which was a mistake. Eventually he lost interest and sold it for nothing to Rupert Murdoch. To be fair to Cudlipp, it was pretty clear to us that Murdoch was going to start a paper, because he owned the *News of the World* and had all those presses standing there idle six days a week. But by selling him *The Sun,* we allowed him to inherit a circulation close to a million, so he had a very good start.

Cudlipp married Eileen Ascroft, who was in charge of the biggest group of magazines in the world [Amalgamated Press]. She was very good, too. It wasn't a very happy marriage because they used to fight all the time. After she died, in rather mysterious circumstances, Cecil became very angry and gave Cudlipp an ultimatum – stop drinking or you will be fired, which was quite serious. Cudlipp was a heavy drinker at that time, especially brandy – if he had a few brandies, he got very difficult to handle. The only person who seemed to be able to handle him when he'd had too much to drink was Marje Proops. After the ultimatum, Hugh decided that red wine wasn't alcoholic – but only the best was good

enough, Chateau Latour. It cost about £20 a time then. The trouble was, he used to force everybody else to drink it with him. Ten o'clock in the morning and at lunchtime and at teatime, he'd be drinking Chateau Latour. People were drinking it like Coca-Cola. Every time I went to see him, I'd have a glass of wine with him. In the end, I said, that's enough – I can't take any more of this. It was very cloying stuff, I found. So I switched to white wine and I've stuck with it ever since.

Cudlipp could be difficult to work with. I remember going to one public dinner where I think he'd had enough to drink and in the course of his speech he pointed at me and said, "That's the man you've got to be wary of – Percy Roberts, who's ruining the *Mirror*. All he's interested in is making a profit". But he could be a lovely man and he was a genius.

The Royal Family were treated very differently back then. When Prince Charles was at Gordonstoun, he wrote an essay on the future of the monarchy, which was pretty critical. Eventually he is supposed to have sold it in a pub, allegedly to pay for the cherry brandies he was drinking in those days. Anyway, whoever bought it offered it to the *Mirror* and we bought it. Then Cudlipp sent it to Martin Charteris, who was the Queen's secretary, with a little note saying "No copy has been made". I saw Charteris later about something else and he was over the moon about it.

Another astonishing unknown royal story is that Freddie Reed and the other royal photographers all had the ambition, especially when she was in warm climes, to get a picture of the Queen in a bathing suit. And they did, but it was given to the Royal household and never published.

Cudlipp hated being chairman – he was a newspaperman through and through. I don't think he could read a balance sheet – anything that interrupted doing a newspaper was a hindrance as far as he was concerned. And he wouldn't take the union situation seriously at all. Probably about 70 per cent of my time was spent dealing with the print unions. They were appalling – there is no other word for it. They were the strongest unions in the country and had us in an absolute

---

perfect womanhood, Mrs Britain, continued, although not without hiccups. Neil Bentley recalls when, one year, Eric Wainwright was sent to check out the suitability of the winner, but asked no questions other than "Where's the pub?", to which he retreated for the rest of the day. As a result, that year's Mrs Britain turned out to be as much an ideal representative of British womanhood as Wainwright was of sobriety. (At the Savoy Hotel lash-up with which the promotion culminated another year, Hugh Cudlipp had called upon a friend of the

Welsh winner to sing "There'll Be a Welcome in the Valleys" [*sic.* the Welsh Cudlipp], and then "My Way".)

When Donald Zec decided to end a 34-year association with the paper and depart to write books, I ended a turbulent executive/editor relationship with Miles – like Cudlipp, as a former features executive he was especially demanding of that editorial area – and went off to write showbusiness interviews and, later, set up a showbusiness department. I travelled extensively,

Landmark: Percy Roberts (second left) congratulates the northern staff and editor, Bernard Shrimsley, who played a major part in taking the Mirror's circulation past five million.

stranglehold. It wasn't so much the outrageous staffing levels, or the rates of pay they demanded, it was demarcation that presented the biggest problem. But there was huge overmanning. Having worked in composing rooms when I was a journalist, I could read type upside down. I remember going into the office of a father of the chapel down in the machine room and I could read upside down what was on his desk. It was a rota for the Christmas period and it was operated so that exactly half the staff produced the paper. No trouble at all. They were something like 100 per cent overmanned and the wage bill was enormous.

We never really got control of it. I used regularly to be got out of bed at two o'clock in the morning to try to solve union disputes. Once or twice I went into the office in my pyjamas – I lived in a company flat across the street and then in a company mews flat in the West End – because nobody else could get there in time. We were often the victims of secondary activity. There'd be a dispute at the Odhams, Watford, print plant, which we then owned – and the *Mirror* chapel would involve itself. Then we'd get a

settlement at Odhams and the *Mirror* people would say that we had to pay them as well. We were virtually helpless.

I tried to stand up to the unions on more than one occasion; I think, in one year, we lost 10 million copies because I refused to pay. We all knew what the trouble was, but the NPA, as it then was, wouldn't agree on anything and wouldn't take on the unions. Except for Rupert Murdoch. He came to see me one day with the chairman of the NPA, Lord [Richard] Marsh, and they asked if I would join a fund to which we would all contribute and from which we would get paid out if stopped by the unions. A sort of safety net, if you like. I said no. But I said what I would agree to was a plan where if any of the four main newspapers, the *Mail, Express, Sun* or ourselves, were stopped, then we would all stop and have a complete shutout. Nobody would get paid at all and we'd get Securicor to take over the buildings.

Murdoch rather liked this idea but said he was not on speaking terms with Vere Harmsworth [head of

Continued on page 138

mainly to and within the United States, and, as was company practice, flew first-class until economic strictures determined that this luxury arrangement was withdrawn. This was but a negligible nod towards prudence: the paper still maintained a vast workforce, even after the subtraction of those distribution departments, "Mickey Mouse" signatories who did not exist, but whose casual payments under assumed names were shared among those who did.

Editorially, the *Daily Mirror* was employing

more than double the number it took to produce *The Sun.* In 1972, the in-house IPC *News* recorded totals of 570 journalists and allied editorial staff in London and 288 in Manchester, where northern editors Len Woodliff, a wartime tank commander with a Military Cross, and then Derek Jameson were fighting every bit as fierce a circulation battle as that in the south, even though Murdoch had resisted printing north of London. There were also, IPC *News* reported, 1,675 further contributors to the editorial operation, which presumably included

Associated Newspapers] and asked me to talk to him about it. So I had lunch with Vere who, somewhat reluctantly I thought, agreed. Then Rupert and I went to see Lord Matthews, who was then running the *Express*, and he said what we were suggesting was a conspiracy. I said, that's right – we've been the victims of union conspiracy for years and it's time it was stopped. He asked how long we thought the lockout would last. I said that, provided nobody got paid, less than a week. He said, I don't believe you. He wouldn't agree, so Lord Matthews was the man who stopped Fleet Street taking on the unions.

Mirror Group seemed to get all the union trouble at that time, particularly from NATSOPA, or SOGAT as it became. One advantage I had at the *Mirror* when dealing with the unions was that, because I'd worked in Nigeria, where there were no demarcation problems, I could have produced a newspaper entirely on my own. It would have needed to be a weekly, but I could have done it.

The linotype piece rate system was a complete carve-up. People were getting paid for making mistakes – they would make a mistake and then get paid for correcting it.

I remember once a dispute with the NATSOPA cleaners that threatened production of the *Mirror*. I had been out to dinner, and, coming back to the flat, dressed in a dinner jacket, I bumped into a union official, an FOC, coming out of the pub. I started going on about the strike and so did he, and then we sat on the bonnet of a car parked in the street and reached an agreement.

There was so much corruption in the unions at that time. I remarried and went on honeymoon to South Africa. The day I got back, I had to make a speech to the wholesalers, which I had prepared in advance. Halfway through I got fed up – I thought, this is the most boring speech I have ever heard – so I ditched it and started to tell them about the Mickey Mouse scam – how men were signing on as Mickey Mouse, or

Prince Charles, or Gordon Richards and were getting paid. Of course, the next day it was all over the papers. I thought there would be trouble with the unions, but not at all – they were fed up to the back teeth with all these creeps coming in and taking money. The Inland Revenue got in touch with me and said they were going to prosecute these people. I said, how? I don't know who they are. How can you prosecute Mickey Mouse or Prince Charles? But it became an issue in Parliament and it was agreed that we would not be permitted to pay anybody without having their National Insurance number and union number. So that virtually stopped it overnight, but not before many people had made fortunes.

When you look back, it was an incredible period, it really was. The problem was, Cudlipp was no manager, although you could say I wasn't much of one, either, I suppose. If Cudlipp promoted someone, he didn't give him a salary increase – he'd say you can put in expenses of £1,500 a year. And that's going back God knows how many years.

Cecil King insisted that I approve expenses and the most extraordinary claims used to appear. Then Cecil stopped all expenses other than approved ones with receipts provided. That stopped a lot of the fiddling. They had to be very careful because the taxman had been told about it and he knew what to look for.

I am told that before my time in London, when the top rate of tax was 90 per cent, the morning editorial conference used to take place at the Savoy and everyone would come back with 20 cigarettes, which were worth several pounds of taxed income.

If I had stayed on, I think I would have been in a position to fight off Maxwell. I certainly would have had a good go, because I had already dealt with him when he tried to buy *The Sun* before Murdoch got it. I did the negotiations with him and formed the conclusion then that he was a bullying crook. **9**

---

the network of district reporters, Ralph Champion's five-strong New York bureau, Peter Stephens and one or two more in Paris, Dennis Martin in Bonn, John Checkley and one other in Rome and stringers (contracted freelances) from Athens to Zanzibar. Group production staff numbered 1,700.

Although now bereft of Donald Zec and the incomparable Peter Wilson, gone from the sports pages on health grounds – sport had caught up with the rest of Fleet Street in 1971

when it was permanently allocated the whole of the back page – the *Mirror* retained some of the biggest names in the business: Marje Proops, now writing the "Dear Marje" column that soon made her the doyenne of agony aunts, Waterhouse, Pilger, new sports columnist Frank McGhee, Geoffrey Goodman, who had arrived from the IPC *Sun* as assistant editor and industrial editor, and Terence Lancaster, ex-*Express* and *People*, who, as political editor, was more day-to-day hands-on than John Beavan had been. With Sydney Jacobson as

Great company: Peter Wilson's farewell dinner in London on 16 October, 1972. From the left: Joe Mercer, Godfrey Evans, Denis Compton, Henry Cooper, the man himself, Alec Bedser, Tommy Farr, Eric Bedser, Terry Downes, Eddie Tomas and Teddy Waltham.

editorial director from 1968-74, and deputy chairman 1973-74, the paper threw its considerable political strengths behind Labour's campaigns in the two General Elections of 1974. With the miners' strike bringing Ted Heath's Government to its knees, the Prime Minister went to the country on 28 February. Winning five seats fewer than Labour, he tried and failed to negotiate a coalition with the Liberal leader, Jeremy Thorpe, and Labour formed a minority administration, hanging on by the slenderest of threads until Harold Wilson called another election for 10 October. This time, Labour squeaked home with an overall majority of just four.

The *Mirror* was elated, but underwent a severe hierarchical shake-up when Jacobson retired and went off to complete a trio of former *Mirror* heavyweights in the House of Lords. John Beavan had become Baron Ardwick in 1970, excitedly leaving his sickbed to rush to the office when Cudlipp leaked the Government's lordly intentions over the telephone. Hugh, knighted in 1973, became Baron Cudlipp of Aldingbourne, West Sussex, the following year. Sydney, another of the *Mirror*'s Military Cross holders and beloved of those who worked closely with him on the paper, became Baron of St. Albans in 1975. When he died in 1988, Cudlipp overcame his hatred of funerals and memorial services to

Abroad spectrum: Peter Stephens (left) ran the Mirror's *Paris office; John Checkley (right) was the man in Rome.*

DEREK JAMESON

First person

Derek Jameson was born in east London in 1929 and educated at Detmold Road Elementary Boys' School, Hackney. He joined Reuters as an office boy in 1944 and became chief sub-editor there before working on the London American *(1960-61),* Daily Express *(1961-63), and* Sunday Mirror *(1963-72). He was then northern editor of the* Sunday Mirror *and then* Daily Mirror *from 1974 to 1976, when he returned to London as managing editor of the daily. He left the following year to edit the* Daily Express *and subsequently was editor-in-chief of the* Daily Star, *editor of the* News of the World *(1981-84) and a successful broadcaster. He and his wife, Ellen, now live in Miami, Florida.*

'In hot metal days, Manchester was a crucible for journalists, especially those with Fleet Street in their sights. All the major titles printed key editions there and maintained large editorial staffs. Jobs were easier to acquire in the "frozen north", as it was universally known. They paid national wages and the brightest and best talent stood a good chance of being recruited to work in head office. Many of the top names in the business came out of Manchester. The Aussie firebrand John Pilger, for instance, started his career in Britain as a down table sub-editor on the Manchester *Mirror*.

The *Mirror* occupied pride of place as the top-selling title in the north, publishing fast-moving editions to embrace the diverse interests of Scotland, north Wales, England north of Birmingham, Ulster and eventually the Irish Republic. From 1955, the daily and its sister *Sunday Mirror* shared the third floor of Withy Grove, a huge Victorian edifice that once published ten nationals under one roof and justly claimed to be the biggest printing centre in Europe.

On the other hand, cynics described it as the largest public convenience in Europe. Its marbled splendour at ground level disguised the fact that the backstairs quarters were little better than a slum, though the *Mirror* papers made a brave attempt at modernisation with the help of partition walls, fluorescent lighting and a lick of paint. Withy Grove was the northern fortress of the Kemsley empire, bought out in its declining days by the Canadian entrepreneur Roy Thomson. His organisation took over all production areas and the plant's various tenants leased its offices and printing facilities for a fee based on the number of pages produced and copies printed.

On the demise of the *Daily Dispatch*, a failing Kemsley national based in Manchester, the Mirror Group smartly stepped into its shoes and took on much of its redundant staff to produce northern editions. Oddly enough, *Mirror* supremo Hugh Cudlipp had worked on the *Dispatch* at Withy Grove before moving to Fleet Street. Kemsley's production boss, who moved over to Thomson, was Fred Bale, a ferocious pigeon fancier. Every time some disaster occurred in the production areas, a shout would go up for Fred and the answer invariably came back: "He's looking after his fucking pigeons!" One of Fred's claims to fame was that he had been Cudlipp's head printer on the wartime *Eighth Army News*.

Withy Grove's composing room was huge, with rows of linotype machines stretching as far as the eye could see. The "stone," as it is known in the trade, was unique in that several rival papers were assembled simultaneously by an army of Thomson compositors. Thus *Mirror* sub-editors would be putting pages to bed in one aisle while their *Telegraph* colleagues did the same a few feet away. Not that it mattered much since the two papers were on different wavelengths, though the situation could get fraught when the *Sunday Mirror* and *News of the World* were in production. One *Sunday Mirror* editor jokingly liked to stand with a huge pair of binoculars, reading *NoW* proofs.

On the *Daily Mirror*, everyone worked under tremendous pressure. At least half the paper was put together independently in Manchester: what was good for Surbiton was likely to be of little interest in Sheffield. Accordingly, Manchester printed ten or more editions nightly to keep readers happy on the basis of their geography. London's pages had to be adapted or discarded altogether to meet local requirements. A huge production feat requiring the services of some 300 journalists – sub-editors and production executives in Manchester and feature writers, reporters and photographers in every district. Sport in general and

attend and speak passionately at Sydney's St. Brides, Fleet Street, memorial, an occasion he employed also to lambaste the Murdoch influence that had produced "the dark ages of tabloid journalism".

Miles was editor for more than three years, during which time the country embraced, although not warmly, decimal currency; the *Mirror* coined the phrase "Bloody Sunday" with its front page on the atrocity in Londonderry, where 13 civil rights demonstrators were killed by Army paratroopers; Britain became a full member of the EEC; and the Vietnam war ended.

Ted Pickering, a former chairman of *Daily Mirror* Newspapers within IPC and not yet a knight, had become chairman of what was now Mirror Group Newspapers when Alex Jarratt moved to Reed. Editorial director Sydney Jacobson retired in 1975, opening up a gap into which Tony Miles was elevated. It was on Miles's recommendation that Michael Christiansen, who in resurrecting his career after his sacking at the *Sunday Mirror* had, I told him, completed one of the most remarkable

Clinched it: Derek Jameson with actress Shirley Ann Field in November 1963.

football in particular accounted for much of this activity.

The cost of this operation – utilising something like a quarter of the *Mirror*'s staff and production budget – was a major factor in the paper's switch to computerised production. Fast and efficient transmission of facsimile pages from London to regional printing centres cut out the need for a separate operation in Manchester. The new technology spelt doom for the large staffs maintained by national titles in the north. The *Mirror*'s northern empire collapsed.

Rupert Murdoch was among the first to see that the money required for a Manchester base could be better employed elsewhere. After launching *The Sun* in 1969, he declined to set up a duplicate operation for its northern editions, no doubt scared off by the cost of producing his *News of the World* at Withy Grove. Instead he took a gamble that the soaraway *Sun* would continue to shine in those faraway areas that could be reached only by editions printing in London as early as 7pm.

When I was appointed northern editor of the *Daily Mirror*, one of Cudlipp's last decisions before his retirement, my brief was simple: stop the onward march of *The Sun*. Rupert's pride and joy, employing many ex-*Mirror* staff, had already taken a million readers off the *Daily Mirror* in the south. My first move was to run the *Mirror*'s own version of Page 3 Girls, often buying up second rights to freelance pictures first published by *The Sun*. Tony Miles, then the editor in London, disapproved but let it go in the wider interest of fighting *The Sun*.

Then I spotted what I saw as *The Sun*'s Achilles' heel. Coming off-stone at 7pm in London, the paper could not

Continued on page 142

comebacks since that of Lazarus, succeeded him as editor. Mike Molloy became deputy, but only briefly – four months later, Christiansen suffered the stroke that effectively ended his journalistic career.

Having introduced daily bulletins commenting on editorial performance – a practice copied from his father, Arthur, whose *Daily Express* communiqués were legendary – the shy Christiansen was a popular figure whose efforts to maintain good relations with his staff included whisking groups off to Lords at lunchtime to drink beer and watch his beloved cricket for a couple of hours. But his ideas could be eccentric, as he had proved years before when, as the assistant editor in charge of *Mirror* features, he decided to run "Upside Down Week" in the paper, with bylined writers switching to areas other than their own. He emerged chastened from Bill Connor's office after suggesting that Cassandra should write the gardening column. "That man is a doughnut masquerading as a ping-pong ball," Connor observed of the bald-domed Christiansen.

First person   DEREK JAMESON

get into Manchester's territory with the most vital ingredient of all – late-night football results. We ruthlessly exploited the situation, running two or three pages of pictures and reports of the top teams in successive editions. Celtic, Rangers, Newcastle, Sunderland, Liverpool, Everton, Leeds and Manchester United all made a powerful contribution to the *Mirror*'s success.

By 1975, the northern editions were putting on 60,000 new readers a month. Sales in February that year were 1,357,972, the highest northern circulation ever recorded. Larry Lamb, founding editor of *The Sun*, confessed that the Manchester *Mirror* had been a major impediment to *The Sun*'s progress.

I moved back south and was by no means the only Mirror man from Manchester to reach the heights in Fleet Street. Larry Lamb had worked there and my oldest friend, Bernard Shrimsley, an earlier northern editor, became editor of *The Sun, News of the World* and *Mail on Sunday*. Dave Banks won his spurs on the subs' table in Manchester before going on to edit the paper. Another northern editor, Mike Terry, became a top features executive on *The Sun*, and Mike Taylor, a former night editor in London, was northern editor before moving back down south to become deputy editor.

The northern *Mirror* also produced an array of legendary characters still discussed with awe in newspaper bars the world over. Men like Maurice Wigglesworth, a blunt Yorkshireman of such ample proportions that it took two belts strapped together to encircle his waist. As the *Mirror*'s night news editor in Manchester, he could terrify the toughest of reporters. It was always done with unfailing courtesy. He called everyone, editorial messengers included, "sir." A typical midnight phone conversation with an erring reporter: "You don't know why we missed t'story? I'll

tell tha why, sir. 'Cos tha's a fookin' idiot, that's why, sir!"

His best exchanges were with his sparring partner, George Harrop, the night picture editor. "Stop pickin' tha' nose, George," he would say. And when George protested his innocence: "If there's one thing I hate worse than a nose-picker, it's a fookin' liar." Once they sat together watching Ada, the ancient tea lady who always wore a Second World War snood, charging through editorial behind a trolley laden with steaming tea urn and plates of cakes and biscuits. "There she goes, George," said Wiggy, "the Angel of Mons."

Then there was Ted Fenna, all six foot and four inches of him, first and perhaps most formidable northern editor of them all. Once, Granada TV was making a *Mirror* documentary and the film crew got a messenger to rush up to him with a piece of agency tape in his hand. "Here's a good story, Ted!" he had to say. "That is a good story," Ted was to retort, studying the copy intently, "let's splash it." It required several takes to satisfy filmmakers. The first attempt was too slow, the second ruined by a ringing telephone, the third too fast, the fourth too stilted… Came the fifth try and Ted bellowed: "That is a good story – and you can shove it up your arse! I'm going for a drink."

That was Withy Grove in the grand days of hot metal. Irreverent, down-to-earth, suffering fools badly. Frantically busy and highly successful. The whole edifice came crashing down with the invention of a copying machine that could reproduce a facsimile page down to the faintest smudge with total accuracy, to be transmitted electronically in less time than it takes to read the headlines. Today, Withy Grove is an entertainment complex called The Printworks. They still sound the klaxon hooters that used to disturb the dead of night as the mighty presses rolled. **,**

Christiansen believed, as Cudlipp had done before him, that the *Daily Express* was the paper from which the *Mirror* could steal readers. To this end he launched an expensive and relatively up-market Europe-embracing editorial venture, with large numbers of staff being dispatched to Britain's EEC partners to file what seemed to be pretty much what they liked. What soon became known to the staff as the "Euro-yawn" was to culminate with Christiansen, accompanied by assistant editor Mike Taylor, editing the paper from Paris, but it was there, in bureau chief Peter Stephens' apartment, that, on 1 May 1975, he was taken ill. Unwisely, he decided to make the return

journey by car. Taylor nobly drove the boss back to London and, it transpired, into retirement, which Christiansen spent running a bookstall.

Molloy, having been acting editor since Christiansen's stroke (a period during which he recycled the *Mirror* Magazine disaster of six years previously and ran The *Mirror* Guide to Sexual Knowledge), was appointed editor on 22 December, his 35th birthday. He inherited an almost empty war chest, he remembers: "Mike had told me he wanted to attack the *Daily Express,* but sending staff all over Europe at vast expense was a brainstorm. He was one of the most talented journalists I ever worked with, but a man who every now and again would have a massive seizure and do something stupid."

Molloy quickly settled to become an inspirational editor, although for a while the paper suffered an identity crisis as it attempted to retain its gravitas while also offering the titillation that characterised its main competitor. To challenge *The Sun*'s appeal to younger working men, pictures of bare-breasted girls were introduced towards the end of 1975 and appeared, although not necessarily every day, nor always quite so unclothed, until early 1980. There was plenty of froth, too – *"If it's fun you're after… from coast-to-coast, your comedy hosts – and their saucy postcard world"* – yet with awards raining down on Waterhouse's brilliant column and Pilger's evocative writing maintaining the standards he had set during the Vietnam war, the paper was still presenting significant popular journalism alongside the trivia. Lancaster and Goodman were both writing weekly columns, and reporter Richard Stott produced a run of investigative series, into deputy Tory leader Reginald Maudling's business affairs and Ernest Marples' tax irregularities – coincidental payback for the old rogue's fleecing of *Mirror* Magazine – as well as the explosive Revie revelations. Mirrorscope

Balancing act: Editor Mike Molloy had to take on The Sun *– but couldn't sink quite so low.*

was long gone, but the idea that tabloid papers should include intelligent and informative commentary and opinion had not.

On the lighter side, the launch at the beginning of 1976 of the *Daily Mirror* Pop Club gave the paper a fillip and even drew guarded praise from senior staff at *The Sun*. Created by television editor and part-time magician Clifford Davis, it was based on the paper's highly successful Punters' Club, which Noel Whitcomb ran distantly and autocratically, deigning only occasionally to speak with the racegoers who paid his salary. Davis wanted to enroll younger readers in a club that would run regular offers of cut-price concert tickets, discounted records, prizes, organised trips to see big rock acts abroad and the like. In doing so, the *Mirror* would establish an invaluable database as well as leave its rivals trailing in the important popular music field.

It was another idea that required old-style investment to succeed in a new-style marketplace. Davis and I went to see Felicity Green, who then controlled the publicity and promotions purse strings. "How many membership cards do you think we should have printed?" she asked Davis. "Two hundred thousand," he said. "Don't be ridiculous," said

Killing fields: John Pilger's powerful reports from Cambodia were backed by Eric Piper's pictures.

Ties are us: Editor Molloy and deputy night editor Ted Graham enjoy a lighter moment with the Queen during Her Majesty's 1976 visit.

Felicity, "we'll print ten thousand." The Club was announced in the paper of 28 January and 50,000 applications for membership arrived the following morning. Eventually there were around half-a-million members and Davis, who, with silver hair and a camel hair overcoat, looked more like an ageing actor manager than a teen tycoon, thrived in a job that saw the paper make and promote its own record and launch the *Daily Mirror* Rock and Pop Awards, which years later were snaffled by the industry to become the Brits.

In February 1976, the Queen, on a tour of Fleet Street, visited the Holborn building, to be greeted by chairman Pickering and shown by Molloy and deputy night editor Ted Graham "how each day's *Daily Mirror* is prepared". After this edifying experience, the paper reported blandly, Her Majesty said: "It has been a most interesting day."

Nowhere near as interesting, however, as that spent by some lucky readers and a group of staff in June the following year, when, with a flash of its traditional panache, the *Mirror* chartered Concorde for "the best day trip ever" – from London Heathrow to Washington D.C. and back. "In your super soaraway *Mirror*…" ran the cock-a-snook-at-the-opposition line at the top of the four-page souvenir issue given to

each of those travelling. Competition winners joined celebrities such as Esther Ranzen and boxer John Conteh – the beginning of a close association with the paper that would end in tears – plus two of the *Mirror*'s own star names, Proops and Waterhouse, a gaggle of executives, including Molloy, Brian Downing and Felicity Green, and various advertising clients the company wanted to impress. One of these was Richard Branson, who was so won over by the experience that, more than a quarter-of-a-century later, when British Airways announced its fleet of Concordes was to be withdrawn from service, he tried to buy them.

The paper made its own headlines when, at 11 o'clock in the morning of Wednesday 31 May 1978, security guard Antonio Castro drove an armoured truck containing £197,500 in cash into the Holborn vanway where each night delivery lorries would collect their loads of papers. He was shot and killed in an audacious payroll robbery that the paper reported starkly the following morning: MURDER AT THE MIRROR.

When on song, Molloy was an exceptional editor. He had an almost unerring eye for hiring talent and the persuasive skills to bring on to the staff a cluster of high calibre journalists, including Joyce Hopkirk, formerly editor of

Stars of the seventies (top left to right): Assistant editor Joyce Hopkirk, feature writer Paul Callan, diarist Peter McKay, (bottom left to right) diarist Peter Tory, and leader writer Joe Haines.

Cosmopolitan and *The Sun*'s first women's editor, who joined as an assistant editor. Relentlessly cheerful, she was a positive influence on the editorial floor although Molloy sometimes found her organisational skills less than perfect. "You couldn't organise a piss-up in a brewery," he exasperatedly told her one day. So, to prove him wrong, she did just that – and put the wrong date on the invitations!

Another recruit was Paul Callan, a Fleet Street scallywag who became the paper's gossip columnist – The Inside Page had run its course – and, later, a descriptive features writer whose prose was first rate when he was sober and only slightly less so when he was not. Peter McKay, now one of the *Daily Mail*'s constellation of star

names, also stayed awhile, contributing his brand of gossip, and later the fine writer Peter Tory, an ex-actor and a part-time pilot, arrived from the *Express*.

The paper's editorials were written by Deryck Winterton and David Tattershall, worthy successors to W.M. and B.B., until the arrival of Joe Haines, formerly head of Harold Wilson's press department and author of *The Politics of Power*, the riveting tale of Wilson's Downing Street years. The serialisation of the book was a circulation-grabber for the paper after Joyce Hopkirk and supersub John Patrick – so good that he was paid an executive-size salary in order that he shouldn't desire promotion away from what he did best – had turned it into a

*Pure sensation:
The Real Joyce
McKinney was
unmasked by an
intrepid Mirror
team.*

superior political soap opera. When Tony Miles read the extract concerning what became the infamous list of those suggested for honours by Wilson's secretary, Marcia Williams, he wanted to know how the paper could be certain she had compiled it. "Because she wrote it on her own lavender paper," someone explained, and the "Lavender List" went into history. Haines had been out of work for a year when, in May 1977, Molloy offered him a role as a features writer for the *Mirror*. A year later, he was the number one leader writer and a key member of the paper's political team.

Another circulation winner was the paper's revelations of the truth behind the extraordinary saga of Joyce McKinney and the manacled Mormon. In September 1977, a 21-year-old missionary from Utah, Kirk Anderson appeared to have been kidnapped from outside a church in East Ewell, Surrey. Anderson turned up to report he had been kidnapped and held handcuffed and manacled for three days. News editor Alan Shillum dispatched Ron Ricketts, one of nature's malcontents but a first-rate reporter, to find out all he could about the suspected kidnapper, Joyce McKinney, a southern blonde with more aliases than respectable ladies normally employ. McKinney and her companion, Keith May, were arrested the next day, and an incandescent performance by Joy, as she preferred to be known, at a preliminary court hearing had Fleet Street eating out of the hand of what appeared to be a foolish but lovelorn young woman. "I loved Kirk so much I would have skiied down Mount Everest with a carnation up my nose," she told the magistrates – and when

Record breaker: From its launch, the Daily Mirror Pop Club was an instant hit.

released on bail pending an Old Bailey trial, promptly skipped the country. What had been an intriguing tale turned overnight into a sensational one and the *Mirror* mobilised a fearsome collection of reporters, including Barry Wigmore and Roger Beam, plus Tony Delano and Chris Buckland, then of the New York office, and Jill Evans in Los Angeles to start digging into McKinney's background.

But it was not until reporter Frank Palmer and photographer Kent Gavin, in Los Angeles on a separate assignment, were diverted to search for proof that McKinney was not what she seemed that the *Mirror* raced ahead of the chasing pack.

held up his hands – and bought a round of drinks for his rivals.

Molloy was directing a challenging newspaper and enjoying its journalistic successes and the awards it was winning for words and, especially, pictures – Gavin and others were following the tradition set by their colleague Arthur Sidey, the ex-messenger who had become the paper's first winner of the British Press Photographer of the Year award in 1963. Shortly before the Mirror Group lockout that gave *The Sun* the opportunity to become Britain's biggest selling daily paper, Molloy called a meeting of the editorial staff and told

Super scoopers: Jill Evans and Frank Palmer would help uncover the amazing truth about Joyce McKinney in the case of the manacled Mormon.

They discovered a set of pictures of the type for which a demure young woman would not be expected to pose. What's more, they found that she was a call girl with a past so vivid you needed dark glasses to view it. Back in Britain, the police had not yet decided whether to apply for McKinney's extradition, so the paper faced a contempt charge if it published. Until, that is, she talked to the *Express*, again picturing herself as a wounded innocent who had been ill used by the Mormons and by Britain. Molloy and Miles decided to go ahead with "The Real McKinney", a blockbuster that made up for the frustrations suffered during much of McKinney's dramatic preliminary court appearance, when the journalists' industrial dispute had kept the *Mirror* off the streets. Palmer, Wigmore, Beam and Gavin shared the Reporter of the Year award for what was a great team effort. And *Express* editor Derek Jameson, lately Molloy's deputy, walked into the Stab,

them: "We've done something unique in newspaper history. We've reversed a trend. We have turned a newspaper's falling circulation around."

He was enjoying, too, the extra-curricular activities that are available to those with the top job. Time had taken care of the pub's Nights of Magic and now Tramp, the then fledging celebrity club in Jermyn Street, became the regular late-night hangout for Molloy and close associates. There they would meet such seventies' icons as Keith Moon, drummer for The Who and a noted boulevardier, who took to turning up at the Stab in a chauffeured Rolls-Royce with his own silver tankard from which to guzzle champagne. Rod Stewart became the editor's friend, with the result that I wrote a three-part series on the singer's life. (A similar exercise on world boxing champion John Conteh had repercussions when, soon afterwards, he spun off the rails, took to

First person   KENT GAVIN

Kenneth George Gavin was born in Islington, north London, in 1939 and educated at Tollington Park Central School, Stroud Green. He joined Keystone Press Agency as a messenger at the age of 15 and subsequently worked there as a freelance and then staff photographer. He joined the Daily Mirror *in 1965, where picture editor Simon Clyne added a final "t" to his Christian name – "The name Kent is one that will be remembered," Clyne told him. Gavin was British Press Photographer of the Year in 1968 and 1969, Royal Photographer of the Decade for both the 1980s and 1990s and his total awards and nominations number more than 100.*

Forever young: Kent Gavin retired from the front line in 2003.

It's been a 38-year-long grand adventure for me. I'd been pestering Simon Clyne for a job when, in 1965, Keystone sent me to cover a visit by the Queen to Ethiopia and the Sudan – my first major assignment abroad. The *Mirror* man, that great snapper of royals, Freddie Reed, was taken ill on the trip, and, as a result, the paper used several of my pictures. When I got back, Clyne gave me a job and started me on a career that's taken me all over the world and into practically every area of journalism. In 38 years, I have worked for five picture editors – Simon was followed by Alex Winberg, Len Greener, Ron Morgans and, now, Ian Down – and nine editors and met more famous people, from royals and presidents to rock and sports stars, than practically any other photographer has had the chance to shake a Nikon at. Whiling away time on a plane recently, I started to make a list of the notable people I've met over the years and managed to recall eight presidents, three queens, five prime ministers and countless sundry royals before even starting on the major stars.

In my early days on the paper, I was covering the funeral of a murdered policeman when I saw a tear start to roll down the cheek of one of the uniformed mourners. That picture was elected news photograph of the year and re-emerged much later as news photograph of the quarter-century. In 1967, the Mirror Group did a deal with Nivosti, the Russian press agency, that resulted in me spending three months in Moscow with access never previously granted to a western photographer. The following year, I went with reporter Alan Gordon out on to the ice floes near the Magdalen Islands, off New Brunswick, and brought back a picture of a hunter clubbing to death a seal pup – "The price of a sealskin coat" was the *Mirror* headline – that's still being used today by crusaders against animal cruelty.

I love sport and covered football from the start – mainly Arsenal, for whom I have a passion that possibly exceeds Piers Morgan's. I first met Bobby Moore, who became a great friend, at the 1970 World Cup. Reporter Roy Rutter and I were sent from Mexico City back to Bogotá when Bobby was detained for questioning about the disappearance from a hotel shop of a gold and emerald bracelet. The sports reporters and photographers on the trip had all hopped on the plane taking the rest of the team to Mexico, turning their backs on a sensational story.

I have been in umpteen trouble spots and war zones: Aden three times, variously with writers Mary Malone, Donald Wise and Stanley Bonnett, as well as Biafra, Czechoslovakia during the Russian invasion, Belfast several times, and, with Don Wise again, Vietnam. Six months after Vietnam, I heard on my car radio a newsflash that a BOAC VC10 had been hijacked and was believed to be heading for Amman. Jordan was on the brink of civil war at the time and Palestinian guerillas opposed to King Hussein had already hijacked two other jets. I called the office and then went straight to Heathrow

---

drinking heavily and one day invaded Molloy's office in a drunk and disturbed state. Eventually I had to stay in the room alone with this previously fine fighter to talk him out from under the editor's desk, where he had coiled himself into the foetal position and was refusing to stir. With great strength of character, he later straightened himself out and became a responsible husband and father.)

Another regular watering hole was Angelo's, an Italian restaurant in Albemarle Street introduced to Molloy and other senior staff by Patric Walker. Astrologer Walker, gay, waspishly funny and a wonderful raconteur, had cast stardust on a previously uncared-for column written over the years by various contributors, including Francesco Waldner, filing from Italy under the considerable handicap of knowing little English. Walker's Charles Street apartment would be the venue for drinks, often in the company of his celebrity chums, before lengthy and convivial dinners in the basement room of Angelo's, where the piano playing of Jimmy Hardwick – still tinkling the

Flash of genius: Among the most moving images captured by Kent Gavin is this picture of a police officer overcome by emotion at the funeral of shot WPC Yvonne Fletcher.

with nothing but cameras and my passport. It took a couple of days to get into Amman, where all three hijacked jets were sitting on the tarmac at Revolution Airport. The guerrillas were in control, and, for six days, me and the other 119 reporters and photographers in the Intercontinental slept in the corridors as the hotel was shelled and mortared day and night.

I must have seen two or three hundred people die and we were shot at by Hussein's Bedouin troops and by guerrillas holding out on the roof. But photographing what was going on was almost impossible. The Bedouins apparently believed their souls were stolen if their images were reproduced and were none too keen on the world seeing pictures of Arabs killing Arabs, either, so at the sight of a camera they would open fire. After six days, lots were drawn to see which of us could leave on a Red Cross plane. I was lucky that day – unlike reporter Ellis Plaice, who was a loser in the lottery and stayed on – and

got back to London, where the *Mirror* splashed on my story and ran several pages inside of shots I had taken inside the "hellfire hotel".

On the whole, the celebrity front-line was a lot easier, although Mick Jagger's 1971 wedding to Bianca in St. Tropez turned into a mini-riot when the world's press tried to get in. For years, I was in and out of Los Angeles like a yo-yo, photographing Hollywood stars, including Joan Collins naked in the pool at her Beverly Hills home. See what I mean about it beating being a war correspondent!

Not quite so successful was a trip to South Africa in 1976 with reporter Garth Gibbs, who had been told by a reliable contact that she had seen Lord Lucan at the Cafe Royal in Cape Town – missing for the past 18 months after the family nanny was found dead at his home. We were away for almost a fortnight, but Lucan didn't show

Continued on page 150

keys today, but now at Joe Allen in Covent Garden – would coax the editor into quietly singing some of the dozens of standard songs that never became lost in the fog of alcoholic amnesia.

If visits to Tramp or Angelo's were not on the agenda, what for a short period became a cut-throat card school would be convened in Molloy's office. Former features art editor Paddy O'Gara recalls: "Mike bought a card table when the Press Club sold up a lot of stuff – it had supposedly belonged to Edgar Wallace,

and Mike paid £300 for it. One night, there were just he and I left in a poker game and when I won he gave me the table in lieu of money. But it never left his office because he won it back soon afterwards. Eventually he gave it to Robert Maxwell as a present."

Writer Christine Garbutt was the only woman in a school in which deputy editor Peter Thompson, writers Sydney Williams and Tony Pratt and sports desk executive Tony Cornell were regulars along with Molloy and O'Gara. As a teenager, Garbutt had been taken by her

First person   KENT GAVIN

and all we ended up with was a highly-expensive spread in the paper, with my pictures of the interior of the restaurant and the headline: LUCKY LUCAN LUNCHED HERE.

And then there was the Joyce McKinney caper, when reporter Frank Palmer and I were dispatched to Los Angeles when news editor Alan Shillum received a tip that there were some extremely interesting – meaning seedy – pictures of McKinney, the ex-beauty queen who was then awaiting trial in London for the alleged kidnapping of her Mormon boyfriend. We turned up nude and semi-nude shots of McKinney and discovered she had been a model for sex magazines and had provided "massage" services in a past that she was pretending had been sweet and innocent. We locked the material in a safe and awaited the end of the trial, but Joyce skipped bail and fled the country. The Director of Public Prosecutions wouldn't say whether attempts would be made to extradite her from the United States and bring her back to be tried, so we were snookered. Until the *Daily Express* found her in Atlanta, Georgia, and promised her own "true" story the following week. The *Mirror*'s sensational exposé started the same day as the *Express* whitewash job.

As the years went by, I found myself concentrating more and more on photographing members of the Royal Family, and, after Lady Diana Spencer came on the scene, the royal beat began to take up about two-thirds of my time. I remember getting the rota pass to photograph the christening of Prince William on what happened to be the Queen Mother's birthday. When Michael Shea, the royals' press secretary, showed me a list of the pictures I would be able to take, I noticed that it didn't include one of the baby with his great-grandmother. I'd been told not to speak to the Queen, so I went up to the Queen Mum and told her how daft this was. Next thing I knew was that the Queen came up to me and said: "Now, why didn't I think of that? Well done!"

Then, when Charles and Diana's marriage had started to go wrong, writer Mary Riddell and I managed to get on board a Concorde flight that was bringing Di back from a visit to New York. I asked if I could have a word and she actually asked her lady-in-waiting to move so that I could sit next to her. She talked with me for about two-and-a-half hours, about her marriage, about how some of the Royal Protection Officers would occasionally touch her up – pretending it was an accident when they laid hands on her – and about the problems of being a princess. The champagne was flowing and I had to keep going to the loo to write down what she had said, so that I could give notes to Mary. Di asked me not to publish some of what she told me about Charles and their marriage, but the rest of the stuff I gave to Mary – and what I could remember after all that champagne made a fantastic exclusive for the *Mirror*.

Mostly on royal stories and tours I worked with James Whitaker, who had excellent contacts in the royal household but a sort of love-hate relationship with the royals themselves. It's all very different since Diana's death, of course. Piers, wrongly I think, believes that royal reporting ended with the death of Diana. But look at the Jubilee, and look at William – he's 21 and at that age his father was getting a lot of press.

Lots of other things have changed, too. Digital technology changed everything – the office stopped being the base to go to every day and then return to for your pictures to be processed. Now we work mainly from our cars and send back pictures on our mobile telephones. I love the technology, but it means that we photographers hardly ever see one another now. The camaraderie has gone and is missed terribly by all national newspaper journalists who can remember the way it used to be. Fleet Street was a watering hole of the giants, frequented by legends, some because of their drinking but many more because of their work. The *Mirror* is still strong photographically, but, in the great days, we had the best set of press photographers in the world – people like Freddie Reed, George Greenwell, Arthur Sidey, Eric Piper, Alasdair McDonald (still with the *Mirror*, happily) and Doreen Spooner. I would hate to have to start my career over again now. However, neither do I want to pack up completely – especially where going to the Arsenal is concerned. **,**

journalist father, a senior executive working for Lord Beaverbook, to parties at Hugh and Eileen Cudlipp's Cheyne Walk home – she danced to rock and roll with impresarios Val Parnell and Lew Grade, and remembers Cudlipp's then "notorious" reputation as a seducer. Somewhere along the way to the *Mirror* she learned to play cards, but was told by Williams, a Machiavellian ex-*Daily Herald* reporter, that women were not welcome. They became so when the school was short of players one night. Williams told her Molloy had decided, "She can

come if she doesn't talk – I am not having my poker school turned into a knitting circle." Making it clear she would always leave at 11pm because she had children at home, Garbutt won about £150 the first evening. "I had never played for more than 10p," she recalls disingenuously, "but I had cashed a cheque for £10 in the Stab and drew a full house in the first game. There was lots of drinking, but I would only sip mine. I remember one game in which it was down to Paddy and me with quite a lot of money on the table. He had two pairs,

True professional: Doreen Spooner was at home with news, fashion or portrait photography.

Loon: The antics of Keith Moon, pictured here with girlfriend Annette Lax, alarmed reporters.

something like threes on tens, but I had twos on Jacks. The table went over, there was uproar, and then the mad Irishman said, "That woman can sure play poker."

For all the carousing, the paper stayed sharp as Molloy refined his editorial team and continued to hire the best talent that could be coerced into joining the staff. I became assistant editor in charge of features and brought in such writers as Ray Coleman, who contributed authoritative pieces and series on rock and roll legends, and Noreen Taylor, whom I coaxed away from a contract at *The Sun* to join a slimmed-down features writing team. Less

successful was Molloy's hiring of Bel Mooney, whose column failed to ignite in the way he wanted (Marje Proops's page was still all-conquering, but the problem of a female columnist was not solved until Anne Robinson was switched from an executive role some years afterwards). Later, Molloy brought in Christopher Ward, by then an assistant editor at the *Sunday Mirror*, as assistant editor (features) and promoted Richard Stott, itchy for an executive role after his investigative successes, to features editor. I became assistant editor (news and pictures), where I was joined for a while by John Edwards, a former *Mirror* man

Mirror *favourites: Boxer John Conteh proved to be a handful when drunk. Rod Stewart (pictured with a* Melody Maker *pop award) would occupy many column miles with his womanising.*

ANTON ANTONOWICZ

First person

Anton Antonowicz was born in 1950 and educated in north London at St. Gilda's Convent, Crouch End, and St. Ignatius Jesuit College, Stamford Hill, and then at Warwick University and the University of British Columbia, where he stayed for three days before becoming a waiter in a Greek restaurant. After working for the Georgia Strait *in Canada and the* Waltham Forest Guardian *in England, he joined the* Daily Mirror *on contract on 21 December 1977, and in May 1979 filled the staff vacancy created when editor-to-be Richard Stott was appointed features editor. Antonowicz has since won nine major awards for his investigative reporting and work as a foreign correspondent.*

Behind the lines: Anton Antonowicz reports from war-torn Baghdad, 2003.

6 When I joined the *Mirror*, I soon realised that good reporters were a dime a dozen there. There were people like Stuart Grieg, who was to tragically die quite young, who were so much better than me. So I decided to try to specialise in investigations. I worked on some of the Shock Issues the paper was doing at the time. One had a fantastic front page, showing a newborn baby that was born a heroin addict because its mother was. For that, John Merritt, a great friend who also died young, and the freelance John Lisners and I were fitted up with tape recorders and went into a south London garage to buy heroin. Not only were we offered drugs, but £20,000 in counterfeit £20 notes as well. The bad guys all got ten years in jail, as I remember.

My first foreign job was in Sardinia, when there was a kidnap of a guy named Rolf Schild, who the kidnappers had confused with a Rothschild. He was rich, but not Rothschild rich. He was held captive along with his wife

and daughter. They were released and so eventually was he, but not before they'd cut off one of his ears. There were only two industries in Sardinia, it seemed – raising goats and kidnapping. It was pretty hairy, but then I think first foreign jobs always are.

I wasn't sent to the Falklands in 1982 but I was in a bar near the office, quite pissed on a day off, when John Penrose called me from the news desk. He said the *Mirror* had had a tip-off about Alfredo Astiz, the man who originally took South Georgia for the Argentinians and was wanted by the Swedes for throwing two nuns out of a helicopter. Apparently, killing women was his thing. The information was that Astiz was being sent back from Britain to Argentina on a British Caledonian flight from Gatwick. Get down there and get on the plane, said Penrose, adding that, if Astiz wasn't on board 15 minutes after the plane was due to leave, I was to get off again. I went with the photographer Mike Maloney. We had no luggage and we booked, first-class of course, on the plane, which was to stop at Rio de Janeiro before going on to Buenos Aires.

Fifteen minutes after the scheduled departure time, I was about to throw a fake epileptic fit in order to get off the plane when, suddenly, a helicopter clattered down and landed right next to us. The "blue-eyed exterminating angel", as he was known, was escorted on board by just one man, who sat with an amused expression on his face throughout the flight. They were in club class, but fortunately I managed to get into the seat immediately behind Astiz. His clothes were all new – the British Government had fitted him out in style from Marks and Spencer – and he had a double crown on the back of his head. I remember that because I spent an awfully long time looking at it while he was refusing to talk to me. I

who had gone, and was to return to, the *Daily Mail.*

Edwards was part of the normal large *Mirror* contingent we sent to cover the 1980 Republican Conference in Detroit where, to save on expense, he, Waterhouse, Chris Buckland and Richard Lay, a freelance, shared a grand house on the lake in Grosse Point, Detroit's most fabled suburb. "A charming family owned the house," recalls Edwards. "They were vacating for one week, going to their lodge also on the lake somewhere. They

provided us with tea and biscuits, and then showed us where the master switch was for all the outside and security lights and the tap that controlled the underground lawn sprinkler system, which was running at the time because of very hot weather. They put the lights on to show us where the switches were and left them on. Then they left. The lights were on and many fountains of water were sweeping the parched lawns. And that's just how it stayed for the entire week – we never worked out how to disengage the lights' master switch or turn off remember also that he ate slaveringly and, remarkably, ate some cheddar cheese with a spoon. He got more and more wound up as I asked him questions – he was trying to watch a film called *The Competition*, about two competitive classical pianists who fall in love while trying to win a big prize. I had seen it previously, and, as it got near the end, I said to him, "The girl wins". He went berserk – he jumped out of his seat and took a swing at me, but missed.

When we arrived in Rio, the Pope was just leaving after a visit to Brazil, so we had a line about the exchange of a dog of war for a man of peace. It all made terrific copy and I received a "herogram" from Richard Stott, who was then assistant editor in charge of news. He sent a message telling me to enjoy a long weekend in Rio – adding that the editor wondered if the girls on Copacabana Beach really were the best looking in the world, which meant we were expected to bring back a feature!

I'd always thought that if I was doing well at the *Mirror* after ten years, it might be time to move on, and in 1989 John Merritt, who was by then working for *The Observer*, and I were offered the joint-editorship of Insight at *The Sunday Times*. Although I had grown up with the *Mirror* – my Polish father learned his English by reading Cassandra and my Irish mother read the paper, too – I hadn't had any substantial pay rises and *The Sunday Times* was offering more. Richard Stott, the editor then, went berserk when I said I wanted to leave and Joe Haines, who had become something of a mentor to me, said, "You're a *Mirror* person" and arranged for me to see Robert Maxwell.

Maxwell knew me – mainly because mine was the only name he could remember! – and he asked me how much *The Sunday Times* was offering and then added, "And if you are going to make it up, don't make it up for more than £3,000 more than they've really offered!" He matched *The Sunday Times* money and then asked me who was going to tell Stott, who liked to control his own editorial salary budget. I said, "You are", but he didn't of course. Stott exploded when he found out, but later, when he left to edit *The People*, he wrote me the nicest letter I ever received from anyone on the *Mirror*.

When Roy Greenslade was editor, I was given all the stuff written by reporters Terry Pattinson, Frank Thorne and Ted Oliver on their inquiry into Arthur Scargill's alleged misuse of miners' strike funds. I locked myself away for a week and turned it into a five-part series, which didn't please the reporters much until they won an award for the story. Then, when Colin Myler was editor, I got a yellow card after I had cocked up a story and a rival paper got something that we didn't. Suddenly I was given an official warning about my attitude and manner. I was told that some of those running the paper thought they would earn brownie points from the chief executive, David Montgomery, by getting rid of me, as I was one of the last "old *Mirror*" journalists left. But they were wrong – whatever you say about Montgomery, he vetoed any ideas of firing me.

When Piers Morgan became editor, he said, "I'm a young guy on a steep learning curve and I just want you to go out and win me awards." Well, seven of mine have come under Piers. My latest big assignment was going to Baghdad during Gulf War 2. It was the worst experience of my journalistic life – you just didn't know what was going to come at you. The Palestine Hotel was like the Hotel California – you could check out, but you could never leave! Quite early on, Piers came on the phone and said there would be no problem if I wanted to pull out, but I hung on. The rooms were filthy and there was nothing to eat. Some reporters had already left and those still there faced the dilemma of whether to go or stay. But, as I wrote in the paper, going places and being there is what journalists do.

What I have learned over the years is that the *Mirror* is not a "product" and the people who buy it are not "customers", they are our readers. The paper is a vibrant, energetic and, sometimes, sensitive entity that needs nurturing rather than simply being required to satisfy the demands of shareholders. I believe that the young reporters of today are, as a group, much better than we were when I started out. There are some terrific people at the *Mirror* – people like, dare I say it, I am in their feelings about the paper. People who love it so much, they won't be going to work for any other.

'

the water. The place became known as the House of All Light. Frankly, Waterhouse and I never ever got to know the name of the street, so it was much simpler just to say to taxi drivers, "Grosse Point... House of All Light." They knew exactly where to go. The drought broke while we were there with the most spectacular storm ever seen. Inches of rain fell in driving wind. The sky was coal black. The house was like a lighthouse. The sprinkler system kept going through all this and the road flooded. Our sprinklers were unstoppable. When

we left Detroit for home, it was all still blazing and soaking."

It was at the same Republican Convention that Chris Buckland's briefcase was, for the British, more of a talking point than anything in Ronald Reagan's Party carnival. A bar the British and Australian press favoured in the Joe Louis Arena, where the convention was being held, was scheduled to open at 3pm, because that's when the delegates arrived. The British and Australians succeeded in getting it to open at 10am, because that was when they arrived. One

Diverse talents: (top row left to right) Art director Paddy O'Gara, columnist Paul Foot, feature writer John Edwards, (bottom row left to right) reporter Richard Stott and feature writer Christine Garbutt.

night, Buckland mistakenly left his briefcase in the bar. Security was tight. His whole life was in the case: passport, mortgage papers, insurance documents, bank statements. It vanished and when, the next day, he went to the FBI to ask of its whereabouts was told that out in the lake that he could see through the office window was a tiny island where unidentified items were often taken and blown up. Buckland was mortified. It wasn't until two days later that the barman who had been on duty the night the briefcase went missing turned up to inform the Brits that he had noticed the case had been left behind and, as he had nowhere to keep it safe, had locked it in the ice cabinet. It was still there, by now sealed inside a block of ice. An ice pick had Buckland back in business in about ten minutes.

Back in Britain, the country had, in May 1979, once again rejected Labour in favour of a Conservative Government. The *Mirror*'s campaign had been as forceful on behalf of Labour as always, but Jim Callaghan's Winter of Discontent had allowed Margaret Thatcher to lead the Tories to victory with an overall majority of 43. Molloy was despondent. Like Cudlipp, he didn't like coming second and the circumstances of *The Sun* usurping the *Mirror* at the top of the circulation tree rankled still.

The paper was producing stunning journalism – John Pilger and photographer Eric Piper's coverage of the slaughter in Cambodia, and Molloy's front page and the quality of the writing when John Lennon was shot dead in New York set standards no other tabloid could match.

Major events, too, like the 1979 IRA murder of Lord Mountbatten and marriage of Prince Charles and Lady Diana Spencer in 1981 – the executive staff jogged down Fetter Lane to watch the royal procession pass along Fleet Street – always brought out the best in the editor, and his intuitive hiring talents hadn't deserted him, either. I was astonished when, in the summer of 1979, he asked what I thought of the idea of signing Paul Foot to write a weekly page, but he went to Foot's home that same evening and persuaded him to come to the *Mirror*. "I'd met Paul at a *Private Eye* lunch," Molloy recalls. "I wanted someone to put some balls into the paper and knew he could, although I did wonder if I could get away with bringing to the paper a Trotskyist and member of the Socialist Workers' Party. Paul was horrified when I told him a company car came as part of his deal. He turned it down but came to me later and asked if he could have a London

Follow The Sun: *Topless models featured from the end of 1975 – but not necessarily every day.*

Another war: *Joe Haines goes for the jugular, attacking* The Sun *during the Falklands crisis.*

Underground season ticket instead. The management refused. They said that if they gave one to Paul, everyone would want one. I just told him to put it on his expenses."

In April 1982, the Falklands War split the inner cabinet that formulated editorial policy, with Geoffrey Goodman and Terry Lancaster in favour, and Tony Miles and Joe Haines opposing the Government's decision to send a task force. Molloy's casting vote decided, not for the last time, that the paper would not support a war. The paper's calls for compromise angered both Prime Minister Thatcher and *The Sun* and the latter attacked the *Mirror* as a "timorous, whining publication" that "has no faith in its country and no respect for her people". Haines' reply in a *Mirror* editorial headlined "The Harlot of Fleet Street" was a masterpiece of invective: *The Sun* had "long been a tawdry newspaper," he wrote, "but since the Falklands crisis began it has fallen from the gutter to the sewer… *The Sun* today is to journalism what Dr Joseph Goebbels was to truth."

The *Mirror* had picked up the *What The Papers Say* Newspaper of the Year Award the previous year and, as the circulation war intensified, launched bingo, first in the northern editions only and then in them all as this temporary sales aphrodisiac swept through the popular press. Molloy tried to maintain balance in the paper and tested a black-and-white, picture-driven supplement, *Picture Mirror,*

which although visually stunning and beloved by staff and freelance photographers alike, failed to impress readers enough to be incorporated as an add-on attraction to the paper. The impetus to close the gap with *The Sun* remained elusive. The *Mirror*'s less brazen image, its general hostility towards Thatcherism and its tendency to occasionally treat serious subjects in a serious manner did not meet the criteria of a red-top revolution instigated by Murdoch that was every bit as radical as Bart's had been in the mid-1930s.

In the mid-1990s, the sociologist Richard Hoggart's examination of English culture, *The Way We Live Now* – a deliberate echo of Anthony Trollope – argued that newspapers generally present a distorted picture of the people for whom they claim to speak, "neglecting some aspects of their personalities and extending others; these actions taken together result in a caricature. To think *The Sun* represents the common norms of English working-class life is like assuming that low-budget, urban violence American films represent life in the towns of the Midwest."

Maybe so, but it was beginning to look as if *The Sun* had won the battle of the red-top tabloids. And in the boardroom at Reed International, never a hotbed of fervour for the *Mirror,* there were those now thinking that it was time for the company to hoist the white flag.

Bill Hagerty was born in 1939 and educated at Beal Grammar School, Ilford, Essex. Trained on local newspapers in east London, he joined the Daily Mirror *from the* Daily Sketch *as a features sub-editor in 1967. After a year on* Mirror *Magazine, he was subsequently features editor, showbusiness editor and an assistant editor. After spells as an assistant editor at the* Sunday Mirror *and* The People*, he left to join* Today*. For six months, he edited* Sunday Today *before returning to Mirror Group as deputy editor of the* Sunday Mirror*. He was deputy editor of the* Daily Mirror *before editing the* People*, 1991-92. He now edits the* British Journalism Review*.

'Older men forget, even old journalists. Unless, that is, they are sensible enough to keep diaries to aid recollection as the final deadline gets closer. I was sensible in this way for no more than 13 months, scribbling the day's happenings: from the beginning of 1971 until the end of January the following year. I was 31 when appointed features editor of the *Daily Mirror*, having spent a joyful year at *Mirror* Magazine. The magazine closed down, but Mike Molloy, its editor, and I must have done something right as we were promptly parachuted into the newspaper's features department, Molloy as assistant editor in charge.

Today, the diary makes fascinating reading only for those who were there at the time. But a few of the entries illustrate perfectly how different national newspaper life was 30 years ago, when the Murdoch *Sun* had risen, but was yet to scorch the *Mirror*'s shirt-tail, and even after all those years conveys how exciting it was – and, I am sure, still is – to be young, relatively well paid, and working on the bridge, or at the very least at the top of the staircase just outside, of a mighty ocean liner of a newspaper that appeared indestructible. Like the glorious summers of youth, real or imagined, one never wanted those balmy days to end…

Wednesday 10 February: I thought it would be a good idea to sign Bobby Moore to do a weekly column, not primarily about football and to run in the features pages. Mike Molloy suggested Pat Doncaster should ghost it. [New editor Tony] Miles thought it a good idea, so I put it to Bobby over the phone and he's keen if the money is right. Later he agreed to it on an initial three-month contract for £60 a week.

Tuesday 2 March: Lunch with Reg Smythe [creator of Andy Capp], who says he knows he is wealthy because he earns £40,000 a year [I was earning £5,600] and is £20,000 in debt – he said when he was getting £40 a week, he never owed a penny.

Friday 11 June: Tony wants to run a competition – Go to Brazil with England's Captain to See Pele Play His Last Internationals. Pele's international career ends next month. Spoke with Pat Doncaster, who is in Los Angeles. Bobby agrees, but there are conditions: he will take Tina, they must travel first-class etc., which is fair enough.

Tuesday 15 June: Pat Doncaster isn't enthralled at the prospect of roaring off abroad again so soon. I went to see Tony early in the evening and he said: "Well you can

go to Brazil with Booby Moore then, cock. You deserve a trip." Percy Roberts cleared the cost only today. I shall be away 12 days. [I was, too!]

Friday 18 June: To the Café Royal for the long-delayed farewell lunch for Lee Howard. With typical *Mirror* efficiency, the whole affair had been arranged, the date confirmed and invitations issued, but no one had bothered to confirm with Lee – he had to phone the previous day to see if it was on. Earlier in the day, the features department moved into new offices, a few yards from the old ones. Cudlipp wandered down "just to see what your new accommodation is like". He has been worryingly friendly of late.

Friday 23 July: Peter Salton [sub-editor] came to me with a reader's letter concerning a series about witchcraft, which ran earlier this week. It had concluded with three "love potions" taken from an American book, one of which included lily of the valley as an ingredient. The letter Salton unearthed claimed that the flower is poisonous! True – he checked with Middlesex Hospital. We decided to run a paragraph of warning on page 2.

Wednesday 10 November: Our Shock Issue on pollution, which I more or less totally rewrote on Sunday and Monday, was at last looking something like in shape when Cudlipp came into Tony's office and, looking at a couple of overnight proofs, said he wanted crossheads – I hadn't used any. So I spent two hours on the stone, cutting all the copy. Lack of bottle was prevalent everywhere. After I left, Mike [Molloy] redid some of the pages to get even more crossheads in.

Monday 6 December: Cudlipp held a lunch for Tony Miles at the Café Royal to celebrate Miles' appointment to the board. There must have been about 70 people there. Cudlipp, obviously having had a few drinks already, mingled before lunch. He was in his gruff but friendly mood – I was talking to Donald Zec when he [Cudlipp] told me I had lovely hair! As one might have predicted, Hugh went too far in his speech, attacking Dennis Hackett [former publicity director] and Lee Howard [former editor; neither he nor Hackett was present]. What Alex Jarratt [incoming managing director and Cudlipp's successor as chairman], attending his first *Mirror* lunch, made of it all, I cannot imagine.

Sunday 19 December: We started work today on the 48-page Christmas *Mirror*, the biggest issue of the paper ever. The decision to go ahead had been delayed because of protracted negotiation with the unions. The journalists eventually settled for an extra £8.50, plus a fiver expenses.

Sadly, indolence or lack of resolve dictated that the diary entries stopped soon after this. But my unwritten memories are priceless…

In 1972, Cudlipp decided that Mike Taylor, the night editor and a potential high-flyer who later became deputy editor, should experience at first hand the Common Market, which Britain was about to join. Cudlipp told Mike to choose a companion with whom to travel on an "educational" month-long tour of mainland Europe. Taylor wanted to take features writer Jill Evans, his girlfriend at

Billboard: Hagerty's by-line picture.

the time, but, unsurprisingly, the editor vetoed that. So Taylor nominated me and I'm still grateful that he did: in two trips, each lasting a fortnight, we visited Holland, Belgium, France, Germany and Italy, without anybody protesting, or caring, that they were outside the Common Market, Spain, Greece and Poland... and Turkey. When we returned, we submitted the required report of impressions gleaned and knowledge gained during our travels. As far as I am aware, Cudlipp never read it.

I cannot recall the year of Eric Wainwright's retirement, or the date his last piece appeared in the paper, although it was some years before his leaving (I do know he was earning £4,172 a year in March 1973 and, understandably perhaps, had not received a salary increase since the end of 1967). He had joined the staff in 1950 and had become part of the fixtures and fittings in Holborn, or would have, had he turned up more frequently. When the time came for his departure, the *Mirror* responded in typical fashion: dinner at The Ritz.

The pre-dinner reception spilled into a ground-floor corridor and a group of us were standing there, glasses in hands, when Her Majesty the Queen Mother and her entourage approached slowly towards us. Standing close by me was Arthur Thirkell, film and theatre critic – don't say to yourself, "A seat in the Thirkle" or you'll be more than 30 years late with the gag – and, presumably recognising him from film premieres or command performances, the Queen Mum paused alongside our dinner-jacketed and still relatively sober group. Thirkell introduced Wainwright and explained it was his farewell party. The Queen Mum beamed, shook Wainwright warmly by the hand and said: "I shall miss reading your articles." The venerable old dear must have had a spectacular memory.

Later, when running a show business department for

editor Mike Molloy, I had the idea of asking Debbie Harry, at the time a superstar with her band, Blondie, if she would be photographed wearing a gymslip and school shirt and tie. Why? Give me a reason why not. The shoot was in the studio a floor below the newsroom, so I went into Molloy's office and said, "Come with me." I wouldn't explain further and Molloy rather grumpily followed me downstairs. When I opened the door to the studio, where rock music writer Pauline McLeod was by now interviewing Ms Harry, Molloy took one look and said, "Jesus Christ!" I've never forgotten Blondie in a gymslip. Neither, I suspect, has Molloy.

On a trip to the United States I was diverted from somewhere to Los Angeles: the office had arranged an interview with John Wayne, still an enormous star in the 1970s. I was driven directly from the airport to the John Wayne Tennis and Country Club at Newport Beach, where the great man was drinking with cronies. He shooed them away and opened a fresh bottle of his specially imported tequila, which we shared. After a light lunch – more tequila – Wayne went out into the sunshine to be photographed by the British freelance, Bob Aylott, whom the picture desk in London had assigned. Wayne agreed to mount the steps to the umpire's chair on an empty tennis court. When he was halfway up the steps, with his back to the camera, Aylott started to take pictures. Wayne was furious, and rightly so: "Are you trying to photograph a pimple on my god-damned ass?" he growled, climbing swiftly back down the steps. Which is when, by talking fast, I prevented John Wayne from unleashing one of the most famous right-hand punches outside of the boxing ring on Aylott's chin.

On another trip, I was arrested on the Santa Monica freeway when driving back to Beverly Hills from a party at which I had been reasonably abstemious and Robert Mitchum had sent out for cigarette papers. No tobacco, just papers. The solo cop in a car made me walk a chalk line on the road, called for my rental car to be towed away and drove me, handcuffed, to a police station where I was breathalysed. He presumably did not want the bother of redoing his paperwork, so left me in a holding cell overnight even though I had, unknowingly, passed the breath test. Next morning, I appeared in court to be charged with illegally crossing a freeway lane and was fined 20 dollars.

During the night, I had demanded my statutory one telephone call – I'd seen it on the movies – and from a phone on wheels that was trundled up to the bars of the cell I made a reverse charge call to the editor and explained my predicament. Molloy broke off the conversation for a few seconds and I could hear another voice, "That was Percy Roberts," he said when he resumed. "He said not to forget that this call's costing a pound a minute."

Recalling co-authoring *The Front Page*, that finest of stage plays about newspaper journalism, Ben Hecht said that he and Charles MacArthur were writing "of people we loved and of employment that had been like no other was ever to be." Hecht also lamented: "Would that our writing had been as fine as our lunches." I know just what he meant, on both counts.

8 CAPTAIN ON THE BRIDGE

It is a few minutes after midnight and therefore the morning of Friday 13 July 1984, and the new proprietor of the Daily Mirror *is about to break his word to the paper for the first, but by no means the last, time. Robert Maxwell, born Ludvik Hoch, has gained control of Mirror Group Newspapers despite assurances that it would not be sold to any individual. Maxwell has promised not to inflame a delicate situation by visiting the Holborn building, but, within minutes of giving that undertaking, is prowling the newsroom and then the executive ninth floor. Tony Miles, now deputy chairman and editorial director of MGN, has gone home, but returns when it becomes clear that Maxwell's visit is not purely social, even though he stomps into the office of chief executive Douglas Long, marches to the drinks cabinet and says: "I am going to have a drink. Anyone else want one?"*

The publisher, as he is to insist he is referred to, has called a board meeting. Bob Edwards, Sunday Mirror *editor and an old acquaintance of the new owner, is already at Maxwell House in the city and is ferried back to Holborn in the boss's Rolls-Royce. Douglas Long, editor Molloy and advertising director Roger Bowes are present, having been at a dinner in the executive dining suite. Other directors are summoned from their homes and a reporter and photographer are sent by the astute night news editor to record this historic event. The board meeting is short, but the directors are informed there will be another later that day. The editors of the three national titles are instructed to be available for lunch at Claridge's. Eventually Maxwell sweeps from the building and into the waiting Rolls. It is a little after 3am…*

Robert Maxwell had long wanted to own a national newspaper. He had flirted with various ideas for a Labour-supporting daily paper and had lost out to Rupert Murdoch when attempting to buy the *News of the World* and then the IPC *Sun*. But Maxwell was nothing if not determined. Like he had on several occasions in the past, he lived to fight another day.

But nobody realised he was waxing his holster and checking his gun was loaded when, in the late 1970s, Alex Jarratt briefed Percy Roberts, who had succeeded Sir Edward Pickering as Mirror Group Newspapers chairman, with one sentence: "Make a profit." Roberts managed it most years, but with the unions often rampant, *The Sun* constantly and hugely outspending the *Daily Mirror* on television advertising, and the cover price of the *Mirror* higher than its main rival most of the time, it was a hard slog. The Reed board, disenchanted and determined to restructure the main company, decided MGN was a luxury it no longer wanted to afford. The 1982 figures of what once had been a money machine – a profit of £2.1million, 80 per cent down on 1981, on a turnover of £250million – did nothing to dissuade them.

Despite the recently knighted Sir Alex Jarratt's affection for the newspapers, most members of the IPC board were opposed to its political views and were concerned that the trades unions would get so out of control that other businesses in the Reed empire would be affected. Jarratt, however, was appreciative of the *Daily Mirror*'s sometimes abrasive but constant relationship with the Labour Party and determined that Reed should not jeopardise it. So in announcing the intention to float MGN as

Gotcha: A proud Robert Maxwell announces that he has bought the Mirror. *A turbulent time lay ahead for the Group and everyone who worked for the papers.*

a separate company, he went out of his way to emphasise that no individual would be allowed to obtain enough shares to control it. Maxwell, lurking out of sight and if not out of mind, must have allowed himself a wry smile.

"Reed had made it clear that they didn't want us," Mike Molloy recalls. "They cut the promotions budgets and insisted we bought inferior Reed paper, which meant we were not as well printed as *The Sun*. And Roger Bowes was having to sell advertising space at a discount to keep the cash flow and profits up. But we weren't helping much. There was a board level spat where two directors weren't speaking to one another and we ended up with some new casting equipment for the foundry that just didn't work and for a long time we were unable to produce an edition for the Midlands. We were running twice as fast just to stay in the same place."

Rumours about a possible bid by Maxwell had been circulating for months in Holborn. Joe Haines reported his concern at a lunch attended by Miles, Geoffrey Goodman, Terry Lancaster and Bob Edwards. Lancaster and Edwards were

unfazed; the others horrified. The *Mirror*'s NUJ chapel decided to seek out a friendly intermediary to discuss with Reed the possibility of a staff buy-out of the *Mirror*, but the plan was jettisoned when Reed asked Tony Miles, chairman and editorial director since Percy Roberts had retired, and Doug Long, who had picked up the chief executive slice of Roberts's role, to look around for a potential chairman for the independent company. They had no ideas, so summoned city editor Robert Head to see if he did. Head suggested Sir Peter Parker, the cultured and highly successful company director – he was again to figure, briefly, in *Mirror* history a decade hence – and Clive Thornton, a determined character who had overcome losing a foot as a child to become admired within the Square Mile for smoothly running the Abbey National Building Society. Miles and Long liked the sound of Thornton, and Thornton, it transpired, liked the sound of the job they were offering.

With Reed keeping a nervous eye on the stock market, which was not behaving at all in a manner conducive to a flotation that would

First person   SIR ALEX JARRATT

Sir Alex Jarratt was born in 1924 and educated at the Royal Liberty Grammar School, Essex, and the University of Birmingham. He served in the Fleet Air Arm, 1942-66, and after university worked in the Civil Service until 1970, when he became managing director of IPC, 1970-73; chairman of IPC and IPC Newspapers, 1974; and chairman of Reed International, 1975-85. He was knighted in 1979. He was chancellor of Birmingham University for 19 years until 2002 and now devotes time to working for Age Concern and various charitable trusts.

'When I joined IPC in 1970, Hugh Cudlipp was chairman and the *Mirror* was financially in bad shape. The Mirror Group board had been desperately anxious that the reverse takeover by Reed should take place successfully and that its editorial freedom should be maintained, but they knew what might happen – the *Mirror* might go down the chute. I handled the Government end of the merger, which is how I came on the scene. I remember Hugh Cudlipp coming to see me for the first time – I was in the Department of Employment and Productivity with Barbara Castle – and saying, "I'll have you know, Mr Jarratt, I am Fleet Street's best editor and lousiest manager." Those were the first words he ever spoke to me.

But editorially, I think the paper was still extremely strong. With Hugh there, it was the usual mixture of highly personal stories and the famous shock horror stuff, plus Hugh's view of leading articles – no sentence more than ten words, no words more than two syllables and you could deal with any subject that exists. Dead right in my view, too. The paper had great social weight at that time, so although the whole empire was financially weak – it had overstretched itself – the *Mirror* was still editorially very strong.

Then along came Rupert Murdoch. And the effect of Rupert on the editorial judgement of the *Mirror* was fundamental. Murdoch sat on the shoulders of the *Mirror* in terms of pricing policy, editorial personality and liveliness. It had the *Mirror*'s style without the *Mirror*'s very serious attempt to deal with major issues. And it was very good on sport. Then came a period of price control, where you had to acquire so many [extra] costs before you could put up the price, and we had these battles where we could have put up the price – the *Mirror* had always led on price – but "by God we've got Murdoch there now…" It caused a lot of confusion financially while the editorial battle was still going on.

Meanwhile, in the background of all this was the final flowering of the total strength of the unions, which caused battle after battle. The inability of Fleet Street to come together to deal with that threat – they tried several times, but someone would always break the line – was disastrous. The attempt in the mid-1970s by the *Mirror*, including me, I might add, as its managing director, to bring in automatic page composition didn't work. The unions made sure that it didn't work until they owned it and commanded it and we had to call it off. It was a major defeat and it blocked us off from making a significant breakthrough in manning and cost control.

I don't know how many times I sat up through the night, eating bacon and egg sandwiches with Percy Roberts and Ted Blackmore [directors] and others on some crazy [union] dispute. The danger was that the disputes had a culture of their own – they almost became enjoyable, for both sides. It was a game. At times, the game could get nasty. There are tribes, aren't there, who just pretend to fight each other but every now and again someone slips and spears somebody? It was like that. There was an atmosphere sometimes in the *Mirror* building of "Keep them talking, keep the presses rolling", almost with a giggle in your voice while you were saying it. So management were part of the problem, although I think our management at that time showed themselves capable of providing part of the solution too. We fought one or two great battles in which we won about 75 per cent of what we wanted. But what we had was the ultimate combination of a perishable product and a powerful production force. The two things don't sit readily together.

Hugh retired and Tony Miles took over and things largely settled down. The *Mirror* was losing circulation to *The Sun* but it had a good run because politically it was able to have a go at Ted Heath and support a Labour Government. The unions continued to be a problem – in many ways the unions made the chief executives of public

realise the price they required, Thornton took stock of a business where the unions frequently had management on the rack, and management and editorial staff eased the pain with conviviality of the liquid kind. Thornton, who barely drank and believed he could appeal to the unions' loyalty in order to turn around the business, hosted dinners for the Group's senior editorial executives and when, in the short gap between two such evenings, I moved from the *Sunday Mirror* to join newly appointed editor Richard Stott at *The People*, I bizarrely twice found myself sitting next to the fledgling chairman. He was pleasant and obviously committed, but patently did not realise quite how daunting was the task ahead. What the Group needed was a Cavalier and the cautious, moderate Thornton was a Roundhead. "In the land of the legless, the one-legged man is king," Paddy O'Gara cynically and memorably observed, but he was wrong – the king was destined never to be crowned.

Thornton drafted an admirable "protective structure" that guaranteed the independence of

Dilemma: Alex Jarratt (second left) with IPC directors Gordon Cartright (on his right), John Chandler and George Bogle.

companies look like amateurs in terms of prestige, autonomy and looking after their own patches. Eddy Shah, who initially had the guts and really was responsible for it, and Rupert Murdoch were weakening their strength elsewhere, of course.

I had written the conditions under which Reed took over IPC, which included Reed not putting pressure on the Mirror Group to use its newsprint and, most importantly, that the *Mirror*'s editorial freedom should be preserved. And we kept to that – Reed never interfered at all. There weren't many people at Reed International who had a feeling for newspapers. They had a feeling for the rest of IPC, the magazines and books, so could see them more readily as a business and one not affected by politics and, to a lesser extent, affected by the unions. The board, roughly speaking, regarded newspapers as profligate, trade union-ridden, something they wouldn't really wish to be associated with – and, for quite a few of them, the *Mirror* was supporting the wrong party. I remember attending my first strategic planning meeting at Reed. There were six divisions and I was in charge of one

and IPC was put down as being the sixth, the last, in terms of importance.

When it came time for Reed to reconsider its whole structure, we began to get rid of things – we sold our interests in Australia and South Africa and the next on the list was the Mirror Group. The board decided that it was something they did not see as being part of the future of Reed – they hadn't done, basically, for some while. They thought the other disposals were more urgent and the overseas sales were completed by 1979-80. And then we began to look at the UK portfolio. By 1982, we announced the intention to float Mirror Group in the autumn of 1983. Investment bankers and stockbrokers advised that we could float it for around £85million.

At the press conference when I announced this, one journalist asked me, "How does it feel not to be a press baron?" and I said, "I've never felt I was one. It was never that sort of relationship." There was a long process ahead, six or eight months of work, which was

Continued on page 162

the newspapers by ensuring that no single shareholder could own more than 15 per cent of the equity. But most of the trades unions rejected his overtures to obtain no-strike guarantees that would, he believed, make the company a viable proposition for potential shareholders. He was nonplussed, Reed were impatient, the staff increasingly worried. Maxwell, watching the city shy away from a company obviously in disarray, made his move on 4 July 1984, tabling an offer of £80 million together with a guarantee of continuing support

for Labour. Reed rejected it.

"The Thornton situation had become surreal," says Mike Molloy. "Tony Miles and Doug Long liked this little guy with one leg – he didn't frighten them like some tough city operator would have done. But after a while, when Maxwell was obviously stalking the company, Ken Hudgell, the company secretary, was actually running the place. Reed denied more than once that they would sell to Maxwell – there were lunches at Browns Hotel that I attended with Miles and Long, the other editors

First person SIR ALEX JARRATT

appropriate and necessary. While that was happening the stock market fell and Mirror Group had a lousy time – I think they made £1million profit, not a loss but not far off. It became obvious that the float we had envisaged was not going to happen and we were told that we would get about half what we had anticipated – £40million plus. So we pulled back, and when that became known, Tony Miles and Douglas Long found Clive Thornton and made a management buy-out proposal.

Clive Thornton hadn't been in the business before but he had made a reputation for himself at Abbey National and he had Tony and Douglas as his lieutenants. The management buy-out bid actually made some progress, but then, one morning, my phone rang and there was our friend, Robert Maxwell, saying he wanted to buy the *Mirror*. I said it wasn't for sale, so he said, "I want to come and see you". I said, "I don't want to see you", so he said, "Well, I'll send a letter – you can't refuse a letter, can you?"

We'd had a previous relationship. Reed had three photogravure plants in this country, on which we printed our colour magazines. One was at Odhams, Watford, and Maxwell owned printers at Watford. I had more trouble than anyone with Odhams Watford, it was a very, very difficult factory, so I sold the factory to Maxwell for a pound. He closed it and paid the redundancy bill; we gave him a contract to print two of our magazines and he actually sold the business to the workers. It was a sweetheart deal. Both sides came out well. He was a remarkable fellow, no doubt about it. He had tried to buy Butterworths from me, but I wouldn't let him near it. We were both flying on Concorde around that time and after lunch I wanted to go for a pee. But Maxwell, who was in a front seat wearing that great big coat of his, got up and stood astride me and boomed, "I want to buy Butterworths". I was trapped in my seat, but I said, "It's not for sale, Bob".

Having told him the *Mirror* wasn't for sale, I got the letter with a formal offer. Two weeks later, during which time I was saying in public and telling him that I was not going to sell and he kept pushing up the price, one or two of my institutional investors rang me up and said, "You

don't really mean we are not going to sell at this price, do you?" We were talking about £113million net, but something around £90million after we assumed some debt – more than twice what we had been told we would get from a flotation. At that price, there was no way that the board could say no.

A lot of people were very upset. Clive Thornton was very upset because he had lost his function. The unions were very furious because they didn't trust Maxwell. And Tony and Douglas were not very pleased, although they shook down with Maxwell fairly rapidly as far as I could gather. I should say in passing that I handed over to Maxwell an actuarially assessed pension fund that was actually in surplus.

I didn't feel bitter in the end about him taking the *Mirror* because, although he was a bastard, when he ran the papers, before he got involved with Macmillans and whatever, he invested more in them than I did. The bitter bit – bitter for the people concerned and bitter for me – was that I had preserved their pension rights perfectly. The Mirror Group ones were more or less recovered [after Maxwell had plundered the pension fund], of course, but some other people are still in trouble today.

The final negotiations came to a crunch on a Thursday night when we received a banker's draft for the money so that we could put it into the bank first thing in the morning – we knew who we were dealing with. And that was it, really. Despite what the unions claimed, I had never said that I would not sell to Maxwell. The unions told me that they did not want me to sell to Maxwell – there's no doubt about that. What I did say, right from the outset, was that it was my intention not to sell to any individual person. I did say that, quite clearly, when I was asked if I would sell to any other proprietor. I went back on that, it's true. I went back on it because the money we would get from a flotation was proving to be less than half of what Maxwell was offering. There was no way the board was going to agree that we should resist his bid and carry on, hoping to float later. They stayed with me in opposing the bid as long as they thought it appropriate, but it became clear that the only way we were going to get the amount of money we had originally hoped for was from Maxwell.

and either Jarratt or Les Carpenter where it was definitely said. They also told us that Maxwell didn't have the necessary funds."

Tony Miles then suggested that Molloy should speak with Neil Kinnock, who had succeeded Michael Foot as leader of the Labour Party after its disastrous General Election of 1983, when the Conservatives had increased their overall majority to 143. Molloy knew Kinnock, who lived near him in Ealing, west London, and Miles urged the editor to obtain a public statement affirming that the Labour Party did

not want the *Mirror* sold to Maxwell. "I pointed out that I did not have a contract and that as Maxwell would probably fire me if he did get hold of MGN, I would like some assurances," Molloy recalls. "So Miles telephoned Carpenter and reported back that Les had said Reed would 'look after me', whatever that meant. I spoke with Neil, who was evasive and shifty – Maxwell had already got to the deputy leader, Roy Hattersley, and promised him that everything would be fine."

Richard Stott later unearthed the severity of

Tall order: Clive Thornton, flanked by Tony Miles and Douglas Long on his appointment as Mirror Group chairman.

If people had not felt hurt, troubled, left out, furious, it would have been marvellous. But I did at the time what I thought was right as chairman of a public company. What I did was not going to be acceptable to many people, I was totally aware of that, but if you are running something, I fear that's something you have to live with. And if I were to start a list of who let down whom over time, then I would have a few things [within the company] to put on the other side of the sheet. I think people are wholly entitled to attack me for what I did, just as I am perfectly entitled to say that what I did was right in the circumstances.

Apart from the proposed management buy-out, there were no other suitors. I've always said that I didn't sell the newspaper to Robert Maxwell; he bought it from me, because he was determined to have it and said so. As chairman, I didn't do the negotiations. Les Carpenter, who was then the chief executive of Reed, did the final negotiations on that Thursday. And they were tough, I believe – Les was a very tough negotiator and he knew Robert Maxwell extremely well because he'd been in the magazine business for years. Negotiations were tough,

yes, in tying up the loose ends of the contract, but not in the sense of haggling over money, because Maxwell kept pushing money across the table. Hence the phone calls from shareholders urging us to negotiate. Institutional shareholders don't command what you do, but nor do you ignore what they have to say.

I didn't meet Maxwell at all during this period. Les asked him not to go to the *Mirror* building when the deal was done and he agreed, but of course he went there straightaway. The man was a rogue, but he had many fine entrepreneurial qualities and you need colourful people in business. He was one of them, but totally flawed. Sad in many ways. What happened was terrible, stupid and terrible. Nobody will ever know the truth about his death, of course – I have two Jewish friends who quite separately have come to reckon that he knew things about Israel's relationships with Russia that might come out because he was in trouble, so Mossad had him killed.

I don't feel guilt about selling to Maxwell, but I have mixed feelings. I regret that I was unable to do what I set out to do and carried my board in agreeing what we should do, namely to float it. I always thought it was the best solution, because with new shareholding you could maintain the editorial freedom that I had helped preserve right up until the *Mirror* left our ownership. I was sad that we did not achieve that. But against that, Maxwell was the sort of man to be in charge of popular newspapers in a highly competitive market that was being led, essentially, by Murdoch. He had that sense of rough and tumble and ability to get in there and mix it, which we didn't.

I believe that if Maxwell had not attempted to become the world's biggest publisher, if he had stayed as a press baron, it may have been uncomfortable working under him but in terms of the determination to win, the enthusiasm he brought and a feeling for being in the business, it could have been all right, you know. **'**

the situation Thornton confronted. The here-today-gone-tomorrow chairman discovered that personal expenses within the company were running at a total of £5million a year and that almost £1.4million of this was claimed for business entertaining. What's more, he had requested, and been provided with, a list of employees whose expenses were more than £8,000 a year. Many of these had, Thornton learned, recently been awarded salary increases – "I cannot continue to present a bleak picture

to trade unions and ask for restraint against this background," he wrote to the board. He suggested that the expenses figure should be halved, but before the axe fell, Jarratt and Carpenter were to whisk the carpet from under Thornton's feet.

Maxwell, determined that this paper would not be yet another that got away, increased his offer. Reed, having cooled on the flotation plan when the projected figure it would achieve was revised from £85million to £45million, decided to listen, and chief executive Les Carpenter met with Maxwell at the Ritz, opposite Reed's headquarters, to negotiate. At an NUJ chapel meeting at the *Mirror*, passions ran high and Joe Haines told the assembled journalists that he would have to be "dragged through the door to work for a monster like Robert Maxwell". Haines somewhat ruefully remembers: "Yes, I called him a crook at that meeting and warned people not to allow him through the front door. Then he bought the Group and I warned my wife that I would be fired that day."

Maxwell had increased his offer to £113million, although assumed debts effectively reduced this to £90million – £5million more than the original amount Reed were told the flotation would realise. There was, Jarratt decided, no way he could keep faith with Reed shareholders without accepting. Appreciating that the *Mirror* management and the unions would vilify him, he did so. Maxwell, elated at having obtained the company for probably no more than £40million on top of the worth of the MGN buildings, proposed paying by banker's draft. Carpenter rejected the idea, but agreed to a cheque that would be paid directly to Reed's bankers after Sir Robert Clark, chairman of Maxwell's bankers, Hill Samuel, had been woken to authorise it. Carpenter re-crossed the street from the Ritz. Maxwell promised Carpenter he would stay away from Holborn that night, summoned his Rolls-Royce and headed off to Claridge's for a celebratory dinner. Arriving in Holborn the following morning to find Maxwell sitting at his desk, Clive Thornton petulantly tore up a copy of the *Daily Mirror* and went home.

Born in what was then Czechoslovakia in 1923, Ludvik Hoch (the name is spelt variously, but this is that used in Joe Haines' official biography) was one of seven children and grew up in extreme poverty. Most of his family died in the Holocaust, but he fled to France, where he fought with a division of the Free Czech Army before being evacuated and transported by sea to Liverpool. He joined the British Army and served in the Pioneer Corps until October 1943, a frustrating time for a young man anxious to kill Nazis but a period during which he learned English and changed his name to Ivan du Maurier, after the cigarettes he smoked. Transferred first to the Somerset Light Infantry and then the 6th North Staffords, Lance-

Corporal Leslie du Maurier, as he now was, crossed to France soon after D-Day and became a lance-corporal and then a sergeant while fighting in Normandy. Further promotion, to staff sergeant, and a recommendation for a commission saw him assigned to work with an Intelligence unit in Paris, where he met Elisabeth Meynard, and, before returning to the front promised her he would win a Military Cross.

Military Cross duly won, for bravery in action when he led an advance across bullet-swept open ground "showing no regard for his own safety", Second Lieutenant Robert Maxwell – he had returned to England to be commissioned in the Queen's Royal Regiment (West Surrey) on 6 January 1945 – received his medal from Field-Marshal Montgomery on 5 March. He married Betty Meynard in Paris on 14 March, when she became Madame du Maurier – his official papers had yet to catch up with his latest and permanent change of name (he had also briefly been known as Jones and Smith, but settled on Maxwell because of what he thought was its solid Scots ring). After VE Day, work with Army Intelligence in Berlin and elsewhere saw him promoted to captain. It was a story straight out of *Boy's Own* and one hinting that Robert Maxwell was likely to go far in life no matter under which name he chose to travel.

His subsequent career, starting when he met Ferdinand Springer, the German publisher of scientific books in Berlin, saw the formation in England of Pergamon Press, which swiftly grew to become a major technical publisher and made its boss a millionaire. A self-described cradle Socialist, he fought the marginal seat of Buckingham for the Labour Party in 1959 as Captain Robert Maxwell, although convention dictates that officers below the level of major do not continue to use their rank. He lost, but won narrowly in 1964 and slightly increased his majority two years later. Losing the seat in 1970, he failed to regain it in the two General Elections of 1974 and withdrew from parliamentary politics. Pergamon had by now made him a very rich man indeed and had won the Queen's Award for Industry. But when irregularities discovered by the American Leasco Data Processing Company caused them to withdraw from a bid for Pergamon after obtaining a 38 per cent majority holding, the Department of Trade and Industry was called in

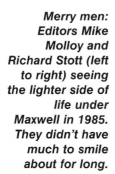

Merry men: Editors Mike Molloy and Richard Stott (left to right) seeing the lighter side of life under Maxwell in 1985. They didn't have much to smile about for long.

to investigate. Its inspectors famously concluded that, "notwithstanding Mr Maxwell's undoubted abilities and energy, he is not in our opinion a person who can be relied upon to exercise proper stewardship of a publicly quoted company".

Anyone who thought this body blow would finish off Maxwell should have closely examined his war record: whatever his failings, he did not lack courage or guile. He fought back and eventually regained control of Pergamon, which was located next to the grand house, Headington Hill Hall in Oxfordshire, that he leased from the council. The bouncing Czech had bounced right back.

After failing to get his hands on the *News of the World* and *The Sun* – and earlier rescue the Labour-supporting *Reynolds News*, which had gone to the wall under its tabloid reincarnation, *Sunday Citizen* – Maxwell became involved with the *Scottish Daily News*, which lasted only six months. He was approaching 60 and still on the outside of the media jungle when the Mirror Group came lurching through the undergrowth towards him. It was now or never – and Maxwell, as he had shown elsewhere, did not believe in never.

(Roy Greenslade has likened Maxwell to both *David Copperfield*'s Wilkins Micawber, the business failure who always believed something would turn up to make him rich, and Mr Merdle, of *Little Dorrit,* who was a Member of Parliament and apparently extremely rich through interests in "everything good from banking to building". A third analogy can be made with J.B. Priestley's James Golspie, the manipulative crook who ruins lives in *Angel Pavement* before departing by sea for Montevideo. But Merdle probably has the edge. He killed himself.)

When the Mirror Group national newspaper editors lunched with Maxwell at Claridge's, he listened as they described the shortcomings of the Group: union anarchy, lack of promotional funding, haphazard management. Back at Holborn, Cap'n Bob – Keith Waterhouse, far away at the Democratic Convention in San Francisco, coined the nickname when Roy Hattersley gave him the news of Captain Robert Maxwell's triumph – met with the *Daily Mirror*'s political team on the Sunday. Molloy suggested the slogan "Forward with the People" should be re-introduced on the front page. Maxwell decided he preferred "Forward with Britain" and that a statement of intent, written by Terry Lancaster to his instruction, should appear under that headline the following day:

"To me, the *Mirror* has always meant something special. I believe it means something special to those who work for it and you who buy it. The British people."

Molloy, knowing that Maxwell would be aware of his approach to Neil Kinnock, was surprised when told he had behaved loyally. Lancaster, guilty of no misdemeanour, was not invited to stay at the *Mirror*. Goodman reluctantly and suspiciously agreed to remain. Haines demanded that he should never be asked to write anything in which he didn't believe and later threatened to resign if even a word of the leading articles he wrote was changed. Maxwell concurred and Haines was promoted to assistant editor. As for the men whose presence on the ninth floor had overnight become redundant, Miles and Long were soon on their way, Miles to Florida and Long to become launch managing director of *The Independent*.

When the dust settled – not that it ever did completely during the publisher's tempestuous reign – there began a period of Maxwellmania that saw an already groggy newspaper at the mercy of a bully who thought he could make it better by kicking sand in its face. The gargantuan publisher in the electric blue suit, a favoured form of dress, believed existing *Mirror* readers could be retained and potential customers attracted by the publication of a great many pictures of his grand self. He was wrong. Many were, however, initially enthralled by Who Dares Wins – bingo dressed up in flashy clothes – which threatened to make one of them a millionaire. Eventually, after *The Sun* had purloined the idea and announced its own £1million winner, Maudie Barrett, from Harwich in Essex, was announced as the *Daily Mirror* millionairess at the Labour Party Conference at Blackpool. "Put the money in the bank and you'll get £2,000 a week interest," Maxwell advised Maudie at the presentation of the cheque at the Blackpool Town Hall. According to Neil Bentley, Maxwell was very much taken with Maudie's dog, Thumper, which Marje Proops, in town with a *Mirror* contingent that made Cudlipp's of years past look puny, erroneously sat on. The paper was filled with pictures of Maudie and Thumper and, mostly, Maxwell. But like all newspaper promotional games, Who Dares Wins soon lost its appeal.

When not in the paper with Maudie and Thumper, Maxwell found other ways of dominating its pages. Photographs of him with world leaders turned up in space he commandeered from editor Molloy at will. Molloy, having initially being taken in by Maxwell's promises of editorial independence, was despondent. "His early days were an absolute nightmare," he recalls. "I went through a very bad period of my life. I was disgusted with the way the Labour Party had folded in the face of Maxwell. The *Mirror* was to me like a country – I had always lived there and it had never been owned by anybody. It was a meritocracy and a democracy. I hated what was happening and thought that the paper was never really going to be the real *Daily Mirror* again, the *Mirror* that was on the side of the angels. I became deeply disillusioned." At some point during the paper's tribulations, Molloy started to write, often closing his office door and scribbling on a pad while the paper took shape out on the editorial floor. By the time he left MGN in 1990, he had published four novels, one of them, for which he received a handsome advance, by a Maxwell company.

The publisher's profile, higher than his rooftop helipad by now, received a further boost when he embarked on a costly barnstorming national tour by private train. In each town visited, the idea was to present to the public a *Mirror* roadshow that would either cement their loyalty as readers or send them dashing to their nearest newsagents to snap up copies of the paper. Molloy and a batch of *Mirror* big names were conscripted to accompany Maxwell and appear at meetings where few readers turned up and, although they made the publisher even more newsworthy, did little for circulation. Indeed, although Who Dares Wins saw sales rise from 3,547,247 in the month Maxwell took control to 3,683,746 by the end of October, within a year they had slumped to an alarming 3,102,427.

There was no area of the company that the new boss didn't prod and, if he found it wanting, swiftly kick in the backside. A few decisions brought about improvements – the timorous locking of the front doors of a great newspaper publishing house at 7pm every evening was immediately ended (they had been closed completely for five-and-a-half months at the end of 1974 when the IRA was especially rampant). And his dynamism certainly enlivened what had become a moribund

First person   BARRY WIGMORE

Barry Wigmore was born in 1946 and educated at Reading Grammar School. He joined the London Evening News *at the age of 20 and became chief reporter before leaving for the* Daily Mirror *as a reporter ten years later. He was joint British Press Awards Reporter of the Year in 1976 with the team that worked on the Joyce McKinney and the Manacled Mormon story. Los Angeles correspondent 1979-83, then chief feature writer in London; he resigned in protest over the lockout of casual journalists by David Montgomery. Barry joined* Today, *where he worked as chief features writer and then became the paper's first New York correspondent until the paper's closure. He now freelances from Florida.*

Far North: Wigmore dressed as a Mountie in January 1997. His mission: to interview the Spice Girls on their tour of Canada.

❝ As the *Mirror*'s chief feature writer, I was in Bosnia early on in the war there when Serbs were fighting Croatians. Photographer Bill Rowntree was with me. We had just got a good story about a pitched battle between armoured cars of the Serb regular army and Croatian militia who towed artillery and rocket launchers behind private cars. With the BBC's Martin Bell and his crew, we had ferried the wounded from both sides to hospital after the armoured cars had been ambushed and hammered with rockets.

Rowntree was wiring his pictures to London and I moved on to suss out where we should go next. It was a small Muslim town that was being ethnically cleansed – i.e. cleaned out – by the Serbs. They did this by laying down a barrage of mortar fire, marching the mortars across the town to drive everyone out ahead of the explosions. They had pounded the town once and were laying down a second barrage. You could hear the mortars getting closer. Crouching in a bombed-out house, I suddenly spotted a red phone lying in the rubble. This was before the luxury of cell phones made calls from the battlefield easy.

To my amazement, I found the phone was still working, so as I'd been out of touch for several hours, I made a quick check-call to the news desk. "Maxwell wants to talk to you," they said. I groaned. "Talk to Phil Swift first." Swift, the deputy editor, was, I think, editing

that day. "Sneaky has been stirring things," he told me. "Just listen to Maxwell, don't argue with him. Then we'll discuss what he wants."

Nick "Sneaky" Davies was foreign editor and a man you wouldn't want to turn your back on in the office. He was doubly dangerous when whispering advice to Maxwell, whose ear he had, while you were out in a war zone. The mortars were creeping along the street as I was put through to one of Maxwell's many secretaries. "The chairman is busy at the moment, hang on," said a Roedean voice.

The mortars pounded. A group of retreating soldiers came through, looking at me as though I was mad. "Putting you through to the chairman." A mortar exploded just down the road.

"What the fuck was that?" bellowed Maxwell.

"A mortar, Bob. I'm covering a war."

"Where the fuck are you?"

Continued on page 168

---

business. But although bulls in china shops doubtless have no intention of damaging the goods, they are likely to end up destroying a great deal of Royal Doulton while on the rampage.

A rash of hirings, often made without reference to the editor, were only partially successful. Harry Harris, who had got to know Maxwell through the publisher's ownership of Oxford United F.C., arrived as chief football writer and although often a figure of fun to the

more erudite members of the staff – his introduction to a report from Jerusalem referring to "the birthplace of the legendary Jesus Christ" was a subject of great hilarity – had good contacts and broke stories. Julia Langdon, who became the first woman political editor of a national daily paper, was a considerable capture; Jo Foley, hired by Maxwell as the third-ranking *Mirror* executive and, apparently, with a promise that she would be Molloy's successor, less so, and she quietly vanished when Richard Stott got the job instead;

I told him. "You cunt, you're in the wrong place."

"You're telling me, Bob," I said.

"Get back to Zagreb and contact the governor. He'll arrange for you to interview President Tudjman."

"The governor, Bob?"

"Yes, you cunt, the governor." He banged down the phone.

I retreated to safety and called Phil Swift again. He made some inquiries and discovered that "the governor" was the former governor of the US state of Maryland, a man of Croatian extraction, with whom Maxwell had done business, and who was now acting as some kind of fixer for Tudjman. In the middle of a war, the Jewish Maxwell was doing some dubious double-dealing to buy up Croatia – or, at least, local newspapers in the region – with a man who had Nazi sympathies.

It took me two days to get to Zagreb, travelling across farm tracks and fields because most roads were mined. I met the ex-governor and interviewed Tudjman, but by now Richard Stott was back in the editor's chair and had no interest in running a piece that was manifestly unsuitable for the *Mirror*.

"I think it's more appropriate for *The European*, Bob," he told Maxwell. "Sorry, it's missed the edition," said Charlie Garside, editor of the European weekly Maxwell had founded, when the story dropped on his desk. It never did see the light of day. But somehow or other, Maxwell seemed satisfied.

The Armenian earthquake was one time when Maxwell was actually useful. It was a massive human disaster. First reports said at least half-a-million were dead. It finally came down to about 50,000 killed, but I still saw more dead bodies there than anywhere else before or since.

As soon as the story broke, Maxwell decided he was going to get involved. Peter Jay, his chief of staff, was ordered to round up medical supplies. He did so, brilliantly, within a few hours. Then Peter, myself, Bill Rowntree again, and, for some strange reason Sam Pisah, Maxwell's Paris lawyer, took off aboard the great man's Gulfstream jet for Moscow. We landed there,

dropped off Peter and Sam to handle the diplomatic side of things, and then the jet took off again with Bill, myself, the supplies, and an old pal of mine, Genady Sokolov, a Russian fixer I had used several times before. No doubt a GRU spook, Genady was also wonderfully cynical about the Soviet system and a dedicated capitalist. We flew to Yerevan, which was as close as any plane other than a helicopter could fly to the epicentre.

We had five days of great exclusives: heart-rending horror stories that I faxed to London via the *Moscow News*. The rest of the Brit pack arrived some time later, having travelled overland from Turkey in a convoy of buses led by Kate Adie. Thanks to Maxwell, we had beaten them all – but it was the only time I found his involvement in a story anything other than a nuisance.

In 1988, I was sent to Australia to cover the bicentennial celebrations. It was a dream assignment: under the general headline *Wigmore Down Under* I had four or five weeks there doing a feature series with photographer Brendan Monks on the quirks and eccentricities of the country and its people. It was enormously successful for us: we had six spreads, plus loads of news splashes and page leads. These covered everything from tracking down the real Crocodile Dundee, upon whom the then new hit movie was based, to The Darker Side of Oz, about the plight of Aborigines in their homelands.

Part of the deal was that I should also cover the cricket: Ian Botham, then playing for Queensland, versus an international all-star team; a three-day Test between Australia and England in Sydney, and, as the last event of the celebrations, a one-day international between the same two countries in Melbourne.

In 27 years as a Fleet Street staffer, I worked for a lot of editors. Richard Stott was the best, and a good friend. But like all editors, he could have towering rages and that last Melbourne cricket match provoked one. Throughout his career at the *Mirror*, Stott hated holidays. He never took his full quota and he did not believe others should either, particularly not his senior staff.

Before leaving London, however, I had cleared it with

George Gale, returning to the scene of his expenses coup of many years before, lasted only a year as a second-time-around columnist. (Keith Waterhouse, convinced Maxwell would find it impossible to resist being "helpful" to a column that was sacrosanct, left for the *Daily Mail* in 1986, but was constantly cajoled by Maxwell to "return home". He declined and flourished without Bob's benevolence, writing more books and for TV and immortalising his former *Mirror* Magazine colleague in a hugely successful stage play, *Jeffrey Bernard Is Unwell*.)

Maxwell also decided to bolster what had become over the years the most editorial-friendly and efficient legal team in Fleet Street. Following the departure of Philip Levy, Patrick Easton eradicated the "them and us" safety-first policy that more often than not resulted in legally sensitive material not making the paper and instilled in the house lawyers a determination to overcome legal problems so that stories would survive as unscathed as possible. After Easton's death, Hugh Corrie and then Charles Collier-Wright continued this him and the news and features editors to take a holiday in Oz after the work was done. Stott suddenly got it in his head that the Melbourne cricket match was all a con to enable me to spin out the trip while I waited for my wife to fly out and join me for the holiday, which was partly true. The first I heard of this was when I checked in with sports news editor Tony Cornell from the press box at the MCG just as the game was starting.

"Well," I told Tony, "I'm here now, so I might as well cover it." He agreed and I duly filed the story and then checked in with him. "Stotty's gone potty," he said. "He's banned your copy from the paper. He says I'm not to use a word of it. I don't know what to do – the agency copy's crap, I've got a big hole in the paper and nothing to fill it with."

"That's easy, Tony," I said, "just use my copy and stick someone else's name on it. I don't mind, as long as you sign the expenses."

"What name can I give you?" he asked.

Just then, across 10,500 miles of phone line, I heard a roar in the background. Keith Fisher, a sports editor of unbridled enthusiasm and flamboyant page designs, had just been shown a scheme for a spread by a layout artist named Bernie. "Great! I love it, Bernie," he yelled. "Love it, Bernie... Love it, love it, love it... Bernie, love it."

And that's how the well-known *Mirror* sports writer Bernie Lovett was born. I understand they still wheel him out of retirement occasionally when there's no one else available to write a piece.

Buckling down: Barry Wigmore gets ready for a 200ft bungee jump over London.

policy. Fortunately, for an editorial staff beleaguered in other ways, so did Maxwell's imports, the experienced Oscar Buesalink and Arthur Davidson.

Molloy did better when, after Maxwell asked him who the one *Sun* journalist he would like on his staff, plumped for John Blake. Then running the rival paper's Bizarre column, Blake had previously snaffled a scoop from under the noses of an opposition that included Paul Dacre, later editor of the *Daily Mail*, Rod Gilchrist, who would become deputy editor of the *Mail on Sunday*, and Les Hinton, subsequently to run Rupert Murdoch's British press operation. Competition was fierce among the Brit reporters covering the sole United States tour of the controversial Sex Pistols, and when Blake heard that the most notorious of the band's members, Sid Vicious, had allegedly been hospitalised after carving a swastika on his chest with a sheath knife, dared to ask the Pistol why he carried a knife. "To stab cunts like you," Vicious snarled, lurching across the room. The band's roadies intervened with a cry of "Sid, don't kill the press," Blake recalls. The tip-off was correct and a white-faced Blake got his exclusive.

After Molloy's conversation with Maxwell, Blake was amazed to be summoned by the publisher and offered any job he cared to name at any salary he cared to conjure from the air. "I negotiated myself a Jaguar car, a flash salary and a fridge full of good wine," says Blake, who arrived to create the showbiz-based White Hot Club for the *Mirror* before moving on to become assistant editor in charge of features and then, for a spell, editor of *The People*.

It was Maxwell's earliest "signing", however, that became the most controversial. Early on the morning of Saturday 14 July he telephoned Hugh Cudlipp at his home in Sussex and asked him to call upon him "in your office on the ninth floor of the *Mirror*". Cudlipp was later to recall that Maxwell asked him what he would like for lunch – the first time he had ever ordered lunch (lamb, well done) four days in advance. Cudlipp had written a letter of congratulation when Maxwell acquired MGN. Maxwell, flattered, had suggested to his senior editorial executives that Lord Cudlipp should renew his association with the *Daily Mirror*. Only Richard Stott, too junior a member of staff to have come under Cudlipp's influence when he ran the show, demurred.

Cudlipp had previously heard – "with horror" that Tiny Rowland, of Lonrho, might buy the *Mirror* and decided that a holder of the MC and a former Labour MP was less undesirable than a man denounced by Prime Minister Edward Heath as "the unacceptable face of capitalism". When he met with Maxwell, he turned down the offer of becoming the "independent chairman" of the company on three grounds – "I've done that, I'm too old and I wouldn't be independent with you as publisher." But, in what he later claimed was the hope of achieving some damage limitation, Cudlipp agreed to become a consultant, although insisting that the agreement should exclude any involvement in political policy. When Maxwell asked him to name his price, Cudlipp asked for £10,000 a year and £2,000 expenses for rail fares to and from Chichester – a deal Maxwell observed wouldn't get him a decent doorman. But the relationship was not fruitful and fell into abeyance after a couple of years. Cudlipp subsequently learned that Stott had said: "What on earth has he

[Cudlipp] to contribute?" "Stott was right," Cudlipp admitted.

Of the current staff, John Pilger and Paul Foot were the two uncompromising star writers who, on the face of it, were completely incompatible with the overbearing Captain. But he gave each a glass of champagne and promised he would not interfere with what they wrote. Pilger lasted for only 18 months, writing little for the paper in that time and being lost in the redundancy shuffle when new editor Stott was required to cut costs. Pilger was not a member of the company pension scheme – a fortuitous and by no means unhappy oversight as it turned out – and at the writer's request Stott and Molloy successfully approached Maxwell to enhance his pay-off. Later Pilger wrote accurately but ungratefully of Maxwell, "If the journalists could not spot the con man, the readers could," and later still rejoined the *Mirror* as a contributor. Foot, the Lefty firebrand with a will of iron, survived Maxwell without his column being contaminated by the publisher's itchy fingers. He did, however, describe that fateful day in 1984 as "the worst Friday 13th of my life". As for Marje Proops, the biggest *Mirror* name of all and intensely loyal to the paper – "Break her in half and she'd be like a stick of rock with '*Daily Mirror*' printed right through her," Cudlipp once observed – Maxwell initially wanted to ease her out of the paper. Wiser counsel prevailed and he was soon employing flattery and charm with a ladle.

The unions were largely keeping their heads down during the early days of Maxwell's reign, weighing up just how tough he really was. They found out when, in August 1985, production of the *Mirror* was disrupted as part of a NGA dispute over Maxwell's decision to save money by having the Group's loss-making *Sporting Life* typeset outside London. He promptly announced the NGA compositors had "dismissed themselves" and suspended publication of all MGN titles. A letter of support for Maxwell's action to *The Times* was signed by the four editors: Graham Taylor, of the *Life*, plus Molloy, Stott and Peter Thompson, who had been promoted from being the daily paper's deputy to take over the *Sunday Mirror* after the Captain had hoisted Bob Edwards upstairs as deputy chairman. A settlement was reached after a stoppage of 11 days, but the damage done to the circulations of the national

Double top: Mary Riddell, a gifted feature writer, later a brilliant woman's editor.

titles was catastrophic. Five days later, SOGAT action prevented publication of *The People.* Maxwell sacked those responsible and when London print workers refused to sanction the printing of extra copies to compensate for a production-damaging dispute in Manchester, he sacked them, too.

When further SOGAT action again impeded production of the *Daily Mirror* and only 28,000 copies were printed, Haines wrote an editorial, signed by Maxwell, that carried the headline "Fleet St: The party is over" and warned: "Fleet Street has been the most inefficient, uncompetitive and old-fashion industry in the country… It looked as if the good life would never end. But now it is about to. THE GRAVY TRAIN HAS HIT THE BUFFERS". With Maxwell about to introduce new colour presses that would at last give MGN papers – the *Daily Mirror* especially – a competitive edge, the 52 Fathers of Chapel of the 13 trades unions with members employed by the company began to negotiate. The journalists gave up their sabbaticals and the right to work a four-day week. Other chapels accepted job losses. Eventually 1,600 employees left the company with proper financial compensation and pension entitlements were enhanced – ultimately a

hollow concession on Maxwell's part, although not so at the time.

Rupert Murdoch, watching with considerable interest as MGN curtailed union strength and put itself on a profit-making financial footing, had his own agenda – a moonlight flit from Bouverie Street to Wapping that would effectively end the print unions as a force in national newspapers. Eddy Shah, whose battle with the NGA at the Warrington, Lancashire, print works of his Messenger group led to Margaret Thatcher's union-curbing employment laws, was the catalyst for the end of restrictive practices and the introduction of new technology. Maxwell, with his shearing of union Sampson-like locks and the innovative introduction of colour presses, drove Fleet Street towards the exit from the dark ages. Murdoch, sharp as a stiletto and twice as deadly, finished the job, but he couldn't have done it without the other two.

As time went past, Maxwell's direct day-to-day involvement diminished, but not enough to revitalise Molloy. Deciding it was time for a change of editor at the *Daily Mirror,* the publisher moved Stott from *The People* and created Molloy editor-in-chief at the 1985 TUC Conference at Blackpool, the sort of vulgar but star-spangled setting that appealed to him. Molloy's decade of editorship had tailed off into disappointment, although even towards the end he was creating outstanding front pages for such disparate stories as the 1984 IRA bombing of the Grand Hotel, Brighton, during the Conservative Party conference and, the following year, the Live Aid concerts to raise funds for famine relief in Ethiopia. "I knew after the first six months to a year that it was inevitable we would part," says Molloy. "He had no loyalty towards anyone and would eventually become tired of everyone, including even his wife. He'd said when he first got the paper that he intended to stay only until he was 65 and I believed him and thought that I might outlast him. When he told me at Blackpool that it was time for a change, I felt this great sense of relief. I didn't want to go on editing. He offered me a pay-off then, or the chance to stay on as editor-in-chief. I chose that and he gave me a generous rise." After researching a proposed new daily paper for MGN, which Maxwell turned into the weekly *European*, and for a while editing, with scant enthusiasm, the

Sunday Mirror, Molloy was invited to leave the Group in 1990 – "Maxwell said, 'I've tried to buy *The Observer* for you and I've tried to buy *Today* for you, but I couldn't get either. So I don't have anything for you to do'." Molloy's reward for 32 years with the company was one year's salary, but Maxwell arranged for his pension to be paid at the age of 55 and later enhanced it. Even then, it wasn't quite the end of Molloy's Maxwellian experiences, as the events of 1991 would determine.

Back in 1985, Maxwell, forever running to keep under the moving spotlight of acclaim, ran to Ethiopia as the one-man saviour of that miserable country's problems. An appeal for money from readers raised millions and a team of the paper's journalists whistled in and out of Addis Ababa. According to Neil Bentley, the operation was partially successful: "I went to Ethiopia to spend £2 million of *Mirror* readers' money. We did it properly, we made sure the money went where it was most needed – it was the best thing I ever did as a journalist. Then Maxwell called me in Addis Ababa and summoned me back to London. When I said I hadn't finished the job, he said, 'Be a sport, Neil. Come home.' But I delivered the rest of the relief supplies before leaving – and Maxwell never spoke to me again except to say, 'How old are you?' and 'I think you should be sensible.' I was properly paid off in 1988 but when I left, there was a residue of £230,000 in the Ethiopia fund." This money was distributed some years later.

Richard Stott, a pugnacious character ever ready to bawl out staff that didn't cut the mustard, was prepared to take on Maxwell when he thought attack was the best form of defence but knew also how to dodge and weave in order to get what he wanted. This and the publisher's increasing commitments elsewhere saw a significant decrease in his appearances in the news pages. The turmoil at Wapping had interrupted *The Sun*'s relentless march up the circulation graph and the *Mirror* rallied. Bright new stars such as Christena Appleyard, who became an assistant editor, and the multi-talented Mary Riddell enlivened the features pages. James Whitaker, having been recruited from the *Daily Star* in 1983, had developed into the most authoritative of royal correspondents and, often in tandem with photographer Kent Gavin, was cresting the wave of stories provided by the tribulations of the nation's first family. Keith Fisher, an alarming extrovert without the need of a microphone no matter the size of the space he occupied, had instilled punch and renewed vigour into the sports pages. And big stories, including a series of domestic disasters, were journalistic challenges the paper met confidently, especially after Maxwell boldly invested in full colour presses ahead of the rest of the field. (Advertising director Roger Eastoe had met Maxwell at a conference in Athens the March before he bought the company, and for an hour they had talked about the editorial advantages and increased advertising potential colour printing could bring to a national paper.)

Stott subsequently acknowledged that colour printing was crucial in the *Mirror*'s success of 1988, when colour pictures of the Clapham rail and Kegworth air disasters made the paper almost leap from newsagents' counters. Lockerbie and Hillsborough followed, with *The Sun* inadvertently giving its rival a boost when it alienated Liverpool and a large section of the north-west of England by blaming drunken Liverpool fans for the Hillsborough catastrophe. Liverpool, although initially enraged by what it considered the *Mirror*'s insensitive colour coverage, turned its fury on *The Sun*, which has never quite regained its standing in that city.

Maxwell was still likely to erupt like a giant Roman candle, but for much of the time was too busy "rescuing" the cash-strapped Edinburgh Commonwealth Games, suing *Private Eye* for libel or calling on the Gorbachevs in Moscow – he took Noreen Taylor along to interview Raisa Gorbachev without bothering to ask the Soviet Union's first lady beforehand, and then the President cancelled the meeting. The *Private Eye* case, brought after the magazine accused him of making donations to the Labour Party in order to get a peerage, ended with Maxwell being awarded £55,000 in damages and his considerable costs. Unwilling to let the matter rest there, he briefed Molloy and John Penrose, now an assistant editor and married to Anne Robinson, to produce a spoof issue of the magazine called *Not Private Eye*. Chaos followed when the convivial Penrose was invited for drinks by the *Eye*'s main shareholder, Peter Cook, and the pair, not altogether sober, ended up back at the *Mirror* building in Molloy's office. They made a serious hole in the drinks cabinet before Penrose passed out and

Couple of swells: John Penrose (above, left) in the company of Derek Jameson. Penrose would later leave journalism to manage the early broadcasting career of his wife Anne Robinson (left), herself a former Mirror assistant editor and columnist. Then, as now, Annie was not universally popular either with those who knew her or those who didn't.

Cook sprayed graffiti on the walls and windows and then made a call to Maxwell, who happened to be in New York, to tell him he was busy drinking £55,000-worth of booze in the *Mirror* building. Cook disappeared fast to escape the resultant security sweep; Penrose woke up under a pile of coats in the photographer's room where thoughtful colleagues had hidden him as security heavies prowled the corridors.

Penrose didn't survive under Maxwell. After suffering several bouts of the publisher's bullying he quit to look after the burgeoning career of his wife. Anne promptly went to Maxwell and demanded an increase in salary to compensate her for Penrose's lost earnings. He gave it to her. (Shortly afterwards Robinson told Joe Haines she was thinking of giving up journalism and trying for a full-time career in television. "Don't do it, Anne," advised Haines. "You're too old.") Deputy editor Phil Walker was fired while Stott was on holiday and although reinstated through the editor's intervention never overcame Maxwell's antipathy towards him. A fine tabloid journalist, although not in sympathy with the *Mirror's* politics, he was paid off when Stott departed and went on to become editor of the *Daily Star.*

Ensconced at the top of Maxwell House, as he

Cast adrift: Editor Roy Greenslade fell out with Maxwell over his constant interference with the Mirror's content.

had renamed the W.H. Smith building that butted on to the rear of MGN when he had acquired it, Maxwell hired former Ambassador to Washington Peter Jay as his chief-of-staff – i.e. prestigious gofer – and continued to veer between being a tyrant and a magnanimous uncle. He could be, and sometimes was, moved to tears by the plight of unfortunates and would dispense largesse with alacrity. He enabled the small daughter of reporter Don McKay to obtain an operation to save her sight, earning McKay's unswerving loyalty. But more often than not his Mr Hyde tendencies were submerged by the eccentric demands of Dr Jekyll. Neil Bentley remembers the publisher departing for Brighton by helicopter from the Maxwell House helipad without a landing area being predetermined. "Find me somewhere to land in Brighton," Bentley was instructed from the sky somewhere over south London. He managed to locate a football ground and the club secretary was coerced from his home to switch on the training floodlights.

When the phrase "Fuck Maxwell" was visible among the graffiti Charles Griffin had included in his drawing depicting the fall of the Berlin Wall in 1988, Maxwell decided Griffin was personally responsible and, not unreasonably had he been right, demanded his dismissal. Griffin protested his innocence and the threat was withdrawn, but Stott was fearful of ever closing his eyes in case, when he opened them, some of his staff had been culled.

There was some slimming down of the

editorial operation, although, compared to what was to come under the next *Mirror* regime, it was mere tinkering and redundancy terms were initially not ungenerous. But Maxwell did then shut down those foreign operations that had survived into the 1980s (Molloy had maintained a Rome operation only until the then girlfriend of the *Mirror*'s John Penrose, Anne Robinson, returned from her stint as *The Sunday Times* correspondent there. Penrose also returned to London and the Rome bureau ceased to exist before Maxwell's arrival). Peter Stephens retired and Tony Delano, who uniquely had worked for the paper in Paris, Rome and New York, briefly returned to Paris until the axe finally fell. David Bradbury was also in Paris, but was then shuttled to New York to work there with Paul Connew, who, when Maxwell decided to close the bureau, jetted to London and went over the head of the editor to appeal directly to the publisher. All he succeeded in doing was alienating the editor and irritating Maxwell. He was fired. So was Bradbury.

Stott had arrested the decline in circulation after the earlier disastrous impact of Maxwell – "It takes something close to genius to lose so much circulation so quickly," *Marketing Week* had wryly observed after his first year – despite Maxwell's insistence that his official biography, written by Joe Haines, should be serialised in the paper (sales dropped by an average 40,000). But the editor's relationship with the publisher was not getting any better and Stott began to consider his future. He had earlier suggested to

First Person GEOFFREY GOODMAN

Geoffrey Goodman was born in 1921 and educated in Manchester and at the London School of Economics. He joined the Daily Mirror *in 1947 as a news reporter after war service in the Royal Air Force, when he was awarded the DFC, and after experience on the* Manchester Guardian. *Fired the following year, he worked on the* News Chronicle, Daily Herald *and the IPC* Sun *before returning to the* Mirror *as industrial editor in 1969. He retired in 1986 as an assistant editor and columnist and Group industrial editor and then co-founded the* British Journalism Review *and edited it 1989-2002.*

I was sacked just before Christmas in 1948. Half-a-dozen reporters were fired, three of whom, me included, were members of the Communist Party. The editor, Sylvester Bolam, and the managing editor, Cyril "Shitbag" Morton, didn't want people they believed to be dangerous lefties around the place. I had hardly ever seen Bish Bolam. I worked to Ken Hord, who was a real bastard of a news editor but good. My closest friend on the paper then was a caption writer and deputy picture editor named Lee Howard, who later moved to news and ended up as editor. When I was sacked, Lee came to The Clachan pub with me and he was weeping.

I went to the *News Chronicle*, where the political correspondent, Geoffrey Cox – later editor of ITN and knighted – took a liking to me. Occasionally I stood in for him in the House of Commons lobby, which was my first step into political and industrial journalism. I was number two in Industry at the *News Chronicle* until just before the General Election of 1959 – I had left the Communist Party in 1951 – when I was offered the industrial editorship of the *Herald*.

When it was decided that the paper would be

Goodman down: Geoffrey fell foul of editor Richard Stott.

relaunched as *The Sun*, about a dozen of us put the idea to the Mirror Group board that the *Herald* should be maintained as an independent Labour paper within the *Mirror* stable. When *The Sun* was sold to Rupert Murdoch in 1969, I was one of those who refused to sign an agreement to join the new paper. Then Hugh Cudlipp and Sydney Jacobson took me out to lunch and convinced me that I should join the *Daily Mirror* as industrial editor. Over lunch, Sydney said to Hugh: "You do realise that Geoffrey doesn't agree with some of our policies?" Hugh said: "I don't give a fuck about that. I promise that, whatever he writes, I will never interfere." And he never did.

In 1970 I was offered a safe Labour parliamentary seat in Leicester, but Hugh said to me: "Don't be a cunt – you'll be wasted on the back benches for years. You'll have more influence here if you stay and write a column." So I became a columnist instead of an MP. I don't think the Leicester CLP has ever forgiven me.

In 1977, when Derek Jameson resigned as Mike Molloy's deputy editor to go and edit the *Daily Express* – he was immediately ordered from the office, I recall – I went with Peter Thompson, another assistant editor, to see Tony Miles about who would succeed Jameson. Miles was editorial director and had all sorts of objections to me getting the job, although he didn't much care for Thompson, either. But he appointed Peter. By then, Joe Haines had come to the paper as leader writer after being Harold Wilson's press secretary. Joe and I often didn't see eye-to-eye and the daily saga between us over the paper's policies would make a riveting play all by itself.

Continued on page 176

Maxwell that he should be allowed to put together a consortium to buy *The People*, the runt of the MGN litter, but the idea now appeared defunct. Maxwell, meanwhile, began canvassing both Molloy and Ernie Burrington, the former notorious drunk who Stott had straightened out when inheriting him as deputy editor of *The People*, for the names of likely editors. A born again Burrington had succeeded Stott at *The People* and had both Maxwell's ear and the inclination to deliver opinion into it

from the corner of his mouth. According to Joe Haines, Maxwell twice saw David Montgomery, who had persuaded Murdoch to buy *Today* for him to edit but was now out of favour at Wapping, but Maxwell's interest waned. From the names that floated to the surface of the Molloy-Burrington think tank, Maxwell plucked that of Roy Greenslade, an assistant editor of *The Sunday Times* with tabloid experience both as an executive at *The Sun* and, previously, casual shift work at the *Mirror*.

GEOFFREY GOODMAN

First person

In 1984, just 48 hours before Maxwell bought the company, Mike Molloy, Peter Thompson and I were sitting in Molloy's office and they asked me if I knew Maxwell. Not well, I said, but I'd had an extraordinary experience with him in 1967 when he had wanted to buy the old *Sun.* He asked me to his office in Fitzroy Square and offered me the deputy editorship of the paper he intended to relaunch. Mike Randall, a former editor of the *Daily Mail,* had tentatively accepted the editorship, he told me, and then he outlined what sounded like a brilliant idea – he said he was doing deals to print just about every television listings magazine in the country and with the profits intended to finance a paper to replace the old *Sun.* He offered me £25,000 a year – an astonishing amount of money back then – so I said I would think about it.

"What the fuck do you have to think about?" he said, suddenly angry. To deflect his hostility, I started a conversation about his experiences during the war and he told me an amazing story. He said that when he was awaiting demob at the end of the war in Berlin, he was sent on a special mission for British intelligence. The whisky was going down as he told me how he had been given the job of breaking into the Russian war hero Marshall Zukov's safe, because a Red Army colonel had informed British Intelligence that it contained plans to strip Germany of a lot of vital heavy machinery and take it back to Moscow. I said I didn't believe him, which didn't please him at all.

Some time after I had left the paper, Thompson was collaborating with another ex-*Mirror* journalist, Tony Delano, on a book called *Maxwell: A Portrait of Power* [Bantam Press, 1988] and they were going to use the story, saying that I thought it was a lie. One morning Maxwell called me at home and said: "I hear you have been co-operating with those cunts Delano and Thompson – you told them what I told you in confidence. And you don't believe the story, anyway." No I don't, I said. So he insisted that I went to see him. There was a bottle of wine on the table. He asked why I didn't believe him and I said that even British intelligence would not get involved with a Red Army colonel.

"What if I show you copies of documents we took from Zukov's safe?" he said. "Can you read German?" I can, so he had some documents spread out on the table. As far as I could tell, they were genuine and proved his story to be absolutely true. Later, I spoke with his solicitors, who also believed the documents to be genuine. So I agreed to go into the witness box and swear to their authenticity if Maxwell's legal action against Delano and Thompson went that far. It didn't. The book was published, but with the episode removed.

The Friday morning after Maxwell took over the paper, he called me at home and asked me to go and see him on the Sunday. When I arrived, Tony Miles, Joe Haines and Terry Lancaster, the political editor, were all waiting to see him. We were called in one-by-one. He said to me: "Will you work for me?" I said: "Well, that depends on what you want to do with the paper." He said he intended to ask Hugh Cudlipp to be his editorial adviser and that he wanted me to be part of a politburo that would run the editorial policy of the paper. So I said: "Okay, as long as I have the freedom to write what I like. If you want to produce a great *Daily Mirror,* I'll stay."

I didn't know that, by then, he had not only guaranteed continuity of Joe Haines's role but also made him an assistant editor, despite Haines's famous quote at a chapel [union] meeting just before the deal went through, where he had described Maxwell as a liar and a crook. Then Terry Lancaster told me that both he and Tony Miles had come to financial agreements and were leaving. I felt very let down by this – I said to Terry, stay on at least until you feel it is so impossible you have to leave. Terry said, "He doesn't want me." It turned out he knew Maxwell better than I did.

I was confronted with a crisis immediately, even before Terry had the chance to leave – it was halfway through the miners' strike and Maxwell wanted me to write a leading article attacking the miners. I refused. Mike Molloy, Terry and I went to see Maxwell – Haines was on holiday – and he said, "This is what I want the paper to say. Take it down, Terry." Terry was struggling to take notes because of the arthritis in his hands. I tried to intervene and Mike eventually persuaded Maxwell to let us work on the piece in the editor's office and show it to him later. In the lift,

Greenslade turned down the editorship of *The People* but accepted that of the *Daily Mirror* and Maxwell suddenly told Stott that he would entertain selling *The People* after all and that he should resume his editorship of that paper forthwith. The publisher plucked me from the deputy editorship of the *Sunday Mirror,* the position to which I had returned to the group after an enjoyable temporary absence at *Today,* installing me as acting editor of the *Mirror* until Greenslade could extricate himself from Wapping. Maxwell took the opportunity to spring-clean in other areas, losing Peter Jay and Patrick Morrisey, the managing director who had arrived with the dubious newspaper production qualification of having put the pink stripe into Signal toothpaste. Burrington moved into management. Geoffrey Goodman had bailed out in 1986, the same year that Edwards – Maxwell's old friend – had metaphorically been dropped down the lift shaft, a fate soon to befall Molloy. It was like a macabre version of the Gay Gordons, with dancers disappearing whenever Maxwell decided to stop the music.

Pay-off lines: Political editor Terence Lancaster was pushed out by Maxwell.

Terry said: "That's it – I'm not going on." He and Miles left soon afterwards.

Later, when he was trying to buy Bristow's helicopter service in Aberdeen, Maxwell said he wanted me to become his industrial relations adviser. I said no and explained that this would present considerable conflict of interests for an industrial editor. He couldn't understand that. Then I had an argument about the way the paper handled the end of the miners' strike – I fought to get space for the implications of what had happened, but Mike Molloy was off that night and I failed. I was very deeply upset.

At the Labour Party Conference of 1985 in Blackpool, Maxwell announced that Richard Stott had become editor and I made a speech at the *Mirror* dinner table, with both Molloy and Stott present, expressing how regrettable I thought this was – the usual Goodman suicide job. I don't think Richard ever forgave me.

The rest of 85 and the beginning of 86 was a miserable time for me. I couldn't stand Maxwell and I began to feel ashamed of myself. I used to go home after Maxwell's notorious Tuesday lunches for senior executives and put on tape my disgust at the personal corruption that was going on – the fawning and the acquiescence. Bob told me he wanted me to retire a few months early and Richard killed my column – absolutely within his right, but a blow nonetheless – and I realised there was no longer a role for me at the paper.

I told Maxwell I was unhappy and took him to dinner at The Ivy. He said: "Well, what do you want to do?" I said I would really like to start a new paper and Maxwell suddenly said that he wanted to start a new evening newspaper in Manchester and asked if I would be the editor! Then he said: "Would you like your column restored?" I said no – it was the editor's prerogative. "I could overrule him," Maxwell said, but I pointed out editors were supposed to be able to make decisions like that. I paid the bill – it was an expensive evening – and on the way out Maxwell asked if I was going to claim the cost on my expenses. I told him no – and I never did.

When I left in May of that year, he put on his grey face, said how sorry he was and offered me my company car for a pound. "Just give me a quid," he said. I did and I kept the car. **,**

If the *Mirror* staff believed a change of editor would make Maxwell less irascible, they were hallucinating. If Maxwell believed he had hired a cipher of an editor and that he could start dictating every dot and comma of the paper, he hadn't researched his new man thoroughly enough. Greenslade, the first *Daily Mirror* editor not to be promoted from inside the organisation since Hamilton Fyfe almost 90 years before, arrived in February 1990 and his relationship with the publisher came under pressure from the start. "To my mind,"

Greenslade was to write, "I was editor of the *Daily Mirror*. In his mind, I was merely another employee and, as such, a servant."

Greenslade got the message almost immediately, having to resist Maxwell rewriting the 12 February front-page headline carrying the release of Nelson Mandela after 27 years of imprisonment in South Africa. When a crowd of 200,000 gathered in Moscow to protest against the Communist Party, the publisher demanded changes to the page-one layout. He wanted involvement in the paper's series on Arthur

Scargill that alleged irregularities during the 1983-4 miners' strike. When, now as Greenslade's deputy, I produced the first after a long absence of Shock Issues, on education, the editor was reprimanded for publishing it "without permission". Greenslade fought to retain his autonomy, hiring John Diamond as a columnist, bringing in Harry Arnold, a former royal reporter who had grown jaundiced at *The Sun*, and axing the Old Codgers, who toddled off into the sunset and their place in newspaper history. But Maxwell's omnipresence continued, despite juggling a great many balls in the air, some of which he dropped (the London *Daily News* had been and gone, the *European* was struggling, and the New York *Daily News* was on the horizon). *Sporting Life* was in trouble and he engaged Charles Wilson, a veteran Fleet Street mercenary and a former editor of *The Times*, to become its editor-in-chief. And he was still buzzing back and forth in his private plane on foreign business trips and even taking breaks on his yacht, the Lady Ghislaine. Yet none of this, nor the impending flotation of the company, slowed down the fusillade of demands for Greenslade to "pop up" to Maxwell's eyrie, reached through a door in the rear wall of the MGN building and then an express lift to the skies.

The political landscape erupted in November 1990 when a challenge was mounted to the leadership of Margaret Thatcher, handsome winner of her third General Election in 1989 with a majority of 101. Greenslade was informed by Maxwell that the publisher and Joe Haines would handle the leadership contest, but Alastair Campbell, the then political editor and as astute as any in Fleet Street, came up with an exclusive suggesting that senior figures in the party were urging the Prime Minister to go. Maxwell trumped it with one stating that six cabinet ministers would resign the following morning if Thatcher did not stand down – but exploded when Greenslade asked him for the source of the story. Campbell investigated in the Commons and the story did not stand up. Greenslade stayed with his original front page and was blamed by Maxwell for having missed "the scoop of the decade". He berated Campbell on the same grounds, even though no ministers had resigned. When Campbell protested that nobody resigned ahead of Thatcher's own resignation, Maxwell replied: "They probably would have done if we had run it."

What was once Cudlipp's circus had turned into the Wacky Races. Maxwell did not rate the John Diamond column and demanded Diamond's resignation. He cancelled the television advertising for Greenslade's new *Mirror* Woman supplement. And when disagreeing with Greenslade's line when Gorbachev sent Russian tanks into Lithuania, barked: "Do you realise that Gorbachev wouldn't do anything without ringing me first?"

Life had its lighter moments. Sitting in the editor's office one night when Greenslade was off, I took a call from the publisher. "You'll never guess where I am?" "Quite right, Bob. Where are you?" "I am a mile above the office [no he wasn't] in my plane and I am talking to you on the telephone. What do you think of that?" he chortled. "Bob, the wonders of modern technology never cease to amaze me." "Quite right, quite right," he boomed before hanging up; the big kid proudly showing off his new toy.

Another night, with the paper once again locked in a bingo war with the opposition, he was foolish enough to agree to appear on television with then *Today* editor David Montgomery in an item designed to pitch the two against one other in an argument about whose game was best. Montgomery spoke first and produced an enormous cardboard cheque, prominently emblazoned with the *Today* masthead. Maxwell had no such prop and was patently irritated. "What did you think?" he asked me when he returned. "Pity about that big cheque of Montgomery's, Bob." "Yes, why didn't I have a big cheque? What kind of cunts have I got working for me?"

On another occasion, when he required my presence urgently in the office – by the time I arrived he had forgotten why – he wanted to send his helicopter the nine miles to Ealing, in west London, to whisk me back to Holborn. I pointed out that there were certain hazards to landing a helicopter in a quiet and not very wide suburban street.

More poignant was the telephone conversation when I had to call him late one evening on an editorial matter. His voice was a croak and I asked, "Are you all right?" "No I'm not," he said. "I have a very bad cold… and nobody cares." The tragedy is that, by then, few did.

Greenslade and I managed to come up with a strategy of cunning mixed with dumb insolence that held Maxwell at bay much of the time. Christmas Day came and went, with Maxwell interrupting a normal working schedule only for a couple of hours during which time he was helicoptered to and from Headington Hill Hall, ate lunch with some of his family and still found time to bark at me over the telephone between mouthfuls. He was irritated when I told him at nine o'clock that I was leaving to have dinner but could be back in 15 minutes if I was needed. He was lonely and the presence of a familiar, if not especially friendly face in the editor's office would provide comfort.

The paper acquitted itself well at the beginning of January during the first Gulf War, although Maxwell's total support for American and British action after Iraq's invasion of Kuwait meant the paper's customary role as a questioning and, where necessary, sceptical observer was blunted. That wasn't the Captain's only involvement in the conflict: at one point he wanted reporter Bill Akass and photographer Ken Lennox, two of a terrific *Mirror* team out in the Gulf, to assist with a plan to sell Maxwell-owned encyclopaedias to the troops.

Greenslade, his frustration boiling over, had the previous month given an interview to Jean Morgan of the *UK Press Gazette*. The article appeared in January and for the editor effectively rolled out a carpet towards the door marked Exit. He probably did not realise just how explosive was the warning shot he directed at Maxwell when admitting that the *Mirror*'s circulation had slipped below three million and forecasting that the situation would get worse. And Maxwell's initial reaction was disarming enough: "What a densely argued point of view." But that was before those flitting around Maxwell's flame, but never getting burned themselves, whispered to him that the interview was pessimistic and destructive. On 21 January, while also engaged in buying the New York *Daily News*, Maxwell wrote a long memo of complaint to the editor, questioning almost every element of the paper. He demanded the appointment of an "authoritative woman's editor" – Christena Appleyard, who had supervised this area, had left the paper – and a sports columnist of similar standing to Harry Harris (the publisher's own appointment and a conduit for him to get his football interests into

the paper). He criticised the features as "dull and unattractive" and attacked the leading articles, written mostly by David Thompson since Joe Haines had become a columnist and consultant to Maxwell. He didn't think much of Tom Hendry's investigations unit, insisted on a date for John Diamond's departure and pointed out that, as publisher, "it is my responsibility to advise, warn and, when necessary, to command".

Greenslade's long reply, dated 27 January, defended his staff before insisting: "I do not have the same freedom as other editors. I cannot send on a story abroad without your permission. This is becoming a nightmare… A daily newspaper editor cannot operate like this. It is making editing impossible." There was more in the same vein in what turned out to be a suicide note. What Maxwell required was unquestioning obedience, something he was not destined again to find in the editor's office at the *Mirror*.

He flirted with the idea of establishing a ludicrous and unworkable three-deck system to edit the paper, with Joe Haines as executive editor, Mike Molloy returning as day editor and me taking over at night. Then he sacked Greenslade – Diamond went too – without any real idea of who would replace him and bizarrely asking his dismissed editor's opinion on possible successors. He sent for me and told me Charlie Wilson, who had become one of his floating factotums, would be the new editor. While I sat facing him, he placed a call to Wilson to give him the good news. From the brief conversation and the look on Maxwell's face, it became clear that Wilson was not enamoured of the idea. "Why don't you make me editor?" I asked. "You're too defiant," he said, looking at me balefully. It was the nicest compliment he ever paid me.

Wilson took over as acting editor during the three weeks it took Maxwell to sort out a mess of his own making. "Now about the leaders…" I began to say to Wilson on his first morning. "I know, I know," he replied, "whatever the old man says goes." No wonder Maxwell wanted him to take the job permanently. But a flurry of activity that included a summons for Richard Stott to catch up with the publisher in America – surprise, surprise, with the flotation of MGN imminent *The People* buy-out was no longer on the table – ended with me being asked to "pop

Sinking ship: When Robert Maxwell fell from the deck of his yacht Lady Ghislaine on 5 November 1991, he was to leave a trail of chaos and scandal in his wake.

up" to the ballroom-sized sitting room above the publisher's office suite. There, a not particularly joyful Stott and an equally subdued Penny, his wife, were being served drinks by Joseph Caetano Pereira, the genial Portuguese butler who still works in the executive catering area at Trinity Mirror. Maxwell, beaming broadly, lifted me bodily from the floor with his right arm circling my shoulders while thrusting a bottle of Czech beer towards me with his left hand. "You are the new editor of *The People*," he said. I knew from Richard's face that the minutiae of his return to the *Daily Mirror* had not yet been ironed out. I knew also that Maxwell, he of short memory, was back where he started: Stott was not the type of editor to roll over and wave his paws in the air.

Nobody on the editorial staff realised it, but this was the beginning of the end of the Captain. Rumours inside and outside the building concerning his precarious financial position were circulating even before he separated Mirror Group Newspapers from the Maxwell Communications Corporation and then decided he would retain absolute control after the flotation by retaining 51 per cent of the shares. He had paid far too much for Macmillan, the American publishing company, borrowing heavily to do so. Pergamon had been sold and potential investors were starting to question the wisdom of leaving the gorilla in charge of the zoo. Ernie Burrington became deputy publisher and then managing director of MGN, Charlie Wilson disappeared back to the ninth floor as editorial director, and the flotation went ahead. It was not a disaster, but neither was the city letting off fireworks and turning cartwheels outside the Stock Exchange.

Then Maxwell, blundering on like a charging elephant despite his worsening financial situation, learned that BBC-TV's *Panorama* was putting together a programme about him. He declined to take part on the grounds that *Panorama*'s purpose was "to dish the dirt" and fired off missives to BBC chairman Duke Hussey and director-general John Birt in an effort to get the programme stopped. When it was broadcast, on 23 September, it revealed that a *Mirror* "Spot the Ball" competition, run at Maxwell's insistence after Greenslade had poured scorn in the paper on a similar *Sun* promotion, had been rigged to avoid paying out £1million. Against his better judgement, Greenslade had become the judge in the competition, and, under instruction from Maxwell that the £1million prize should not be won, placed the ball in the unlikeliest positions imaginable on the published football photographs. Greenslade was later to write that he was "haunted" by carrying out Maxwell's instructions. Maxwell reacted to the television programme exactly as one would expect: writs cascaded from Maxwell House like ticker tape, although none of them stuck.

The *Panorama* hoo-ha had barely died away before the *Mirror* was plunged into a fresh scandal. A book by the renowned American reporter Seymour Hersh claimed that Maxwell and foreign editor Nick Davies, known in the office as "Sneaky" because his talent for machination matched his undoubted journalistic qualities, were Israeli spies. In the House of Commons, MP George Galloway then claimed Davies had been involved in arms selling. Davies denied everything   so did Maxwell, but then he would – and the paper leapt to Sneaky's defence. Too soon, it seemed, when a former wife announced that letters she had found confirmed Davies had been party to an arms deal in Ohio. Never been to Ohio, said Davies, and Stott continued to back him – until the *Daily Mail* obtained a photograph of the foreign editor with an arms dealer's wife. The picture had been taken in Ohio.

Stott wanted to fire Davies instantly, but in a final twist to a fantastical story, Maxwell demurred. The wretched romantic ambitions of an aged and vastly overweight man who, when he gazed into the looking glass could perhaps still see the dashing handsome army officer of 45 years before, dictated that he should try to protect someone who had gained the affections of the woman Maxwell lusted after. All but estranged from wife Betty, he had developed a passion for one of his senior secretaries, Andrea Martin. Andrea, in turn, had fallen in love with Davies, whom she subsequently married. Maxwell felt that, for Andrea's sake, he could not be seen to be vindictive towards Davies. But Stott persisted and Davies was sacked – not for spying, but for lying.

Meanwhile, there was tension in the boardroom as directors began to become concerned over large amounts of money that were being transferred out of the business to what were ostensibly sound investments. Financial director Laurie Guest was especially concerned and said so, but the directors were so in the thrall of the publisher that they reacted slowly. Maxwell's behaviour appeared unchanged. He was still fielding half-a-dozen telephone calls at once, often utilising several of the eight languages at his disposal. At the end of October he called Mike Molloy at his home and said he had a job for him. "I need my old friends around me," he said. "I miss you. I'll see you next Thursday afternoon." Then Ian Maxwell, the older of the two sons involved in MGN and the not infrequent butt of his father's fury, called Molloy and repeated the message: we want you back. The summons to Maxwell House never came. In the early hours of 5 November, Maxwell went missing from the Lady Ghislaine off the coast of Tenerife.

Among the acolytes Maxwell had gathered around him over the years was photographer Mike Maloney, good at his job but with an ego that, although not in Maxwell's league, could house a barrage balloon. Four years after the Captain went over the side, Maloney was to write of a time when he was sent to photograph the Lady Ghislaine for a brochure Maxwell intended to produce. One night, after Betty Maxwell had retired to bed, the publisher demanded, "Let's liven this place up" and began shuffling around one of the yacht's grand salons in approximate time to the music pouring from its state-of-theart sound system. Maloney switched on the disco lights and the two of them moved around the small dance floor, face-to-face and snapping their fingers to the strains of Chris Andrews' "Yesterday Man". The irony of the song's title was lost on Maloney, but the picture he painted would have been touching and sad had it not been so funny. It remains an indelible memory of the Captain who deserted a sinking ship to tumble from the deck of one that was completely seaworthy.

9 REWRITING HISTORY

It is a gloomy Friday evening late in October 1992 and the Daily Mirror *newsroom is packed to overflowing. It is almost a year since Robert Maxwell's death, yet the atmosphere in the room is again one of fear and loathing and there are no smiles on the faces of the assembled journalists as they contemplate the arrival of a new boss, David Montgomery. Many of them know Montgomery, now a few days short of his forty-fourth birthday, of old. Some can remember when he was a sub-editor on the* Mirror; *others worked with him when he transferred to the* Sunday People. *Since then he has edited the* News of the World *and* Today *before giving up editing newspapers in an attempt to run them. The idea that a company so recently manhandled and financially abused by one of the greatest rogues in Fleet Street history should now fall into the hands of a dour Ulsterman with limited managerial experience is viewed by most of them as God's cruel joke. But Montgomery has promised to give assurances about job security, union recognition and editorial independence.*

Daily Mirror *editor Richard Stott descends from the ninth floor, clutching not tablets of stone but a piece of paper bearing Montgomery's signature. Stott reads Montgomery's promises, made "without difficulty or reservation": "The editorial independence of our newspapers will be preserved and vested in the editors, with continuing support for the left of centre tradition of all titles. I have definitely got no plans for job cuts in editorial departments, nor has the board considered any. We will create the conditions in which the journalism will flourish and increase the value for money of all titles.*

Union recognition will continue. The editors of all titles remain in their positions. Our aim is to build a strong independent company."

There is no applause, no cheers from the journalists, who had threatened an office sit-in that would prevent publication of the paper unless these pledges were made. Most of them feel they have been down similar routes before. Does Montgomery intend to keep his word, or are they again being dealt a bad hand from a crooked deck? Upstairs, in the office that has seen King, Cudlipp and Maxwell in control of the company, David Montgomery is still shuffling the cards...

Did he fall, did he jump, or was he pushed? These are the questions those at the *Mirror* and just about everyone else in the country were asking in the immediate aftermath of the Captain's plunge from the deck of the Lady Ghislaine. It had dominated conversation in office and pub as the paper once again found itself generating its own news. Stott's front page, THE MAN WHO SAVED THE MIRROR, has since been widely ridiculed, but despite subsequent discoveries, there remains a large element of truth in the sentiment. The paper was in a parlous state when Maxwell moved in and, despite those who survived his reign undoubtedly deserving a campaign medal, his introduction of colour and occasional flashes of editorial nous meant it was in better journalistic shape when he departed. Most newspapers published laudatory obituaries before the extent of the damage to the company was known.

The know-alls who sniped at those who worked for Maxwell for failing to realise in time that he was a crook were as predictable as their arguments were facile. He'd hoodwinked almost everyone, including journalists from other papers, over the years. There wasn't a gun big enough to train on everyone who had, in Cudlipp's phrase, supped with the devil. Presidents and prime ministers, royals, lords, ladies and many more of the great and the good accepted his hospitality and were taken in by the man in the electric blue suit – until *Panorama* raised doubts and the splash of his body hitting the Mediterranean signalled the need to turn their heads in the opposite direction. One who didn't do that was fellow

for reacting too slowly, or not reacting at all, when alarm bells began to ring at MGN. Of those attending Maxwell's last board meeting on 29 October, five were concerned that the publisher's dealings and double-dealings had gone way beyond the bounds of probity. None of them raised such doubts at the meeting. Yet £98million of the Group's funds had gone missing within the past six months. The two non-executive directors, Sir Robert Clark – soon to re-emerge in a superior role – and Alan Clements, met with Maxwell privately once the board meeting had concluded and told him an audit committee needed to be set up to

Brothers grim: Ian (left) and Kevin Maxwell took control after their father's death.

media baron Lord (Conrad) Black, who later said of Maxwell: "He had a number of unattractive aspects, but he did have an astonishing career and was a memorable figure. He was a good natural publisher in many ways. When he had the *Mirror* he arrested its decline and gave Murdoch a real run for it. He beat him to the punch on editorial colour and the combined sale of the *Mirror* and the *Daily Record* was equal to *The Sun*'s and sometimes slightly ahead of it. He was a scoundrel of historic proportions. He was capricious and ill-tempered and the way he treated his people was a disgrace. But a uniformly bad man – the conventional opinion of him now – he wasn't." It was a fair and accurate epitaph.

As Richard Stott subsequently illustrated, some of the company's directors were culpable

scrutinise financial controls within the company. But they failed to mention this to any of the other directors. Patently, most of those around the boardroom table were frightened of Maxwell.

There was chaos after the Captain's bloated body was found. Kevin Maxwell, the nearest to a chip off the old block in terms of blinkered drive, assumed control of the Maxwell Communications Corporation, with brother Ian, the more affable of the pair, taking over as MGN publisher and signing a *Mirror* article promising the paper would continue as before. In Maxwellian tone, it was headed: "My pledge to you". Tributes from all over the world had flooded into Maxwell House and the publisher's body had been buried on the Mount of Olives in Jerusalem before accountants in London

Maxwell's legacy: Both present and former employees reacted to the plundering of the pension fund.

discovered a hole in the company pension funds big enough for the massive coffin to have been carried through sideways. Soon it became clear that £426million had gone, £350million of which was money from the Mirror Group scheme. With the board's collective nerve waning by the minute and around two-thirds of MCC's stock exchange value having evaporated, dealings in MCC and MGN shares were suspended and Kevin and Ian resigned. At the *Mirror*, Stott ignored objections from Charlie Wilson and others in the crumbling hierarchy and prepared a front page announcing MILLIONS MISSING FROM THE MIRROR, accompanying it with an editorial promising the paper would diligently investigate the fraud – "warts and all". The story, it transpired, consisted of little *but* warts. Centre stage was the announcement of a Serious Fraud Office investigation into the vanished millions – the Maxwell brothers were eventually found not guilty of the fraud charges brought against them – while hovering in the wings were such sideshows as the disclosure that Maxwell had bugged the offices of some senior staff and

revelations about his sexual escapades. Did he fall, did he jump, or was he pushed? Despite durable conspiracy theories claiming that he was murdered by Mossad agents, the evidence suggests that he fell or threw himself from the Lady Ghislaine, with the torn muscles and ligaments discovered at the post mortem indicating that he might have tried to clamber back aboard. Maxwell was not built for clambering.

The General Election of 9 April 1992 came and went, with Labour slashing the Tory majority but failing to prevent John Major's return to Downing Street. Labour leader Neil Kinnock resigned, to be replaced by John Smith, but the drama being played out in Holborn was every bit as compelling as Labour's soul-searching. A bemused Ernie Burrington, resisting any desire to reach for a stiff drink, took over as chairman of MGN with a salary increase of £30,000 to £200,000 a year. But he resigned after two months and walked away with an annual pension of £120,000, or £80,000 plus £250,000 in cash. The staff was awarded a 3 per cent increase in salary for having coped with the trying times since the papers had been left in the lurch – "We will not make a profit for 1991 after providing for the money which has disappeared and for the unexpected liabilities the company has inherited," Burrington had written to the staff on 8 April 1992. The journalists were enraged by Burrington accepting a raise of almost 18 per cent, especially those who had protected him in the distant past, when his drinking so nearly resulted in the sack, and who felt he had spurned them after his unlikely elevation to executive stardom. Silent executive director Sir Robert Clark, astonishingly to many observers now with mouths permanently fixed wide open, became the new chairman.

The board had decided to put up the price of the *Daily Mirror* by two pence, an increase viewed with horror by editor Stott but with glee by *The Sun*. Circulation began to fall and although the Group was still afloat, it was in administration with no guarantees that it could weather the storm. Stott had already begun investigating a possible buyout by the staff. Production director Ian MacDonald, circulation director Ian Herbertson and advertisement director Mark Pritchett all backed the idea, as did I at *The People* and Joe Haines, still anguished at having been fooled into writing his flattering biography of the giant fraudster. The Glaswegian Charlie Wilson and Bridget Rowe, brassy editor of the *Sunday Mirror*, said they were in, but from then on played hokey-cokey with the proposition as another option was presented. Roger Eastoe, the deputy managing director, remained neutral, a stance which, when continued, was destined to bring misery to the *Mirror*. Former British Rail chairman Sir Peter Parker, the man overlooked when Clive Thornton was installed as the last and momentary pre-Maxwell chairman, agreed to front the bid, which was being managed by the Electra venture capital group and included John Sharkey, a skilful businessman from the advertising industry, for extra gravitas.

On Friday 2 October, lunching in the Gay Hussar in Soho with Marje Proops, I looked up to see David Montgomery, accompanied by a slim, bearded man, passing our table on their way out. Montgomery waved, almost shyly. I didn't know it, but the buyout was about to be torpedoed. The consortium of banks that effectively owned Mirror Group had been

On the fence: Roger Eastoe would survive to serve on David Montgomery's board.

negotiating with Montgomery and his lunch companion, Lord Hollick – recommended for his peerage by Neil Kinnock after the then plain Clive chaired the left-leaning Institute for Public Policy research think tank – and believed the pair were the best bet for the banks to get back their money. Hollick was the key. Hambros, the merchant bank of which he was a non-executive director, was putting together a rescue operation for MGN that included the "expertise" of Montgomery. But Montgomery had no standing in the city – "They were casting around for some non-executive directors to support the project," Hollick later recalled, "to accept the call to arms, if you like. David Montgomery was not someone I had previously worked with or knew. It was a time when the paper and the whole organisation was in great danger, so I thought there was an important public role to play there."

Before either Hollick or Montgomery could play any sort of role, both the journalists and the board had to be won over. Montgomery succeeded with his written assurances in persuading the reluctant editorial staff to cooperate. The board approval necessary to ratify the new management was distorted when Haines quit as a non-executive director and

Eastoe, his neutrality rampant, abstained from voting. Montgomery was in. So was Hollick, for just four months. Clark, the busted flush from the Maxwell era, was chairman, Montgomery, an ex-Rupert Murdoch employee with a hatred of *Mirror* culture and a determination to change it, was chief executive. Editorial direction was in the hands of Wilson, another former Murdoch man who, when Stott had told him of the staff buyout proposal, said he was "in with both feet, matey". The *Daily Mirror* may have been rescued, but there were those on the staff who would have preferred the paper to have thrown itself into the Mediterranean in Maxwell's considerable wake.

Had he made inquiries of the man he didn't know, Lord Hollick would have found that in certain quarters, Mirror Group being one of them, Montgomery's qualities were far from appreciated. When a young sub-editor at the *Daily Mirror*, he was alarmingly ambitious and headstrong to the point of ignoring instruction. In Manchester, where Montgomery had started with the Group, reporter and fellow Protestant Ulsterman Alastair McQueen became explosively irate when his copy was rewritten by the former Plymouth trainee, inaccurately thought McQueen. Then, when I was standing in as editor in London late on an evening when Montgomery had been left in charge of the backbench, I made sure I told him before I left for the night that he was no account to change the front-page lead story without contacting me. Something prompted me to telephone the office before I arrived home. Sure enough, "Monty" – he was given the soubriquet "Rommel" after someone observed, "But Monty was on our side" – was in the process of changing the splash story. Later, as assistant editor in charge of features at the *Sunday People*, I intervened when he had reduced a young woman features writer to tears in a corridor of Orbit House. The rumour mill alleged that I hit him. I did not, but it is indicative of his popularity that there were no tears of regret when he quit shortly afterwards to go to the *News of the World*.

As soon as he took over at MGN, that same rumour mill was predicting that my history with him, plus the fact that I had sacked his then wife, Heidi Kingstone, from *The People* magazine, meant I would not survive for long. The rumour was correct in that, on 11 November, he fired me, but wrong about the

reasons. When he had asked me why I did not take *The People* sharply downmarket, I'd pointed out that Bridget Rowe's *Sunday Mirror* was already rolling about on the market floor and it didn't seem sensible for the two MGN Sunday titles to compete head-to-head down there. He disagreed and I went. Then we heard that David Banks, a former *Mirror* backbench executive, had boarded a plane in Australia en route for Holborn Circus. Stott speculated to me that Banks was returning to replace him. Don't be ridiculous, I told him, and so did Montgomery: Banks was coming to edit *The People*, he informed Richard. Two days later he sacked Stott over a breakfast table at Claridge's. When Stott reminded him that, at their last meeting, he had said he thought everything at the *Mirror* was going well, Montgomery now famously replied: "I was tap dancing." He later had the gall to argue semantics, but the truth was, to misquote the master of the fractured epigram, Sam Goldwyn, that Montgomery's agreement wasn't worth the paper it was written on.

The blood-letting began immediately. David Banks, collected by Montgomery and Wilson from Heathrow, snoozed in the car on the journey to Holborn and then discovered a wholesale clearout of editorial casual staff had begun. As Stott has observed, the banks wanted savings and they wanted them fast, and the only way to achieve that was by enormous cuts in personnel. But Montgomery seemed to want to do more: in dumping some of the best and most experienced *Mirror* journalists, it was as if he

Tribute: The Mirror's memorial edition on the death of Princess Diana.

The future's orange: Ulsterman David Montgomery took over as chief executive of the crippled Mirror Group with a determination to cut costs and wipe away the old Mirror culture.

wanted to eradicate the past. His unfulfilled previous period with the Group had left him with a loathing of all things he considered either Cudlippian or part of a *Mirror* culture that was profligate and soft. His antipathy towards Cudlipp became clear after Hugh died and the *British Journalism Review* approached the Mirror Group to obtain sponsorship for the journalistic award it was creating in the name of its former revered editorial director. He refused even to discuss the idea. Later he was to say: "The behaviour of Cudlipp and his acolytes at the end of his tenure was pretty appalling. I think there were aspects of the Cudlipp era, which I saw with my own eyes, which were like the last days of Rome… *The Sun* had just started and there was a huge amount of arrogance and complacency and squandering of resources. The culture was a legacy that affected the *Mirror* for many years." As previous chapters of this book show, Montgomery was partially correct. What he failed to notice, because it was not in his nature, was that the Cudlipp era was also one of exuberance and fun, words not prominent in the Montgomery lexicon.

The savagery of the staff cuts was too much for Hollick, who bailed out in March 1993. "The paper needed to be restructured, yes," he said later. "There was a need to sort it out and that is never an easy thing to do,

Protest: Marje Proops, determined as ever but increasingly immobile, was supported by former editor Roy Greenslade when she attended the Mirror AGM to add her support during the pensions crisis.

professional qualities and attributes you would say, 'I'd like to hire them – they're good people.' There was a sort of cleansing that went on there that I thought was inappropriate and I felt very strongly that while the paper needed to be restructured, it also needed considerable investment."

Montgomery didn't just try to remove those people to whom Hollick referred; he succeeded. Alastair Campbell, the political editor who made no secret of his closeness to, and support of, the Labour Party, was ousted: "Monty and I agreed we weren't going to get on and that it would be better if I went," he recalls. "I had tried for a while to make it work, but then David Seymour was brought in as group political editor without my knowledge. Monty said he thought I should be able to work with Seymour and that the *Mirror* would still be a Labour paper but its policies needed a new direction and to be sharper – all that guff that really meant I wasn't wanted. I said I didn't think it right to bring in someone over my head and that was that. I think he knew the nature of the job and he knew my personality and that was what he was suggesting wouldn't work."

New editor Banks made a point of informing Campbell that Seymour's appointment was not his decision, which of course it wasn't. Amanda Plattell, later a Conservative Party spin doctress but at the time part of Montgomery's management team, was later to claim the trophy sacking of Campbell, who remembers that "she

Bowing out: Lord Hollick eventually found he could not support Montgomery's methods.

whatever industry you do it in, and in a newspaper group it is particularly difficult because it is done in the full glare of publicity. But I felt the approach that David had at the time was unnecessarily brutal. I felt he was trying to remove from the company people who were independently minded, who were vocal, many of whom had been active trades unionists and many of whom were distinguished journalists who by reference to any sort of normal criteria of

Leader writing: Alastair Campbell, then Mirror *political editor, interviews Labour leader Neil Kinnock. When Campbell was forced out under Montgomery, Kinnock wrote an article for the* Evening Standard *condemning his friend's dismissal.*

David Banks was born in 1948 in Warrington, Lancashire, and educated at Warrington Grammar School. He joined the Daily Mirror *in Manchester, transferred to London and became an assistant night editor before moving to New York as night managing editor of the* Post*. After considerable experience abroad, he returned to the* Daily Mirror *as editor in 1992 and became editorial director in 1994. Later he became a television columnist for* The People *and a successful radio broadcaster. Following health problems, he is now a freelance broadcaster.*

In at the deep end: David Banks was summoned from Australia to edit the Mirror.

There were rumours going around that I was going to be offered the editorship of the *Sunday Mirror* or *The People*, but David Montgomery called me and asked if I would like to edit the *Daily Mirror*. I asked what had happened to Richard Stott and he said something like it was all over. I didn't have to think about it very much. He told me to get to London as quickly as possible as the paper would be without an editor until I arrived. Within a week, I was on my way back, believing that Richard Stott had gone from the *Mirror* and Bill Hagerty from *The People*, too, a week or ten days before.

I arrived at Heathrow on a wet Sunday and was met by Montgomery and Charlie Wilson. I was knackered and fell asleep in the back of a very hot Jaguar, waking up just as Charlie was saying something about if there was going to be a strike, why didn't they have it full out. Nobody will be happy about Stotty going, he said. I said, what – he's gone, hasn't he? They said, no, we have to do that this morning. So suddenly I was

involved in the demise of a fellow editor.

I was to be dropped off with Charlie at the *Mirror* building before Montgomery went to meet Stott at Claridge's to do the deed. I remember sitting in the back of this car with my stomach somewhere round my tonsils. It was the beginning of months of unpleasantness. It had been made clear to me, and I had been promised, that I wouldn't in any way be implicated in the demise of an editor, but that I would be coming along to steady the ship.

I arrived at the *Mirror* presumably at the same time that Monty was getting rid of Richard. It was a bizarre day. I held a meeting of executives immediately and reintroduced myself – I knew most of them. I explained to them that Richard had gone and that it wasn't personalities that were important, but the paper – it was the *Mirror* we all cared about. They were obviously concerned about Richard, but I was appealing to them to get the paper out, which they all agreed to do. The irony was that after everyone had gone back to their posts and were briefing their staffs, the picture editor came in and said none of the casual staff could get into the building. Their passes wouldn't work and they had been told to go home. So I said, this is ridiculous – who's stopping them? I called Charlie Wilson and said: "The casuals can't get in – how I am going to put the paper out?" And he said, "Haven't you told the executives that all the casuals are sacked? I thought you heard that in the car." And I said, "I was asleep in the bloody car."

Continued on page 190

dotted the i's and crossed the t's and was perfectly nice, actually." The political editor's demise spurred Labour into action it had noticeably failed to display when Robert Maxwell gained control of the Group: Neil Kinnock, a friend of Campbell's, wrote a long and unprecedented article for the *Evening Standard* condemning the political editor's departure and in the House of Commons 170 Labour MPs signed a lack-of-confidence Early Day Motion questioning Montgomery's political perspicacity. The paper's support of Labour immediately became slavish –

Montgomery, like Clark and Wilson no Labour supporter, didn't need further flack from the party the paper had traditionally backed. What's more, it would have been commercially disastrous to shift the *Mirror*'s political allegiance. With Haines gone for good and David Thompson following, Seymour, a former *Mirror* writer I had taken to *Today*, became also the paper's leader writer. He still is, doubling up as readers' editor to deal with errors and complaints.

Anne Robinson followed Campbell to *Today* before going on to conquer the world. Features

First person DAVID BANKS

At that point, I guess you have to make a decision. You either tell your executives that you had no knowledge of this and that it is none of your doing, which is so weak and toadying in a way. Or you say to yourself, I'm part of this – I've agreed to do the job, I've taken the money. So I called a second executive meeting, where I told them that I had decided we were over-manned to the extent that we shouldn't have the dependency on the casuals that we had. And that I had decided at that point to stop the casual system. That first day, that horrific first day, led to months of union problems and general unpleasantness.

On the Wednesday, Rupert Murdoch called to offer me his congratulations and to say, "You'll have a tough time against Kelvin, but give 'em hell". It was bizarre – his was the only friendly voice I heard that week, from management or union. It sounds as if I am moaning and whingeing, but I'm not really – I took the money, I should have known what I was getting into and I was in it.

It never properly settled down. You could never concentrate 100 per cent, or even 75 per cent, on journalism and the business of editing. My entire first year was completely unsettled. I had real problems with Paul Foot because he was having problems with Montgomery and management, and was standing out against what he saw as an improper course of action. Of course, I understood that, but I was quite firmly on the other side. I was in an impossible position. We had some good journalistic moments and some low ones, but most of the time it was a matter of trying to keep the ship afloat. I always adored the *Mirror*, right from boyhood, and I was determined that nothing appalling was going to happen to it during my editorship, that at least it would carry on. That was my whole ambition.

Looking back, Montgomery managed to bring the company out of administration. He was a great money-saver. I don't think at that stage of his career he was a great creative force, but he was a great cutter, a slasher, a burner – an unattractive thing to have said about you. In a way he did half the job. He helped pull the *Mirror* back from the awfulness of the immediate post-Maxwell period. Where he went awry was that he couldn't supply the rebuilding process. He never had the time for journalism,

he never ever boasted about our journalism. He only ever boasted about [in-paper] games, about buy-ins, about promotions. It was impossible to get him to focus in any way on the journalism. I don't think he likes journalists, really – he sees them as something of a hindrance.

One of the phrases that will always be associated with David by people who worked for the *Mirror* at that time was "old culture". He wanted to eradicate old culture – everything that had gone before, good or bad, was old culture. The great joke was going into the pub and asking for two gin and tonics and a pint of old culture. It was almost a Polpot reworking of the paper's identity. Everything had to be rethought or restarted. Overmanning, old styles of journalism, John Pilger – that was all old culture. It was all uniformly bad. Mind you, Charlie Wilson had been as close to Robert Maxwell as anybody and he survived, which was a puzzle. But that was Monty's downfall – he should have concentrated just on making the *Mirror* a great paper again, on bouncing it back to the top of the pile.

The management just carried on regardless, really, putting up with Monty's rages and imperious behaviour. I guess rather as they had with Maxwell. I used to say to my fellow editors that I would much prefer an accountant to be running the bloody place than a former editor, because there was no question that he was "The man" and everything had to be decided by and done through him, in management and major editorial decisions. And he held the purse strings very, very tight. It was a difficult time.

After a little less than two years I became unwell and exhausted – in hindsight, I was developing the first signs of leukaemia – and Montgomery saw this before I did and suggested that I should stand down and become editorial director. Frankly, I agreed to do it because I was knackered, dispirited, demoralised. I don't think I was ever intended to be the editor for bad times. If I was going to be successful, it was going to be on my own terms and I was never editor on my own terms. And so, in the middle of 1994, there was nothing about the *Mirror* that I so thoroughly enjoyed at that point that I wanted to stay on.

---

writer Barry Wigmore also joined *Today*, en route to a successful career as a freelance in the United States. Brian Bass, a vastly experienced journalist in both news and features, told new features executive Richard Holledge to fuck off when Holledge criticised the soon-to-be-cancelled Friday *Mirror* Xtra supplement for which Bass was responsible. "Then I remembered that I had told Montgomery to fuck off years before when he changed my page layouts on the backbench," Bass recalls, "so I wasn't surprised when I was asked to move to a

very junior role in news production. To be fair, I was properly paid off and Amanda Platell was very helpful."

At high managerial level, McDonald and Herbertson were fired, but Wilson and Eastoe swiftly adapted to the new regime, with Wilson later even editing the *Independent* for a while when Montgomery obtained a controlling interest and started to trim away fat that by now was difficult to find at the struggling paper.

Paul Foot, who, with the assistance of Bryan Rostron, produced a consistently outstanding

Putting his case: David Banks makes one reader's dreams come true in September 1993 – Diane Brooks from Nottingham had won a competition to pay off her mortgage. But Banks found the constraints on his editorship left little to smile about.

So I became editorial director, although I have always held the belief that editorial directors, since Cudlipp at any rate, are not worth the paper they are printed on. An editor is an editor is an editor and nobody should push him around or tell him what to publish. So I didn't do that, but I was there if they wanted to talk to me and any experience I had that I could parley I would do. Then I got interested in radio and in doing other things. I was still editorial director, but at the same time I was doing a breakfast radio show for LBC and I was doing a morning television show for Live TV. Eventually I quit to go off and do that kind of thing full time.

My time at the *Mirror* was not enjoyable, but it is not something that I would be happy to leave off my CV. And you are what you are – you make decisions and you go along with them. I don't think there is anything I have done that I have regretted, but certainly that era comes close. I had been very successful up until that time, but all I managed to do in the best part of two years as editor of the *Mirror* was keep my head above water. It's a great shame – I would love to have been a triumphant *Mirror* editor, but it wasn't to be. I've expunged a lot of it from my memory. I much preferred working for Rupert Murdoch, I know that. **,**

column, had outlasted Maxwell, but the carnage all around as dozens of colleagues were shown the door repelled him. One day he asked for volunteers to march seven times around the building "blowing trumpets", presumably in the hope that the walls would tumble as they once had in Jericho. There were no trumpets, but some 40 members of staff circled the building seven times anyway.

Tim Minogue, a sub-editor employed on a casual basis, who had become an NUJ activist as the swell of firings continued, had lost all his

work on the *Mirror* when the casual staff was locked out early in Montgomery's cost-cutting programme. After signing an individual contract, he continued working on the *Sunday Mirror* and also speaking out on behalf of the journalists, particularly in the trade paper *Press Gazette*. Returning to the office along New Fetter Lane one lunchtime – he had escaped only to buy a sandwich – he saw the demonstration and exchanged greetings and shook hands with Paul Foot. The following morning he received a letter from editor Colin

True colours: Amanda Platell would go on to find a role with the Conservative Party.

Myler, sacking him for unspecified "gross misconduct". When he entered the building in order to obtain clarification from Myler, he was stopped and escorted out by Brendon Parsons, an editorial executive and close confidant of Montgomery, and two members of the security staff. Soon afterwards, Foot presented a column devoted entirely to what was happening at the *Mirror*. When Banks rejected it, Foot refused to supply a substitute piece and resigned. The NUJ provided legal assistance for Minogue, Foot and others to pursue claims of wrongful dismissal against the paper, most of which were settled by the group shortly before reaching court. (The NUJ struggled and failed to survive in the building, despite another Montgomery assurance, and now has no official recognition in the group, having been replaced by Steve Turner's British Association of Journalists.)

When later accused by me of having wasted valuable talent in his culture-changing purge, Montgomery replied: "I've never heard anybody actually specify a piece of talent we have wasted." I cited Foot, Campbell and Robinson. "I don't think Foot contributed much at all, except a bitter political philosophy," said Montgomery. "He wasn't terribly productive. And he chose not to work with me, rather than the other way round. The other people made

their own decisions about life. I don't think any of them made a particular contribution to the newspaper... They had their talents, but they were for hire."

For all this activity, and perhaps partly because of it, the circulation slumped, falling by around 200,000 in the first year of Montgomery's tenure. A flurry of publicity came with publication of pictures of the Princess of Wales working out at a private gymnasium, which provoked accusations of intrusive journalism, a writ from Diana and condemnation from Lord MacGregor, then chairman of the Press Complaints Commission (the Group's papers temporarily withdrew recognition of the PCC). But generally the paper lacked such excitement. Something had to give and it was Banks, a naturally jovial hulk of a man who had found the editorship both distressing and dispiriting. In 1994, he was "promoted" to become editorial director for a while and Montgomery switched Colin Myler from the Sunday title to edit the *Daily Mirror*.

In March of that year, the paper went through a genuine culture shock when it moved away from the building it had occupied for more than 30 years. Down came the red, white and blue matchbox and in its place appeared a far more handsome building, although so big it broods over Holborn Circus, dwarfing everything around it. It was not, however, to be home to the *Mirror* – it is now the headquarters of Sainsbury's and, the transitory nature of newspapers being what it is, few of those busying themselves there every day realise their workplace stands on the site of what once was the world's greatest newspaper and periodical empire. Of the four historic plaques that were inlaid in a wall of the entrance lobby – depicting Bartholomew, King, Cudlipp and Bill Connor – Connor's survived and was given to Bill's widow. The others vanished – "an act of corporate vandalism," the company admitted long after Montgomery had departed. The pictures of members of the *Mirror* staff that crowded the walls of the Stab in the Back disappeared, too, and soon afterwards the pub became a branch of Pizza Express. Vagabonds, the Fetter Lane bar that had challenged the Stab as the *Mirror*'s main watering hole, withered and moved to the Barbican, where it remained, renamed The Edge, until the death of popular proprietor John Mullally.

All change for Canary Wharf: The Mirror's old ways were left behind after the move to 1 Canada Square.

Montgomery relocated the Group to 1 Canada Square in a Canary Wharf far bleaker than it is today. There a *Daily Mirror* that, in some past eras, had been floated out of the loading bays on a wave of alcohol became the product of what basically was a temperance hotel without the beds. Although by now happily married to his third wife, Sophie, the former Countess of Wooton, and being abundantly rewarded for clawing back £30million of the banks' money and, admirably, patching up the pension fund, Montgomery's demeanour remained austere. His demands for sobriety – no bad thing bearing in mind the Group's tipsy history – were such that the editorial staff soon became wary of being seen even in the same street as a bar, let alone enjoying a drink inside one. Such was the frigid atmosphere around the place that there was talk among those survivors from the crew of the

Captain's leaky ship of producing lapel badges that read: "Come back Maxwell – all is forgiven". But they didn't dare. Their disillusion could, however, be expressed in another form. West Country district man and skilled musician Geoff Lakeman had mourned the departure of such venerated reporters as Ron Ricketts, Ed Vale and John Jackson by writing a song that is still sung when ex-*Mirror* men and women get together:

The Boys of the Byline Brigade
No more will we see them parade
The ink in their veins, it has gone down the
*   drain*
The lead in their pencil's beginning to fade
We're ending a chapter and turning the page
For the Boys of the Byline Brigade.

They once did a bloody fine job
In the army of dear Captain Bob
It's Fleet Street they led, with their middle-
*   page spread*
With scoop and a splash, well they cut a fine
*   dash*
Now hear the death rattle, they've fallen in
*   battle*
The Boys of the Byline Brigade.

No more will the telephone ring
It's an end to their globetrotting fling
Farewell with a sigh to the Bank In The Sky
Goodbye, you old hack, to the Stab In The Back
They'll carry you off in your own mink-lined
*   coffin*
The Boys of the Byline Brigade.

The Boys of the Byline Brigade
Exclusives were their stock in trade
With cheque book in hand they'd all make the
*   first bid*
But they'd sell their old granny for twenty-five
*   quid*
Farewell to the headlines, they've met their
*   own deadlines*
The Boys of the Byline Brigade.

Authors Chris Horrie and Adam Nathan later observed: "The difference between Maxwell and Monty, senior *Mirror* people decided, was that while Maxwell had been a compulsive liar, Monty was compulsively sneaky. When Maxwell told you something, you knew it was a lie, so you knew where you stood, but nobody ever got close enough to Monty to know where they stood".

The Murdoch infiltration of MGN continued

On song: Geoff Lakeman wrote a lament for the Mirror days and ways of old.

with the recruitment by Montgomery of former *Sun* editor Kelvin MacKenzie, brought in as managing director of Live TV, the Group's fledgling cable tabloid television operation. MacKenzie had been openly contemptuous of Montgomery when they were both at News International. Now he was to work closely with him, while, for the time being, engaging in open warfare with Janet Street-Porter, who was in charge of Live's programming. The *Independent* deal went through, with *Independent on Sunday* editor Ian Jack welcoming Montgomery's arrival with a leading article that commented: "Mr Montgomery is not popular among journalists, having fired a good editor of the *Daily Mirror* and many others of his staff." Jack warned Montgomery to keep his tanks off the editor's lawn and, unsurprisingly, departed soon afterwards. Monty also bought Midland Independent Newspapers, a major regional group, and titles in Northern Ireland. The empire was growing and he began to display signs of delusions of grandeur. With his high business profile determining that his private life came under press scrutiny, he took to telephoning then *Mail* editor-in-chief David English and asking for items about him to be left out of Associated's papers. "I have to keep pointing out to him that he is not a proprietor!" said English.

Street-wise: Janet Street Porter has a laugh with another Goofy on the Thames.

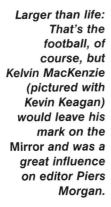

Larger than life: That's the football, of course, but Kelvin MacKenzie (pictured with Kevin Keagan) would leave his mark on the Mirror *and was a great influence on editor Piers Morgan.*

Montgomery was now on good terms with the Labour Party, where, after John Smith's premature death and Tony Blair's succession as leader, Alastair Campbell – who had notoriously thumped and been thumped by the *Guardian's* Michael White in the Commons when White rejoiced at Maxwell's death – had arrived to head Blair's press team. "We decided to be grown up about it [he and Montgomery's past history]", says Campbell. "He wrote me a very nice letter and I said the past was the past and it was important that the party and the *Mirror* should have a good relationship in the future. Later, Montgomery became a not insignificant figure in the Northern Ireland peace process. He had good contacts and good ideas and was extremely helpful."

Myler had managed to stabilise circulation, but Montgomery was not satisfied. His method of choosing editors appeared to be hit-and-miss, with more misses than hits. He later bafflingly attempted to explain this: "Quite a few people want to be editors and not all of them will be successful editors and the trick probably is to spot those people who have great talent and ability and are ambitious and want to be editors [but] who actually won't make it in the job. And probably we don't really know for sure until they try… Editing requires a particularly tenacious sort of individual, someone with a lot of stamina for a start, particularly with daily papers, and a lot of focus and single minded-ness… And you don't really discover that, and

the people don't discover that for themselves, until they have a go. What I've learned is that when you get it wrong you should do something about it and I managed not to do something about it fast enough in some cases."

Having decided he had got it wrong with Myler, he talked with new ally MacKenzie before looking towards Wapping – where else? and approaching Piers Morgan, wunderkind editor of the *News of the World*. When Morgan agreed to move to the *Mirror*, Myler, whose reconstruction of the staff had included the inspired hiring of the soon-to-be award-winning Brian Reade, was eased upstairs as managing director. Morgan, raw but possessing the dynamism lacking in the *Mirror*, arrived on 1 November 1995 and soon found out exactly how his new paper differed from the sex, sport and scandal sheet he had left. With his eyes fixed firmly on the rear lights of the *Mirror's* nemesis, he swung the paper into *Sun* mode, famously with a front page before the England v Germany semi-final of football's Euro 96 tournament: "Achtung! Surrender! For You Fritz Ze Euro 96 Championship Is Over". It was a colossal xenophobic error of judgement, although Morgan still defends it as "a bit of a laugh". For this, MPs and former *Mirror* luminaries Joe Haines and John Pilger castigated him in the press, although Pilger was soon to revise his evaluation of the new editor enough to write for him.

Morgan also soon realised that some of the

First person　　　COLIN MYLER

Colin Myler was born in 1952 in Widnes, Cheshire, and educated at St. Patrick's RC school and SS John Fisher and Thomas More High School, Widnes. He was associate editor of the Sunday Mirror. *After becoming deputy editor, he was promoted to editor in 1992. He was made editor of the* Daily Mirror *in 1994 and managing director of the title in 1996. He is now managing editor of the* New York Post.

'I was appointed editor of the *Daily Mirror* by the then chief executive, David Montgomery, at the end of March 1995. Montgomery's brief was short and simple: stop the circulation slide and improve the paper.

According to Montgomery, the paper was "listless and drifting". He wanted it to have more direction and more energy. He also wanted it to be staffed by younger, multi-skilled journalists – the new-breed of smart, computer-wise whiz-kids who could do everything on screen; design a page, sub, pull in pictures, pull in ads, and send the page to the plant. It was Montgomery's vision of a "paperless newspaper office". It sounded straight out of an Arthur C. Clarke sci-fi novel. But he was serious.

Here we go, I thought, yet another Fleet Street revolution. The days of the splash sub were numbered. But did these wonder kids exist? They did, and some were already at the paper – although not enough of them. But they were the least of my problems. Every new editor can tell tales of how they rescued their new paper from the throes of death. It's a bit like going to a new hairdresser or dentist for the first time – the bad state of the hair/teeth is often exaggerated. But David Banks had experienced an awful, at times traumatising period at the paper, introducing and overseeing extremely difficult new working practices that were resisted by the staff, particularly by the huge numbers of casual staff the *Mirror* had traditionally relied on. A plan implemented to introduce new contracts was bitter, brutal and protracted. Morale was pretty low, new direction and fresh blood was badly needed.

The problem I faced was why would anyone want to leave *The Sun* or the *Daily Mail* to go to the *Mirror*? I decided to go for Peter Cox, *The Sun*'s night editor, as my deputy. I met Coxy, told him about my plans and he excitedly, and quickly, accepted my offer. I knew he was a good production journalist and I knew also he would target four or five key subs from *The Sun* to bring with him. So did Kelvin Mackenzie, still *The Sun*'s editor, and that's why Coxy never joined me.

On the day he was to start, he called to say Kelvin had arranged for him to speak to Rupert Murdoch that afternoon in New York. Rupert offered him a "once-in-a-lifetime" job at the *New York Post*, which he had to accept, he said. It was a disappointment, but not a huge surprise. Coxy's reign at the *Post* ended rather ingloriously after a few months and I subsequently did hire him, although not as deputy editor. He was, however, pivotal in me prising away from *The Sun* Simon Cosyns, at the time the brightest designer in tabloid journalism.

I took two key people with me from the *Sunday Mirror*, sports editor David Balmforth and John McShane, a hugely experienced news editor. Sue Carroll, a terrific operator, was running features at the *Daily Mirror*; Ron Morgans was running pictures. I immediately redesigned the paper to open up an op-ed spread and redesigned the leader to run alongside the left-hand op-ed read. The idea was to give the *Mirror* a more quality feel and put more intelligent, relevant reading into the paper, to differentiate us from *The Sun*. I wanted more in-depth news stories, more intelligent and relevant features, and more exclusives, particularly in sport, where *The Sun* had gained ground on what once was the *Mirror*'s supreme strength.

I introduced a Monday soccer section, beefed up our pre-printed Saturday "magazine" section and set out to hire some high-profile columnists. I wanted to bring Anne Robinson back to the *Mirror*. I knew she was unhappy at *Today* and I persuaded Montgomery that she would be a great asset to the paper if I could get her to return. He was still upset at her bitter denunciation of him after he took control of the *Mirror*, but, to his credit, said that if I wanted her, I should go get her. I met her several times, once at her London home. As always, Annie was charming. She played hard-to-get, but, I thought,

staff remained bruised by events of the immediate past – "There was a residual problem and a tension with the older *Mirror* types, who had seen the damage and devastation caused by the culling," he was to say – and that the chief executive was someone who wished to very much be involved in the editorial process. "I didn't much like the way things had been done before I got here, or the way that people like Paul Foot and others were portrayed as the people who had done in the *Mirror* and were responsible for all its malaise," he recalls. "It

wasn't true. These were great journalists who should have been treated with more respect. Having said that, I think there is a slightly rose-tinted view from *Mirror* people of that era about the problems that Montgomery inherited after Maxwell and what they would have done to have solved them. The Mirror Group could have gone under – purely financially, it could be argued that Montgomery saved the *Mirror*. I don't think he cared much about the heritage and history. He cared about getting the company commercially back on track and if that needed

Lost opportunities: But Colin Myler brought in some great names.

Anne have made a difference? Absolutely. Cheapness was, sadly, a fundamental, transparent management failing that ran right through the company. Their aspirations were always to win the Premiership. Unfortunately, their strategy, when it came to hard cash, was more Accrington Stanley. It was always stressed to me that the *Mirror* could never invest in the business like, say, the *Mail*, because it had to service and satisfy investors. The *Mirror* was not allowed to compete financially with *The Sun* or the *Mail*.

Nothing new then, or, to some extent I suppose, now. I did, however, poach from the *Mail* one of their rising stars, Martin Clarke. I made him news editor, and, within two months, Paul Dacre realised his mistake in letting him go and appointed Clarke editor of the *Scottish Daily Mail*. I continued to hire the "paperless multi-skilled wunderkinds" and managed to put together a great, young team. I relaunched, from London, editions for Northern Ireland and Eire and a Scottish edition. All on the cheap and, considering the foresight and investment of other UK-based newspaper groups in Ireland, too little, too late. Inexorably, the circulation continued to decline, but at a slower rate. At least we were attracting good journalists from other papers and hiring fresh young talent, like Brian Reade, who I picked up from the *Liverpool Echo*.

Sue Carroll returned to her natural home with *The Sun* at Wapping, but her departure allowed a great journalist, Fiona McIntosh, to flourish. She went on to edit *Elle* magazine. News hit the ground running. Michael Barrymore had travelled to America to enter a drug and booze rehab clinic. Allan Hall, the *Mirror*'s American editor, found him, got great pictures and a first-hand account of Barrymore's tortuous battle with booze and drugs. It was a great tabloid exclusive and a coup for a paper that in most circumstances would have lost it to *The Sun*.

Promotions had moved into a new phase – tied to TV game shows. The *Mirror* spent a fortune with a Des O'Connor show. It was the usual format – game card in paper, play live with the show, produce a winner, pay Des

Continued on page 198

desperate to get back to the paper that she always regarded as her maternal home. She loved the *Mirror* and *Mirror* readers loved her. At *Today*, she told me, she felt starved of reader reaction. The fact was that she was a star and missed the big stage. She wanted £250,000 a year and a string of the usual "no interference" clauses in her contract. They were all manageable and I was pretty pleased to have got her. But it never happened. At the last minute, Monty said he really couldn't welcome her back. But it was really about the M-factor – money. He just didn't want to pay her.

Later, I tried to poach Richard Littlejohn from *The Sun*. After a memorable five-hour lunch at Luigi's in Covent Garden, Littlejohn agreed to join for £250,000 a year. He was ripe for a change, his friend Kelvin having left the editorship of *The Sun*. But again Monty wouldn't pay and Littlejohn went to the *Daily Mail* instead. Would he and

brutality to do it, then that's what was going to happen. David's personality did not lend itself to sorting these things out in a way that left him very popular. He is a very tough character, but I never had a problem with him. He was very good to me. Over Achtung! Surrender! he called me in on the Monday morning and said, 'You've dropped a right clanger here, but we'll back you'. David was probably the most interfering of the people I've worked for, but you must remember that if you ask people who worked for him when he was an editor, some of

them have a very high regard for him. So I had no problem with him giving me his views."

Those people of the pre-Montgomery *Mirror* era, and others too, were soon unenamoured by what they saw as another major Morgan gaffe. On the eve of the Major Government's 1996 budget, the *Mirror* was gifted the details of what the Chancellor would be announcing the following day. Morgan decided against running the story and now says: "The documents appeared to be genuine, but we didn't know if they had been stolen, which raised a potential a fortune and move on, hoping to attract new readers and keep them. I don't remember that it succeeded. All I know is that dealing with prima donnas like O'Connor, and particularly agents, was a nightmare and all too time-consuming.

The political stance of the paper remained pro-Labour. Montgomery was close to the Labour hierarchy, although they were cautious of him. Monty's erstwhile benefactor, Lord Hollick, had helped him land the *Mirror* prize he longed for. But their marriage was short-lived and ended bitterly and publicly. Hollick never really understood tabloid journalism, hated tabloid journalists even more, and sneered at what he regarded as crude and tacky elements of the business. I remember having to make a promotions presentation to him when I was editing the *Sunday Mirror*. We were advertising on TV an ABC of sex – the usual after-9pm watershed sexy, in-your-face ad with a glossy part-work as the attraction. Hollick looked at me as if I had walked in with something on my shoe and made some comment like: you poor thing, is this what you call serious journalism? Later, Montgomery brushed aside his comment with, "Don't worry, he doesn't understand newspapers."

I knew John Smith, the Labour Party leader, quite well. I liked him and believed he could, and would, eventually lead Labour to power. His sudden death was a true tragedy. I was with him at a Labour dinner the night before he died. He was in good form. We chatted, he made a great speech, and I stayed overnight at the Hilton hotel. I was just about to leave for the office after breakfast when the newsdesk rang. They'd heard that Smith had collapsed and was on his way to hospital. Minutes later, I was called in my car and told it was not looking good. The next call, before I arrived at the office, was to say it was believed he had died. We had a major practical problem – half of the paper was already printed. Our presses at the time dictated that we had to pre-print the features part of the paper. I said we would have to lose the pre-print and start again. It was a huge technical operation.

It was my biggest challenge as an editor. The loss of a Labour leader, particularly one with so much promise and expectation, meant there would be much focus on how we treated the story. I cleared the first 20 pages or so and set to work. Most of the story fell into place quite easily. The challenge, as always for an editor, was the front page. There were plenty of photographs to choose from, particularly from the dinner the night before, an event the *Mirror* had sponsored. But "the last picture" was hardly novel, nor would it be exclusive. I had a different idea. I called Charles Griffin, then the *Mirror*'s resident cartoonist and a brilliant caricaturist. I said I wanted him to draw John Smith outside 10 Downing Street with a plaque behind him that read: *John Smith should have lived here*. Griffin did it brilliantly and it made a fantastic front page. I was very proud of it and the paper. Griffin and the paper

Top draw: The front-page tribute to Labour leader John Smith, illustrated by Charles Griffin.

were duly recognised when awarded "Image of the year" at the *Press Gazette* annual press awards.

Montgomery was restless and appeared uncomfortable. He said he was unhappy with the executive structure within the company and wanted to change things around. He was spending increasingly more time travelling, particularly to America, talking to investors and potential investors, and he said he wanted to restructure the management of the papers. He wanted me to become managing director of the *Daily Mirror*. I was stunned and said I would like to continue editing. I didn't feel the job I had started was anywhere near completed, but his mind was made up.

He was very persuasive and complimentary. But he knew one thing that I didn't – but was soon to find out. Piers Morgan from the *News of the World* had already been hired to replace me, although Montgomery was nervous about the direction he might take the paper. The real hand behind the hiring was Kelvin MacKenzie, who Montgomery had welcomed into the fold by giving him Live TV to run. Montgomery's instincts about Piers were right. He took the *Mirror* downmarket and head-to-head with its nemesis, *The Sun*. "Achtung! Surrender!" said it all.

First person — EUGENE DUFFY

Eugene Duffy was born in 1962 and educated at Blessed William Howard High School, Stafford. He joined the Staffordshire Newsletter *as a trainee reporter in 1978, moved to the* Worcester Evening News *and then the* Gulf Daily News, *Bahrain. He was a casual reporter/news desk Daily/Sunday Mirror 1986-90 and joined the staff of the* Daily Mirror *as deputy night news editor in 1990. Currently, he's the associate editor, news.*

Job on the line: Eugene Duffy would field the Captain's call.

Two o'clock in the morning and time is dragging. The wires are dead, 24-hour TV news is still to be invented and it's a struggle to stay awake. Then the voice booms out: "What's cooking, mister?" Maxwell has arrived.

He's standing over a desk, glaring down at photographer Chris Grieve, who has his feet on the desk and is watching MTV. Maxwell has no idea who he is, only that this is the foreign desk, where Nick "Sneaky" Davies normally sits and reports on the world (more often than not as Cap'n Bob wants it reported). Grieve is panic stricken, but manages to blurt out that he's listening to Bruce Springsteen talking about unemployment in America (he's actually singing *Born in the USA*). Maxwell hasn't a bloody clue. "Excellent, let me have some copy." Then he's off, stomping down the empty newsroom and back to his lair at the top of Maxwell House.

A typical night at the *Mirror* in the Maxwell years when "The Publisher" dominated everything. The newsdesk phones ran with six lines and a special Maxwell Hotline. When Bob rang down you could see the newsdesk staff collectively push back their wheeled chairs to make sure they weren't the one to pick up the phone.

The then news editor, Tom Hendry, was the one who bore the brunt of the Captain's daily tirades, an experience never to be forgotten. Maxwell was like any

playground bully. If he saw you were afraid, he'd kick you from pillar to post. Occasionally you could stand up to him and get away with it. But not often.

Working on the night news desk for many years, as I had, put you on the front line with Maxwell. By mid-evening his office closed down and he would direct his calls and demands through the newsdesk. Often we would spend hours trying to track down bankers, directors, lawyers all over the world. We would also take the calls from people desperate to talk to him. One such call: "This is the office of the Turkish President, Mr Turgut Ozal. Can we speak to Mr Maxwell please?" I dialled Maxwell's private office and explained who was calling. "Tell him I'm not here, he's after money," snarled Bob and slammed down the phone.

When he was bored, he would ring for a read-through of the other papers, obsessed with any reference to himself or Maxwell companies. On many such occasions, even when he was calling from his private jet as it carried him across the Atlantic, he fell asleep. What to do – hang up or carry on? Many a time, night desk late man Tony Bushby would drone on for hours on end, fearful that to stop would cost him his job even though all he could hear were the publisher's snores.

Continued on page 200

can of worms. I had a long meeting with Charlie Wilson and Montgomery and, given the possible commercial impact of stuff leaked from the budget, we jointly concluded that as we had not independently established the veracity of the documents, we could not run it. The stuff we had – only a few proposals, not the juicy stuff – was very dull and therefore not much of a story. I suggested giving the material to the Government very publicly and making a big noise about it. If it turned out to be fake, then

there was no harm done. If it was genuine, then we had behaved responsibly. It worked well – we were all over the TV news and sold an extra 40,000 papers. With hindsight, what I should have done is tell the Government we had it, wait for the inevitable injunction and run 'Tories Gag The *Mirror* Over Leaked Budget'. That way we'd have got all the publicity and I'd have maintained journalistic credibility."

Three months before the General Election of

Much has been written about Bob and his eastern Europe connections, and, one night, his closest relationship to a foreign power was laid bare. The newsdesk phone rang; Bob was calling from Moscow. "Eugene the Duff," he boomed. "I've been a very silly boy." He'd left a letter in his bedside cabinet – could I go and fetch it? "It's addressed to Mikhail fucking Gorbachev, so you can't miss it, mister."

Eventually I was able to persuade the security staff that the publisher really was on the line and that I had to retrieve the letter – immediately. Twenty minutes later, letter in hand, I was back on the line. "Fax it, now – and don't read it," he demanded. "Certainly, Bob." The letter was from the Israeli Prime Minister, offering a restoration of full diplomatic relations between his country and the Soviet Union. Maxwell was the messenger trusted by both sides.

"Did you read it?" he asked after the fax went through. "No, Bob," I lied. "Don't take me for a cunt, mister," he said before hanging up. Relations between the two countries were duly restored and later Bob got his reward – a grave on the Mount of Olives, with the Israeli Premier and President leading the mourners at his funeral.

The circumstances of Maxwell's death have given rise to a thousand theories. My own memories of his last weekend are crystal clear and I think I was the last person at the *Mirror* ever to speak to him. Every night news desk shift began with one question – where is the publisher and what number is he on? Bob insisted on that night's *Mirror*, and any article relating to him published elsewhere, being faxed instantly to his hotel or the Lady Ghislaine, his private yacht.

For weeks the other papers, particularly the *Mail on Sunday*, had been hammering Maxwell with questions over the *Mirror* pension fund. On that final November Friday evening, I came into the office and asked the editor's secretary for Bob's weekend numbers. "He's not to be contacted," she said. "He's away on the Lady Ghislaine and mustn't be disturbed." This had never happened in all the years Maxwell had owned the *Mirror*. I accepted the secretary's explanation although I was certain that, at some point, Bob would be on the phone, screaming for his cuttings. But that night there was no call.

On the Saturday, I sat in as night news editor for the *Sunday Mirror*. Same thing – Bob remained out of touch. Sunday, about 11pm at the *Daily Mirror*: "Who's that?" "Eugene, Bob." "Ah, Eugene the Duff, what's cooking?" I

ran through the day's news events. There was a big story in Israel. "Send me some cuttings." He explained he was due back the next day to address a Jewish business meeting in London. He sounded fine.

Tuesday afternoon, driving to work, the radio news: "*Mirror* publisher Robert Maxwell is missing at sea." There were few tears, only from those who knew for them the days of Maxwell's silver shilling were over. And within days the dramatic story took an even more dramatic turn as Maxwell's rape of the paper's finances was discovered. The scandal threatened to kill the paper.

The staff worked on, most of us blind to how serious the situation really was, putting our faith in Richard Stott, the editor, to bring us all through. Then David Montgomery arrived. The paper was down and now it was to get a good kicking. Out went Stotty. Out went over a hundred casuals. Out went dozens of production staff who refused to accept the scrapping of the four-day week.

Night after night there'd be mandatory chapel meetings on the editorial floor. Security guards gathered at every door ready to escort us all out into the street if we didn't go back to work. And in the end Monty won, of course. Friends and colleagues such as Paul Foot, who were the face of the *Mirror*, headed out the door. The paper changed direction, chasing "aspirational" readers, those with money in their pockets who would attract better class, more lucrative advertising.

For a brief while we even had a cardboard cut out of Montgomery's perfect *Mirror* reader placed at the entrance to the newsroom. She was known as Swindon Woman – the deputy manageress at Boot's, who went skiing in the winter, the Mediterranean in the summer, had private health cover and wanted to drive a Volvo. Around the same time the red circulation graph fixed on the wall outside editor David Banks' office went for a walk never to be seen again. David, a lovely man, followed soon after.

Then it was Colin Myler's turn to run the ship: giant promotions on the front page and Monty's script followed to the letter. It wasn't pretty, but somehow the *Mirror* ship at last settled. Perfect time, therefore, for a new editor. Step forward Piers Morgan.

For some reason, from the day Piers started in the job he became Public Enemy Number One for many former *Mirror* staffers. They seemed not to have known, or to have forgotten, how truly awful many of the Maxwell and Montgomery – he'd gone not long into Piers' reign – days were. The critics were party to regimes where staff spent

1 May 1997, Morgan further infuriated *Mirror* traditionalists by dropping the word "Daily" from the title. But its politics didn't change: The *Mirror*'s support of Blair was absolute and the "souvenir issue" of 3 May, when the full impact of the Tory devastation was known, featured a front page that deserved a place in the gallery of

the paper's finest: IT'S TIME TO DO. The death of the Princess of Wales the following September also saw the paper produce powerful and memorable journalism. Morgan wasn't out of the wood yet – indeed, he was soon voluntarily to walk into a tree and suffer serious self-inflicted wounds – but he was proving a

Hand in the till: The front page that told the world what Robert Maxwell had been up to.

more time at lunch than at work. Where on-the-spot dismissals and ritual office humiliations were acceptable parts of life at the *Mirror*.

All Piers wants is great stories: His mantra: "Just give me the bullets, I'll fire them." But it has been a rollercoaster ride:

- The Budget papers leak that wasn't published.
- The Di video hoax, when *The Sun* stunned the world with video shots purporting to show Diana cavorting with her lover, James Hewitt. It seemed too good to be true, and it was – within 48 hours the *Mirror* revealed the video was just two lookalikes playing to the camera. It was the biggest own goal since *The Times* published the Hitler diaries.
- Trevor Rees Jones, when Piers secured the first interview with the bodyguard who survived the Paris crash in which Princess Di died. We sold unbelievable numbers of papers. The interview ran over several days, starting on a Saturday as a taster with just one quote: "Hello, I'm Trevor".
- The Home Secretary Jack Straw's son offering to supply drugs to *Mirror* investigative reporter Dawn Alford, Achtung! Surrender!, Blair's first election victory, 9/11, the Paul Burrell saga, Omagh, the City Slickers affair, the second Gulf war...

Yet for sheer intensity – and an example of how the *Mirror* responds when a massive story breaks – none can compare with the death of Princess Diana. I was on holiday but at home on the night of the accident in Paris. My deputy, David Leigh, called me to say there'd been a crash, that Diana had "hurt her leg" but that Dodi Fayed was seriously hurt. Leigh's main problem was that half the news team were at chief reporter Harry Arnold's wedding in deepest Kent.

It was by now midnight on Saturday and not one mobile phone at the wedding party would answer. By 1.15am I was in the office and a makeshift team of six were on their way to Heathrow for a dawn flight to France. An hour before the PA newsflash, we knew, through our own contacts, that Diana was dead. It was only around 6am that the Arnold wedding party got to hear the news – and then only because reporter Sydney Young needed to use the bathroom.

Very much worse for wear, he awoke to hear a strange buzzing noise at the foot of his bed. Peering down he saw his trousers slowly shuffling across the bed. "I *must* be pissed," he thought before staggering to the bathroom, grabbing the trousers on the way and then realising it was his vibrating pager that had caused the trousers to move.

Syd picked up his messages – "Ring the fucking office: Diana and Dodi dead." He woke his wife, Jackie, told her to wake the rest of the *Mirror* guests and headed straight back to London. Jackie started banging on doors: "Wake up. Syd's gone, Di's dead and Dodi's dead too." Alas, most of the slumbering hacks were still so drunk that all they heard was "Syd's gone" and assumed it was Syd who had died. If, in the hour that followed, Kent Police had stopped any of the cars heading towards London, many of Fleet Street's finest would have spent the day in the cells for driving under the influence.

I remember, in the early days after Diana's death, Piers asking Syd: "This must be the biggest story you've every covered?" Syd thought for only a moment. "Well, the Kennedy assassination was pretty big too." The greatest journalistic double of all time, perhaps? Syd was a great district man, too, based near Bristol and working without direct supervision much of the time.

Sydney Young, supposed to be out on a "doorstep," on his mobile phone to the newsdesk... Me: "Bloody hell, Syd, I can't hear a word – is there a tractor next to you?" After dodging the desk for years, Syd is finally forced to confess: "Okay, Eug, you've got me. I'm mowing the lawn."

fast learner.

Charlie Wilson eventually came to the end of an MGN road along which he had danced, normally to someone else's tune, for more than eight years, pausing only to commandeer a wheelbarrow to carry away the share options he had been awarded in addition to his top-of-the-

range salary. Chairman Clark went – quietly, of course – too, leaving Roger Eastoe, the most famous neutral power after Switzerland, as the only surviving senior executive of the Maxwell era. Montgomery saw himself succeeding Clark, but the institutional shareholders didn't. The new chairman was Victor Blank, a

Sydney Young was born in 1933 and educated at Ardwick Technical School in Manchester. He left at 15 with a certificate in how to duck and dive to become a £1-a-week tea boy with the now-defunct Holiday and Edwards News Agency. He spent 37 years on the Daily Mirror, *seven of them as head of the Belfast office during the troubles, three in the New York bureau and 25 as district reporter in Bristol. He's sort of retired, but still lives on "his patch".*

'In another time and another place they would probably take a trip to a log cabin somewhere above the snowline with their traps, an axe and a shared desire to live the life of a loner. They wonder how their office-bound fellow hacks can stick it on the "taxi ranks" of Fleet Street newsrooms. Not for them the drudgery of commuting to London in the short-term hope of a foreign trip or – the ultimate horror – promotion to the newsdesk to become a "reporter with the nerve taken out".

National newspaper district men like to think they belong to an elite band. Others less charitable describe them as eccentric, self-centred egotists. They are all of this and many other things besides.

Their role was born in the days before motorways, bleepers, mobile phones, e-mails and all that other arty-farty stuff. The papers relied on the district men to cover the hard-to-reach patches. Some towns had two reporters. In the 1960s, when the *Daily Express* tried to start an ill-fated regional printing plant, it had four in Bristol alone.

Enlightened news desks realise that even though they can now cover the entire country from London, the on-the-spot district man (and with one or two famous exceptions they have all been men) has his roots deep in his community and a vast network of informants. To maintain their way of life, they guard their patches with passion and zeal – one northern *Daily Mirror* man's area was known as "God's Little Acre" – and see the rare intrusion of a London staffer as a gross insult to their manhood and a threat to their livelihood. A forgetful or harassed news editor who sends anyone into a district man's territory without first smoothing ruffled feathers risks, at the very least, a three-day sulk.

Although the bosses and their bean counters still choose profit over professionalism by paying off some of the long-time district men, they cannot kill the legends

they become – like the late, much-loved Tom Merrin. Brighton-based Tom went, they claimed, because he broke the cardinal rule for district men that says, "Thou shalt be available 24 hours a day". He did not hear his news desk bleep when it went off at 2.30am one day, and the *Mirror* dispensed with one of its smartest and most colourful reporters.

One of Tom's triumphs was when he discovered the Sun had bought up boxer Terry Marsh – just acquitted of shooting promoter Frank Warren – and had got him hidden away somewhere on Tom's patch. Knowing any reporter's enthusiasm for the better things in life, Tom started to hit every five-star hotel in town. No luck – until persistent Tom made a second call on all the hotels to ask the night porters: "Has anyone ordered all the papers for the morning?" Bingo! Mr Smith had and he had booked in with a Mr and Mrs Jones, who were in an adjoining room.

Next morning, Tom and a photographer were in the dining room when the unsuspecting boxer and his wife met a star-struck "punter" with shiny, jet black hair and more than his fair share of East End charm. Any chance of an autograph and a picture for the kids – they'll be so excited? A few words from Marsh and Tom went whistling on his way with a very economical splash story.

Tom was the first *Mirror* district man to really embrace new technology, but complained constantly that his Tandy was not back-lit like some of the more modern laptops. Finally, the *Mirror* relented and told him he was getting a new one. "Is it back-lit?" asked Tom. "No, but it's got Windows." "I don't care if it's got fucking lace curtains," said Tom. "I want one that's back-lit."

He shared the district men's dislike for office rules. One year, the *Mirror* introduced some American-born self-assessment forms. At the check box that asked "What are your ambitions for next year?" Tom wrote: "To give Michelle Pfeiffer a good seeing to."

District men still thrive, although there are fewer now. The *Mirror* closed its Welsh district office about ten years ago, but still has one-man district shows in Cornwall, Bristol, the east Midlands and the north-east. Birmingham, which for years was a two-man operation, is also down to one since Bill Daniels retired.

Clive Crickmer, now retired as the *Mirror* man in the

merchant banker and the deputy chairman of Great Universal Stores, with a solid City reputation and an open mind.

The arrival at the *Mirror* of MacKenzie, tunnelling out of the News Bunny warren at Live TV to become Montgomery's deputy, helped steady an editorial operation that still swayed erratically under the conflicting influences of editor and chief executive.

Montgomery, although insistent outside the company that he rarely interfered editorially, had developed an affection for poster front pages, probably influenced by the brash and bold projection of the New York *Daily News* (had he fully realised the *Mirror*'s debt to the *News*'s typography in the 1930s, he might not have been so keen). By filling the front with a series of inconsequential stories, he quickly

Fishy tale: Syd Young is the old trout on the right.

screen. "He always beat the *Daily Record* with their 'summer has arrived' piece about a new sighting of Nessie," said Stott of Geoff, whose self-taught skills with the accordion still keeps him in demand at folk concerts.

Doug Slight, who had the patch before Geoff, wrote to Ken Hord, then the *Mirror*'s editorial manager, to complain that his Ford Escort office car was having terrible trouble coping with the hills in Devon and Cornwall, and a four-wheel drive Land Rover would make life easier. Hord said, sadly he was unable to meet the request – but would send Slight a map showing him how to avoid the hills!

The late and much-loved Frank Palmer, author of many fine crime books and a Reporter of the Year award-winner, was as honest as the day is long. One hot summer's day, Phil Mellor made a post-3pm call from the London newsdesk to Palmer's Nottingham home and asked: "I suppose you were in the garden with the *Nottingham Evening Post* fluttering gently over your face?" Sleep-befuddled Palmer asked: "How did you know that?"

A fully paid-up Luddite, Palmer resented the passing of writing stories on the back of a fag packet in a pee-filled public telephone box. A colleague, tired of trying to explain how to operate a first-generation laptop, sent him an idiot's guide. The first instruction, which took Palmer a day or two to master, said: "Lift the lid." Switching on took a little longer.

Richard Stott once felt it necessary to punish Frank Palmer and myself for some long-forgotten misdemeanor. He ordered us to London to see what it was like "at the sharp end". And it *was* tough for two thoroughly spoiled free spirits whose motto, coined by Palmer according to the sneering editor, was "File for three – home for tea".

He put us in the Tower (the hotel that is) for a week and although the hours were long, the news desk softened the blow by giving us not very demanding jobs at press conferences that were short on copy and heavy on booze. Evenings were spent downing even more drink in the Stab, the office pub across the street from the Holborn Circus office. At the end of our time on punishment block, Stott invited us to his office and filled us with neat vodka and gin from the editor's bar. As we made our unsteady way out of his office, he said sternly: "Let that be a lesson to you."

north-east, is cricket mad and still believes he is a demon bowler. For many years, the London news desk imported him as a ringer on for their cricket team and were willing to cover his costs. The bean counters never questioned why a Geordie should be charging exes to write about coastal erosion in Essex every summer.

Richard Stott, a *Mirror* editor who understood the value of district men, once said about Geoff Lakeman that it was easy to tell when summer had arrived – it was when a picture story about the paper's multi-talented district man in Plymouth swimming with dolphins appeared on his

devalued the technique. When MacKenzie, a legend to many of the *Mirror*'s new, young members of staff, turned up on the editorial floor, he looked around and asked: "Where are all the journalists?" He appeared stunned by the small number left after Montgomery's cleansing of all departments.

But MacKenzie introduced stability, instructing the backbench to adopt the sole use of Tempo heavy condensed type for the lead story and reverting to sensibly balanced front pages unless there was a major event that warranted a page-one wipeout. Morgan, a huge fan of MacKenzie, latched on quickly. Montgomery largely withdrew from editorial involvement, leaving the legacy of a central command nightdesk with the news, picture and feature desks grouped around the hub like satellites, and his much vaunted "Academy of Excellence", which was supposed to establish a layer of highly-paid super journalists who could do everything. The first idea, originally set up to maximise manpower, was such a success as a cohesive production unit that other papers subsequently adopted it. The Academy became a joke – what was the point in training a crack splash sub to scan pictures?

MacKenzie's other main contribution before bailing out in June 1998 to acquire Talk Radio – former boss Murdoch provided the funding – was to suggest that City of London should be treated as the mixture of showbusiness and a Las Vegas casino it had become. He introduced Anil Bhoyrul and James Hipwell, two sharp financial journalists, to Morgan, who loved the City Slickers idea but was to come to love it less in the fullness of time.

Montgomery, his star waning by the day, unloaded the company's stake in the *Independent* to Dr Tony O'Reilly's Irish Independent group, but the sale did not prevent MGN's share price dropping low enough for it to arouse the interest of two regional newspaper groups with ambitions beyond their current station. Trinity and Regional Independent Media were prepared to slug it out for the dubious privilege of adding national titles to their successful local chains. Neither, however, was interested in Montgomery coming along as part of the package.

In a little more than six years, Montgomery's stewardship of the company had seen 600 jobs lost and the *Daily Mirror* shed around half-a-million circulation. But not everybody lost out. The banks who'd been fooled by Maxwell got their money back and Montgomery walked away a rich man: on top of his considerable salary, share options cashed in for almost £750,000 and a pay-off estimated at £1.4million meant he did not immediately have to look for somewhere else to proffer his talents, although, given his temperament, he may well have done so. At Canary Wharf there was no jubilation when it was learned that he had gone – a staff buffeted and browbeaten by what many considered callous management were nervous that although they were escaping from the frying pan, they could be falling into the fire.

It didn't turn out like that. As we shall see, the *Daily Mirror* was about to be given the opportunity of regaining its dignity, poise and *joie de vivre*. Ironically, it was the culture introduced by the man who had wanted to rewrite history that was soon to be forgotten.

10 **BACK TO THE FUTURE**

It is the evening of Thursday 7 November 2002 and a chill breeze is blowing along Bride Lane, just south of Fleet Street. Inside the nearby St. Bride's Institute, Piers Morgan, editor of the Mirror, *is delivering the Hugh Cudlipp Memorial Lecture, an annual event organised by the London Press Club to celebrate the life of the greatest tabloid journalist of all. The* Mirror *has, over the past week, scooped the rest of the national press with the revelations of Royal butler Paul Burrell, the theft case against him having collapsed in the High Court. Morgan is understandably in good spirits.*

"I've been studying the Cudlipp heritage rather a lot in preparation for this lecture," he tells an audience containing a sizeable contingent of former Daily Mirror *journalists, but no members of Morgan's staff. "It seemed ridiculous for the current* Mirror *editor to deliver such a speech without addressing the big question that has occupied the minds and columns of our constantly increasing phalanx of media experts during the last year: do we at the* Mirror *of today really deserve to be mentioned in the same breath as Hugh Cudlipp?" Morgan, while paying tribute to the Cudlippian* Mirror, *goes on to address that question, admitting, "It's certainly been a rollercoaster journey to get to a position of people even daring to suggest it." Lady Cudlipp, present in the audience this evening, had taken him aside after the paper had won the Newspaper of the Year*

and Hugh Cudlipp prizes at the 2002 National Press Awards, Morgan reveals, to tell him, "I think Hugh would have rather liked what you're doing with the paper."

Then he quotes Cudlipp from 1984: "Mirror newspapers are now rarely mentioned in any significant sense; even more rarely quoted. The Daily Mirror *must and can regain its position among the world's most quoted and influential newspapers... Popularity isn't enough." And Morgan concludes: "I think, on balance, that he might have rather enjoyed what we are doing with his paper now."*

The majority of those in the audience, including some Mirror *veterans who have been among Morgan's sternest critics, applaud warmly. The editor thanks them – and hurries away to climb back aboard the rollercoaster...*

On a Sunday morning six weeks before Morgan's success at St. Bride's, Sly Bailey was having breakfast and browsing the business sections of that day's newspapers. The chief executive of IPC Media paused to read an article in *The Sunday Times* about the resignation the previous Tuesday of Philip Graf, chief executive of Trinity Mirror. Headhunters had been briefed to find a replacement for Graf, she read. "Wow! Fantastic! What a fabulous job," she thought to herself. Bailey had for three years been COE at IPC – the much-changed magazine publishing house that once was part of Mirror Group – and in July 2001 had pulled off the considerable coup of selling the

New powers: John Allwood (left) took the reins until Philip Graf assumed control of Trinity Mirror.

company to AOL Time Warner for £1.15billion, the biggest ever transatlantic media deal. The daughter of a financial journalist, Bailey grew up in a newspaper reading-household before starting in publishing by selling advertising space at the *Guardian* – "Whatever the bottom rung of the ladder is, I started from it," she says.

Shortly after *The Sunday Times* had pressed the Wow! button with Bailey, she received a telephone call that resulted in her being short-listed as a replacement for Graf. "There were other strong candidates," she recalls. "But I met Victor [Blank] – a girl chooses her chairman very carefully! – and discovered there was a chemistry, if you like, that suggested we could have a good relationship and work well together." On 12 December it was announced that Sly Bailey would be the chief executive of Trinity Mirror, becoming one of the very few women to run national newspapers (the *Financial Times* is currently among Marjorie Scardino's many responsibilities at Pearson; in the late 19th century, Rachel Beer edited the *Observer* and *The Sunday Times* simultaneously and was also proprietor of the *ST*). Bailey started her new job on 3 February 2003.

Philip Graf, the only child of a Belfast bakery foreman, also grew up in a home where a newspaper, the *Belfast Telegraph*, arrived every day. After reading law at Cambridge and working for an oil company, his passion for newspapers led him to Thomson Regional Newspapers, where he worked in marketing, advertising and research before returning to Belfast and the Thomson-owned *Telegraph*. He subsequently joined Trinity in Liverpool and by 1993 was chief executive of a thriving regional newspaper group with feet itchy to walk even taller. Its takeover of the Thomson group in 1995 transformed Trinity into a major player in newspaper publishing and when, in September 1999, it edged out Regional Independent Media in the tussle for the Mirror Goup – capturing a company larger than itself for £1.24 billion – Graf was thrust into both the hot seat and spotlight previously occupied by Montgomery.

Graf, affable, cheerful and liked by those who work for him, is a very different brand of Ulsterman to his predecessor. John Allwood, temporarily chief executive after Montgomery's departure, had already begun to rationalise the business on Graf's behalf, rendering Live TV anything but – it was lamented by few – by the time the new boss settled behind his desk at what was now Trinity Mirror. But Graf soon discovered that, compared to paddling in out-of-town shallows, diving into the deep waters of the pool previously known as Fleet Street was nail-bitingly hazardous. Scrutiny by the city and sniping from Trinity Mirror's rivals seemed constant. And the editor of the *Daily Mirror* didn't make the going any easier when, as the 21st century began to ease its way out of the cradle, he dropped the company, and Graf, into the deep end of controversy.

In January 2000, Bhoyrul and Hipwell, the expensively-suited Slickers who had turned the *Mirror*'s city pages into a Harry Enfield "loadsamoney" lookalike, heavily plugged the shares of computer company Viglen Technology. At 3.22pm on the day they wrote a story that, when it appeared the following morning, would double the firm's share price, Morgan invested £20,000 in Viglen on the stock market. Uproar ensued when the *Daily Telegraph* found out. Morgan claimed he had not seen the *Mirror*'s Viglen story until he read the first edition at 11.30pm on the evening. An internal inquiry was launched immediately and resulted in Bhoyrul and Hipwell, who had been buying shares they had tipped, being fired for "gross misconduct". Morgan was exonerated

Sharp practice: City Slickers Bhoyrul and Hipwell had been buying shares they had tipped and were sacked for gross misconduct.

within the company of serious wrongdoing, but fiercely rebuked by the Press Complaints Commission in a judgement that ran to 14 pages. He had, decided the PCC, "fallen short of the high professional standard demanded by the [PCC] code" and was accused of failing adequately to supervise the slickers. Following this, and the revelation that a number of *Mirror* staff had been involved in playing the stock market, the Department of Trade and Industry launched an inquiry. Dozens of staff were interviewed. It was a banana skin that the journalists had thrown down and then stepped on, with the *Mirror*'s traditional stance against share buying by its City pages staff – they were paid well on the understanding that they could not play the market – having been lost when Graf's predecessor instilled his "new culture" within the company.

Graf and chairman Blank stood by their man after the internal investigation, with Graf commenting: "We had very few letters from readers about what happened. I think that's important. I think people didn't see it as greed as much as foolishness and were able to distinguish between the Slickers' behaviour and what Piers was being lambasted for." Piers, distraught at the hideous personal and corporate publicity, locked himself away in his office for six days. There had been managerial discussions concerning his future, or lack of it, at Trinity Mirror, but chairman Blank and his board decided that their mercurial but accident prone editor deserved another chance.

When Morgan could eventually bring himself to talk about what *The Sun* promptly labelled

"Mirrorgate", he was contrite: "It was a terrible failure on my part to understand the potential problems of what was going on – running a column of that nature, which was tipping stuff all the time, and with share prices rocketing, and people on the staff buying shares in the middle of it. My involvement in it was tiny, but explosive PR-wise. I totally hold up my hands to the enormous failure of my managerial competence on the floor during that period – it

Standing by their man: Trinity Mirror chairman Victor Blank and his board supported Piers Morgan.

JESSICA CALLAN

First person

Jessica Callan was born in 1975 and educated at More House School, then Stowe and Buckingham University. She has been with the Daily Mirror's *3am column since its inception in July 2000.*

'My first memory of the *Daily Mirror* was aged eight, when I took part in an Easter egg tasting feature. I recall the fondly remembered agony aunt Marje Proops combing my hair before the photographs were taken and my howling every time she roughly dealt with a knot. Needless to say, letting a child tuck into as many chocolate eggs as she likes results in one thing. After posing for the picture with chocolate smeared all over my face, I was promptly sick.

Twenty years later, I am in charge of the 3am gossip column at the paper. The column was the brainchild of Piers Morgan and the then showbusiness editor, Richard Wallace. When Matthew Wright left, they decided they needed a whole new breed of showbusiness columnist – a team of feisty women who would strike fear into the hearts of celebrities the moment they walked through the door.

We were to stay up until the wee small hours – hence the name 3am – and report on the late-night antics of celebrities. Our brief was to write about stars behaving badly, celebrity punch-ups, and their bawdy bedroom behaviour.

I met up with Wallace, who explained what they wanted and I leapt at the chance. I already knew Polly Graham, Matthew's deputy on his column, who was to be on the team, but Wallace kept the identity of the third girl secret until I had signed on the dotted line. It turned out to be Eva Simpson, from the *Daily Star*, who was already a good friend.

Right from the column's launch on 3 July 2000 we were a talking point. Fleet Street was fascinated, and, needless to say, didn't waste any time in criticising us. We were soon dubbed the "3 Absolute Mingers" and "the dogs at dawn". It merely tickled us and Piers relished the fact that we were being talked about.

Journalists have always bitched about one another, but today, with the internet as an everyday tool, online gossip columns mean everyone reads the same stuff on websites that are updated throughout the day. We make almost a daily appearance in the Media Monkey web column, as well as Popbitch. But if you dish it out, you've really got to be able to take it. Besides, if we're honest, we're all quick to laugh at gossip about our rivals.

Before we had even reached the end of our first month, Noel Gallagher slagged us off in front of an audience of 80,000 fans at one of Oasis's concerts at Wembley Stadium. We had dared to suggest that the thought of Noel sunbathing naked in his garden at his villa in Ibiza in full view of the locals might not exactly be a pleasant sight. He retaliated by saying we were "15 times uglier than Matthew Wright". We loved it.

Unfortunately, you can never count on the readers to back you up. When we conducted a poll to see who they thought was the ugliest, us, Matthew or Noel, they disloyally voted for us. Overwhelmingly. We even checked the phone lines for sabotage, but to no avail!

As our pictures were at the top of our page, it meant we were quickly recognised by celebrities and, even worse, by the bouncers and bodyguards, so storming the VIP sections at parties was much more difficult. This often meant lurking in the shadows and eavesdropping.

Some celebs would pick fights with us if they didn't like what we had written. *EastEnders* actor Steve Mcfadden called us up and said we were a bunch of cunts and threatened to stop us from doing our job when he next saw us. We merely ran a full transcript – well, almost – of the entire conversation. Liam Gallagher had a go too and slapped Polly's backside at a party before loudly asking her when she last had sex and telling her he thought she was fat.

We were also encouraged to name and shame agents and PRs who lied to us – something we could have done on a daily basis. One hilarious occasion was when we phoned Kylie Minogue's publicist and told him that we were running a story the next day that she had split from her boyfriend, James Gooding. Murray Chalmers, Kylie's publicist at Parlophone Records, said he'd call us back, but the next thing we knew he had put out a statement through PA from Kylie, confirming her break-up from

was a very bad episode for the *Daily Mirror* and a very bad episode for me. I am not a crook, but I understood that people on the outside could look at it and say, "Oh, come on…" It was very wrong of us not to regulate the City Slickers, it was wrong not to have the staff signing the share portfolio registers, it was all wrong… However, from what I have been told by other journalists, it wasn't a patch to what was going on at other newspapers for a long time. I think it was a huge wake-up call to a lot of papers to change their systems. But I shouldn't have been

buying shares as editor of the *Mirror* and not a week goes by without me reflecting what a shame it was that it happened, because it will always be there, always ticking away underneath me and will always be a stick to beat me with – and quite rightly so. With hindsight, it was bloody stupid."

Since the story exploded and the DTI involved itself – the Department never announces when an inquiry is completed or suspended, so, for all the editor and management know, it could be ongoing –

Street fighter: Jessica Callan sees off her rivals.

Gooding. We were outraged.

But we soon hit back. As well as naming Murray in the column and dubbing him "Murray Charmless", we also got a snapper to doorstep him and published a picture of him wearing a hideous jumper with a reindeer on the front. Chalmers retaliated by excluding us from Kylie's birthday party, claiming we weren't banned, just "uninvited". Don't you just love PR speak? We still got stories from the bash and Murray soon asked if he could make peace.

We also ran stories on celebs propositioning us. I had the dubious honour of Blackburn striker Dwight Yorke asking me if I wanted to have a threesome with him and his then girlfriend, the glamour model Jordan. This really was one of those classic occasions of making my excuses and leaving. Piers was delighted with the tale and said that was exactly the sort of story he wanted to see us getting, but much to my horror, most of my male colleagues – including the editor – expressed doubts over

my protestations that I didn't take Dwight up on his kind offer!

Other showbusiness journalists were quick to slag us off – especially our then rival at *The Sun*, Dominic Mohan – but even quicker to imitate us. The *Daily Star* started a column, headed up by three girls and called The Bitches (how proud their mothers must be), and the *Daily Mail* nicked our Wicked Whispers section. Mind you, I have to admit I stole that idea in the first place. My father, Paul, was a *Mirror* writer in the 1980s and told me, when I started the 3am column, that it was almost 20 years to the day that he had headed up the *Mirror*'s gossip page team. In the best traditions of the business, I nicked Wicked Whispers – usually highly libellous stories told without actually naming the celebrity involved – from him. It had been one of his regular gossip features. Needless to say, I claimed it as my own idea. Well, dad always repeated to me from an early age: "Take all the glory and spread all the blame."

I think Piers was as stunned as we were by all the attention the column got. It started with a big piece about us in *The Observer*, followed by features in *Heat* magazine, *The Guardian, Marie Claire*, the *Evening Standard* and *The Daily Telegraph*. Most startling of all was when *Vanity Fair* said they wanted to shadow us at several parties. They ran a piece over several pages on us in their English and American editions, complete with catty comments from other journos. Funniest of all was Mohan's quote: "Why are you doing a piece about them? Why aren't you writing about me?"

Although life today as a *Daily Mirror* journalist and gossip columnist is no longer like it was back in my dad's day, the so-called golden era of all-day sessions in the Stab or El Vino and the "bank in the sky" where expenses were dished out, life is great as a 3am girl. In the past three years, we've had the usual comings and goings of any department. Some people just aren't suited to the life of a gossip columnist. There is an art to working a party and there is immense pressure in bringing in exclusives every day while at the same time tackling savage hangovers. Yes, I guess some things never change...

Morgan no longer buys shares: "I own some only in Trinity Mirror and Arsenal Football Club – the first because I am allowed to and the second for compassionate reasons, and Arsenal's are performing very badly. I took a view that whatever I bought into, there was a potential risk of conflict of interest. There are even as an Arsenal shareholder, I suppose. If I have a conversation with the boss of Arsenal and he tells me they're buying Ronaldo and I think it might affect the share price, there's a conflict of interest."

Members of the *Mirror* staff are still allowed to buy shares, but are required to register them with the company. "Not that many are buying, after what happened," said Morgan. "What made it so much worse was at the time share prices were all exploding – it was the gold dust-dot-com period when things were just flying. The thing about the famous Viglen shares is that, when it all blew up, I hadn't actually sold them and they had come right back almost to where they'd started. So the negligible profit that I made, which went to charity, was nothing

Hello, boys: Sue Carroll checks out the male strippers at Stringfellows for a Mirror feature.

like what people said about me doubling my money overnight. Yes, they had doubled overnight, but I hadn't sold them."

The chastened Morgan threw himself into restyling the *Mirror* and bringing in fresh talent to strengthen a writing staff that by now included Tony Parsons, Sue Carroll and Brian Reade as columnists and Oliver Holt, coaxed from *The Times,* to follow Wilson, McGhee, Ken Jones and the colourful cricket writer Chris Lander in producing authoritative sports copy

and columns for pages now edited by Des Kelly. Morgan and showbusiness editor Richard Wallace came up with the idea of the 3am Girls, a column in which a team of energetic and tenacious young women reporters would scurry around London by night, harrying celebrities and providing hot gossip copy by the yard. Then, when stories in other papers suggested political sharpshooter Paul Routledge had been blocked by Downing Street from joining Lord Hollick's *Daily Express,* Morgan snapped him

Making the Mirror *today (left to right): Columnist Tony Parsons, sports writer Oliver Holt and executive news editor Richard Wallace.*

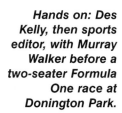

Hands on: Des Kelly, then sports editor, with Murray Walker before a two-seater Formula One race at Donington Park.

up to write abrasive copy that remains a constant thorn in the side of the Government ("I think Piers only hired Paul as a stunt because he thought we were stopping him going to the *Express*," says Alastair Campbell, "which we weren't").

Deputy editor Tina Weaver launched the acclaimed M magazine supplement – "One giant leap for womankind", although the leap was to be curtailed on cost grounds by Sly Bailey – while James Steen, ousted editor of Muhammad Fayed's *Punch*, arrived to launch and edit The Scurra, a gossip column as scandalous as it sounded. The experienced Kevin O'Sullivan headed up the showbusiness operation when Wallace climbed higher up the executive ladder. The Pride of Britain Awards, an old-style but original *Mirror* promotion, was the idea of associate editor (features) Peter Willis. It immediately seized the public's imagination and with prime time television coverage projected the *Mirror*'s credentials as a caring newspaper into millions of

Mag lady: Tina Weaver created M magazine.

living rooms – "It's incredibly patriotic, compassionate and humane and it salutes the little guys rather than celebrities," said Morgan, although part of the event's pulling power is a high celebrity quotient at the event.

Soon it was time for loose cannon Morgan, his confidence by now fully restored, to roll dangerously across the deck of the *Mirror* once more. His dislike of rival editor David Yelland was intensified by the Mirrorgate jibe and further fuelled after Yelland discovered that Marina Hyde, a *Sun* journalist and a friend of Morgan's, had been exchanging e-mails with the editor of the *Mirror*. Yelland sacked her, having her escorted from the building. "Yes, it got nasty," Morgan recalled. "We started off joshing with each other in the papers and then it got increasingly unpleasant. When the shares thing happened, he went absolutely potty, splashing with stories about me every other day. It went on and on and on. The idea that I wouldn't retaliate when every day I would read stuff in *The Sun*, calling me a

Tribute to courage: The Pride of Britain awards have carried on the Mirror's great caring tradition.

poisonous, horrible, lying, cheating little spiv, and then have to be permanently arguing the toss with people in the street who'd read it and want to shout abuse at me, is absurd. No one seems to question Yelland's behaviour in all this, but I say check the cuttings and count the number of times my name appeared in *The Sun* and his in the *Mirror*. You'll find he did more about me by a massive long way. In terms of the damage caused by me to him and him to me, it's like chalk and cheese. I make no defence of it. I thoroughly enjoyed whacking the little sod, to be perfectly honest. He will never be somebody I can consider a friend."

After the discovery of the e-mails that had winged back and forth between Morgan and Hyde – Morgan zealously guards details of their personal relationship – News International launched an inquiry that culminated in an internal hearing. Morgan went to Wapping to give evidence on Hyde's behalf: "I found the whole idea of News International sacking people for e-mailing competitors absolutely farcical, because, as they knew, I have had e-mail correspondences right from the top of that company, including their chairman. If I had brought those to that meeting, it would have brought the whole pack of cards down. But I

decided not to. I decided to go there and make the point strongly that I found their behaviour very objectionable. I would never sack anyone for e-mails. E-mails to me are private conversations – I find the whole idea that an e-mail should be public property repugnant. I got there to find the chief librarian reading my e-mails – e-mails, by the way, that both parties had deleted the moment they received them. They got hold of a year's worth of e-mails, printed them out and allowed all sorts of people to read them. They tried to make out that she was giving me the news list every day, but out of the thousands of e-mails that we exchanged that year I think they found one e-mail with a diary story she had submitted at *The Sun* that they had rejected. She sent it to me saying, "Can you see anything wrong with that?" I said, "No, we'll lead on it", laugh, laugh, but we never used it. It all caused a lot of personal problems for me that were way out of kilter with what Yelland had to suffer through us taking the piss out of his hairstyle." Yelland refused to speak publicly about the affair, except to insist he behaved honourably throughout.

Morgan felt bruised, too, by his experience when appearing as a guest on the television satirical quiz show, *Have I Got News For You?* Savaged by, in particular, *Private Eye* editor and permanent panellist Ian Hislop, Morgan then misread the audience and ended the show red faced and obviously irritated. The lampooning of Hislop in the *Mirror* did not begin until later and reached a crescendo after the sacking from the show of host Angus Deayton for extra-curricular sex and drugs activity that filled tabloid pages for weeks.

"My antipathy to Hislop really started after the Angus Deayton thing," Morgan was to insist, "when I watched the way he carved up Deayton on screen and thought, 'That's pretty rich'. He took a high moral position and really did him in and was very sanctimonious. We were talking about it and wondering why he never gets it and I said, 'I'll tell you why – most journalists and especially editors are terrified of upsetting the editor of *Private Eye*.' Well, they run everything they hear about me anyway, and have done for ten years, and I'm therefore in a brilliant position to dish a bit back to him. I know I'll get it back with bells on, but so what? – I'll get it anyway. So I love poking fun at him – and he absolutely hates it. He came down here to Canary Wharf to do a book signing and we had placards out, 'Gnome Go Home' – incredibly puerile, utterly pathetic, but all the staff that carried them were volunteers and

thought it was hilarious – and he went absolutely potty. He edits the number one piss-taking magazine and he's on the number one piss-taking television programme, so if he can't have the piss taken out of him, what has the world come to?"

Between Morgan's vendettas, the world moved on. So did the *Mirror*. The events of 11 September 2001 had a profound effect on the editor and the future direction of the paper. Without having to trot down the road to Damascus, he was converted to a more serious agenda and a more questioning policy of a Government that had moved smoothly into a second term on 1 June. The fact that the Government had been wooing Rupert Murdoch's recent New Labour converts at News International since winning the 1997 Election – and Blair had even flown to Australia at Murdoch's invitation prior to that – irritated Morgan, and Alastair Campbell believes: "What turned the *Mirror* away from us was the very positive line we took in nurturing *The Sun*. But we did not, as Piers believes, leak the 2002 election date to [*Sun* political editor] Trevor Kavanagh. Trevor wrote two stories with a date for the election – one was wrong and one was right. Anybody could have done that."

Morgan was further mortified when the *Mirror* found out that the Prime Minister's wife

Enemies at the gates: Private Eye's **Ian Hislop and David Yelland of The Sun.**

Cherie trifles: Cherie Blair takes a stand with the Mirror *in the days before the fall-out with Piers Morgan.*

was pregnant at the age of 45. "It was a good tabloid story," he now says, and "I agreed it with Tony and Alastair that we would have it exclusively. Then, at six o'clock that evening, they told Cherie what we had agreed and she picked the phone up and told Rebekah Wade [then deputy editor of *The Sun*]. And then they all lied to me about it and I found out the truth three months later. She did it just to get one over on us and for a Labour Prime Minister's wife to do that to the *Daily Mirror* struck me as rather bizarre."

The annoyance was not one-way traffic. Cherie's developing antagonism towards Morgan was illustrated when *Mirror* chairman Blank and chief executive Graf entertained her and the Prime Minister to dinner. "Cherie walked in and straight away said to Victor, why don't you fire Piers?" Graf recalls. "Then she sat next to me at dinner and gave me 15 minutes of the same message. We had a fairly forthright conversation on the subject, which I offered to continue over lunch sometime. But she never got back to me."

The company's faith in the editor, blunders notwithstanding, was demonstrated when, in April 2001, Tina Weaver moved to edit the *Sunday Mirror* – Des Kelly replaced her as

deputy editor – and Morgan was appointed editor-in-chief of both *Mirror* titles. But 9/11 and the subsequent retaliation on the Taliban in Afghanistan launched Morgan on a journalistic course and would lead to commendation and censure in equal measure and, ultimately, rejection by a significant number of *Mirror* readers.

The paper's coverage of the tragic events of September 11 was exemplary and its critical stance on the American pursuit of Osama Bin Laden found favour with many of those concerned that the deployment of American firepower in Afghanistan, and Tony Blair's unwavering support for the actions of President Bush the younger, was solving few of the problems of international terrorism and doing little for the impoverished people of a sad country. Looking back, Philip Graf comments: "At the end of the day, what you need is a newspaper with a strong set of values that the editor and the journalists believe in and that resonate throughout the paper. What the paper was trying to do was take a distinctive position and show people that the *Mirror* stood for something again." It showed the public and it showed the industry, which rewarded it with three major awards in the space of four months.

Celebrity squared: Supermodel Naomi Campbell lost her legal battle with the Daily Mirror.

The *Mirror* was flying again and in the spring of 2002 announced a relaunch that would change the face, the tone and even the name of the paper – to the delight of traditionalists, it reverted to being the *Daily Mirror,* although the red masthead disappeared in favour of a title reversed white-out-of-black (or, occasionally, a colour background) and underlined in red. Introducing the new look and new feel, Morgan wrote: "The truth is that the *Mirror* relaunch started on September 11. That was the day when we threw away the trivia-led news agenda that had dragged us for so long into the redtop gutter with *The Sun* and the *Star*." He had, indeed, already introduced a phalanx of writers old and new: John Pilger and, briefly, Paul Foot – the anti-establishment columnist who "hadn't contributed much" in the jaundiced view of the departed Montgomery – plus Christopher Hitchens and the *Guardian*'s Jonathan Freedland were drafted in to address the drama being played out on the international stage. Matthew Norman had been added to the paper's impressive roster of columnists and Lorraine Davidson began reporting from Brussels on the Euro debate. Only the reintroduction of the

Cassandra byline, perched above a series of insipid columns, failed to enhance the editorial package. Morgan kept the identity of the writer secret, possibly to protect him from the wrath of those who could remember Bill Connor's unmissable prose.

So high had Morgan's profile become – he was later to host *Tabloid Tales* for the BBC, appear impressively on the political forum *Question Time* and become a multi-media celebrity – that his name became a regular fixture in most papers, other than his own. Sometimes he relished it and his sense of humour rarely deserted him: "Sir, your media diary reported that I 'poured very inebriated out of a taxi, to attend the leaving party of one of my 3am girls," he wrote to the *Daily Telegraph* in October 2002. "Can I just state, for the record, that it was actually out of a rickshaw."

Together with its more responsible character, the *Mirror* promised to eschew the celebrity dross that had filled so many column inches in the past. Wrote Morgan: "We have stood up to control-mad celebrities, abandoning copy approval and fighting the likes of Naomi Campbell on points of important free speech principle." The changes were about "becoming a serious paper with serious news, serious sports, serious gossip and serious entertainment." Exactly of what "serious gossip" consisted was not defined, but the message was plain: the *Daily Mirror* was to be the quality choice among the popular tabloids. What's more, in future the best was going to cost less. The *Daily Mirror* slashed its price to 20p, later increased to 25p. Wherever he was in the world, Rupert Murdoch heard the news and reacted the way everyone except, presumably, the Trinity Mirror board, knew he would. He thrust his hands deep into his pockets.

The *Mirror* strategy was doomed to fail. Murdoch had the money and he had the authority to use it. He would, it soon became clear, hold the price of *The Sun* as low, or lower, than that of the *Mirror* for as long as it took to smash its rival's resolve. Trinity Mirror had sparked a price war that it just could not win. The company's share price soon reflected the trouble the flagship was in.

"The pricing policy didn't work the way we wanted it to," Philip Graf was to recall with considerable understatement. "The objective was to persuade people to try the relaunched

Brian Reade was born in Liverpool in 1957 and educated at local schools and Warwick University. He joined the Reading Evening Post as a reporter in 1980 and became a Fleet Street freelance before returning north to the Lancashire Evening Post and Liverpool Daily Post as a sub/football writer. He moved to the Liverpool Echo as a columnist/feature writer before joining the Daily Mirror in 1994. He now writes two columns a week, one at the front and another at the back of the paper. Since joining the Mirror, he has won two major awards, including Columnist of the Year (2000).

'It would be pushing back the boundaries of convenient intro-writing to say the *Daily Mirror* has always been in my blood, but to be honest I can't remember a time when it wasn't in my house. My life-long socialist mum adored the paper because it was daily confirmation that she was right and the enemy was wrong, plus she'd got the hang of the crossword by about 1962. The *Mirror* educated her, fired her anger, and pandered to her admirable prejudices, most of which are the very same ones that today earn me a living.

In the 1970s, the *Mirror* was all the raw material a teenager obsessed with football, politics and sex needed. Idealism was fed by John Pilger, Paul Foot and radical campaigns, such as Troops Out Of Ireland. Humour was garnered from Keith Waterhouse, Andy Capp and the Fosdyke Saga strip, football knowledge from the likes of Frank McGhee, and adolescent desires were taken care of by pictures of Linda, 22, from Essex, in the days before the paper became a nipple-free zone.

When I stumbled into journalism and the riveting world of Wokingham District Council Environmental Sub-Committee meetings, it was hard to imagine ending up as a columnist on the *Mirror*. To get two columns, and a free rein to attack or celebrate every aspect of life, was like winning both the Lotto and the Superball and being twice presented with the cheques by a naked Dani Behr in a jacuzzi.

There had been better times to become a feature writer on the *Mirror* than the summer of 1994. Unbeknown to me, half the department was being shown the door and I

walked into a bloodbath. Everyone over 40 – grand or years old – felt under threat, whether real or imagined. If you had both 40s under your belt, it tended to be real. I realised the true extent of the newsroom decimation within minutes, when I asked where I should sit and was told curtly that it didn't matter. All the graves were still warm. Climb into any.

I totally understood the antipathy to newcomers back then. Anyone given the job of a long-serving journalist because they were cheap, cheery and from the provinces deserved the contempt of those who remained. Had a union delegation kindly asked me, a former NUJ father of the chapel, to pack my bags and scoot back to Liverpool, I would have.

The downbeat atmosphere wasn't helped by the paper's obsession with lightweight froth. Every serious news story had to be bettered and being bettered, meant putting our own gimmicky slant on it. The ethos was not about telling the news but making it and "getting talked about". Occasionally it worked. Like during the 1997 General Election campaign, when David Pilditch (a reporter hugely underestimated simply because he likes to sleep in wheelie bins and fall in love with Grimsby trawlerwomen) dressed up as a chicken to hound John Major. He and a Tory press officer got involved in a row that turned into full-scale fisticuffs and made the lead story on the lunchtime news. It was hilarious and brilliant and it worked because it typified the *Mirror* at its best – irreverent, fearless and kicking the shit out of lantern-jawed public schoolboys.

Others were not so funny, and as someone who was dressed on numerous occasions by joke shops and the fashion department, I have to hold my hands up and say, yes I was that desperate for a byline.

It was Piers Morgan who gave me my break as a columnist. He had only been on the paper a few weeks when he offered me a weekly TV column. He also provided me with my proudest moment in journalism – writing the narrative for the first ten pages of the paper on the day of the 1997 General Election. To be able to expunge all your demons about 18 years of Tory rule and

paper over a period of time. It wasn't intended to start a price war."

But start one they did, and the structure of Trinity Mirror meant that there were institutional shareholders who were tying a white handkerchief on to a stick almost as soon as Murdoch retaliated. Sly Bailey, viewing the episode after she became chief executive, did not disguise her condemnation of what was a serious self-inflicted wound: "I don't think for a minute members of the management team sat around the table and said, 'I'll know what we'll

do – we'll have a price war'. But let's face it, that's what happened. Price cutting is not the way to drive loyalty. The way to drive loyalty is to produce a great, compelling newspaper and marketing that as a value proposition. I do not believe reducing the price of the newspaper is the way to build long-term loyalty. I don't think it's where we should be spending our money."

Editorially, Morgan compounded the fracture by too frequently and too stridently hammering the paper's anti-war stance. Readers grew tired of the same old diet, which became more

Arena of history: Brian Reade reports from Japan on the eve of the World Cup clash between England and Argentina in 2002.

urge the country to vote them out on such a historic day for both the Labour Party and the *Mirror* was an incredible honour.

After that, Piers gave me a general column, and, a few months later, a sports column, which was my passport to a return to Liverpool. And that is how it's been for the past six years. So to say I owe him one is an understatement.

Piers gets stick from time to time, and will undoubtedly have the words "Achtung! Surrender!" at the top of his obituary, but the paper has improved massively since he became editor. This may put me in a minority, but I was never more proud of the *Mirror* than during the invasion of Iraq. Circulation was lost but the paper's courageous stance and outstanding journalism won it much credibility.

The joy of writing an outspoken column on a paper you have read all your life is that, on most occasions, you tend to have most of the readers on your side. Being anti-Tory/monarchy/hunters/poseurs/Lords/knights/fat cats and everything else Establishment puts you at one with the

Mirror audience. You get the odd death threat. A BNP supporter once told me not to walk through Oldham when it was dark or I would be shot. Which was a shame as I'd just booked a fortnight in a Glodwick B&B. And a football fan once sent me dried excrement, which tumbled off the written page like coffee granules, right into my scrambled eggs.

The bizarre thing about that was it was shortly after 9/11 and an outside security firm was opening all our mail to check for anthrax.

This letter had been opened, inspected and put back in the envelope. Which was nice of them, but personally I'd have preferred anthrax on my breakfast to dried turd.

Interference at editorial level is rare. Although I have had this type of conversation a few times:

Desk: "Don't you think this might be a bit upsetting to members of the Royal Family?"

Me: "No. Besides it's all true and not a word is libellous."

Desk: "Yes, but the Queen Mum/Princess Margaret/Diana died only last week. Could you tone it down a tiny bit?"

But generally I am left to my own bigoted devices. That says a lot about the *Mirror*. Unlike most other tabloids, where columnists tend to toe the editor's/proprietor's line, our columnists aren't picked for their views but for their ability to provoke. We have commentators who can at times sway to the right, like Tony Parsons, Sue Carroll and James Whitaker (did I say at times?), and those on the left like Paul Routledge, Matthew Norman and me. Which is how every newspaper should be.

Continued on page 218

unpalatable by the day after British troops had flown out to support the Americans in Iraq. He later acknowledged the error. After she had replaced Graf, Bailey reinforced the message: "Piers and I have discussed the paper's policy on the war very frankly. I supported it absolutely – it was a war unlike any other – but the relentless nature of our coverage is what readers found difficult. A lot of the images on television were too difficult to deal with and having 18 or 20 pages of coverage every day in a strident manner when you are not sure how

you should behave or how you feel – especially when we had troops on the ground – was a complicated message for many of them."

Graf, by now approaching 57 and with ten years as Trinity's chief executive behind him, had been considering moving on before the *Mirror*'s price-cut disaster: "I'd been in the newspaper business for 30 years and I wanted to go off and do something different with my life," he was to say. "I gave plenty of notice, saying I would stay until a successor was found, and in some ways I was sorry to leave. It had been

This sounds like total flannel, but it's true. In the nine years I have been at the *Mirror*, the one thing that has truly set the paper apart is the quality of those who work there. Not just as journalists, but as people. It's the first paper I have worked on where if a junior reporter is doing a story with a senior one, the rookie always receives his name first on the joint byline. To my knowledge, no other paper has that rule. Elsewhere fear comes before favour.

Whenever you do a job on the road you may not have the best expenses, or get booked into the best hotels, but you undoubtedly have the best colleagues. Maybe I'm biased, but there is something about genuine *Mirror* journalists – especially those who joined the paper because they love and appreciate its history – that makes them stand out from the pack.

Feather brain: Reporter Pilditch in famous chicken get-up.

Dream assignments? Well, you don't get much better ones than interviewing Muhammad Ali at his home, plus two nights drinking Chicago dry with photographer Roger Allen. Or covering Miss World in the Seychelles with the legendary snapper Kent Gavin, who's convinced that 18-year-old Miss Israel, despite being breathtakingly gorgeous and dating Tel Aviv's version of Lord Rothermere, has the hots for him.

When it comes to memorable pieces of journalism, the two that truly took my breath away never appeared in the paper. Then *Mirror* executive Brendon Parsons' unforgettable "my tornado hell" report from the Caribbean, which moved everyone on the paper to tears – of laughter – when it landed on their screens, strangely failed to make the paper. Neither did the note Chris Hughes (one hell of an operator) once shoved through Michael Barrymore's door, trying to persuade him to open his heart after another breakdown. It started: "As our front-page said today Michael, you are indeed Awight! Awight! Awight."

My mum died in January 2003, very suddenly, of cancer. As she lay in hospital, embarrassed at how she looked, she would try to get rid of anyone who visited her bedside. Her last sane words to me were, "Go and get the *Mirror* for us, son." When I brought it to her, she was in no fit state to read it, but glanced at the back page, saw a lead on David Beckham and said: "Remind me, when I get out, to stop buying the Daily Manc" (an affectionate Scouse term to describe the paper whenever it over-indulges our dear Mancunian neighbours).

She never did get out, but if she had, she would still be buying the *Mirror* every day for the rest of her life. Because to her and millions like her, it is more than a paper, it is part of their identity. No matter how many accountants, management consultants, pension-stealing megalomaniacs and brutal opportunists pass its way, the *Mirror* can only ever be a paper of principle. A paper of the Left and for the underdog. If it ever tries to be anything else, it will cease to exist. ❜

challenging and tough and fun and I wouldn't have missed it for the world. There were some great people and some, er, interesting people and being associated with a paper like the *Mirror* was a privilege." He had restructured the management of the company during the latter part of his tenure. Roger Eastoe, by now managing director of the company's national titles, ended an association that threatened to be eternal – "Roger was a highly respected advertising man, but we needed a new style of management and I felt he didn't fit with that," said Graf – and Mark Haysom stepped into the job from a role as director of a large clump of regionals. Another regional director, Stephen Parker, was elevated to managing director of all the regional newspapers, and Joe Sinyor, a keen businessman with no publishing experience, arrived from Sony to become chief executive of all titles. With Eastoe gone, Paul Vickers, a lawyer with a passion for the press and now company secretary and group legal director, and

All change: Piers Morgan dates the emergence of a more serious approach from September 11.

Head girl: Chief executive Sly Bailey set her agenda with B-words.

Vijay Vaghela, the former treasurer who Sly Bailey was to appoint financial director, were the only senior managers remaining from the Montgomery years. Well, almost: the chipper Wally Cowley, circulation sales director of the national papers, had survived even longer than that. Wally, although previously in a less senior role, holds a Maxwell service medal and bar.

When Sly – "Sylvia" sexed up – walked into the COE's office at Canary Wharf, the *Mirror* landscape changed. So, after a while, did the executive management staff. Joe Sinyor departed before his face had become familiar. Mark Haysom went, and Ellis Watson arrived as general manager – "We targeted Ellis and went out and got him," said Bailey. "This business isn't just about cash, it's also about the wherewithal to go out and get what you want: our message is, come and work at the *Mirror* – that's the place to be. Come and join us – it's challenging, it's exciting and we're having fun."

Whether or not the *Mirror* editor will see it that way remains to be seen. The big fear about Trinity when they had taken over the group was that they would be unshakeably parochial –

indeed, they could hardly believe some of the high salaries paid in the editorial department – but the naivety at national level worked to Morgan's advantage in that, under Graf, he had established what was almost autonomous control of the editorial budget. The paper was hugely overspent one year and with the circulation having slipped below two million for the first time since the 1930s, Bailey immediately instigated financial restraint. The fall below the important circulation threshold approximately coincided with her arrival and she was, a member of staff noted, "terrified and worried and furious all at the same time". The *Mirror* had been facing the biggest price differential ever between it and *The Sun*, and had strayed too far down the road signposted "Serious". The paper must be about "Baghdad and the Beckhams, the BBC and Bollywood, Blair and Big Brother – sometimes serious, sometimes fun," said the new chief executive.

At the end of August she announced her management strategy to the city and a few days later the *Daily Mirror* met its obligation to implement its share of company-wide job cuts.

Among those made redundant were *Mirror* men and women who, over the years, had become as much part of the paper as was the title piece itself: photographer Kent Gavin, reporter Harry Arnold, medical correspondent Jill Palmer and golf and snooker correspondent Tony Stenson, one of several long-serving members of the sports department now working for sports editor Dean Morse. ("You know, the Montgomery era was very sad," said sports desk secretary Chris Kelly, who joined the desk in 1966, "but after that, morale picked up again. That's what professionals do. The days of flying paper planes across the office may have gone – there's not much paper about, anyway – but the atmosphere's still good. This is the Premiership champions of sports departments.")

Sitting at her desk, Sly Bailey reflected on the restructing programme aimed at saving £25million and when asked about Morgan's future replied: "I am very confident we have a highly talented editor, but I don't think the guidance has been provided in terms of direction." She also insisted: "But why should it not still be fun? If you can't have fun in this business, I'm not sure I know where you can. My job is to create the right kind of innovative creative environment where people can do their best work. If you have an environment where the editorial team are not working hard, that are not enjoying themselves, that aren't having fun, you can see it in the pages of the newspaper."

On the editorial floor, Piers Morgan, still only 38 years old, was busy bringing out the next issue of the *Daily Mirror.* Recently he has been embroiled in controversy once more, paying £125,000 to Tony Martin, the farmer jailed for shooting and killing a teenage burglar. The Press Complaints Commission had said the *Mirror* would have to show the story was in the public interest and that payment was necessary to secure it. Morgan said the case "raises fundamental questions in the public interest about serious issues such as people's rights to defend to defend their homes, burglars' rights and the issue of legal aid for thieves to sue their victims." Within a few days the buy-up added 400,000 to the paper's sales and the executives were coming to work with smiles on their faces.

Another day, another paper, another front seat

Blood money: In July 2003, the Mirror *bought up Tony Martin, jailed for killing a young burglar.*

in what all those years before Philip Gibbs called "the peep-show of life".

"I can't think of any other job that would bring me as much fun and excitement as this one," Morgan has said. "God, it was fun," wrote Hugh Cudlipp. "So far as journalism was concerned I didn't do a stroke of work in my life. It was a pleasurable mental exercise. I was paid frugally at first and sumptuously later on, but was always surprised I was paid at all for the editorial side of my activities: what for – enjoying myself and informing and entertaining others? Who would mind working around the clock if every day is punctuated by the impulse of events, when the only routine is the exceptional and the unexpected, and when the norm is the abnormal?"

The news, good and bad, keeps coming. The *Mirror* story goes on.

First person PIERS MORGAN

Piers Morgan was born in 1965 and educated at Chailey Comprehensive and Lewes Priory, Sussex. After a gap year, during which he discovered "the lure of money and journalism", he left a job in "boring" insurance and attended the NUJ College at Harlow, Essex. After experience at the Tooting News *and casual reporting shifts at* The Sun, *he joined that paper, and, shortly afterwards, at the age of 23, was appointed to run the Bizarre music and gossip column. He was made editor of the* News of the World *when 28, moving to edit the* Daily Mirror *in 1995 at the age of 30.*

The Mirror *Award Judges: Paul Burrell, Richard Branson, Miriam Stoppard, Mel B, and editor Piers Morgan gather at Richard's house.*

' I had what my mother remembers as a rather odd interest in newspapers from the age of six or seven. She tells the story of how I picked up the *Daily Mail* front page and said, "Mum, what's this about this woman who's been rapped?" It was spelt R-A-P-E-D, of course. So I'd always wanted to be a journalist, but it was my mother who drove me and got me on the course. I was doing all sorts of weird odd jobs during my year off before university and then working at the Lloyds insurance market and she said, "Come on, do what you really want to do".

I'd been writing for local papers, about cricket, since I was quite young, just sending stuff in. I had my first piece in the *Mid-Sussex Times*, about a cricket tour of Malta, when I was 15. They paid me £15 for 1,500 words. I then sold it to *The Cricketer* magazine, who ran a truncated version and paid me £10. So I'd earned £25 from a trip to Malta, learned you could be quite well paid in journalism and also experienced the thrill of the byline.

I ran Bizarre for five years and it was great fun. I turned down promotion at *The Sun* because I wanted the high profile of the column and I was enjoying it so much. Looking back, I was never ruthlessly ambitious. I never really could believe the speed at which things happened. I've never been fired and I've never actually applied for a job in journalism. I know both will happen, but I've been incredibly lucky so far. I didn't go after the editorship of the *News of the World* – it just came out of the blue. I was 28 and doing a pop column – it was a really weird experience. I think Rupert Murdoch just took a punt and luckily it came off.

I didn't covet the *Daily Mirror*, either – I just got offered it. When David Montgomery first approached me, I thought about it and I wasn't really sold on the idea. I didn't see myself as a natural *Daily Mirror* editor. I wasn't massively left of centre – I'd always been a Thatcher boy from East Sussex. I had begun to see Tony Blair quite a lot and he was becoming much more acceptable to middle England, so I was probably shifting fairly fast to becoming quite Blairite without realising it. But my natural instincts would not have been the *Daily Mirror*, and certainly I would not have been most people's choice – a right-wing editor of the

News of the World, working for Murdoch, and who'd been on *The Sun*, was hardly the ideal person, you would have thought, to revive the fortunes of the *Mirror*. However, Montgomery came back to me and I took the decision to leave the *News of the World* because the *Mirror* was a daily paper and I was getting a bit bored with the pace of a Sunday. I wasn't absolutely convinced that I was the right person for the job. I just thought I'd be mad not to do it.

And when I got here, I certainly didn't revive the paper's fortunes at all, not for quite a long time. I was interested only in going toe-to-toe with *The Sun* and trying to take them on at their own game and blow them out of the water. Montgomery wanted to score a hit against Rupert, I think. He said the *Mirror* had been receding in its clout and credibility – no one was taking it very seriously then.

I have studied the history of the paper. Since Cudlipp sold the [IPC] *Sun* to Murdoch, you can't really chart when the *Mirror* has ever really competed properly against his [Murdoch's] firepower, his resources, and his aggression. Funnily enough, the only time it ever really competed was when Maxwell ran the show, because he was just as big and aggressive and rich as Murdoch. Maxwell's period ended in total chaos and corruption, I know, but you ask the journalists who have been here throughout when the most exciting time in terms of competitiveness was and they will always say when Maxwell ran the show, because that was the only time we financially punched our weight.

The truth is that if you are owned by somebody who loves newspapers and has a billion pounds, you're going to be much better off than if controlled by a plc company trying to run national newspapers up against those people. The paper has wrestled with that dilemma

Continued on page 222

for years. I have taken it in a different direction and tried every trick in the book to be competitive editorially – and we have been, from time to time, very competitive, certainly when it comes to the big stories. In the past seven years we have won a team reporting award five times, we've been newspaper of the year a couple of times, we've had a very good run of winning awards, but in terms of circulation, whenever Rupert wants to get out his financial gun and spray us, it's always very painful.

I've loved every minute of my time here, the good, the bad and the ugly. It has been an extraordinary time. But my conclusion is that no matter how good a team you put together journalistically – we have a very good one right now and there have been good people here for 35 years – the paper will never compete financially with Rothermere or Murdoch because it doesn't have the money. That's the challenge as we go forward.

The first two or three years, I struggled with the readership. I didn't really understand *Mirror* readers. I couldn't really define them. You are talking about people who live in the same streets and in the same kind of houses as those who read *The Sun*, so it is a very fine dividing line in their thinking about how they want their paper to be. Essentially, they don't like the more prurient stuff, they don't like the more racist, xenophobic, hateful stuff. The average *Mirror* reader – the core, staple reader – has a basic extra dimension. They have a sense of compassion and humanity that is not necessarily a requirement for reading a paper like *The Sun*. That's the difference – they have a different thought process. You can never over-estimate the power and compassion of the *Mirror* readers.

I made mistakes early on, such as Achtung! Surrender! Obviously I'm sorry if that offended anybody, but I still think it's funny – I don't think that taking the mickey out of the Germans can be described as the biggest offence of all time. It was never intended to be as xenophobic as it was made out to be – it was meant to be a bit of a laugh. But what it taught me was that *Mirror* readers are different to *Sun* readers, no question. I can tell from the letters I get. To begin with, we have been around for 100 years, which means some readers have been reading it for 70 or more years. I get letters from them talking about "their paper". It's not my paper, it's theirs and they feel very strongly about it.

They don't want too much trash. They don't want it to be overtly titillating. They want it to be thought provoking and challenging, but not too heavy – I learned that lesson with the Iraq thing, which got too attitudinal, too screamy for many readers. The *Mirror* in its heyday, when there wasn't much competition and it had a huge staff to produce small papers, was a working class tabloid that had fantastic success that we shall never enjoy again. It resulted from a freakish set of circumstances really – including the war – and it was this period that made the *Mirror* a national institution. I am very aware of the heritage, but I don't think the model of that time can possibly be compared to today's paper. I am not

whingeing about it, that's just the reality. There are a lot more papers now, there's the internet, there's 24-hour television news on four or five channels, there's radio everywhere. Do people any more pick up their morning paper to read the news? They buy it for lots of other reasons, be it promotions, or sports reporting, or TV programmes, or bingo, or whatever it is. We are in a very fast moving, multi-media age. It is no surprise to me that sales of popular newspapers are diminishing slowly. They will continue to do so, not at the rate that people predicted, but they will diminish because there are people walking around with little computers in their pockets that, at the push of a button, will flick up every paper and show every page.

I came to realise there was no real upside to trying to compete directly with *The Sun*, because they had more money and the paper's brand was so powerful in the area of tacky, pump-it-up, stack-'em-high, exposé-driven tabloid stuff. So we began to move back to what I suppose could be described as heartland *Mirror* stuff. We began to do more foreign reporting, more with Anton Antonowicz, and generally making a greater commitment in the paper to serious stuff. And then came September 11. I could see almost immediately that this was going to be a defining period for us. To begin with, here was a story of such enormity that it would run for months. It was so serious that it was really dominating people's thought processes here like nothing had before.

So we just went for it – and produced brilliant newspapers, I thought. That slightly lulled me into thinking that in peacetime – if I can use that phrase – when things went back to normal after September 11, we could carry on being just as attitudinal and aggressive about world affairs and hope to sell as many papers. But fear was no longer a stimulus for readership – i.e. people had got back to feeling more cosy about life – and we slightly overdid it.

We were very critical about Afghanistan, which actually was totally in keeping with the *Mirror*'s position historically on most conflicts. It's very rarely been gung-ho about it. And then came the Iraq war, so we bounced into another very serious thing. But this time it was on television all day and I now realise the difference between this and even the last Gulf War was 24-hour television coverage, which made people feel much more patriotic than normal, much more emotive and engaged as they watched our boys being shot at every morning. Once it had started, they were not in the mood to read me banging on about why we were anti-war, not while they were watching what they were watching. It was a misjudgement of the power of television. Afghanistan didn't resonate with the public in the same way because they couldn't see it.

Then there was a rather ill-judged price war, in the sense that it didn't work! I signed up to the idea and we were doing very well when we launched it in the spring of 2002. We had won a lot of awards and *The Sun* didn't really know where it was going and wasn't very confident. I thought we could seize on that by getting rid of the red

Man in the middle: "One day you're a halfwit, the next you are a genius. The truth is, I've probably been somewhere in the middle," says Piers Morgan.

top and being demonstrably a different sort of paper than *The Sun* or the *Star*. I wanted to be somewhere a bit different, capitalising on what we'd achieved with the post-September 11 stuff. The idea was to be cut-price for a year, nationally. And then – the financial element again – we couldn't afford to do it. We launched it, and after a short period of time, we kept the cut-price in half the country and went back to full price in the rest. Murdoch kept *The Sun* at 20p nationally for five months. It devastated our sales in the areas where we were again full price – 12p was the biggest price differential the *Mirror* had ever had to put up with. That taught us a lesson – there is no point in going toe-to-toe with Murdoch in a price war, not unless you are prepared to match him pound-to-pound all the way.

After that, I lightened the paper a bit – I think post-war

everyone wanted a little more frivolity in their lives and we do need to mix the serious content with celebrities, with football, with sex – all the components of a successful tabloid paper. But I am not going to change the overall position of the *Mirror* – we'll remain slightly above the others in the red-top sector and try to drive home what I think is the heartland essence of the *Mirror*, but with a contemporary edge. I feel personally happier with the paper than I have ever done. I acknowledge that, because of the price thing and the Iraq short-term problem, we did badly. But I think it was a knee-jerk reaction to the negativism on the front page after the war had started and many of those who felt like that have come back.

John Pilger gets the biggest response of any columnist we have, for and against. The trouble with him is that he obviously has a lot of agendas, which cause a lot of controversy. I think sometimes people find it hard when we splash on a Pilger piece – they think it's the paper speaking. I have to be careful as we go forward that we don't make John Pilger the voice of the *Mirror*. He's the voice of John Pilger. I love having him in the paper, he stirs things up and he is a great journalist, but no one would pretend that he doesn't have agendas, in the same way that Christopher Hitchens does the other way. And I think Jonathan Freedland writes for a tabloid in a nice, easy way. I also think I need to rein back from going too big with it all – great big spreads of 2,000 words – but writers like these give us an edge. I think the new Cassandra column is well written, too. It doesn't pretend to be the original Cassandra, but I think the person who does it – no, I won't reveal who! – does a very good job. It hasn't created quite the waves I'd hoped it might, but we're working on that. And I like having a bit of the heritage back in the paper.

Dropping below two million was a watershed, I admit. We have suffered a lot commercially over the past few years. Promotionally we have been beaten up. We have not had the advantage of the promotional firepower of *The Sun* and *Mail*, which sometimes has been four to one against us. But we shall regain some of those readers who left us over price. We'll regain readers who left us because of our stance on the Iraq war, because already they don't feel as emotive about it. I would like to concentrate on being over two million because a focal point like that can motivate everybody. We don't want to look at being three million – if we are selling an average of two million copies in four or five years' time, it would be a triumph.

Reversing the decline is something the *Mirror* has failed to do, apart from little blips every now and again, for 35 years. I've actually done better in seven years, in terms of rate of decline, than what was done the previous seven years. Not brilliantly – I don't pretend I have done brilliantly circulation wise. But I want people to accept that, given the competitiveness and the firepower of our rivals, it is slightly irrational to judge the *Daily Mirror* purely on circulation performance. Given that we can't fight a fair

Continued on page 224

fight, we should be judged in other ways as well to get a better assessment of how we are doing.

You know, when we first cut the price, we were doing well and everybody was talking up the *Mirror*. It reminds me that, in this world, one day you are a halfwit and the next minute you are a genius, and I have been in one camp or the other for about ten years. The truth is probably that I have always been somewhere in the middle. I'm not a bad editor. I don't pretend to be any great genius, but I do give it everything I've got and I'm trying to get the paper to a position where it can be more resilient against better-resourced competitors.

Sly Bailey's view of all this is that she wants to sell newspapers, which seems to me to be an extremely healthy view for a chief executive of a national newspaper group. We have discussed at length what happened with Iraq – I still believe we were absolutely right and that we will be totally vindicated as time goes on – and the price war and everything else, and she has made it abundantly clear to me that my job is to edit the paper without interference from other people, including herself. And she understands, as everyone does, I think, that despite everything that has happened, the branding of the *Mirror* has never been stronger. There's not anyone in the western world that doesn't know that we are the anti-war *Daily Mirror*.

I deliberately choose to keep a high profile. People always look at me aghast when I say so, but I actually enjoy it. In my experience, most journalists quite like going on telly; they just don't get asked very often. I get asked a lot and probably do about a tenth of it. I find it amusing and entertaining and normally of some benefit to the paper – unless I do *Have I Got News for You* and get buried. Clearly that's not of massive help to anybody, least of all myself. But if I go on *Question Time* and turn in a creditable performance, I can't see that it's anything but quite good for the paper. It doesn't interfere with how I edit the paper at all. If you are not the biggest financial player in the market, anything you do to get the name of the *Mirror* out there has got to be worth doing.

I encourage all my staff to do whatever they can to raise their profiles. I would like them all to be famous, for them all to be on telly with the *Mirror* logo in the background. There's nothing like getting a free ad on the telly.

I totally accept that I am a celebrity of sorts. I have no problem with that at all. I never make any complaint about what is written or said about me, but I will retaliate. Anyone who wants to get it on with me knows the rules of engagement and that's fine.

Politically, for 18 years the *Daily Mirror* was slavishly loyal to Labour – almost *Pravda*-like in the Alastair Campbell years – and there was really no other paper supporting Labour. They were in opposition for a long time and didn't really have any friends in the media, and the *Mirror* was their paper. That all changed when Blair got into power. *The Sun* backed him, with brutal commercial instincts, six weeks before the election. As a

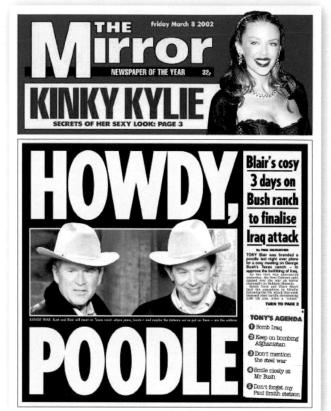

Bush fire: The Mirror *attacked Tony Blair's 'cosy' relationship with the US President in 2002.*

result, Blair felt beholden and started dishing out all these sweeties that we assumed we'd be getting to Associated and to *The Sun*. He did so in response to their support and I found it pretty reprehensible that Alastair would allow that to happen – as I told him at the time – but we carried on being great supporters of Labour for a couple of years afterwards, just taking it every week, seeing all the interviews and best stories and election dates and all the rest of it appearing in rival newspapers. I think that was wrong, a misjudgement by Number 10. I think it was an insult to the *Mirror* after what we had done for them and to our readers, who had been so supportive and were now expected to buy *The Sun* to read about policy initiatives being brought out by the Government.

The Cherie thing [the much-publicised rift between the Prime Minister's wife and Morgan] was a sideshow, really. She just doesn't like me and I'm not a massive fan of hers. I thought she overstepped the mark when she demanded my head on a plate when she sat with my chief executive over dinner, but I later discovered that is something she is not averse to doing regularly with people she doesn't like. She said she thought my moral compass was wrong. Well, I would say that having watched her own moral compass over the past year, we

Fighting for peace. The Mirror makes a stand against the war on Iraq.

are probably about the same. I think it is not really justified in that we've done nothing to Cherie in the paper at all. I remain a supporter of Tony Blair. I like the guy. He's a very charming bloke and I have always got on very well with him. But I totally disagreed with him siding with a very right-wing Republican administration over Afghanistan, and particularly Iraq. The idea that I have to defend myself for a position that surely, if you look at it from a left-of-centre *Mirror* reader's perspective, is absolutely where that reader would be.

I have never done anything in my career where I have had such a huge positive reaction from people in the street. They'd say, "Keep going on Iraq, keep going on the weapons of mass destruction." The British people don't like George Bush. Tony Blair likes him, because he loves the power he thinks it gives him in America, he loves the standing it gives him abroad and I understand that.

Alastair and I still have a great laugh together, about everything from politics to football, as we always have done. If asked about the *Mirror* or me by people when he was at No. 10, Alastair would say we had lost the plot, we were off message, we'd gone mad... the usual Alastair

stuff. But when he sees me or talks to me, we always get on fine. I think the Government has gone mad on a number of issues, but that's politics. Cherie's problem is, I think, that she takes everything terribly personally – you are either on message completely or you are an enemy. Tony is much more pragmatic about it and I have a good relationship with him, as I did with Alastair. Tony is a bit fractious because of the Cherie thing and Iraq, but if I were to see him now, he would be very civil and polite, as he always is.

I would like the *Mirror* always to be a Labour-supporting newspaper, but at a time when fundamentally there is no opposition, where Blair's mandate is so huge and where there has been more than slight disappointment about Blair's achievements and a real unease about his foreign policy, I think we are perfectly entitled, as a Labour-supporting paper, to say to our big mates, "Oi, we don't agree with you about these things". They know they can't take us for granted and that's healthy for democracy and for the independence of the *Daily Mirror.*

There has been speculation about my future from the day I got here. One media correspondent wrote recently that it was only a matter of time before I was sacked. I checked my cuttings file and he's said the same thing three times in the past seven years. Well, I'm still here. I have told Sly Bailey that I won't leave here voluntarily. I don't want to be a full-time television presenter, I don't want to go and edit another newspaper, I believe passionately in the *Mirror*, I love the paper now and I think I have really got to understand the readers. If someone comes along who can do a better job, that's fine – it is a competitive market place. I don't see that person at the moment, but one day there will be someone else in this job. It may be next week, next year, in ten years, but all I can say is that when I do go, it will be because I have been sacked.

I think I am a much better editor than I was even a couple of years ago. We have a very highly-motivated, good team of journalists here, who are very supportive of me and if I thought I'd lost the dressing room, if you like, then I would step aside, but I don't feel that at all.

I would love to do ten years. That would take me to 40 and I've always thought 40 to be a bit of a crossroads, although now I am getting near 40, I feel I wouldn't mind doing it until I'm 50. I really wouldn't. I can't think of any other job that would bring me as much fun and excitement as this one. Every ex-daily newspaper editor I meet says that nothing they have done since has been a patch on it.

I love what I do, I get very well paid for it and we have a great time, even when things are bad. When we were winning all those awards and we were all geniuses, I said to the staff, don't rest on your laurels too long. Trust me, I know how this business works – in a year's time we'll all be halfwits again and there will be a new challenge. And that's where we are.

11 THE MEN (and Marje) WHO MADE THE MIRROR

The four men who were mainly responsible for the creation of the Daily Mirror *that revolutionised the newspaper industry in the mid-1930s and that was selling more than 5,000,000 copies daily by 1964, were a disparate quartet. A semi-illiterate, Machiavellian in-fighter; an aloof, intellectual snob related to the founding Harmsworths; a mercurial Welshman with precocious talent and flair; and an irascible but kindly former advertising copywriter who would become the voice of the paper and set an unparalled standard in the art of column writing. In addition to these must be included a woman who arrived later at the paper, the extraordinary daughter of a publican who became one of the* Mirror*'s greatest assets and, ultimately, a national treasure.*

The strong roots they established brought undreamed-of success and contribute still to a paper that remains a potent force in the very different publishing climate of the 21st century.

HARRY GUY BARTHOLOMEW OBE 1885-1962

Walter Burns: "That's lousy! Aren't you going to mention the *Examiner*? Don't we take any credit?"

Hildy Johnson: "I'm putting that in the second paragraph…"

Walter: "Who the hell's going to read the second paragraph?"

– **Ben Hecht and Charles MacArthur,** *The Front Page.*

He chained typewriters to desks, tapped the telephones of his executives and once suggested to a non-editorial colleague: "Let's walk through the newsroom. Watch them squirm. They need their hate symbols, these boys, and I'm here to fulfil a bloody need. When they hate my guts, I know I'm getting across. So's the paper." A real-life Walter Burns, Hecht and MacArthur's unscrupulous editor, he was, said Cassandra, a mixture of horseradish sauce and honey, barbed wire and blue ribbon. Bart was not everybody's cup of tea, but his personality was a powerful brew that invigorated even if it sometimes left a bad taste in the mouth. His hobby was shooting rats in a cellar.

One of two sons, he was born in 1885 to a shipping clerk father and singing teacher mother.

Educated at elementary school, he became an office boy at the *Illustrated Mail* at the age of 14 and, having impressed proprietor Alfred Harmsworth, was sent to classes at the Slade School of Art. He worked in the engraving department of the *Illustrated Mail* before moving to the struggling infant *Daily Mirror* in January 1904, just as it was about to be relaunched as a picture paper.

Cecil King recorded that Bart was one of two brothers and that Wally Roome, an early general manager of the paper, used to tell a story about Mrs Bartholomew asking son Harry to rescue sibling Claude when he became involved in Glasgow with a girl that his mother thought unsuitable. Harry dashed to Glasgow and returned having married the girl, Bertha, himself. She was, wrote King, "a vulgar old thing who kept Guy under her thumb" and had been married before, giving birth to a daughter who died. She and Bart adopted a son, Peter, credited by Robert Allen and John Frost in their book on the *Daily Mirror* as Lieutenant-Colonel Peter Bartholomew DSO and referred to by King later as a commercial television company manager in Cardiff. King maintained that Bertha, who did not like it to be known that she was seven years older than her husband, was actually 13 years his senior, a disparity revealed only after her death.

King also claimed that Bart's fanciful imagination made it difficult to learn the truth about his early life: "However, he clearly had very little schooling, and appeared at the *Daily Mirror* in its earliest days as manager of the process engraving department. He claimed to be a Jew, which was untrue; that he was brought up in a charity school (I doubt this); that he was related to General Bartholomew (perhaps); that his grandfather drove a cab in Horsham – but there was no mention of his father."

Other sources place Bart at Hannen Swaffer's side when young Guy joined the *Mirror*, working as assistant art editor. Hugh Cudlipp quoted Swaffer singing the praises of his deputy: "If the staff had gone home, 'Bart' would develop a negative, make a print and then make a block, which he handed to me finished." He certainly worked under Swaffer for a while and rose fast. As a superb technician in the art and picture departments, was made a director by Northcliffe in 1913, at one of only two *Mirror* board meetings that the founding proprietor chaired before withdrawing from the company. Bart played a

major part in the launch of the *Sunday Pictorial* in 1915.

After his brother was killed in action in the First World War, he relinquished his reserved occupation status and applied for a flying commission with the Royal Flying Corps. Turned down because of his poor eyesight, he became a war photographer with the Canadian Army – Allen and Frost claimed that Lord Beaverbrook pulled the necessary strings – and his work was published in the *Mirror* and exhibited at the Imperial War Museum.

After the war, he developed the Bartlane process of picture transmission with a Captain Macfarlane, of the *New York Daily News*, and was largely responsible for the technical development of the *Mirror*. He became editorial director of the *Daily Mirror* in 1934 and was responsible for the paper establishing a rapport with, and becoming the champion of, the working and lower middle-classes. He succeeded John Cowley as chairman of the company in March 1942 and reigned autocratically and capriciously. He was awarded an OBE in 1945 after turning down a higher honour for his work with the submariners' paper, *Good Morning*.

Bart was deposed after a board rebellion led by Cecil King in December 1951. Despite his lack of pretension and relatively modest lifestyle, few liked him or regretted his departure. When visiting El Vino, in Fleet Street – a not infrequent occurrence – he would stand at the bar with his back to the door, drinking quietly and talking secretively with Bill Jennings, the company secretary, or another of his small band of cronies. Wounded beyond measure at his dismissal, he disappeared from view. There has never been a biography published of the man who rescued the *Mirror* from probable oblivion.

New Statesman: "He was the first Englishman who really understood pictures and strips and realised that no one reads more than a few hundred words on any subject."

Hugh Cudlipp: "He was heavily jowelled, white-haired at an early age, with a handsome face rarely creased into a smile; in men he evoked thoughts of self-preservation, and the response of women in his presence was of apprehension rather than affection in spite of his physical attributes and the aphrodisiac of power. One could imagine him in infancy winning bonny baby contests, though those who knew him in maturity would have earnestly hoped that the mothers of rival entrants were warned of his proximity, frisking his pram for contaminated dummies or poisoned rusks."

Cecil King: "Bart's spirit and influence became more and more perceptible in the paper. Eventually his drunkenness reached such

proportions that something had to be done. He had got to the point of insulting distinguished guests at lunch, repeatedly alleging, for instance, to the head of the Australian Radio Control Board, Sir Lionel Hook, that 'all Australians were crooks'…"

Hugh Cudlipp: "King was my tutor, Bartholomew my tormentor."

CECIL HARMSWORTH KING 1901-1987

"Early in life I had to choose between arrogance and hypocritical humility. I chose honest arrogance and have seen no occasion to change."

– Frank Lloyd Wright (1867-1959)

The nephew of Alfred and Harold Harmsworth, later Lords Northcliffe and Rothermere – respectively the founders of the *Daily Mirror* and the *Sunday Pictorial* – Cecil was the second son and fifth child of the fearsome Geraldine (Harmsworth) and Lucas White King, a civil servant who became the Commissioner of Rawalpindi in India and then turned to academia at Trinity College, Dublin. As a favour to his sister, Rothermere persuaded Lloyd George to bestow a knighthood on a man who, Cecil maintained, had been "devitalised" by Geraldine.

Cecil grew up largely in Ireland but was educated at Winchester, where he was unhappy, and Christchurch, Oxford, where he read history. Starved of love by a malevolent and selfish mother – she would beat him with a walking stick and later return to examine the weals – Cecil was at an early age surrounded by tragedy. An elder brother was killed at Ypres and a younger boy drowned in the Irish Sea when the boat on which he was travelling was torpedoed during World War One. Then a childhood sweetheart died of a brain tumour at the age of 15 and Cecil's sister succumbed to flu in a post-war epidemic.

On occasions in his life King contemplated

suicide. "It is said that to love other people you must first love yourself," he wrote in 1969, "…but… at least until recently I have hated myself." An unhappy marriage to his first wife, Margaret (Margot), and sexual suppression led to him being unfaithful with a series of mistresses. "Sex was more than an interest; it was a consuming need," observed Ruth Dudley Edwards. This first marriage produced four children, two of whom, journalist Michael and assistant editorial manager (Cecil) Francis, went on to work for the Mirror Group. Cecil's need for a woman who would treat him like a king as well as adopt his surname led to the poisonous Ruth Railton, whose displays of devotion included, on occasion, sleeping at the foot of his bed. Viciously possessive, Ruth alienated his family. Her DBE, supposedly for her almost tyrannical running of the National Youth Orchestra, was awarded after King had lobbied Prime Minister Harold Wilson.

Autocratic, aloof and a towering presence at 6ft 4ins, King was the moneyed class antithesis of Bartholomew and Cudlipp. He was also the only one of the *Mirror*'s big four not to be honoured by his country. Famously, he refused when Wilson offered to make him a life baron and appoint him to a junior ministerial post, believing that he should have a hereditary peerage. After all, his uncles had both been viscounts. As for a junior job in government, this was treated with disdain by a man who was to write: "I have a greater gift of foresight than anyone I have met... My judgement is very good... some have thought me the best talker in London... I am regarded by my colleagues as a master of timing."

Family connections had determined that he should follow a career in newspapers. After Oxford he had brief spells at the *Daily Mail* and *The Times* before Rothermere sent him to Glasgow for ten months to work in every department of the *Daily Record*. A period back at the *Mail* in the promotions department, where he said he learned that cost-cutting and penny-pinching could "cut the heart out of a newspaper", was followed by a year's travelling, with his wife, on behalf of the Associated newspapers-controlled Empire Paper Mills, and then the job of assistant advertisement director of the *Daily Mirror*.

Promoted to run the advertising department, he was made a director in 1929 and then, in 1935, a director of the Sunday Pictorial Company by Rothermere, even though by now Uncle Harold had publicly severed his connections with the papers. King was so unpopular with the other members of the board – being a Harmsworth had its downside – that he was not allowed to see the financial figures and the company secretary, Bill Jennings, had to use subterfuge to get them for him. Chairman John Cowley went so far as to tell him that the company wasn't big enough for both of them. Recalled King: "I said I had no intention of leaving and heard no more about it!"

In charge of the papers' political coverage while Bartholomew controlled just about everything else, King was accused by Winston Churchill of leading a fifth column during World War Two. He defended the *Mirror*'s position with great skill and the paper continued to express the public's dissatisfaction with the country's leaders. He had appointed Cudlipp editor of the *Sunday Pictorial*, of which King had been made editorial director, before the war and the two men resumed their formidable partnership when Cudlipp returned from army service (King, then 38, had been exempted on health grounds).

By 1951, the 69-year-old Bart, who had sacked Cudlipp two years earlier, was "in his dotage and had to be disposed of", King was to write. He masterminded Bart's removal, replaced him as chairman and brought Cudlipp back from the *Sunday Express*. King's acquisition of Amalgamated Press and then Odham's built the company, now the International Publishing Corporation, into the world's largest newspaper and magazine publishing house. For four years he was an outstanding chairman of the British Film Institute. His judgement had been "very good"; his administrative skills unchallenged; his anti-establishment stance and sympathy with the proletariat crucial to the company's great success. His remoteness, which included leaving the office by 5.30 every day – he was usually in bed by 9.30pm – meant he remained detached from the majority of the staff, however, and his sense of humour was, at best, rarefied: when Cudlipp brought his Afghan Hound into the office, King asked its name. "The Caliph of Baghdad," Cudlipp told him. King looked puzzled: "But what do you call him for short?" "Cecil Harmsworth King," replied Cudlipp, mischievously. King did not laugh.

Eventually megalomania – a condition not unfamiliar within the Harmsworth family, as Lord Northcliffe's madness testifies – set in and King came up with an ill-conceived plan to replace the Labour Government with one headed by Lord Mountbatten and featuring Cecil himself in an exalted role. Cudlipp reluctantly led a coup that saw King ousted on 30 May 1968.

Bitter at his treatment, he subsequently went to live in Ireland and published a number of intriguing books, including volumes of his diaries. He died on Good Friday 1987. Ruth, her hostility to King's friends and family undiminished, protected him in death as she had in life. When she died, in February 2001, few mourned.

Maurice Edelman (1966): "King's constant theme has been that newspapers must use power with responsibility. A second – and related – theme has been that the commonsense of the people should be trusted. That is not to say that the people can't lose their commonsense and indulge in a fit of hysteria. At that point, King would say, it's the duty of the press to recommend reason and restraint."

Hugh Cudlipp (1976): "Beneath the cultivated, shy exterior, but not far beneath, there was a repressed pride, an expectation of deference from others, a smooth superiority and an urge for revenge I have not witnessed in other men. He was a social misfit in any stratum of society."

Keith Waterhouse: "'Ten years from now,' pronounced Cecil King, 'there will be three national dailies left in Fleet Street – *The Times*, the *Daily Mail* and the *Daily Mirror*.' Forty years later, Rupert Murdoch was making exactly the same prediction, but with *The Sun* substituting for the *Mirror*. When Cecil Harmsworth King died, his prophecy long expired, his obituary appeared in more national newspapers than had existed when he had originally made it."

LORD CUDLIPP (HUBERT KINSMAN CUDLIPP) KBE OBE 1913-1998

"It's a newspaper's duty to print the news and raise hell."

– Wilbur F. Storey, proprietor
***Chicago Times*, 1861.**

Why Bessie and Willie Cudlipp, of 118 Lisvane Street, Cathays, Cardiff, should have produced three sons all of whom would become national newspaper editors is a mystery that will never be solved. The premature death at 57 in 1962 of Percy, the oldest and probably most brilliant, cut short a career that had included editorships of the *Evening Standard*, *Daily Herald* and *New Scientist*. Reg, long since retired to Sussex, edited the *News of the World* from 1953 until 1959 and never again worked in newspapers, instead becoming director of the Anglo-Japanese Institute in London. Hubert, the youngest boy, most flamboyant and ultimately most famous, edited the *Sunday Pictorial* and subsequently, mostly as editorial director of Mirror Group, shaped much of modern popular journalism. Bessie and Willie also had a daughter, Phyllis. Remarkably, she did not go into journalism.

Willie was, said Hugh, "a genial, pleasant commercial traveller who did more travelling than commerce". Bessie, a policeman's daughter, was "volatile, impulsive, a tireless raconteur". Hubert took after his mother.

From Gladstone Elementary School he scraped through the examination to attend Howard Gardens Secondary in Cardiff but left at 14 to follow his brothers into journalism with the *Penarth News*. Then came evening papers in Cardiff and Manchester – he learned more during a spell as a district reporter in Blackpool than he would have in a year at university, he said: "The Golden Mile was irresistible, an orgy of the bizarre, with its big wheel and exhibitions, barkers with loud hailers beckoning the crowds to step inside and splash a tanner. Freaks, midgets, albinos… The Original Gipsy Rose Lee and The Genuine Buffalo Bill (from Leeds). Beach shows, treasure hunts and the "*Daily Mirror* Eight", high-stepping go-go girls touring the seaside resorts to save an ailing newspaper; the go-go girls were still going when I joined the *Mirror* in London in 1935 and I had the pleasure of meeting them." Adopting the name Hugh along the way, he arrived in London at the age of 19 as features editor of the *Sunday Chronicle*. He moved to the *Daily Mirror* as assistant features editor three years later.

Appointed editor of the *Sunday Pictorial* when only 24, his tenure there was twice interrupted: during World War Two he ran army newspapers, reaching the rank of Lieutenant-Colonel, and after his return, in 1949, was fired by Bartholomew after leaving out of the paper a dispatch from Africa sent by Cecil King. Cudlipp decided the story, about a riot in Enugu, Nigeria, in which a dozen African miners had been killed, not of "world-shattering importance… and wouldn't have sold a copy". But Bart saw his opportunity to remove a blossoming rival power and Cudlipp moved to the *Sunday Express*, remaining in Lord Beaverbrook's employ until King took over at Mirror Group and recalled him.

As the younger man's educator, King taught him how to evaluate the long view when making decisions and, said Ellis Birk, "sent him lots and lots of books. Hugh pretended to read them, but never actually read a single one." Lady Cudlipp concurs: "Hugh hardly ever read a book all the time I knew him. If there was something he thought he needed to read, he'd give it to me and I would tell him what it said."

Cudlipp resumed his *Sunday Pictorial* editorship, swiftly becoming editor-in-chief of the *Pic* and the *Mirror* and subsequently Group editorial director and, after King was deposed, chairman of IPC. Unhappy in a role for which he was unsuited, he engineered a reverse takeover in which Reed International gained control of the Group. He retired from the chairmanship of Mirror Group Newspapers in 1973 – his annual salary was £33,000 – having announced that it would be "an unpardonable vanity" to continue beyond the age of 60. "Old men are tiresome in journalism," he later wrote, "and I did not want to be a tiresome old man like Bartholomew, jealously and cantankerously bullying instead of gently persuading younger performers with new approaches." His bullying days, usually when in the grip of too much alcohol, were over.

Cudlipp was married three times, first, in 1938, to Bunny, a champion swimmer. The liaison was unhappy and his wife died in childbirth. He made no mention of the marriage in his *Who's Who* entry and rarely spoke of it, but many years later was to recall: "It was an absolutely disastrous marriage that ended in an extremely sad way."

His second wife was the journalist Eileen Ascroft, who had been sacked from her job as a *Mirror* features writer by Bartholomew after he discovered she was among members of staff who had used his office door as a dartboard during what Cudlipp, who was there, described as a "modest office beano". She and Cudlipp married after she had divorced her first husband in 1945 – Bunny had died five years previously – and remained so until Eileen died of an overdose of a prescribed sleeping drug in April 1962. The couple had become close friends with another

journalist, Jodi Hyland, with whom they were socially involved as a couple. After some time, Cudlipp began an affair with Hyland and then, shortly before her death, Eileen told Jodi of her relationship with a married man for whom she intended to leave Hugh. This was H.W. "Tommy" Atkins, the Mirror Group's director of publicity and promotions, who died, less that a decade younger than the *Daily Mirror*, only months before the paper's centenary. Cudlipp never knew of the affair. At the inquest into Eileen's death, the coroner determined that there was "no question" of suicide – a view supported by Ascroft's plans for a future with Atkins – but so well known was the turmoil within the marriage that rumours contradicting the coroner flourish even today.

The following March, Cudlipp married Jodi, who still lives in the Chichester home they shared and remains a fierce protector of his reputation. Being married to Hugh was "a bit like living with Battersea Power Station," she said. She stopped work after they married: "It was her decision," he said, "But if she hadn't given up her job, I would most certainly have persuaded her to do so." He was to remain childless – Eileen had miscarried a baby – and in 1973 told television interviewer and former *Mirror* reporter Desmond Wilcox: "I would like to have had a reasonable size family. I feel that, at the age of 60, I'm not quite so in touch with the young as I might be because I'm not surrounded by children and grandchildren. I think my greatest regret is that I wasn't a happy daddy, a role which I might have performed with some efficiency and zeal."

His main relaxation was sailing, although he stayed in constant touch with the office by radio telephone and was often accompanied by members of the *Mirror* staff, in particular Willie Soutar, the art editor, and always by Jodi and their parrot, Bertie, which spouted pro-*Mirror* propaganda. After *The Sun* made inroads on the *Mirror* circulation, he thought of changing Bertie's replacement's name to Rupert, Cudlipp told Desmond Wilcox, but believed Murdoch's papers were so seedy he might be sued by the parrot. The Cudlipps also kept a dog, Georgie, which forever treated Cudlipp suspiciously after he used it to wipe the mist from the windscreen of the car.

Awarded an OBE in 1945, knighted upon his retirement in 1973 and made a life peer the following year, he lived happily in retirement with Jodi, and another parrot, in Chichester. He was on the board of the Chichester Festival Theatre, attended the House of Lords and wrote copiously, mainly for the *British Journalism Review*, although he also completed an unproduced play. He retained for his entire life what could be a lacerating turn of phrase – when asked by a film company in 1997 to do a "profile-interview" about the first Lord Rothermere, he replied: "I enjoyed the enormous pleasure of never meeting him and even greater privilege of never working near him as an editor. In my last few years, I honestly cannot be persuaded by a fat cheque or a share option in First Circle Films to waste time working on a TV profile for BBC2 of the lascivious, gluttonous, Hitler-grovelling, penny-pinching, power-mad, boring old so-and-so."

He severed his connections with the *Mirror*, apart from a brief and, he acknowledged, unwise spell as consultant to Robert Maxwell and irregular but frequent lunches with former colleagues.

He died of cancer on 17 May 1998, but not before writing a note to some of his lunching companions, among them Geoffrey Goodman. "Millions of people are putting up with the double-cancer problem in circumstances far less congenial than mine," he wrote. "How many others can doze off with a full view of the illuminated steeple of Chichester Cathedral?"

Acute breathlessness, he continued, made impossible the social chit-chat they had enjoyed over "two or three bottles" – "Who wants to sit next to a Trappist monk who can't drink and who can only breathe deeply when looking at a steak he can't eat?" And he concluded: "Thanks for the memories – no reply of any sort needed."

At his request, there was no memorial service.

Ellis Birk: "He was the greatest tabloid editor of all time. His particular skill was to articulate brilliantly extremely complicated events and to convert them into words that ordinary people could understand."

Cecil King (1969): "In the popular paper field in my time, Hugh Cudlipp has been the outstanding editor anywhere in the world."

Geoffrey Goodman (2003): "…the notion that Cudlipp needed King in the *Mirror*'s castle to bring out the full orchestration of his genius is, in my view, rubbish. Hugh Cudlipp… was the greatest popular journalist produced by Fleet Street in the 20th century. I remain convinced he would have achieved that eminence even without Cecil King."

Richard Stott (2003): "Hugh Cudlipp was the living proof that great newspapermen should not hang on beyond their sell-by date."

WILLIAM NEIL CONNOR 1909-1967

"For a country to have a great writer is to have another government"

– **Aleksandr Solzhenitsyn.**

Cassandra is to journalists probably the most famous name among British newspaper columnists, even today, 46 years after the writer's death. Yet William (Bill) Connor was so much

more than a columnist to the *Daily Mirror*. He was at the very forefront of the paper's progress from soon after his defection from the advertising industry in 1935. He wrote stories and dialogue for strip cartoons, was briefly an Old Codger, producing pithy replies to the daily Live Letters page, and edited a culture and arts publication the paper acquired, *Public Opinion*. (This was a failure and Cecil King was later to observe: "Connor was a great journalist but not a great editor.") But he took the first step to everlasting renown when Bartholomew inquired of him: "Do you think you could write a column?" So was Cassandra born.

Connor himself had entered the world some 28 years earlier, the son of an Irish father and Scottish mother. Educated at Glendale Grammar School in Wood Green, north London, he went to work for a company called Arks Publicity and then, at the age of 23, became a copywriter at the J. Walter Thompson advertising agency. There he met Basil Nicholson and Philip Zec, both of whom were to make major contributions to the success of the *Mirror*. Famously, one of the accounts on which Connor worked at the agency was Harpic, the lavatory cleanser, and Cudlipp later credited him with having written the "immortal, purchase-compelling prose: old fashioned brush-work is out-of-date". At J. Walter Thompson, Connor learned how to write with brevity and punch and under pressure.

Nicholson was the first to join the *Mirror*, as features editor, and when Zec and Connor followed, Cassandra soon catapulted Bill Connor to national prominence. In a column that appeared up to five times a week, and is not to be confused in any way with the *Mirror*'s 21st century reincarnation of the title, Connor deflated pomposity, attacked hypocrisy, defended the weak and went for the throats of the strong and powerful if he thought they were out of line. He could frighten and wound with idiosyncratic prose that often defied the rules of grammar. He could be wildly funny, tear-jerkingly sentimental and as fierce as a lion with a sore paw.

He visited Berlin on a number of occasions during the late 1930s and robustly attacked Nazism and British appeasement. His unsigned poster page on Hitler – WANTED! FOR MURDER… FOR KIDNAPPING… FOR THEFT AND FOR ARSON – remains a masterpiece of popular journalism. His attack on a ministerial reshuffle during the early days of the war – "Talk about musical chairs. The trouble is that this particular game is being played to a funeral march. Ours." – so incensed Winston Churchill that he complained that the writer was "dominated by malevolence". Cassandra wasn't right all the time and his persecution of P.G. Wodehouse for his misguided but hardly wicked Berlin wartime broadcasts was unedifying (after Cassandra lampooned the humorist's silly-ass name, Pelham Warner, Wodehouse retaliated by innocently wondering whether Connor's initials, W.N., stood for Walpaurgis Nacht). But mostly Cassandra unerringly reflected the thoughts of the man and woman in the street.

Connor joined the Army in 1942, to work, mainly with Cudlipp, on army newspapers. Cassandra's return to the *Mirror*, on 23 September 1946, was marked by one of the best-remembered introductions in journalistic history (even if few of those recalling it get it exactly right): "As I was saying when I was interrupted, it is a powerful hard thing to please all the people all the time."

With little exposure outside the paper, his pseudonym became among the best-known names in the country as he covered everything from the funeral of Churchill to interviews with statesmen and movie stars. For two decades his column, on which he wrote his own headlines, dominated popular newspaper polemics. And although his confidence was damaged by a bruising experience in the witness box during the successful libel action brought against him and the paper in 1959 by the American entertainer, Liberace, his talent remained undiminished. (Donald Zec, however, believes Connor was never quite as ferocious after the trial: "The thought that something he had written was an outrageous piece of journalism and very over-the-top brought about almost a physical change. His face erupted during the trial and from then on he was never quite as forceful a writer.")

Mike Randall, assistant editor in charge of features for three years in the 1950s, recalled Cass's office, "empty save for the litter of discarded first paragraphs lying all over the floor". The writer would be in the pub across the street, oiling his writer's block with several drinks. Frequently he would return what seemed impossibly late, but still meet his deadline. He kept a harmonium in his office.

Failing health could not stem the torrent of words that flooded from him with the unparalleled journalistic skill for which he was knighted in January 1966. He died of cancer in April of the following year, three weeks before his 58th birthday.

Hugh Cudlipp (1967): "Outwardly, he was

stubborn, cantankerous, prickly. Except in the benign moments, which were not infrequent, conversation with him was a boisterous affray; as a marathon reader of books and magazines, his mental ammo was abundant. But the explosive verbal combats ended as a rule with the twinkling eyes peering over the steamed-up spectacles.

"Inwardly, he was a warm and friendly cove, always pressuring the firm and his friends to be generous to a pensioner or to a journalist who had fallen by the wayside."

Donald Zec (1967): "Cassandra of the *Daily Mirror* was loved because, in this uneasy business of putting words together and making them soar if not sing, he was the master."

Cassandra: "One of these unfine days I shall find myself, I suppose, in a celestial – or more likely hellish – waiting room preparing myself for an interview with St. Peter – or the Prince of Darkness.

"And then either His Reverence or His Irreverence will say to me: 'Now, how did you spend your time on earth?'

"'Well, your eminence – or your Lowness,' I shall say, 'I wrote a great deal of nonsense in my time, but I had a fine time doing it. I saw a lot of things and I met great numbers of people. I knew plenty of crooks (this will go down well with the Prince of Darkness) and I knew at least one eminently good man (this may curry favour with St. Peter, but I doubt it).

"I witnessed bits of five wars, saw Vesuvius blow up, swam the Thames at Shadwell, saved Deal Gasworks from the Royal Artillery – a complicated yarn this, but I'll tell you about it one day – made a 42-egg omelette next to the leaning tower of Pisa, and heard Toscanini give his first concert after Mussolini at the Scala, Milan. I can also grow tomatoes and I understand the minds of cats perfectly…"

REBECCA MARJORIE PROOPS 1911-1996

"Advice is like snow; the softer it falls, the longer it dwells upon, and the deeper it sinks into, the mind."

– Samuel Taylor Coleridge.

Marje Proops was born in London, or thereabouts, in 1911, or thereabouts – her age was something she never discussed – and claimed she became a socialist at the age of five when she noticed the difference between the clientele in the public and saloon bars of the pub her father ran. He ran lots of pubs, but Marje, like many but not all Jews, grew up disinterested in drink.

She went to school in Dalston and Hackney and married Sydney Proops in Shacklewell Lane

synagogue, Dalston, in November 1935 when she was 24 or thereabouts. They had a son, Robert.

Marje became a freelance fashion artist and occasional writer, and, in 1939, was sent to see Esme Zelger, the woman's page editor of the *Daily Mirror*. When Zelger had disappeared to show her portfolio to the features editor, a "terrifying-looking" man burst into the room and asked her if she could cover Ascot fashions for the paper. She remained in awe of Hugh Cudlipp ever after: "I don't know what adrenalin does, but whatever it does, mine does it like mad when he's around," she told the television interviewer Desmond Wilcox. "When he says, Come up and have a drink', I tremble with a mixture of fear and excitement."

Her first sketch for the *Mirror* appeared in September 1939 with the signature "Sylviane". When Esme Zelger became woman's editor of the *Daily Herald* in 1945, Marje went with her and was a reporter and feature writer for a short while before being appointed fashion editor at the handsome salary of £23 a week. Until 1953 she was working for another Cudlipp, Percy, during that time the *Herald*'s editor.

She became woman's editor of the *Herald* in 1950 and by 1953 was also writing a radical column. When the paper's advice columnist died, Marje took over, writing under the name Mary Marshall. Soon after Percy Cudlipp was fired, Hugh re-entered her life and in June 1954 she returned to the *Mirror* as a columnist.

She had no shorthand and never learned to type, writing all her copy in longhand before passing it to a secretary for typing or putting into a computer. "Marje is a great communicator," her great friend and former colleague Felicity Green was to say. "To watch Marje work is really an eye-opening experience. She writes everything in longhand, and her pen is just an extension of her hand. She writes almost without hesitation. It just pours out of her like liquid gold."

As a star of Cudlipp's circus, she travelled extensively: to Paris with woman's editor Ailsa Garland and, later, Felicity Green; to Hollywood to interview Marlon Brando and dance with Groucho Marx – when she was ill, Cary Grant visited her at her home – and to anywhere in the world Cudlipp decided would benefit from the Proops-eye view. With the launch in February 1955 of the Woman's *Sunday Mirror* – later Woman's *Mirror* and eventually merged with *Woman* magazine – she began a light-hearted advice column.

In May 1997, Cudlipp made contractual arrangements to ensure she did not have to retire at the statutory age and launched the Dear Marje page that was to make her the doyenne of agony aunts and even more of a household name than she had been previously.

With her unsatisfactory marriage having settled into a comfortable if dull partnership, she embarked upon a 20-year love affair with Phillip Levy, the unmarried head of the *Mirror* legal department. It remained a secret until she revealed it in her authorised biography, written by Angela Patmore and published in 1993.

Later in life, she was ill on several occasions, with a 50-a-day cigarette habit necessitating in 1979 an artery bypass that caused a minor stroke and left her with paralysis down one side of her face and in her right hand. "We thought we'd never see her back at work again," said Mike Molloy. "But she just bloody well fought back. She recovered from the stroke and forced herself to write again. Marje is a tough woman." She never smoked again.

Marje worked for nine different *Daily Mirror* editors. She loved her son, her grandchildren and her cats, and was loved by her staff and most of her colleagues. In 1969, she was awarded an OBE, but absurdly never a damehood, and was also elected Woman Journalist of the Year. She wrote two books, *Dear Marje* and *Pride, Prejudice and Proops*. She was a loyal and generous friend and a dangerous enemy.

Phillip Levy died in 1987, Sydney Proops the following year. A standing-room-only crowd attended her Golders Green Crematorium funeral after Marje Proops died in November 1996 at the age of 85. Or thereabouts.

Geoffrey Goodman: "Her pulling power was enormous. The *Mirror* formula as it developed through the fifties and sixties was uniquely geared to the mood of the country, orchestrated by the genius of Cudlipp and brilliantly executed by his journalists. And Marje fitted into that package with her supreme pulling power. She's the world's woman."

Bernard Levin: "Does Marjorie Proops do good? I cannot see how anybody… can be in any doubt that she does an enormous amount, possibly – of direct, practical good, at any rate – more than any single individual in the country."

Mike Molloy: "The point about Marje is that she's immensely wise. We always used to refer to her as the Heart of the *Mirror*, because she had a direct link with the readers. 'Agony aunt' is used as a pejorative term often by the smart and the sophisticated and the cynical, but for many years, for millions of people too frightened to ask questions, there was nobody to turn to but Marje."

Appendix 1
Strips With Everything

On 12 May 1919 the Daily Mirror *introduced its readers to two new stars. "Uncle Dick" – the pen-name under which Bertram Lamb chronicled their escapades – recruited Austin Payne, a Welshman and former artist with* Comic Cuts, *to make a dog and penguin come to life in a daily feature. Searching for names to give his progeny, Lamb had recalled his wartime batman, who answered to the nickname Pipsqueak. And so The Adventgures of Pip and Squeak became part of the* Mirror *journalistic armoury. Within nine months, Pip, the dog, and Squeak, the penguin, were joined by a large-eared rabbit named Wilfred. Unlike its chums, the rabbit did not speak, but expressed itself in a bizarre language that consisted mostly of the words "Gug" and "Nunc". The public took to this odd trio with a fervour that promoted them both from the printed page and into newspaper folklore. The age of the strip cartoon superstar had arrived.*

The Americans may lay claim to having invented the strip, but, as early as 1908, W.K. Haselden was dividing his cartoons into panels, or frames, and running stories over consecutive days in the *Daily Mirror*. His "Mr Simkins On His Holidays" was told in 16 episodes in 1908 and reproduced in *Reflections*, the annual collection of 100 Haselden cartoons published by the *Mirror* for many years. At the outbreak of war in August 1914 he created "Big and Little Willie", a cartoon send-up of the German Emperor and his son, the Crown Prince. After the 1918 armistice, the crown prince himself was reported to have confessed to a *Mirror* photographer that the cartoon had been "damnably effective", although it might be

argued that lampooning German royalty did not make much difference to the lot of the infantry trapped in the mud of Flanders fields and that tossing copies of the *Mirror* into the German trenches did more for the paper's circulation than for victory.

There were other characters created and discarded by Haselden along the highway to the full-blown strip, including vivacious young flapper Joy Flapperton and the officious Colonel Dugout. These and sundry other figments of Haselden's lively imagination appeared in the paper and the *Reflections* series, which right up until 1930, at least, were sold for one shilling.

NB: One shilling became five decimalised pence; a farthing was a quarter of an old penny and "a bob" slang for a shilling.

The cartoon historian Denis Gifford recorded that Haselden's style, with a boxy square format, is considered by purists to exclude him from any claim that he invented this particular art form. Some insist that Harry Foxwell, who would go on to draw "Tiger Tim" and "Teddy Tail", was the true father of strips when he gave birth to "Helpful Horace", a two-panel feature that made its debut in the *Sunday Pictorial* in 1915. Others promote the work of Bud Fisher, whose "Mutt and Jeff" first appeared in the United States in 1923 and in shape and form is a seminal work from which the strip cartoon of later years directly descended.

But Haselden's idea of publishing daily story cartoons pre-dates all other claimants. And the entry of Payne's Pip, Squeak and Wilfred into the field was the first cartoon work to trigger a nationwide response, with appreciative letters

Animal magic: Pip, Squeak and Wilfred were the Mirror's first cartoon favourites, appealing to a wide section of the readership. The dog, the penguin and the rabbit were promoted with a deal of gusto. Their fan club, the Wilfredian League of Gugnuncs, gained 350,000 members withIn five months of its launch. The terrible trio starred in panto and made many public appearances – not all of them without mishap.

arriving from all areas of society and, on a birthday anniversary of the pets, a congratulatory greeting in rhyme arriving from Viscount Ullswater, a former speaker of the House of Commons. The strip was also commercially marketed with flair, another cartoon first. Albums of the trio's adventures were published, in colour, and by 1926 the *Pip, Squeak and Wilfred Annual* was selling alongside *Wilfred's Annual,* both priced at six shillings. Reunions of the Wilfredian League of Gugnuncs – launched in January 1927 and attracting 350,000 members by late May – drew crowds to the Royal Albert Hall as the strip's fame grew and it expanded into the *Sunday Pic*. The animal pals had their portraits painted and a model manor house, known as Mirror Grange, was constructed as a "home" for them and put on show in 1930 to raise money for handicapped children in Sussex. They also featured on the pantomime stage and even made public appearances, after one of which, in front of 20,000 at Clacton, Essex, Hugh Cudlipp recorded, "Uncle Dick" was fined 50 shillings (£2.50) for allowing the animals to perform on the beach without muzzles. On another occasion the penguin bit a mayor on the nose and,

elsewhere, pecked the hand of his minder, one Bert Canty, who, much to the distress of the mothers that had brought their children to see the animals, began to curse loudly. "How sweet they are," the Queen reportedly observed at a garden party where the terrible trio were on display, but Her Majesty wisely kept out of pecking range.

Bertram Lamb died in 1938, but the strip continued into World War Two and then Austin Payne continued to supply a P, S & W adventure for the weekly, and ultimately unsuccessful, Children's *Mirror*. But even if they had by now lost their superstar status, the odd trio were to have a second, eight-year lease of life when revived in the daily paper in 1953 by the head of the strips department, Hugh McClelland, who drew and scripted the new episodes.

Back in the pioneering days of this seductive art form, other papers were swift to climb aboard the strips bandwagon as it rolled into the imagination of the public. But having been a trailblazer, the *Mirror* stayed ahead of the rest with innovative work such as Tich, which made its first appearance on 21 November 1931 and introduced pantomime multi-frame cartoons in which the eponymous character acted out a joke without speech bubbles or captions. The signature on Tich, "Dart", concealed the identities of brothers Stephen and Frank Dowling, who would be vital members of the *Mirror*'s strips team for years to come.

On 21 December the following year, the most famous female British strip figure of all time – the male and overall title is held by Andy Capp, more of whom later – quietly bowed in with the arrival of Fritz, believed by his new owner to be a visiting German count until a gift-wrapped Dachshund is revealed. "Jane's Journal, the Diary of a Bright Young Thing" was the gentle and genteel introduction of the girl who was soon to put the strip into the strip cartoon. Written from early in its life by Don Freeman and drawn until May 1948 by W. Norman Pett and then for the rest of the heroine's 26-year reign by his former assistant, Michael Hubbard, the strip broke new ground as Jane discarded her clothes with increasing frequency. She did not disrobe completely, however, until World War Two determined that she should strip for victory. That's when Jane's audience expanded to include other nationalities of Allied troops and the U.S. forces' paper in the Far East, *Round-up*, described her as "a highly patriotic comely British lass whose one affliction at odds with her otherwise sterling character (if affliction it be) is that she has just one hell of a job keeping her clothes on". Did the British 36th Division really gain six miles the day Jane took everything off? So claimed *Round-up*, which, under the headline JANE GIVES ALL observed, "Maybe we Americans ought to have Jane, too."

Jane proved to be a successor to Pip, Squeak and Wilfred and a precursor to Andy Capp as another rare example where characters climb from the pencilled frame and enter real life (with Ruggles, as we shall see, it was the other way around, with real life climbing in). There were eagerly-awaited Jane books and because of the character's celebrity, the model who inspired Norman Pett – he worked in his Cotswold cottage and dispatched his work to London on the train – became one herself: Christobel Leighton-Porter was constantly in demand for personal appearances. Initially Pett used his wife as a model, but then saw pictures of Leighton-Porter, an artists' and photographic model from Eastleigh in Hampshire, and it was

her face and figure that he used as reference from then on. Leighton-Porter toured in a stage show of "Jane of the *Daily Mirror*" and later recalled transfixing entire regiments and receiving 62 proposals of marriage in one week. The writer Ali Kefford recorded that Christobel's favourite moment from the fame Jane brought was when the showgirl, demurely dressed, met the then Lord Chamberlain. "Tell me, my dear," he said, "what do you do in your act?" "Well," explained Christobel, "at one stage I turn my back to the audience, take off my bra, and then cover my breasts with my hands as I turn round." There was a short silence before the Lord Chamberlain remarked: "You must have very large hands."

When Jane eventually drifted into the sunset with boyfriend Georgie on 10 October 1959 ("Jane, darling, now's the time to say goodbye to the past – we've got lots to do, planning ahead – let's quietly disappear and start again… together") an era ended. And neither Bob Hamilton's Patti, who replaced Jane four days later, nor Daughter of Jane, drawn by "Maz" – Alfred Mazure – in 1963, could recreate it.

Such was the brush-fire success of strips that Harry Guy Bartholomew, ever ready to seize an opportunity to steer the paper into new areas, had begun to take a personal interest in the department when he became editorial director in 1934. He decided to try to repeat the success of Pip, Squeak and Wilfred and the more recent success, Jane, and was fortunate that soon to arrive on the staff was Basil Nicholson, the advertising man who believed that if a picture told a thousand words, then a cartoon could convey an entire novel. An enthusiast of the American style strip, in which continuing storylines had long since been introduced, on 11 March 1935 Nicholson launched Ruggles, inspired by an American success named The Gumps and chronicling the lives of a suburban middle-class family. The signature, Blik, again cloaked the work of the Dowling brothers and Steve Dowling was to draw every frame of the strip during its 22-year existence. Nicholson called upon his former colleague from the world of advertising, Bill Connor, to help out with the scripting of some of his new projects, but Ruggles was written first by Frank Dowling and then by Ian Gammidge, who was joined for a while by Connor when it evolved into a "real-

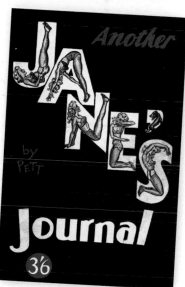

*Girl power:
Christobel
Leighton-Porter
(left) was the
model for Jane,
drawn by W.
Norman Pett
(above, with
prototype for
Jane's
Dachshund,
Fritz).
Below left:
Pett's sketches
for the strip
cartoon that
really did strip.*

life" feature, in which actual people appeared alongside the fictional family.

Nicholson's next brainwave was prompted by Little Orphan Annie, Harold Gray's all-American girl who had become a national institution and years later would have a Broadway musical devoted to her. The *Mirror's* answer was Belinda Blue-Eyes, another little girl in search of her long-lost dad, and it was Bill Connor, not yet Cassandra, who provided the early script for, inevitably, Steve Dowling's art. Soon Steve was joined by his brother and the modest pair adopted the signature "Gloria" to disguise their handiwork. Later Belinda was drawn by Tony Royle and scripted by Don Freeman.

Next came Buck Ryan, not surprisingly yet another offering from the Dowlings, but created by Jack Monk and inspired by Chester Gould's square-jawed American detective, Dick Tracy. Ryan bowed in on 22 March 1937 and, together with Zola Anderson, foe turned friend, and Twilight, whose black hair fell across her face in the style popularised by the blonde movie star Veronica Lake, became yet another long-running success story. Monk wrote and drew the strip until 31 July 1962.

For a while Hugh McClelland had his own popular strip in the paper, with the sheriff of Deadwood Gulch, Beelzebub Jones, providing offbeat western adventures in the company of "depitties" Lem and Zeke and the tiny Tumbleweed. Beelzebub ran for eight years, whereas some of McClelland's other quirky ideas, drawn and scripted by him, bit the dust faster than a Deadwood Gulch villain. Dan Doofer, launched in December 1945, lasted only seven months and was replaced by Sunshine Falls, set in a small town in McClelland's homeland, which ran for a year. The introduction and rapid withdrawal of new ideas was in the *Mirror*'s strip tradition – various characters had swiftly come and just as swiftly gone over the years. Longer-lasting was McClelland's Jimpy, about a boy determined to make good as a magician after being thrown out of the Royal College of Magic – Harry Potter is testimony to Hugh's foresight. Jimpy pursued his ambition for six years after debuting on 5 January 1946.

Other strips were to come and go over the years, but two figures that loom large in the history of *Mirror* cartoon department arrived within five years of one another, before and during the war. The most remarkable was Captain A.R.P. Reilly-Ffoull of the Gallopin' Gertshires, the squire of Arntwee Hall, Much Cackling, Gertshire, whose power of personality soon overwhelmed the original eponymous country bumpkin hero of Just Jake after its launch on 4 July 1938. "Stap me!" became a favourite expression of those enamoured of the Captain's eccentricities in a strip that was wholly British in humour terms – as off-the-wall as a squash rackets ball. The squire and Just Jake's other stalwarts, Eric the butler, Maida Grannitt and Titus Tallow, delighted the more unconventional *Mirror* readers until its creator, Bernard Graddon, died of pneumonia after attending an office party during the bitterly cold Christmas period of 1951.

The other giant to move into a strips collection that, even during the eight-page *Mirrors* of World War Two, usually filled a page-and-a-half of space – pre-war they had been littered throughout the paper – was Garth. Steve Dowling's finest achievement, the mysterious space age muscle man arrived on 24 July 1943 and was to become one of the longest-running features ever to appear in the paper at over 50 years. Garth was written by the indefatigable Don Freeman, the staff writer before Gammidge arrived and the man who developed the character of the strip. John Allard and Frank Bellamy were successively to take it over from Dowling and other artists and writers involved over the years were Martin Asbury, Peter O'Donnell – later to create the huge hit Modesty Blaise for the *Evening Standard* – Jimmy Edgar, Angus Allen and Philip Harbottle.

From that first adventure, when he arrived on an island and discovered that by eating the local foliage he developed super-powers, Garth established a following that spilled over from the usual strip cartoon addicts to sci-fi buffs. It also included at least one member of the royal family – when celebrating the strip's fiftieth birthday in the *Mirror* in 1993, writer Garth Gibbs recalled that 15 years previously, when covering the opening of the new wing of a factory in Wales, the Duke of Edinburgh approached him and said: "I have been to Norway for the past week – can you tell me what your namesake in the *Mirror* is doing?" Garth finally departed for cartoon heaven in March 1997.

Hugh McClelland surprisingly left the *Mirror* for the *Daily Sketch* in the 1950s – he had served in the RAF during the war, during which time Tony Royle acted as a conduit between Bartholomew and the artists – and Phillip Zec and then Julian Phipps took over responsibility for a department that was striking a chord each day with a large percentage of the readership. A 1949 survey of the press had noted that "Much of the popularity of the *Mirror* strips may be due to their blending of reality and fantasy in such a way that people are easily stimulated into identifying themselves with the strip characters." They could do so especially with the family strips that continued the *Mirror* tradition of keeping up with changing tastes in the field. The Flutters, drawn by Len Gamblin, and The Larks, with artwork by Jack Dunkley, were both written by Ian Gammidge and lasted until February 1971 and February 1985 respectively. The Flutters, featuring the rakish gambler Bert Cert, was another gem of comic book creation that only growing social sophistication could render obsolete.

Social sophistication did nothing to dent the popularity of the *Mirror* strips' department's star of stars, however. Andy Capp has proved, to this day, indestructible, even though his creator is dead. Capp swaggered out of the brain of staff artist Reg Smythe after Hugh Cudlipp

Great days: The strips page in the Daily Mirror *of 1954 featured Buck Ryan, Ruggles, Belinda, The Flutters, Garth and the the second coming of the pioneering trio Pip, Squeak and Wilfred. Although much changed, the strips page is a vital Ingredient of the 21st-century paper.*

instructed Bill Herbert, who by now was running the department, to come up with a new daily character to help build circulation in the north. The brief was, according to Cudlipp, for someone "realistic, down-to-earth, essentially northern in flavour". Smythe, a wartime corporal in the Western Desert, came up with a hard drinking layabout who spent most of his time leaning on the bar of his local pub, playing snooker or lying prone on the sofa while his long-suffering wife, Florrie, flung reprimands or plates from the kitchen. Reg was born in West Hartlepool, in the north-east of England, and so was Andy.

The strip appeared from 5 August 1957 and was an instant hit. It was quickly promoted into all editions of the paper, strutting in on 14 April the following year. Reg, slight and shy, was overwhelmed. Was he to be rewarded for creating a cartoon Hercules that soon would bestride the world, translated into more language's than Andy knew existed? Not immediately, and not especially generously, according to John Edwards, then a *Mirror* features writer and subsequently – and still – a columnist with the *Daily Mail.*

Edwards remembers when the American cartoon genius Al Capp, creator of L'il Abner, visited London in the early 1960s and Michael Christiansen, then the assistant editor in charge of features, thought it would be a good idea for Al to meet Andy. Smythe and Edwards, who was to write about the encounter, went for lunchtime drinks and canapés with the great Al in his suite the Savoy.

"Reg had never been to a suite at the Savoy before," says Edwards. "He was surprised and excited. He and Al got on fine and Al drew L'il Abner meeting Andy. Then Al Capp told Reg that Andy Capp was becoming a cult in US and that he (Reg) must be making a fortune. Reg said he wasn't at all. I believe he was getting something like £7,500 a year, a lot then but not much to Al. Al said he had a syndication set-up of his own and would be quite happy to represent Reg in the U.S. and would guarantee him a fortune. Reg talked of nothing else as we walked back to the office.

"Christiansen was pleased with the stuff and almost as an aside I mentioned Al Capp's offer to represent Andy in the U.S. His face went white and he marched me into his office and told me to repeat what had happened. I left his office and that was it. Only it wasn't. Just before going over to the Stab for the evening at around 6pm, Reg tapped on the glass window of the features department and asked me to go to his studio. There he said he had been called to see Cudlipp mid-afternoon and, referring to my conversation with Christiansen, Cudlipp told him that something had to be done for him financially. Between about 3.30pm and 6pm Reg had his salary increased to around £20,000, plus a cut of the Christmas annuals and other ancillary rights – massive sums of money for those days. In thanks, Reg gave me a gold pen. I subsequently lost it."

Much later Andy made the giant leap from the printed page to the stage and TV screen. Among the actors to portray the world's most lovable rogue were Tom Courtenay, in Andy Capp, a 1981 musical by Alan Price and Trevor Peacock, and on television by James Bolam, who in 1988 starred in a six-part series written by Keith Waterhouse. Smythe, who became a very rich man, lived in London for some years, but never really settled. Ian Gammidge fondly remembers their lunches together – "Ten gins and sardines on toast – that sort of thing" – but eventually Reg returned to Hartlepool and continued to draw Andy, and reap the benefits of Al Capp's generosity, until he died in 1998. As for Andy, he's still propping up the bar in Hartlepool and driving Florrie to distraction. That Garth's record longevity will be surpassed there can be no doubt.

Later members of the *Mirror*'s strip club included the oddball northern family portrayed in The Fosdyke Saga, commissioned by then assistant editor Mike Molloy from Bill Tidy for *Mirror* Magazine, which closed before it could make its debut but then featured in the paper from March 1971 until February 1985, and The Perishers, originally drawn by Dennis Collins, a fine landscape artist. Roger Hargreaves' simple but brilliant The Mr Men and Ian Reid's The Greens also came and went. Only The Perishers, launched in 1958 as a British answer to Charles Schultz's worldwide hit Peanuts, survives, now drawn by Bill Merlin with stories and script by Maurice Dodd, who has been with the strip since it was six months old and for a while both wrote it and supplied the art work. The Perishers was another strip that strayed from the page, with a 20-episode animated BBC series in the early 1980s and a stage musical performed by children.

There were also a number of strips offering advice to readers – Patsy on cookery, Mr Digwell, the gardener, Mr Crabtree on angling and Keeping Up With The Jones, a financial advice saga that failed to appeal. Also coming out of the department was the now almost forgotten daily single-frame gag featuring Useless Eustace, drawn by Jack Greenall from 1935 until Jack's retirement in 1974 and thereafter, until Eustace collected his bus pass in 1985, by Peter Maddocks. Eustace might not have lingered so long, but there were countrywide gambling sweeps on the first and last letter of the cartoon's caption that prolonged its anachronistic existence. Mike Molloy, soon to be the paper's editor, also contributed a single-frame series, Virginia, which ran for two years from June 1974.

Charles Roger succeeded Bill Herbert and then Willie (Bill) Soutar, long-time news art editor of the paper, and John Allard took over as head of a diminishing department. Allard joined the paper as an apprentice cartoonist at the age of 15 in 1943 and was sent to the St. Martin's School of Art. Now retired to Essex, he recalls Steve Downing, who had evacuated his family to the West County, where he was a captain in the Home Guard, visiting London once a week and often drawing the latest episodes of Ruggles and Garth on a board perched on his knees as the train rumbled towards the capital. Allard who was Dowling's assistant for many years, became solo artists for Garth for two-and-a-half years and also drew illustrations for features.

Allard, by then strips boss, was involved in two less-than-successful developments when Robert Maxwell took control of the group. "Maxwell revived Jane for about five years," he remembers. "He reckoned it was one of his great ambitions because he remembered reading the strip in the war. His idea was that Jane awoke from a long sleep and discovered wonders of the modern world. John Burns was the artist and Ian Gammidge did the script, with assistance from Arthur Smith, the science reporter. That lasted for about a year and then we reverted to the formula of the old strip. Roy Greenslade killed it when he was editor after he was showing some youngsters around the office and a girl asked, "Why do you have this naked strip cartoon in the paper?"

Maxwell made other forays into the area of strips. He snapped up Flook when the *Daily Mail* made the furry little creature redundant, but Wally Fawkes's whimsy didn't appeal to *Mirror* readers. And Captain Bob introduced a weekly insert for children featuring old Mickey Mouse cartoons. "Maxwell barged in on the negotiations of the contract with Disney and ended up signing a three-year deal," says Allard. "The idea was that it would attract advertising, although it brought in very little." In 1986 the excruciatingly titled Buckingham Dallas, Lucy's "comic adventures" of the Royal Corgis, wasn't. Another new strip fared better. In 1992 the soccer strip Scorer made an appearance, taking on *The Sun*'s Striker in the sports pages. Sport hated it and every now and again would leave it out. There was a plot line running in which Eve, sexy wife of the club chairman, was about to proposition the hero, Dave Storry, and the following day's installment did not appear. The phones didn't stop ringing all morning and we suddenly realised what a hit we had. Richard Stott was the editor and he agreed with me that we should move Scorer on to the strips page, which by then had shrunk to around half-a-page, with only five strips. Scorer was responsible for the strips getting a whole page once more."

Scorer, much expanded, is still scoring as the only proper story strip left in the paper and A Man Called Horace has been avoiding anything wild in the West since May 1989. And the full-page depth occupied by the strips since Allard negotiated it back into the paper – this time in full colour – remains. The great days of strips may have gone, and many of legendary names consigned to the inanimate cartoon graveyard by the power of television, but the feature remains an integral part of the *Mirror*'s appeal. As Reilly-Ffoull would say, "Stap me!"

Appendix 2
The Editors

There have been 19 editorships of the *Daily Mirror,* filled by 18 editors. The average length of tenure during the first 100 years, counting Richard Stott's two periods in the chair as a single editorship, is just over five-and-a-half years. The current editor, Piers Morgan, boosts the average, having completed eight years the day before the paper's one hundredth birthday.

1903-04: Mrs Mary Howarth, the first woman to edit a national daily newspaper. Plucked by Alfred Harmsworth from running the women's features pages at the *Daily Mail* and dispatched back there less than three months later when Hamilton Fyfe "drowned the kittens". Never to be heard of professionally again.

1904-07: Henry Hamilton Fyfe, born London, September 1869, the son of a barrister and journalist, James Hamilton Fyfe. Educated at Fettes College, Edinburgh, the school that has produced many distinguished old boys, including Tony Blair. Married 1907, no children. Followed in father's footsteps as a reporter on *The Times,* later becoming a sub-editor, secretary to the editor and drama critic. Editor, *Morning Advertiser,* 1902-3. After leaving the *Mirror* became, subsequently, drama critic of *The World*; special correspondent, *Daily Mail*; war correspondent with French, Russian, Romanian, Italian and British armies; Hon. Attaché, British War Mission to USA 1917; part of Lord Northcliffe's propaganda team in Germany, 1918; editor, *Daily Herald,* 1922-26; political writer, *Reynolds News,* 1930-42. Fyfe was a prolific author, writing novels, plays and a biography of Northcliffe. He died on 15 June 1951.

1907-15: Alexander Cockburn Kenealy was born 1864, the son of Dr Edward Kenealy QC, MP, godson of Lord Chief Justice Cockburn and brother of Dr Arabella Kenealy, a novelist and writer on medical matters. Educated at University College School, London, and in France, he moved with his family to the United States and shortly before his 18th birthday joined the staff of the *New York Herald*. His obituary in *The Times* claimed that, two years later, he was appointed the *Herald*'s special correspondent with Robert E. Peary's first Arctic expedition, but as Peary's initial foray into the Arctic, to collect meteorites, was not until 1896, it seems more likely that Kenealy covered part of the 1893-95 expedition to chart the ice cap of Greenland. In 1895, he joined the *New York World*, where he was correspondent with the American fleet during the Spanish-American war, and moved to the *New York American* to write humorous articles before returning to London in 1904 as news editor of the *Daily Express*. Joined the *Daily Mirror* the same year. He wrote two humorous books, *The Letters of Alphonse de Mouton* and *The Preposterous Yankee*, both under the name of Montague Vernon Ponsonby. Kenealy died on 26 June 1915 and was survived by his mother, five sisters and three brothers. He was buried on 1 July in a churchyard at Hangleton, near Portslade, Sussex. Mourners at the funeral included Lords Northcliffe and Rothermere,

Harry Guy Bartholomew, successor E.D. Flynn, future editor Leigh Brownlee and a number of senior members of the *Mirror* staff.

1915-19: E.D. Flynn, an American and a friend of Kenealy's. The paper's unknown and forgotten editor.

1920-31: Alexander Campbell, born in Yorkshire in or around 1885, was educated at Ilkley Grammar School before becoming a junior reporter on local newspapers. Moving to the *Leeds Mercury*, he became an assistant editor and filled the same role at the *Daily Record* in Glasgow before, as editor F.R. Sanderson's deputy, helping to launch the *Sunday Pictorial* in March 1915. After working on the aborted *Evening Mirror*, he was appointed by Rothermere as a director and editor of the *Mirror*, where he was to become the second longest serving to date. Weighed down by Rothermere's use of the paper as his personal blunt instrument, Campbell was to write that this was a period when "news was subordinate to political dogma; a galling melancholy task". He established himself as a crusading editor, however, with campaigns against greedy house agents and the promoters of snowball schemes. He and the *Mirror* helped raise money for hospitals and he was a life governor of the Children's Hospital Great Ormond Street. Later, he was a writer, mainly on social issues, and reported from home and abroad. Looking back on his days as editor, when the circulation war was dominated by gifts of free insurance and competitions, he reflected: "I have heard it said that those were the days. To remember or forget? If those were the days, there was something to remember – and quite a lot better forgotten." He died in 1961.

1931-34: L (Leigh). D. Brownlee, a former schoolteacher who had won a cricket blue at Oxford and played for Gloucestershire. "He should have been sporting editor of *The Times*," wrote Cecil King. "He was very knowledgeable about cricket, but quite the wrong man to produce a popular paper." Fired when circulation fell to a low of just over 700,000.

1934-48: Cecil Thomas, the son of a Cambridgeshire rector, was chief sub-editor and then night editor of the paper before becoming the longest-serving *Mirror* editor to date. But he

had been appointed when chairman John Cowley had rejected Harry Guy Bartholomew for the job and Thomas remained in the editorial director's shadow throughout his tenure – he was "Sancho Panza to Bartholomew's Don Quixote," wrote Cudlipp. Cudlipp also recorded that Thomas was financially treated with "degrading meanness" by Bart, who allowed him no expenses. On occasion, usually in front of visitors, Bart would creep up on Thomas and hit him over his bald head with a plank of wood – balsa, but initially terrifying for those witnessing the assault. The good natured Thomas never complained. He was of rotund and rather bucolic appearance, according to Cecil King. Former art editor Bill (Willie) Soutar, who joined the paper illegally as a tape room messenger in 1934 when he was only 13, recalls that Thomas had been an electrical engineer prior to his journalistic career.

1948-53: Sylvester Bolam joined the *Mirror* in 1936 as a sub-editor and, apart from a ten-month break at the *News Chronicle*, remained with the paper for almost 17 years. Born in 1906, he was an economics graduate of Durham University and began in journalism in 1926 as a reporter on the Newcastle Journal before joining the *News Chronicle* in Manchester. After a brief dalliance with the *Chronicle* in London, he returned to the *Mirror* as deputy chief sub-editor and during World War Two was joint night editor with Ted Castle. He became sole night editor and then deputy to Cecil Thomas before being appointed editor in March 1948. Shortly afterwards, the sales of the *Mirror* overtook those of the *Daily Express*. Former art editor Willie Soutar remembers him clearly: "Bolam was a great character and quite religious, a Jew, a smallish man who looked like a bird, a sparrow, with a huge moustache and spectacles. He usually wore a Norfolk suit, with britches, and his preferred mode of transport was a great big motorbike. There he was, looking like a little bird and roaring down the street on his bike." In 1949, Bolam was sent to prison for three months after his paper's reporting of the arrest of Haigh, the "acid bath murderer", was judged to be contempt of court. He returned to edit the paper, but his imprisonment had affected his health and he left after "a disagreement with the management" in January 1953, dying suddenly three months later, on April 27, while smoking a cigarette after breakfast. He was 47.

1953-61: Jack Nener, born in 1902, entered journalism at the age of 14 as an apprentice on the *South Wales Daily Post* in his home town, Swansea. He worked his way up through editorial production at the *Mirror* to become Bolam's deputy and then to succeed him, working largely to Hugh Cudlipp's direction. Tony Miles said of him: "If Hollywood had asked a casting agency to supply someone to play a rough tabloid editor, a character like Jack Nener would have been sent along as the man most suited to the role. All the main ingredients were there: crinkly silver hair, dapper bow tie, gravelly voice, gruff warmth, volcanic temperament." In January 1958, during a heated public debate on press intrusion, he wrote in the *Mirror*: "This is a vigorous, outspoken newspaper. We will not hesistate to expose the buffooneries of public personalities when it is in the public interest to do so... But we believe in the dignity of human beings. We believe that news obtained at the cost of personal distress is not worth printing." When an argument between the two correspondents in the paper's Paris bureau became so bad that one of them complained to London, Nener flew to France to deal with the crisis himself. One of the injured parties moaned pathetically that his colleague wouldn't share the office newspapers with him, and Nener snapped, "Then for Christ's sake order two fucking sets!" and returned to London on the next plane. Of no great physical stature himself, he married the very tall *Mirror* writer Audrey Whiting: Cudlipp referred to the wedding evening as the Night of the Long Wives and an executive competition for an apt phrase for the union was won by "Jack and the Beanstalk". He retired to the south of France but later returned to London, where he died in 1982.

1961-71: Leon Alexander Lee Howard, born 18 June 1914, was, wrote Tony Miles in the *Mirror*'s obituary of its former editor, "one of those remarkable men who now and again emerge in Fleet Street and leave a legend behind them". Privately educated, Lee Howard's early career is unknown, but he served with distinction in the Royal Air Force during World War Two, winning a DFC in 1944. Experience as a navigator and cameraman with the RAF Operational Film Production Unit was followed, after his discharge, by a junior executive role on the *Daily Mirror* picture desk. Handsome and blonde when young, he was in later years

modestly to recall that shortly after the war he turned down the offer of a screen test and film contract because of his love of journalism. He became editor of the Women's *Sunday Mirror* in 1955 and then of the *Sunday Pictorial* in 1959 before taking over at the *Mirror*. He was also a successful novelist, writing, under the name Leigh Howard, *Crispin's Day* (1952), *Johnny's Sister*, (1954) and *Blind Date* (1955), the last of which was filmed the year after publication by Joseph Losey with a cast that included Hardy Kruger and Stanley Baker. He also wrote *No Man Sings* (1956) under the name of Alexander Krislov. He was twice married, to TV critic Sheila Black and, after their 1973 divorce, to *Mirror* Rome correspondent Madalon Dimont. He spent several years of retirement in Rome, where he was known as "Il Professore", and welcomed visiting former colleagues usually wearing a caftan and with a giant bottle of Soave ever present by his side. He died in November 1978 at the age of 64. Lee Howard listed his recreations in *Who's Who* as writing and journalism.

1972-5: Anthony Miles was born in 1930 and entered journalism in Uxbridge as a reporter on the *Middlesex Advertiser*. After working on the *Brighton Argus* and a Fleet Street features agency, he arrived at the *Mirror* as a features writer in 1954. He was then successively editor of the award-winning Inside Page and assistant editor in charge of features and, during its short but praise-filled life, Mirrorscope, until promoted to associate editor in 1968. He succeeded Lee Howard in 1971 and edited the paper until Sydney Jacobson's retirement, when he became editorial director. He was deputy chairman of MGN from 1977-79 and, briefly before Robert Maxwell bought the company, in 1984. In between he was chairman and editorial director, 1983-84. He had been a member of the Press Council and a director of Reuters while with MGN. Subsequently, he worked and lived in Florida. Affable until roused, he was renowned for arguing with restaurant waiters and, when editor, issuing perplexing instructions – "I'm just going out, I don't know where I'm going but if you need me, I'll ring you," he famously told assistant editor Mike Taylor one evening.

1975: Born in 1927, Michael Christiansen was the son of one of the most famous of Fleet

Street editors, Arthur, who, for 24 years, ran the day-to-day editorial business of Lord Beaverbrook's *Daily Express*. They were the only father and son both to edit national newspapers in the 20th century. Michael was educated at Hill Crest School at Frinton, Essex, and in the United States at St. Luke's College, Connecticut. He joined the *Daily Mail* as a reporter in 1943 and then served in the Royal Navy, 1945-47. He became chief sub-editor of the *Mail* in 1950, remaining with the paper until he moved to the *Daily Mirror* in 1956. He was deputy editor of the *Sunday Pictorial* for a year before returning to the daily paper as assistant editor (features), 1961-64. He edited the *Sunday Mirror* from 1964 but was removed in 1972, accepting demotion and becoming *Daily Mirror* deputy editor to Tony Miles, whom he succeeded in 1975. His stewardship of the *Mirror* lasted for only four months before he suffered a stroke on 1 May 1975. Deputy Mike Molloy took over. Michael Christiansen died in 1984.

1975-85: Mike Molloy was born in Hertfordshire but moved to Ealing in London and was educated at the Junior School there and the Ealing School of Art. Having obtained a temporary job as an editorial messenger at the *Sunday Pictorial* during a break from college, he never returned, remaining with the paper until joining the *Daily Sketch* after *Pictorial* editor Colin Valdar moved to edit that paper in 1958. Molloy returned to Mirror Group in 1962, where he became successively *Daily Mirror* features art editor, editor of *Mirror* Magazine and assistant editor in charge of features. Appointed deputy to Michael Christiansen in 1975, he edited the paper after Christiansen's stroke and was formally appointed to the job in December of that year. After ten years, he became Robert Maxwell's editor-in-chief and also edited the *Sunday Mirror* for a short period before leaving the company in 1990. Earlier he drew a pocket cartoon, "Virginia", for the paper – based, she claimed, on the prattling of his long-term secretary, Jill Scott – and during his editorship started to write novels, publishing four while at MGN and another in 1991. A remarkable achiever in several fields, he subsequently exhibited his paintings and has, to date, written three books for children. In a booklet produced for his farewell dinner, writer Peter Donnelly observed of him: "Snappy

dresser. Smart suits. Bow ties… He'd kill for a bacon butty and he's a bit of a bloody know-all." Mike Taylor, his main rival for promotion in the 1970s (and for a while his deputy), always claimed that Molloy had the edge over him because, unlike Taylor, he never dressed up in the parrot suit that was occasionally dusted down and brought out to entertain Hugh Cudlipp at company dinners.

1985-89: Richard Stott was born in Oxford in August 1943 and educated there and at Clifton College, Bristol. He entered journalism on the *Bucks Herald* in Aylesbury in 1963 and two years later moved to the Ferrari press agency in Dartford, Kent. Having worked as a casual reporter on the *Daily Mirror*, he joined the staff in 1968 and remained in the news department until 1979, latterly filling an investigative role and being elected the British Press Awards Reporter of the Year in 1977. He was features editor for three years and then an assistant editor, 1982-84, until being appointed editor of *The People*. He replaced Molloy as editor of the *Daily Mirror* in 1985, but returned to *The People* at the end of 1989 when Robert Maxwell agreed to a plan whereby Stott would be allowed to buy the title. This failed to materialise and Stott returned to edit the *Daily Mirror* for a second time, 1991-92. Sacked by David Montgomery, he went on to be the last editor of Rupert Murdoch's *Today* and remains the only journalist in history to have held five national newspaper editorships and the only man to have twice edited the same two national titles. He has since written regular columns for the *News of the World* and, currently, the *Sunday Mirror*. At an out-of-town editorial conference he once ordered a bottle of port and when the wine waiter snootily pointed out the vintage he had chosen was extremely expensive, replied: "In that case, we'll have two!"

1990-91: Roy Greenslade was born on New Year's Eve 1946 and entered journalism in 1962 as a trainee reporter with the *Barking Advertiser*. After four years, during which he became a sub-editor, he moved to the *Lancashire Evening Telegraph* in Preston and then the *Daily Mail* before being recruited by Murdoch's infant *Sun*. A trade union activist early in his career, in 1971 he left to become a mature student at Sussex University – paying his way by working casual sub-editing shifts in

Fleet Street – and obtain a degree in politics. Having written a book, *Goodbye to the Working Class*, he returned to national newspapers full-time in 1979 with the newly launched *Daily Star,* then the *Daily Express* and the *Star* for a second time until appointed assistant editor in charge of features at *The Sun*, under Kelvin MacKenzie's editorship, in 1981. After three years as a managing editor of *The Sunday Times,* he was appointed editor of the *Daily Mirror* in February 1990. His unwillingness to accept Maxwell's interference in the day-to-day editorial management of the paper led to a turbulent relationship, and, after mounting hostility on both sides, Greenslade departed in March 1991. He has since become a media commentator, writing regularly for *The Guardian*, and is a visiting professor of journalism at the London College of Printing. Greenslade is married to former *Mirror* features writer Noreen Taylor.

1991-92: Richard Stott (see above).

1992-94: David Banks was born in 1948 in Warrington, Lancashire, and educated at Warrington Grammar School. He worked at the *Warrington Guardian*, *Newcastle Journal* and the *Daily Express* in Manchester before joining the *Daily Mirror* there. Transferred to London, he became an assistant night editor before moving to New York as night managing editor of the *Post*. Subsequently night editor of *The Sun* in London, managing editor of the *New York Daily News*, deputy editor of the *Australian*, editor of the *Sydney Daily Telegraph* and then the merged *Telegraph-Mirror*. Returned to the *Daily Mirror* as editor in 1992 and became editorial director in 1994. Later a television columnist for *The People* and a successful radio broadcaster.

1994-95: Colin Myler was born and educated at Widnes, Cheshire. He joined *The Sun* as a reporter in London in 1974 and later worked for the *Daily Mail* and Granada TV in Manchester. He returned to London as news editor of *The People*, was the launch news editor of *Today* in 1985 and returned to Mirror Group in 1990 as associate editor of the *Sunday Mirror*. After becoming deputy editor, he was promoted to editor in 1992. He was made editor of the *Daily Mirror* in 1994 and managing director of the title in 1996. Subsequently he edited the *Sunday Mirror* for a second time. He is now managing editor of the *New York Post*.

1995-: Piers Morgan, born 30 March 1965; family name Pughe-Morgan. Educated at Chailey Comprehensive and Lewes Priory Sixth Form, Sussex, and Harlow Journalism College. With Lloyd's of London 1985-9; joined Surrey and South London newspapers as a reporter in 1987. Showbusiness editor, *The Sun*, 1989-94; editor, *News of the World*, 1994-95. The first *Mirror* editor since Fyfe never to have worked for the Group in any capacity prior to his appointment.

BIBLIOGRAPHY

Allen, Robert and Frost, John: *Daily Mirror,* Patrick Stephens, 1981.

Brendon, Piers: *The Life and Death of the Press Barons,* Secker & Warburg, 1982.

Cassandra At His Finest and Funniest, A *Daily Mirror* book published by Paul Hamlyn, 1967

Crossman, Richard (Morgan, Janet, ed.): *The Backbench Diaries of Richard Crossman,* Hamish Hamilton and Jonathan Cape, 1981.

Cudlipp, Hugh: *Publish and Be Damned!,* Andrew Dakers, 1953.
        At Your Peril, Weidenfeld and Nicolson, 1962.
        Walking on the Water, The Bodley Head, 1976.
        The Prerogative of the Harlot, The Bodley Head, 1980.

Davis, Clifford: *How I Made Lew Grade a Millionaire and Other Fables,* Mirror Books, 1981.

Delano, Anthony: *Joyce McKinney and the Manacled Mormon,* Mirror Books, 1978.

Edelman, Maurice: *The Mirror – A Political History,* Hamish Hamilton, 1966.

Engel, Matthew: *Tickle the Public – One Hundred Years of the Popular Press,* Victor Gollancz, 1996.

Fyfe, H. Hamilton: *Sixty Years of Fleet Street,* W.H. Allen, 1949.

Gavin, Kent, with Hagerty, Bill: *Flash! Bang! Wallop!* David & Charles, 1978.

Gibbs, Philip: Adventures in Journalism, Heinemann, 1923.

Gifford, Denis: *Stap Me! – The British Newspaper Strip,* Shire Publications, 1971.

Goodhard, David and Wintour, Patrick: *Eddy Shah and the Newspaper Revolution,* Coronet, 1986.

Gray, Tony: *Fleet Street Remembered,* Heinemann, 1990.

Greenslade, Roy: *Maxwell's Fall,* Simon & Schuster, 1992.
        Press Gang: How Papers Make Profits from Propaganda, Macmillan, 2003.

Greenwall, Harry J: *Northcliffe – Napoleon of Fleet Street,* Alan Wingate, 1957.

Griffiths, Dennis (ed.): *The Encyclopedia of the British Press, 1422-1992,* Macmillan Press, 1992.

Haines, Joe: *Maxwell,* Macdonald, 1988.

Hastings, Max: *Editor – The Inside Story of Newspapers,* Macmillan, 2002.

Hoggart, Richard: *The Way We Live Now,* Chatto & Windus, 1995.

Horrie, Chris and Nathan, Adam: *Live TV – Telebrats and Topless Darts,* Simon & Schuster, 1999.

Jameson, Derek: *Touched By Angels,* Ebury Press, 1988.

King, Cecil: *Strictly Personal,* Weidenfeld and Nicolson, 1969.
        With Malice Towards None: A War Diary, Sidgwick & Johnson, 1970
        The Cecil King Diary, 1970-1974, Jonathan Cape, 1975.

Maloney, Mike, and Hall, William: *Flash! Splash! Crash!,* Mainstream, 1996.

Matthews, T.S.: *The Sugar Pill,* Victor Gollancz, 1957.

Mercer, Derrik (editor-in-chief): *Chronicle of the 20th Century,* Longman, 1988.

Orwell, George: *My Country Right or Left, Collected Essays, Journalism and Letters,* 1940-43, Secker & Warburg, 1968.

Patmore, Angela: *Marje – The Guilt and the Gingerbread,* Little, Brown, 1993.

Pilger, John: *Distant Voices,* Vintage, 1992.

Randall, Mike: *The Sunny Side of the Street,* Bloomsbury, 1988.

Regan, Simon: *Rupert Murdoch: A Business Biography,* Angus & Robertson, 1976.

The Romance of the Daily Mirror, A *Daily Mirror* Newspapers Ltd. book, 1924.

Seymour, David and Emily (edited): *A Century of News: A Journey Through History with the Daily Mirror,* Contender, 2003.

Smith, A.C.H.: *Paper Voices,* Chatto and Windus, 1975.

Stott, Richard: *Dogs and Lampposts,* Metro, 2002.

Taylor, A.J.P.: *English History,* Oxford, 1965.

Taylor, S.J.: *The Reluctant Press Lord,* Weidenfeld and Nicholson, 1998.

Williams, Francis: *Dangerous Estate,* Longmans, Green and Co., 1957.
        The Right to Know: The Rise of the World Press, Longmans, Green, 1964.

Wintour, Charles: *The Rise and Fall of Fleet Street,* Hutchinson, 1989.

Zec, Donald: *Some Enchanted Egos,* Allison & Busby, 1972.

Files of the *Daily Mirror, Mirror* Magazine, *British Journalism Review, Press Gazette, Campaign, Marketing Week, New Statesman, The Oldie, The Guardian, The Sunday Times, IPC News* and other in-house Mirror Group publications, *Royal Commission on the Press 1975.*

PHOTO CREDITS

Page 42: Cyril Maitland. Page 81: Dame Elizabeth Taylor Collection. Page 86: Braithwaite. Page 91: Mike Maloney. Page 96 (top right): W.E.G.H. Page 97: Bill Robson. Page 102 (Top left): W.E.G.H. Page 108 (bottom right): George Greenwell. Page 113: Tom King. Page 115 (lower picture): Eric Piper. Page 117: Bela Zola. Page 143: Harry Prosser. Page 145 (top left): Doreen Spooner. Page 151 (top right): Allan Olley; (bottom left): Monte Fresco. Page 154: (top centre and bottom left) Alisdair MacDonald. Page 163: Peter Stone. Page 165: Bill Rowntree. Page 167: Mark Rogers Big Pictures, USA. Page 175: Doreen Spooner. Page 180: Mike Maloney. Page 184: Arnold Slater. Page 186: Martin Spaven. Page 187 (bottom left) Roger Allen. Page 188 (top left): Kayte Brimacombe. Page 191: Phil Spencer. Page 192: Alisdair MacDonald. Page 193: Paul Webb. Page 194 (upper): Bill Kennedy; (bottom): Mike Maloney. Page 195: Chris Grieve. Page 206: Bill Rowntree. Page 207 (upper): Ian Derry; (lower): Bill Rowntree. Page 209: Tony Ward. Page 210 (upper): James Vellacott; (bottom left): John Shenton; (bottom centre): Bob Powell; (bottom right): Tim Anderson. Page 211 (top): Chris Turvey. Page 213 (left): Alisdair MacDonald; (right): James Vellacott. Page 214: Andrew Stenning. Page 217: Andrew Stenning. Page 219: Harry Page. Page 220: Roger Allen. Page 223: David Sandison.

The publishers would like to thank Peter Cook, John Mead and George MacPhee of the Mirrorpix Library for their valuable help in the picture research for this book.

INDEX